Studies in the New Perspective on Paul

Essays and Reviews

Don Garlington

Wipf and Stock Publishers
Eugene, Oregon
2008

Studies in the New Perspective on Paul: Essays and Reviews

By Garlington, Don

Copyright©2008 by Garlington, Don

ISBN:978-1-60608-004-7

Printed by Wipf & Stock Publishers, 2008
199 West 8th Ave., Suite 3
Eugene, Oregon 97401

All rights reserved. No part of this publication may
be reproduced, stored in a retrieval system, or transmitted
in any form or by any means, electronic, mechanical,
photocopying, recording, or otherwise, without the prior
permission of the publisher and author. The only exception
is brief quotations in printed reviews and articles. (First rights
belong to the original publishers of the articles herein published.)

Library of Congress Cataloging-in-Publication Data

Garlington, Don, Studies in the New Perspective on Essays and Reviews

For Jimmy Dunn,
Teacher and friend, who introduced me
to a whole "New Perspective" on Paul

CONTENTS

Preface	vii
The New Perspective on Paul: Two Decades On	1
Faith's Obedience and Israel's Triumphant King: Romans 1:5 Against Its Old Testament Backdrop	31
"Even we Have Believed:" Galatians 2:15-16 Revisited	67
Role Reversal and Paul's Use of Scripture in Galatians 3:10-13	99
Imputation or Union with Christ? A Response to John Piper	137
Imputation or Union with Christ? A Rejoinder to John Piper	197
Review of John Piper, *The Future of Justification*	229
Review of D. A. Carson, et al., *Justification and Variegated Nomism I*	239
Review of Simon Gathercole, *Where is Boasting? Early Jewish Soteriology and Paul's Response in Romans 1-5*	287
The New Perspective, Mediation and Justification: A Reply to S. M. Baugh	311
Covenantal Nomism and the Exile: A Reply to I. M. Duguid	341
Review of Gordon Wenham, *Story as Torah*	379

PREFACE

The following collection of essays follows upon its predecessor, entitled *In Defense of the New Perspective on Paul*. This second edition differs from the first in that five new chapters have been added, and the review of Mark Elliott's *The Survivors of Israel* has been deleted as being less relevant to the discussion. The change of the main title to *Studies in the New Perspective on Paul* is due to my conviction that the "New Perspective," so-called, actually represents a return to the original context in which Paul proclaimed the gospel of Christ. Therefore, it is not a thing to be "defended," but stated in the most positive terms possible. Apart from this book, two other essays of mine are germane to the NPP debate: "A 'New Perspective' Reading of Romans 1-4," posted on the paulpage.com (this material is currently being incorporated into a monograph on Romans), and "Paul's 'Partisan *ek*' and the Question of Justification in Galatians," forthcoming in *Journal of Biblical Literature*.

As before, all abbreviations of primary sources conform to *The SBL Handbook of Style: For Ancient Near Eastern, Biblical, and Early Christian Studies*. eds. Patrick H. Alexander, et al. (Peabody: Hendrickson, 1999). It is to be noted that the method of documentation of secondary literature is retained from the original publications, in some cases conforming to the *SBL Handbook* and in some cases not.

59 Shoredale Drive
Toronto, Ontario, M1G 3T1
Canada
dongarlington@yahoo.com

THE NEW PERSPECTIVE ON PAUL:
TWO DECADES ON

1. Introduction

The so-called New Perspective on Paul (NPP) has been likened to a Copernican revolution.[1] Whether one is inclined to defend or assail it, the fact remains that Pauline studies will never be the same again. Some may try to ignore it, but apparently it is not going away, at least not anytime soon. And while many may wish that it would go away, it is my impression that much of the controversy that has surrounded the NPP is rooted in a visceral reaction on the part of various theological traditions. If any proof is needed, one need only peruse the various web sites on which is posted some very "emphatic" material indeed. The purpose of this essay, then, is to attempt to clarify what the NPP is and what it is not, and then to ask what kind of a future it may expect.[2]

Before proceeding, two qualification are in order. (1) I say the "so-called" NPP for at least two reasons. One, the NPP is like the New Hermeneutic—it is not that new anymore. That the "perspective" is not so "new" is confirmed by the fact that certain scholars believe that we have now entered into the "post NPP era."[3] Two, those of us who espouse one version or the other of the NPP like to think that the perspective is not so much new as a return to the "original perspective" of Paul in relation to his Jewish contemporaries. Thus, what to many may appear to be "new" is for others of us rather "old" indeed.

(2) There simply is no monolithic entity that can be designated as the "New Perspective" as such. It is surely telling that D. A. Carson, a noted (hyper)critic of the NPP, acknowledges that it cannot be reduced to a single perspective. "Rather, it is a bundle of interpretive approaches to Paul, some of which are mere differences in emphasis, and others of which compete rather antagonistically."[4] What goes by the moniker of the "New Perspective" is actually more like variations on a theme; and, in point of fact, this generic title is flexible enough to allow for individual thought and refinement of convictions. Consequently, the take on the NPP represented within these pages is quite individually mine. Though I am much indebted to E. P. Sanders, J. D. G. Dunn, and N. T. Wright for numerous insights, this representation of the NPP does not correspond precisely to any of these scholars.

2. The New Perspective on Paul: What it is and What it is Not

What it is

The New Perspective is an attempt to understand Paul (and the NT generally) within his own context.

The actual phrase "New Perspective" was coined by J. D. G Dunn, in his Manson Memorial Lecture of 1982.[5] Dunn bases his "New Perspective" on E. P. Sanders' (re)construction of pre-destruction Judaism, as embodied in Sander's epoch-making *Paul and Palestinian Judaism*.[6] As Sanders himself explains:

> Covenantal nomism is the view that one's place in God's plan is established on the basis of the covenant and that the covenant requires as the proper response of man his obedience to its commandments, while providing means of atonement for transgression…. Obedience maintains one's position in the covenant, but it does not earn God's grace as such…. Righteousness in Judaism is a term which implies the maintenance of status among the group of the elect.[7]

In another place, Sanders summarizes his position under the following points:

> (1) God has chosen Israel and (2) given the law. The law implies both (3) God's promise to maintain the election and (4) the requirement to obey. (5) God rewards obedience and punishes transgression. (6) The law provides for means of atonement, and atonement results in (7) maintenance or reestablishment of the covenantal relationship. (8) All those who are maintained in the covenant by obedience, atonement and God's mercy belong to the group which will be saved. An important interpretation of the first and last points is that election and ultimately salvation are considered to be by God's mercy rather than human achievement.[8]

Dunn further clarifies Sanders' outlook:

> This covenant relationship was regulated by the law, not as a way of entering the covenant, or of gaining merit, but as the way of living *within* the covenant; and that included the provision of sacrifice and atonement for those who confessed their sins and thus repented.... This attitude Sanders characterized by the now well known phrase "covenantal nomism"—that is, "the maintenance of status" among the chosen people of God by observing the law given by God as part of that covenant relationship.[9]

In the heat of the debate over these issues, and the inevitable confusion on the part of many, Dunn calls to mind that the phrase "covenantal nomism" does indeed consist of two parts: *covenant* and *nomos* (law).

> It is important to note...that Sanders did not characterize Judaism solely as a "covenantal" religion. The key phrase he chose was the double emphasis, "covenantal nomism". And Sanders made clear that the second emphasis was not to be neglected. The Torah/law was given to Israel to be obeyed, an integral part of the covenant relationship, and that obedience was necessary if Israel's covenant status was to be maintained. Even if obedience did not earn God's grace as such, was not a means to "*get into*" the covenant, obedience *was* necessary to maintain one's position in the covenant, to "*stay in*" the covenant. So defined, Deuteronomy can be seen as the most fundamental statement of Israel's "covenantal nomism". Given the traditional emphasis on Judaism's "nomism" it is hardly surprising that Sanders should have placed greater emphasis on the "covenantal" element in the twin emphasis. But in his central summary statements he clearly recognized that both emphases were integral to Judaism's self-understanding.[10]

In short, the pioneering (ad)venture of Sanders, as championed by Dunn, Wright, and others, has argued powerfully that Jews of the Second Temple period (and beyond) were not Pelagians before Pelagius. The rank and file of the Jewish people operated with an intelligent consciousness of the way God's covenant with them operated and of their place within that covenant. And while there may well have been exceptions to the rule,[11] the literature of this era is reflective of the sort of popular piety encountered by Paul in the synagogue and in the market place.[12]

But notwithstanding his substantial agreement with Sanders' take on the Second Temple sources, it is Dunn who levels the criticism that "Sanders' Paul hardly seems to be addressing Sanders' Judaism."[13] In other words, the Paul of Sanders takes his countrymen to task for precisely the same reason that Luther did! Dunn thus distances himself from Sanders' Paul by defining the apostle's phrase "the works of the law" not as a generalized principle of obedience for the purpose of earning salvation, but as those works done in response to the covenant in order to maintain the bond between God and Israel (the works of "staying in"). Dunn does maintain that "the works of the law" encompass the whole Torah, but within the period of the Second Temple certain aspects of the law became especially prominent as the boundary and identity markers of the Jewish people: prominently circumcision, food laws, purity laws, and sabbath.[14]

Dunn is frequently misrepresented on this point, as though he restricts "the works of the law" to the "boundary markers," without allowing that the whole Torah is in view when Paul employs the phrase. But just the opposite is the case. He states, in point of fact, that circumcision and the other ordinances were *not* the only distinguishing traits of Jewish self-identity. However, they were the focal point of the Hellenistic attack on the Jews during the Maccabean period. As such, they became *the acid tests of one's loyalty to Judaism*. "In short…the particular regulations of circumcision and food laws [et al.] were important not in themselves, but because they *focused* Israel's distinctiveness and made visible Israel's claims to be a people set apart, were the clearest points which differentiated the Jews from the nations. The law was coterminous with Judaism."[15] No wonder, Dunn justifiably issues a note of protest.[16]

Strictly speaking, then, the NPP has to do with the historical issue of Paul's relation to Second Temple Judaism, with special reference to his phrase "the works of the law." In short, the NPP seeks to understand the NT in such a way that *balances text and context*. To be sure, it is the text that receives the priority. But the NT was not written in a vacuum, and any reading of it has to be sensitive to the issues that were being debated within its own milieu, not ours. Before we ask what the NT *means*, we have to ask what it *meant*. In the end, it all boils down to the basic hermeneutical task of determining both the "meaning" and the "significance" (application) of the text.

The issue of justification, as such, was not on the original agenda of the NPP. But since the two have been merged in popular thinking, they will be considered together in this paper. However, it has to be clarified that there is no such thing as "the NPP position on justification." That is a misnomer.

The New Perspective is rooted in the architecture of biblical eschatology

Though commonplace and hackneyed at this point in time, it is necessary to reiterate that salvation history transpires in terms of an *Already* and a *Not Yet*. The work of Christ has been *inaugurated* by his first coming and will be *consummated* at his parousia. This schema might appear to be too simple and too obvious to call for any comment. However, it is just this fundamental datum that has been either bypassed or suppressed in the contemporary debates respecting justification. On the part of many, there has been a failure to recognize that salvation is not finally complete until, in Paul's words, we are eschatologically "saved by his life" (Rom 5:10).

Rom 5:9-10 stands out as fundamentally paradigmatic for Paul's soteriology, and yet it has been surprisingly neglected in the whole "New Perspective" debate. According to Paul's formulation:

> v. 9: if we have been justified by Christ's blood, then (how much more) shall we be saved from (eschatological) wrath.
>
> v. 10: if we have been reconciled by Christ's death, then (how much more) shall we be saved by his (resurrection) life.

I have treated the passage elsewhere.[17] Suffice it to say here that the past redemptive event in Christ has given rise to hope in the believer, a hope which has as its primary focus the future eschatological consummation of the new creation. Or, as Neil Elliott puts it, vv. 9-10 "relocate the soteriological fulcrum in the apocalyptic future: the gracious justification and reconciliation of the impious is made the basis for sure hope in the salvation to come."[18] Paul thus polarizes past and future as the epochal stages of the salvation experience, with the assurance that although the consummation of redemption is still outstanding, the believer can take comfort that God's purposes cannot fail.

In this argument "from the lesser to the greater" (*a minori ad majus* or the rabbinic *qal wahomer*), Paul asserts that Christ's sacrifice must eventuate in the final salvation of his people in order to accomplish its goal. The salvific process is commenced with present justification, but it will not be consummated until we are finally saved. And "the process of consummating the work of salvation is more like an obstacle course than a downhill ride to the finishline. For the destiny of Christians does not go unchallenged in a world opposed to God's purposes. The powers of evil in the form of afflictions and trials threaten continuity in their salvation."[19] Thus, C. E. B. Cranfield's remark that deliverance from eschatological wrath is, in relation to justification, "very easy" fails to appreciate the formidable nature of the "obstacle course."[20] Given the "tribulations" (Rom 5:3) that attend the life of faith this side of the resurrection, the great thing, from the perspective of the present passage, is yet to be accomplished.

It is none other than this Already/Not Yet paradigm that underlies Paul's explicit statement that it is the "doers of the law" who will be justified in eschatological judgment (Rom 2:13; cf. Jas 1:22). Again, detailed commentary has already been provided.[21] It is only to be noted here that "doing the law" is tantamount to perseverance, in keeping particularly with Lev 18:5 and Deut 4:1, 10, 40; 5:29-33; 6:1-2, 18, 24; 7:12-13, all of which provide the semantic origin for Paul's own language (cf. Luke 8:15).[22] Scholars such as Yinger and Gathercole are quite right that the language is realistically intentioned and far from hypothetical: there is a phase of justification that is yet outstanding. As Brendan Byrne formulates the matter:

> The process [of justification] is not complete. Though they [believers] stand acquitted in a forensic sense, the obedience of Christ is yet to run its full course in them; they yet hang with him upon the cross (Gal 2:19). The process of justification will only be complete in them, as it is in him, when it finds public, bodily expression in the resurrection-existence, the "revelation of the sons of God" (Rom 8:18-21).[23]

I hasten to add that synergism or some such notion of "contributing to salvation" is hardly in view; it is, rather, "righteousness," or the expected conformity of one's faith and life to the demands of the covenant. Klyne Snodgrass speaks pointedly to the issue:

> It is not necessary to recoil from this idea in fear of some theory of "works righteousness" or in fear of diminishing the role of Christ in the purposes of God. Nor is there any idea of a "natural theology" in the pejorative sense of the term. The witness of all the Biblical traditions and much of Judaism is that none stands before God in *his or her own righteousness*. There is no thought in Romans 2 of a person being granted life because he or she was a moral human being, independent of God. The whole context of 1.18f. assumes the necessity of recognizing God as God and honouring him with one's life. The description of those who work the good in 2.7, 14-15, and 29 shows that the obedience is a direct result of the activity of God.[24]

One may legitimately talk of obedience as the precondition of eschatological justification, or perhaps better, vindication. Yet "obedience," in the Jewish context, is but *faithful perseverance* and the avoidance of idolatry (the central thesis of my *Obedience of Faith*). At stake is not "works" in any pejorative sense, but one's loyalty to Christ from conversion to death. Such is of the essence of biblical faith. J. D. Crossan and J. L. Reed put it succinctly and well:

> Faith does not mean intellectual consent to a proposition, but vital commitment to a program. Obviously, one could summarize a program in a proposition, but faith can never be reduced to factual assent rather than total dedication. Faith (*pistis*) is not just a partial mind-set, but a total lifestyle commitment. The crucial aspect of faith as commitment is that it is always an interactive process, a bilateral contract, a two-way street. Faith is covenantal and presumes faithfulness from both parties with, of course, all appropriate differences and distinctions.[25]

What counts for Paul is being and remaining in Christ. If for the sake of a theological formulation we wish to categorize Paul's thought, then the "basis" of justification, now and in the judgment, is *union with Christ*.[26] I would hasten to add that obedience as the precondition of eschatological justification is no more radical than Paul's similar demand of confession of Christ as the prerequisite of final salvation (Rom 10:9-10).

A number of scholars, including Gathercole, believe that in both Jewish and Pauline eschatology there is a tension between election and grace, on the one hand, and final vindication according to works, on the other.[27] Yet Yinger's thesis is precisely that, in the Jewish milieu, there is no actual tension between the two categories; the tension exists only in the minds of Western (systematic) theologians. Ps 62:12, normally considered to be the source of Rom 2:6, actually says: "to you, O Lord, belongs *steadfast love*, for you requite a person *according to his work.*" Apparently, the Psalmist is unaware of any "tension." Therefore, as far as *perseverance and works* are concerned, Paul's criteria for future justification are not at all different than his Jewish contemporaries. Nonetheless, there is one radical difference—*Christ himself* (see below).

A particular aspect of the Already/Not Yet framework of eschatology deserves special mention, namely, return from exile. The idea of a new exodus has hardly escaped the notice of scholars, but only of late has it received the recognition it deserves, particularly with the brilliant and influential work of N. T. Wright.[28] The return from exile motif informs us that there is to be a time when Israel's deliverance from bondage is complete, when Yahweh himself becomes the righteousness of his people (Isa 61:10; Jer 23:6; 33:16). In Paul and other NT writers, the prophetic expectation of Israel's return to the land is projected into the "eschatological now." This means that in one sense the exile is at an end, and yet in another it is not. Believers have been "liberated (literally "justified") from sin" (Acts 13:39; Rom 6:7, 18), and yet they await the final deliverance from the bondage of the old creation, the present evil age (Rom 7:14-25; 8:18-25; Gal 1:4). Given this backdrop to Paul, justification is by the nature of the case liberation from sin, not merely a forensic declaration.[29]

The New Perspective is in line with the character of a biblical covenant

Every covenant is established unilaterally by the sovereign grace of God; and yet the human partner to the covenant is far from a nonentity. Quite the contrary, both privileges and obligations are entailed in covenant membership.[30] It is just the Christian believer's fidelity to the (new) covenant relationship that eventuates in eschatological justification. Such is far from synergism or self-salvation, simply because the covenant is established by grace and maintained by grace. By virtue of God's free gift of Christ and the Spirit (e.g., Rom 5:15-17; 8:1-17; 2 Cor 9:15), the Christian is enabled to bring forth fruit with perseverance out of a good and noble heart (Luke 8:15). The believer's righteousness, therefore, is none other than his/her conformity to the covenant relationship and its standards.[31] This is *both* a righteousness that comes "from God" (Phil 3:9 = Isa 54:17) *and* a righteousness that forms the precondition of eschatological vindication (Matt 12:33-37; Rom 2:13 [= Ps 18:20; 24; 62:12; Prov 24:12]; Jas 2:14-26). As Yinger has shown, the notion of an eschatological vindication based on the "works," or better, "the fruit of the Spirit" borne by the Christian (Gal 5:22-24) is simply in line with OT and Jewish precedents.[32]

What it is Not

The New Perspective is not an "attack" on the Reformation

The NPP is an attempt to understand the NT within its own historical context. Without in any sense attempting to despise or repudiate the significance of the Reformation, the NPP simply recognizes that the four hundred years prior to the NT era are more important than the four hundred or so years between the Reformation and us. For this reason, the NPP is a recognition that the issues that have arisen since the Reformation are not necessarily the issues of the NT itself. Luther's fundamental historical mistake was to assume that a direct equation could be drawn between the life and faith of Second Temple Jews and his perception of the Roman Catholicism of the sixteenth century, especially the brand of Catholicism represented by Johann Tetzel and the sale of indulgences. The NPP seeks to remind us that the Reformation itself was precisely spearheaded by a desire to bypass centuries of tradition and return to the original source documents of the Christian faith.

The New Perspective is not incompatible with the foundational concerns of the Reformers

The NPP is supportive of the central mottoes of the Reformation, among which are the following. (1) *Sola Fide*. Regardless of the NPP's distinctive definition of "works of the law," the root issue remains the same: only faith in Christ can justify and sanctify. Every other "gateway to salvation" is precluded.

(2) *Sola Scriptura*. The charge has been leveled, at least in some quarters, that this historical approach to Scripture is in danger of placing Jewish literature on a par with the canon itself. But precisely the opposite is the case: the object is to read the NT on its own historical terms and not those imposed by tradition, even Protestant tradition. It is in this regard that the NPP attempts to honor a frequently neglected motto of the Reformers—*ad fontes* ("to the sources").

(3) *Solus Christus*. This is the most important slogan of all. A historical, as opposed to a confessional, reading of the NT removes the stress from the "grace" versus "legalism" model and places it on the christological paradigm. It is not as though Paul and his Jewish opponents differed on the definition of such central issues as grace, faith, righteousness, and the relation of works to final judgment. Paul inherits these categories from the OT, as shared in common between him and his Jewish antagonists. The point of difference, rather, resides in *Paul's christology*, with all its manifold implications. It is *in Christ*, not the law, that one becomes the righteousness of God (2 Cor 5:21). At one time the righteousness of God was disclosed precisely in Israel's Torah;[33] but not anymore, because "now," eschatologically, God's righteousness has been revealed in the gospel and through faith in Jesus Christ (Rom 1:16-17; 3:21-22). In contrast to so many of his Jewish peers (e.g., Sir 24:9, 33; Bar 4:1; Wis 18:4; *T. Naph* 3:1-2), for Paul the law is simply not eternal.[34]

All this means that even more basic than *sola fide* is *solus Christus*. For all that Protestantism has insisted that justification is the "article of standing and falling of the church" (*articulus stantis et cadentis ecclesiae*), *christology* really is. *The church stands or falls with Christ*. The actual showcase of Paul's thought is *not* justification, as time-honored as that notion is in traditional theology. It is, rather, union with Christ or the "in Christ" experience. From this vantage point, Col 1:18 exhibits the very life blood of Paul's preaching—that *in all things he may have the preeminence*. At the end of the day, it is Paul's "christological eschatology" that demarcates him from his Jewish compatriots.[35]

Certainly, the core question in a document such as Galatians is not "grace" versus "legalism," after the traditional understanding. Rather, it is *the choice between Christ and the Torah*.[36] Beverly Gaventa says it so well:

> Although the issue that prompts Paul to write to Galatian Christians arises from a conflict regarding the

law, in addressing that problem Paul takes the position that the gospel proclaims Jesus Christ crucified to be the inauguration of a new creation. *This new creation allows for no supplementation or augmentation by the law or any other power or loyalty.* What the Galatians seek in the law is a certainty that they have a firm place in the *ekklēsia* of God and that they know what God requires of them. It is precisely this certainty, and every other form of certainty, that Paul rejects with his claim about *the exclusivity and singularity of Jesus Christ.*[37]

That christology is at the heart of Paul's controversy with the circumcision party is underscored by the relation of the Messiah to the Torah in the theology of the latter. J. Louis Martyn very helpfully distills the thinking of the opponents as regards the Christ of the law. The Jewish Christian missionaries (the "Teachers," as Martyn calls them) viewed Jesus as the completion of the ministry of Moses:

> They view God's Christ in the light of God's law, rather than the law in the light of Christ. This means in their christology, Christ is secondary to the law.... For them the Messiah is the Messiah of the Law, deriving his identity from the fact that he confirms—and perhaps even normatively interprets—the Law. If Christ is explicitly involved in the Teachers' commission to preach to the Gentiles, that must be so because he has deepened their passion to take to the nations God's gift of gifts, the Spirit-dispensing Law that will guide them in their daily life.[38]

The New Perspective is not a conscious repudiation of the creeds of the church

The church's creeds are to be used as any other tool of exegesis, but they are not effectively to be exalted to the status of primary authority. The NPP recognizes that the last word has not been said on anything. Methodologically, it is an endeavor to think in historical/biblical-theological categories, a *historia salutis* rather than an *ordo salutis*. For example, in Galatians, Paul's discussion of faith and works is not topical but historical (e.g., 3:2-3 and 3:12).[39]

The focus of the New Perspective is not merely on sociology or the identity of the new covenant people of God

It is true that some exponents of the NPP have emphasized sociology to the virtual exclusion of soteriology, even in a letter such as Galatians. Yet a more balanced approach seeks to maintain that soteriology remains fundamental. It is certainly notable that Sanders himself thinks that "Paul's argument [in Galatians] is not in favor of faith per se, nor is it against works per se. It is much more particular: it is against requiring the Gentiles to keep the law of Moses in order to be 'sons of Abraham'."[40] He adds further that "we have become so sensitive to the theological issue of grace and merit that we often lose sight of the actual subject of the dispute." Thus, the subject of Galatians is "the condition on which Gentiles enter the people of God."[41] Nevertheless, much more is at stake than a sociology or group identity, one enclave distinguishing itself from another. If the topic under discussion is "how to enter the body of those who would be saved," then "the topic is, in effect, soteriology."[42] Charles Cousar speaks to the same effect: "The issue under debate, raised by the agitators' demand for circumcision, was basically soteriological, how God saves people."[43] See Acts 15:1.

This affirmation of soteriology as lying at the root of Galatians is a necessary corrective to N. T. Wright's otherwise excellent treatment of justification and righteousness language in the NT. Wright is insistent that justification, and consequently the subject matter of Galatians, does not tell us how to be saved; it is, rather, a way of saying how you can tell that you belong to the covenant community, or, in other words, How do you define the people of God?[44] To be sure, such issues are to be weighed in light of the covenant context of "the righteousness of God" and similar ideas. On this Wright is undoubtedly correct. Galatians does indeed address the question, "Who is a member of the people of God."[45] Likewise, it is true that "justification, in Galatians, is the doctrine which insists that all who share faith in Christ belong at the same table, no matter what their racial differences, as together they wait for the final new creation."[46]

That much said, it must be countered that Wright has constructed a seemingly false dichotomy between the identity of the people of God and salvation. Sanders is closer to the mark: Galatians has to do with how to enter the body of those who would be saved. This means that to belong to the new covenant is to be among the community of *the saved*.[47] And justification does, in fact, tell us how to be saved, in that it depicts God's method of saving sinners—by faith in Christ, not by works of the law—and placing them in covenant standing with himself. If justification is *by faith*, then a method of salvation *is* prescribed: one enters into the realm of salvation *by faith*.[48]

The New Perspective is not a denial that in the theology of Second Temple Judaism works count in the final judgment

Apart from earlier researchers, we are indebted to Yinger and Gathercole for establishing beyond any reasonable doubt that the obedience of the people of God is the *sine qua non* of a favorable verdict on the day of judgment.[49] Gathercole's book in particular serves as a useful and welcomed corrective to an imbalance on the part of some practitioners of the NPP. It is true, as he notes many times, that there has been a tendency to play up sociological matters (Jewish distinctiveness and self-identity) and to play down the Torah's own requirement that people really and truly "do the law."[50] Consequently, Gathercole is on target in his insistence Israel's boasting is grounded not only in election, but in actual performance of the law. To the degree that he has redressed the balance in favor of a reading of Judaism and Paul that more accurately reflects the actual data, we are in his debt.

The problem, however, is Gathercole's quantum leap from works as the precondition of final salvation to "earning salvation" or synergism. Yinger, on the other hand, has rightly called attention to the continuity between Judaism and Paul as pertains to the relation of grace and works. Yinger correctly maintains that Paul and Judaism alike are no more "monergistic" or "synergistic" than each other. Indeed, Paul's stance toward works in relation to the final judgment is entirely consistent with Jewish precedents. Once again, in my estimation, the real point of contention between Paul and Judaism is christology, not the relation of works to judgment.[51]

The New Perspective is not an attempt to exonerate ancient Judaism in every regard

The pioneering work of George Foot Moore and others might very well be susceptible to this charge.[52] By contrast, Longenecker's treatment of "The Piety of Hebraic Judaism" is a model of balanced scholarship.[53] He demonstrates, in the words of Israel Abrahams no less, that there are both "weeds" and "flowers" in the garden of Judaism, and that the elements of nomism and spirituality must be kept in proper proportion to one another.[54] My only observation here is that the "weeds" of this garden consists not of "legalism" as classically defined, but of Israel's idolatrous attachment to the Torah to the exclusion of Jesus the Messiah, who is the "end" of the law (Rom 10:4). The Jewish people have preferred to "maintain" their own righteousness rather than submit to God's latter-day righteousness as now embodied in Christ (Rom 10:3).[55] For Paul, such unwarranted and *uneschatological* devotion to the law is no less than idolatry.[56]

The New Perspective is not a denial that there are schemes of self-salvation in various religious traditions

It goes without saying that Paul would have adamantly opposed any scheme of self-salvation based on human performance (Eph 2:8-9 and Titus 3:5 have direct applicability). Nevertheless, historically speaking, he has in his sights the works of fidelity to the Mosaic covenant ("staying in") that would stand one in good stead on the day of judgment. In this regard, the Reformers were correct that if justification is not by Jewish tradition, then it is not by church tradition either: salvation is not by "religion," however conceived. This is the hermeneutical "significance," or application, of the historical principle at stake: only Christ can save, not religion, tradition, or any other extra-christological consideration.

To hone the issue more precisely, Paul does combat a works-principle, but in the case of Israel these are the works of "staying in" rather than "getting in," because the nation was already in the covenant and had an awareness of its election. The Jewish conviction was that one remained loyal to the covenant relation as exemplified by works and on that basis could expect to be vindicated in the final judgment as God's faithful one. Over against this, Paul says two things: (1) the final judgment has already taken place in Christ; (2) Torah observance has nothing to do with it—only faith in Christ counts. On this construction, "grace" *is* set in contrast to "works;" but as regards Israel, the works are specifically those *of Torah*. Grace means that one is not obliged to observe the Mosaic system *in toto* to be regarded and accepted as one of Yahweh's faithful ones. Gentiles do not first have to become "honorary Jews" in order to be "members in good standing" in the covenant community. *In Christ*, one becomes the righteousness of God by faith alone. This means that hermeneutical significance of "works of the law" is any religious system or tradition that would challenge the preeminence of Christ.

3. The New Perspective and Roman Catholicism

Frequently, a comparison is made between the NPP and Roman Catholicism, normally in a decidedly antagonistic tone. In my view, this comparison is both right and wrong at the same time. But before proceeding, I would voice my opinion that labels such as "legalism," "synergism," and "self-salvation" have been very unfairly attached to Tridentine Catholicism. The ghost of Pelagius is too often and too unjustly trotted out as a legitimate grounding of the Catholic understanding of justification.

On the one hand, there are resemblances between the two, in particular the relation of faith, works, and final judgment. Catholic exegetes are quick to point out that the only place in the NT where the words "faith" and "alone" occur together is Jas 2:24: "You see that a person is justified by works and *not by faith alone!*" The point is well taken and needs to be pondered much more carefully by Protestant interpreters. If that had been the case, the supposed tension between James and Paul, especially on the part of Lutheran commentators, would have been eliminated altogether. This is not the place to argue in detail; just suffice it to say that James 2 and Romans 2 (not to mention Rom 4:18-25) are perfectly compatible if viewed *eschatologically*.[57] Both speak of a justification to transpire at the end of this age, and both are emphatic that works are not optional. Classic Catholicism and the NPP are in accord in this regard: while phase one of justification (the Already) is by faith alone, phase two (the Not Yet) takes into account the works that are the tokens of fidelity to the Lord and his covenant. For both, initial faith is complemented by the fruit that accompanies perseverance (Luke 8:15).

On the other hand, this agreement in principle has to be qualified in light of the place of tradition in Catholic theology. It is notable that Dunn's book, *The Partings of the Ways*, was originally delivered as a series of lectures at the Gregorian Pontifical University in Rome. In the course of those lectures, Dunn paused to consider the place of tradition.[58] His immediate concern was that of priesthood in the Letter to the Hebrews in relation to the Catholic doctrine of priesthood. Dunn confesses to some bewilderment at the way the argument of Hebrews can be "so lightly ignored or set aside by those Christian traditions which wish to continue to justify a special order of priesthood within the people of God, a special order whose priestly ministry is distinct in kind from the priesthood of all the faithful."[59]

Dunn concedes that an argument from tradition as over against Scripture can carry decisive weight. But to use Heb 5:1 to justify Christian priesthood in the manner of the Second Vatican Council, while ignoring the clear thrust and argument of the letter as a whole, seems to him to constitute a form of eisegesis and special pleading that cannot really be justified from tradition. He confesses to no quarrel in principle with tradition taking up and developing a possible but less probable interpretation of some text. But can it be justified in making doctrinal use of an interpretation that runs counter to the main point of the text itself? In this case, he remarks, it is no longer simply a matter of tradition interpreting scripture, but of "tradition riding roughshod over scripture."[60]

If I may build upon and extrapolate from Dunn's remarks, the difference between my version of the NPP and Roman Catholicism revolves just around the relation of tradition to final judgment (justification) by works. If my perception is correct, then what is stake in the latter's doctrine of judgment is not "good works" in the most generic terms, but a commitment to the Tridentine standards, including such articles of faith as papal infallibility, the mass, the sacraments, the perpetual virginity of Mary, and prayer to the saints. By contrast, the obedience of faith in Paul bypasses all forms of tradition, Jewish, Christian, or otherwise, and focuses fidelity solely and exclusively on Christ. The latter-day justification of the people of God hinges on union with Christ and the observance of all things that he has commanded the church (Matt 28:20), and nothing other than that. In short, what is required for a favorable verdict in the last day is allegiance to Jesus and *his law* (1 Cor 9:21; Gal 6:2). It is in this regard that the Reformers made a right application of Paul's denial that justification is not by "works of the law." That is to say, if justification is not by Jewish tradition, then it is not by church tradition either.

4. The Contribution of the New Perspective to the Law/Gospel Debate

The relation between law and gospel has been debated vociferously from the time of the Reformation. And while the debate will never end, at least I can say with some degree of confidence that the NPP has a decided bearing on the issues at hand.

(1) The NPP suggests that the nomenclature of "law and gospel" needs to be abandoned in favor of "old covenant" and "new covenant." From the Reformation onward, interpreters have sought to perform a "balancing act" between the role of "law" and "gospel" respectively. On the one hand, it is evident that the believer is justified by faith apart from the works of the law (Rom 3:28; Gal 2:16); and that Christ is the "end" of the law (Rom 10:4; Gal 3:23-25). On the other hand, Paul believes that at least certain aspects of the law of Moses remain intact for the Christian (e.g., Rom 7:12; 13:8-10; Gal 5:14; Eph 6:1-3). Traditional approaches to the subject have sought to tackle the problem from the vantage point of the *loci* or a systematic theology. Yet while this avenue has yielded some fruit, it is essentially wrongheaded, because the Bible is simply not constructed in a topical manner. Its own method of organization is historical, not "systematic."[61] Therefore, the traditional contrast of "law and gospel" is more properly to be conceived as the contrast of two distinct covenants, "old" and "new," as they assume their position along the timeline of salvation history.

Since "law and gospel" are more properly to be conceived of as "old covenant and new covenant," the NPP seeks to focus attention on the salvation-historical significance of texts.[62] As the eye canvasses the time-line of redemptive history, it can be seen that "the law (of Moses) and the prophets" give way to "the gospel of the kingdom" (Luke 16:16; Matt 4:23; 9:35; 24:13). While this is not the place to engage the unity and diversity debate,[63] it may be said that enough diversity between "old" and "new" is in evidence to warrant the conclusion that "the law of Christ" (1 Cor 9:21; Gal 6:2) has displaced "the law of Moses." It is in this sense that Paul writes that "the law is not of faith" (Gal 3:12). To say that the law is "not of faith" is to affirm that the law and faith belong to distinctly different historical realms: the former does not occupy the same turf in the salvation-historical continuum as the latter. This comes as no surprise given that Paul's salvation-historical paradigm is established at the outset of Galatians 3, with the juxtaposition of "Spirit" and "flesh," designating respectively the age of the Spirit and the age of the flesh.[64] For this reason, if one seeks to be justified by the law, one is severed from Christ and falls away from the era of grace back into that of the Torah (Gal 5:4).[65]

At variance with a number of NPP scholars, it is just because of this old covenant/new covenant schema that I would submit that Christ and his people have superseded Israel as the chosen people.

As Wright puts it so insightfully, the NT represents the climax of a story, the story of Israel. The NT writers as a whole take Israel's history and redraw it around Jesus and his people.[66] This has manifold implications for both eschatology and ecclesiology.

(2) By stressing the place of the NT within its own historical environment, the NPP endeavors to address the actual issues being debated in the first-century context. In brief, those debates centered particularly around the ongoing role of the Torah, the place of Israel in God's redemptive purposes, and the admission of the Gentiles into the people of God. At heart, what demarcates the NT's message to Israel is not the allegation that Second Temple Jews were attempting to "buy their way into heaven" by merit or any other means of self-salvation. Rather, by its insistence that Jesus of Nazareth is the purpose and goal of Israel's history and Torah (Rom 10:3; Gal 3:23-25), *christology* is made the decisive factor: *what the people of Israel were seeking in the law is to be found in Christ.* Perhaps the most trenchant expression of this "Christ versus Torah" outlook of the NT is to be found in the Fourth Gospel. According to John 1:17, "The law indeed was given through Moses; grace and truth came through Jesus Christ." And even more striking is John 5:39: "You search the scriptures because you think that in them you have eternal life; and it is they that testify on my behalf." In essence, the NPP argues that justification and membership in the covenant community do not hinge on any set of traditional beliefs, religious or cultural.

(3) Because the NPP is rooted in the basic architecture of biblical eschatology, it serves to clarify that there is no tension between "law and gospel," or "grace and works," when both are assessed within the framework of a biblical covenant. In *qualitative terms*, as perceived by traditional systematic theology, "gospel" as good news is not to be juxtaposed to "law" as an alternate means to salvation. From beginning to end, it is grace that establishes the covenant and enables its participants to persevere and bear fruit (Deut 30:11-14; Luke 8:15). In simplest terms, this is the Already and the Not Yet of biblical redemption. From this eschatological perspective, it is by virtue of the twofold gift of Christ and the Spirit that individuals come to faith and then render to King Jesus "the obedience of faith" (Rom 1:5; 16:26). In Mosaic language, this is none other than the mandate of Lev 18:5 and Deut 4:1, 10, 40; 5:29-33; 6:1-2, 18, 24; 7:12-13 that Israel "do the law" and "live" as a consequence.[67] As such, the obedience expected of the church is none other than that demanded of Israel. If "doing the law" was the precondition of the Israelite's enjoyment of life in the

land, then no less is expected of the Christian believer, whose obedience is directed toward the Christ of the gospel (John 14:15; 15:1-11; Jas 2:18-26; Rom 2:6-11).

Traditionally, Protestant theology has had grave reservations about connecting works of any sort with the ultimate justification/vindication of the believer. Nevertheless, writing of Jesus' own teaching on judgment, I defer to Scot McKnight:

> Jesus should...not be made subservient to the Reformation; his theology stands on its own in its thoroughly Jewish context. Reformation theology needs to answer to Jesus, not Jesus to it. Jesus did not talk about earning salvation; he talked about what covenant members are obliged to do (or strive to do) if they wish to be faithful.[68]

5. Is There a Future for the New Perspective?

The survival of any theological movement depends on the consent it continues to command on the part of its adherents. In the course of biblical study, countless trends have arisen, evoking popular sentiment for a while, but ultimately finding themselves consigned to the ash heap of history. The same may eventually happen to the NPP. Yet I would submit that a genuine "Copernican revolution" has transpired in our understanding of the NT message in relation to contemporary Judaism: Pauline exegesis will never be the same again. But even so, as NPP scholars continue to scour over the biblical and Jewish materials, numerous adjustments and course corrections on their part will call forth qualifications, clarifications, and refinements of the original "Sanders/Dunn Trajectory."[69] Indeed, Dunn himself, addressing the matter of balance in the scholarly treatments of texts, counsels that those who come in on the next phase of the debate will have the responsibility to ensure that the pendulum settles in a truer position.[70]

At heart, it is just the issue of *balance* that will determine the fate of the NPP and that of its alternatives. To take a concrete example, in my review of Gathercole's *Where is Boasting?* I criticized the book for what appeared to be a lack of such balance. Building on an observation of Dunn, I maintained that if Sanders has been criticized for polarizing in favor of election at the expense of obedience, Gathercole is in danger of polarizing in the opposite direction. Gathercole chides Sanders for his systematic methodology; yet Gathercole's own determination to have works as the basis of final salvation is as systematic as Sanders' approach ever was. Only this is a systemization in reverse: whereas Sanders is open to the charge that his approach resulted in a downplay of works, Gathercole's systemization gives rather short shrift to election and the covenant. In a subsequent recension of the review, I concede that his endeavors to balance election and works in Judaism are more pronounced than I originally gave him credit for. The phrase "short shrift" was chosen to say that in comparison with works, election/grace are more in the background than the foreground of Gathercole's book, not that the latter are bypassed altogether. I take his point that *election and works* are the twofold basis of final salvation. I also take the point that Sanders had already substantiated the factor of election and that there was no need for Gathercole to reproduce his discussions. Yet by that very standard, if Gathercole's treatment of texts is acknowledged to be balanced, then so must Sanders' be. However, it is just such a balance that Gathercole is unwilling to grant to Sanders when he ascribes to him a "minimalistic" understanding of covenant faithfulness that reduces righteousness to "mere intention."[71] I think Sanders' handling of the Dead Sea Scrolls proves otherwise.[72]

It would be pointless to engage in a tit-for-tat row about the degree of balance and fairness in scholarly management of the materials. In a rejoinder to my review,[73] Gathercole appeals to such witnesses as George Brooke, Peter Stuhlmacher, Seyoon Kim, and John Barclay to the effect that he had indeed struck the balance between election/grace and works. But even with the above concession, I must reaffirm that I (and James Dunn) did not come away with the impression that Gathercole had assigned anything like equal weight to the former as compared with the latter. And certainly, I must still maintain that Gathercole's primal mistake is to translate the "works" of Judaism into "earning salvation." None of this is intended to make Gathercole a whipping boy or to make a case that the NPP is somehow inherently superior. It is simply to illustrate that if any (re)construction of Paul in relation to Judaism is to survive into the future—NPP or otherwise—it must be prepared to make "course corrections" in light of the most recent data. It is not a question of the truth changing, but rather of our perception of the truth. At the end of the day, the NPP or any other movement will command consent in the eyes of evangelicals only to the degree that it is able to spiral between text and context and bring the "significance" (application) of the text into line with its "meaning."

It is just in bridging the two horizons of the meaning and significance of the text that a work like Gathercole's has much to offer. He has amply demonstrated that boasting in the Judaism prior to and contemporary with Paul entails two elements: election/national privileges and actual performance of the Torah. His book thus serves as a useful and welcomed corrective to an imbalance on the part of some practitioners of the NPP. As he notes many times, there has been a tendency to play up sociological matters (Jewish distinctiveness and self-identity) and to play down the Torah's own requirement that one really and truly "do the law." Perhaps the divide between the two on the part of certain notable scholars is not as stark as Gathercole would have us believe. Nevertheless, to the degree that he has redressed the balance in favor of a reading of Judaism and Paul that more accurately reflects the actual data, we are in his debt.

So, is there a future for the NPP? Most definitely, as long as it is able to weigh the historical materials fairly and accurately (balance), bridge the horizons between text and context, and especially as long as it endeavors to preserve the very lifeblood of Paul's preaching of Christ—*in all things he is to have the preeminence* (Col 1:18).

---

[1] D. A. Hagner, "Paul and Judaism: Testing the New Perspective," in P. Stuhlmacher, *Revisiting Paul's Doctrine of Justification: A Challenge to the New Perspective* (Downers Grove: InterVarsity, 2001), 75, 105. Hagner himself is quite sure that this Copernican revolution is taking us down the wrong path. But, I would ask, If the revolution is *genuinely Copernican*, how can it be taking us down the wrong path? Apart from Stuhlmacher's book, mention can be made of only a few negative reactions, more or less, to the NPP: M. A. Seifrid, *Justification By Faith: The Origin and Development of A Central Pauline Theme*, Novum Testamentum Supplements 68 (Leiden: Brill, 1992); D. A. Carson, P. T. O'Brien and M. A. Seifrid (eds.), *Justification and Variegated Nomism. Volume 1: The Complexities of Second Temple Judaism* (Grand Rapids: Baker, 2001); A. A. Das, *Paul, the Law, and the Covenant* (Peabody: Hendrickson, 2001); S. Kim, *Paul and the New Perspective: Second Thoughts on the Origins of Paul's Gospel* (Grand Rapids: Eerdmans, 2002); S. J. Gathercole, *Where is Boasting? Early Jewish Soteriology and Paul's Response in Romans 1-5* (Grand Rapids: Eerdmans, 2002); S. Westerholm, *Perspectives Old and New on Paul: The "Lutheran" Paul and His Critics* (Grand Rapids: Eerdmans, 2004). Another category of literature is comprised of works that offer some criticisms of the NPP and yet agree in the main that Paul does not take issue with a merit-based system of soteriology, e.g., K. Kuula, *The Law, The Covenant and God's*

Plan. Volume 1. *Paul's Polemical Treatment of the Law in Galatians*, Publications of the Finnish Exegetical Society 72 (Helsinki/Göttingen: Finnish Exegetical Society/Vandenhoeck & Ruprecht, 1999), esp. 65, 73. Various non-NPP scholars champion the analysis of the rabbinic materials by F. Avemarie, *Tora und Leben: Untersuchungen zur Heilsbedeutung der Tora in der frühen rabbinischen Literatur*, Texte und Studien zum Antiken Judentum 55 (Tübingen: Mohr-Siebeck, 1996). Yet it is to be noted that Avemarie acknowledges the grace-element in these sources, although he believes that there is a tension between grace/election, on the one hand, and works, on the other. Most strikingly, Avemarie grants that throughout this literature it is possible to speak of a "covenantal nomism." The Torah of the rabbis cannot be divorced from this context in which the law was given: in this sense, Sander's coinage of the phrase, says Avemarie, is certainly justified (ibid., 584, n. 40).

[2] Another attempt to allay the fears of evangelicals respecting the NPP is the excellent introduction to the subject by M. B. Thompson, *The New Perspective on Paul*, Grove Biblical Series (Cambridge: Grove Books, 2002).

[3] For example, B. Byrne, "Interpreting Romans Theologically in a Post-'New Perspective' Perspective," *Harvard Theological Review* 94 (2001), 227-41; and R. H. Gundry, in a personal communication.

[4] Carson, in the Introduction to *Justification and Variegated Nomism*, 1.

[5] Dunn, "The New Perspective on Paul," *Bulletin of the John Rylands University Library of Manchester* 65 (1983), 95-122. The article is reprinted in Dunn's *Jesus, Paul, and the Law: Studies in Mark and Galatians* (Louisville: Westminster/John Knox, 1990), 183-214.

[6] Sanders, *Paul and Palestinian Judaism: A Comparison of Patterns of Religion* (Philadelphia: Fortress, 1977). It is frequently overlooked that there have been precursors to Sanders in relatively recent times, apart from earlier scholars like G. F. Moore, such as R. N. Longenecker, *Paul: Apostle of Liberty* (New York: Harper & Row, 1964); M. Limbeck, *Die Ordnung des Heils: Untersuchungen zum Gesetzesverständnis des Frühjudentums* (Düsseldorf: Patmos, 1971). Practically contemporaneous with Sanders are N. T. Wright, "The Paul of History and the Apostle of Faith," *Tyndale Bulletin* 29 (1978), 61-88, and U. Wilckens, *Der Brief an die Römer*, Evangelisch-katholischer Kommentar zum Neuen Testament 6. 3 vols. (Zürich/Neukirchen: Benziger/Neukirchener, 1978-82).

[7] Sanders, *Paul*, 75, 420, 544.

[8] Ibid., 422.

[9] Dunn, *Romans*, Word Biblical Commentary 38 a, b. 2 vols. (Dallas: Word, 1988), 1.lxv. See additionally Dunn's *The Theology of Paul the Apostle* (Grand Rapids: Eerdmans, 1998), 335-40.

[10] From Dunn's review of *Justification and Variegated Nomism*, *Trinity Journal* ns 25 (2004), 111.

[11] The factor of diversity within Second Temple Judaism is often raised as an objection to the NPP, as exemplified by *Justification and Variegated*

Nomism. In lieu of a full discussion, I note only that NPP scholars are not unaware of the phenomenon of diversity. See J. D. G. Dunn, *The Partings of the Ways: Between Christianity and Judaism and Their Significance for the Character of Christianity* (Philadelphia: Trinity Press International, 1991), 18; id., *Jesus Remembered*, Christianity in the Making 1 (Grand Rapids: Eerdmans, 2003), 265-86; D. Garlington, *'The Obedience of Faith': A Pauline Phrase in Historical Context*, Wissenschaftliche Untersuchungen zum Neuen Testament 2/38 (Tübingen: Mohr-Siebeck, 1991), 263-64. As far as the thesis of *Justification and Variegated Nomism* is concerned, I would repeat a comment from my review of the book (*Exegetical Essays* [3rd ed.; Eugene, OR: Wipf & Stock, 2003], 339, also posted at http://www.thepaulpage.com). At this stage of the game, the editors would appear to be engaging in piece of presumptive reasoning: Second Temple Judaism was diverse; therefore, there were legalists in Paul's day; therefore, Paul is arguing against the "legalists" (as opposed to the "covenantal nomists"). Time will tell how this apparent agenda will unfold, but one senses that the entire enterprise may well prove to be reductionistic.

[12] Some critics of the NPP have attempted to argue that whereas this literature is the product of scholarly enclaves, the "common people" or "lay Jews" would have embraced a more naïve notion of works-righteousness salvation. See, e.g., D. J. Moo, *The Epistle to the Romans*, New International Commentary on the New Testament (Grand Rapids: Eerdmans, 1996), 216-17. However, such an idea is rooted purely in silence and is, for that simple reason, completely incapable of demonstration.

[13] Dunn, "New Perspective," 121.

[14] Apart from his pioneering article, "New Perspective," Dunn's position is reiterated in many places. See, for example, *Theology of Paul*, 354-66; 371-72; 358-85; *Partings of the Ways*, 135-39; "4QMMT and Galatians," *New Testament Studies* 43 (1997), 147-53; "In Search of Common Ground," *Paul and the Mosaic Law*, ed. J. D. G. Dunn (Grand Rapids: Eerdmans, 2001), 309-34.

[15] Dunn, "Works of the Law and the Curse of the Law (Galatians 3.10-14)," *New Testament Studies* 31 (1985), 526 (this essay is likewise reprinted in *Jesus, Paul, and the Law*, 215-41). See further his "Yet once more—'The Works of the Law': A Response," *Journal for the Study of the New Testament* 46 (1992), 99-117.

[16] Dunn, *Theology of Paul*, 358, n. 97.

[17] D. Garlington, *Faith, Obedience, and Perseverance: Aspects of Paul's Letter to the Romans*, Wissenschaftliche Untersuchungen zum Neuen Testament 79 (Tübingen: Mohr-Siebeck, 1994), 74-79.

[18] Elliott, *The Rhetoric of Romans: Argumentative Constraint and Strategy and Paul's Dialogue with Judaism*, Journal for the Study of the New Testament: Supplement Series 45 (Sheffield: Sheffield Academic

Press, 1990), 229. See further J. C. Beker, *Paul the Apostle: The Triumph of God in Life and Thought* (Philadelphia: Fortress, 1980), 176-81.

[19] J. M. Gundry Volf, *Paul and Perseverance: Staying In and Falling Away* (Louisville: Westminster/John Knox, 1990), 81. G. C. Berkouwer also identifies continuity in salvation as the central problem of perseverance (*Faith and Perseverance*, Studies in Dogmatics [Grand Rapids: Eerdmans, 1958], 12).

[20] Cranfield, *A Critical and Exegetical Commentary on the Epistle to the Romans*, International Critical Commentary. 2 vols. (Edinburgh: T. & T. Clark, 1975, 1979), 1.266.

[21] Garlington, *Faith, Obedience*, 44-71; Gathercole, *Boasting*, 124-34; K. L. Yinger, *Paul, Judaism, and Judgment According to Deeds*, Society for New Testament Studies Monograph Series 105 (Cambridge: Cambridge University Press, 1999), 143-82.

[22] The terminology is picked up by several Jewish sources. 1 Macc 2:67 employs the exact phrase "the doers of the law" to designate loyalist Jews who would be vindicated against the Gentiles by divine justice. Similarly, 1QHab (7:11; 8:1; 12:4-5) speaks of "the doers of the law" as those who observe the community's rules (*halakoth*).

[23] Byrne, "Living Out the Righteousness of God: The Contribution of Rom 6:1-8:13 to an Understanding of Paul's Ethical Presuppositions," *Catholic Biblical Quarterly* 43 (1981), 578.

[24] Snodgrass, "Justification by Grace—to the Doers: An Analysis of the Place of Romans 2 in the Theology of Paul," *New Testament Studies* 32 (1986), 80-81 (italics mine). "Judgment according to works is not the contradiction of justification by faith, but its presupposition. The significance of faith and participation in Christ for obedience are assumed for Paul" (ibid., 86). See further G. C. Berkouwer, *Faith and Sanctification*, Studies in Dogmatics (Grand Rapids: Eerdmans, 1952), 108-13.

[25] Crossan and Reed, *In Search of Paul: How Jesus's Apostle Opposed Rome's Empire with God's Kingdom. A New Vision of Paul's Words and World* (San Francisco: HarperSanFrancisco, 2004), 385-86.

[26] Cf. my *Faith, Obedience*, 70-71.

[27] Gathercole, *Boasting*, 226, 265.

[28] Wright, *The Climax of the Covenant: Christ and the Law in Pauline Theology* (Minneapolis: Fortress, 1991), 137-56; id., *The New Testament and the People of God*, Christian Origins and the Question of God 1 (Minneapolis: Fortress, 1991); id., *Jesus and the Victory of God*, Christian Origins and the Question of God 2 (Minneapolis: Fortress, 1996). See additionally J. M. Scott (ed.), *Exile: Old Testament, Jewish, and Christian Conceptions*, Journal for the Study of Judaism: Supplements 56 (Leiden: Brill, 1997); C. M. Pate, *Communities of the Last Days: The Dead Sea Scrolls, the New Testament and the Story of Israel* (Downers Grove: InterVarsity, 2000); id., *The Reverse of the*

Curse: Paul, Wisdom, and the Law, Wissenschaftliche Untersuchungen zum Neuen Testament 2/114 (Tübingen: Mohr-Siebeck, 2000).

[29] As contra J. Piper, *Counted Righteous in Christ: Should We Abandon the Imputation of Christ's Righteousness?* (Wheaton: Crossway, 2002), 69-80.

[30] See S. McKnight, *A New Vision for Israel: The Teachings of Jesus in National Context* (Grand Rapids: Eerdmans, 1999), 33-39; S. J. Hafemann, "The Covenant Relationship," *Central Themes in Biblical Theology: Mapping Unity in Diversity* (eds. S. J. Hafemann and P. R. House; Grand Rapids: Baker Academic, 2007), 20-65.

[31] Recently, Mark Seifrid has sought to weaken the connection of righteousness and covenant ("Righteousness Language in the Hebrew Scriptures and Early Judaism," *Justification and Variegated Nomism*, 415-42).

[32] Yinger, *Paul, Judaism, and Judgment*, 19-140.

[33] The consciousness of the Torah = righteousness equation comes to the fore in various Second Temple texts. According to this literature, Israel was to "walk in *obedience* to the law" (CD 7:7), that is, "to observe *the whole law* of the Lord" (*T. Jud* 26:1; *T. Gad* 3:1; *T. Asher* 6:3), to "walk in perfection in *all His ways*" (CD 2:16), "*obeying all His instructions*" (CD 7:5; cf. 1QS 1:3-5), "to act according to *the exact tenor of the Law*" (CD 4:8) and to "cling to the covenant of the fathers" (1QS 2:9; 1 Macc 2:50). In short, Israel was to observe "*the righteousness of the law of God*" (*T. Dan* 6:11) and live "the life of righteousness" by walking in "the ways of truth and righteousness" (4 Macc 13:24; Tob 1:3). It was as true of first-century Judaism as of the earlier Maccabean martyrs: "We should truly bring shame upon our ancestors if we did not live in obedience to the Law and take Moses as our counselor" (4 Macc 9:2). Because the law was eternal (e.g., Sir 24:9, 33; Bar 4:1; Wis 18:4; *T. Naph* 3:1-2), those who sought to enter the covenant were obliged to "be converted to the law of Moses *according to all his commands*" (1QS 5:8).

[34] On the eternity of the law in Jewish literature, see W. D. Davies, *Torah in the Messianic Age and/or the Age to Come*, Society of Biblical Literature Monograph Series 7 (Philadelphia: SBL, 1952); R. Banks, *Jesus and the Law in the Synoptic Tradition*, Society for New Testament Studies Monograph Series 28 (Cambridge: Cambridge University Press, 1975), 49-64, 67-85; id., "The Eschatological Role of Law in Pre- and Post- Christian Jewish Thought," *Reconciliation and Hope: New Testament Essays on Atonement and Eschatology Presented to L. L. Morris on His 60th Birthday*, ed. R. Banks (Grand Rapids: Eerdmans, 1974), 173-85.

[35] See my *Obedience of Faith*, 255-57.

[36] See T. D. Gordon, "The Problem at Galatia," *Interpretation* 41 (1987), 32-43.

[37] Gaventa, "The Singularity of the Gospel: A Reading of Galatians," *Pauline Theology. Volume 1: Thessalonians, Philippians, Galatians,*

Philemon, ed. J. M. Bassler (Minneapolis: Fortress, 1991), 159 (italics mine). Similarly, S. J. Hafemann concludes that the essential distinction between Paul and Qumran (and I would say Judaism more broadly considered) is not the law per se nor the nature of the eschatological community as such, but his understanding of the person and work of Christ and their impact on both the law and the nature of the people of God ("The Spirit of the New Covenant, the Law, and the Temple of God's Presence: Five Theses on Qumran Self-Understanding and the Contours of Paul's Thought," *Evangelium, Schriftauslegung, Kirche: Festschrift für Peter Stuhlmacher zum 65. Geburtstag*, eds. J. Adna, S. J. Hafemann and O. Hofius [Göttingen: Vandenhoeck & Ruprecht, 1997], 188-89).

[38] Martyn, *Galatians*, Anchor Bible 33a (New York: Doubleday, 1997), 124-25.

[39] See my *An Exposition of Galatians: A New Perspective/Reformational Reading*, 2nd ed. (Eugene, OR: Wipf & Stock, 2004), 151-52, 162-65.

[40] Sanders, *Paul, the Law, and the Jewish People* (Philadelphia: Fortress, 1983), 19

[41] Ibid., 18.

[42] Ibid., 45, 46.

[43] Cousar, *Galatians*, Interpretation (Louisville: John Knox, 1982), 61.

[44] Wright, *What Saint Paul Really Said: Was Paul of Tarsus the Real Founder of Christianity?* (Grand Rapids: Eerdmans, 1997), 119, 120-22, 131.

[45] Ibid., 121.

[46] Ibid., 122.

[47] In this regard, Hafemann is correct in insisting that the context of Paul's usage of "works of the law" is the contrast between the two covenant eras within the history of redemption, not (merely, I would say) a material or socio-ethnic contrast. "Hence, to continue to maintain allegiance to the old covenant once the new has arrived not only denies the saving efficacy of Christ's work, but also leads at times to a false boasting and ethnically based 'legalism' [I prefer "nomism"] as a by-product" ("Spirit," 178, n. 24).

[48] A very telling consideration is that "righteousness" and "salvation" are placed in synonymous parallel in some conspicuous passages in the Prophets and Psalms: Isa 45:8; 45:21-25; 46:13; 51:5–6, 8; 56:1; 59:17; 61:10; 62:1-2; 63:1; Ps 24:6; 51:14; 71:15–16; 98:1-3, 8-9 (LXX 97:2-3, 8-9); 4 Ezra 8:36, 39–40; CD 20:20; 1QS 11:11–15; *1 Enoch* 99:10. Noteworthy as well are Ps 35:27-28 (LXX 34:27-28); 72:1-4 (LXX 71:1-4, 7); 85:11-13 (LXX 84:12-14); 96:13 (LXX 95:13); Isa 9:7 (LXX 9:6); 11:1-2, 5; 45:8, 22-25; 51:5-6; 53:10-11; 61:11; Jer 23:5-6; Mal 4:2 (LXX 3:20). See the further assemblage of passages by R. H. Gundry, "The Nonimputation of Christ's Righteousness," *Justification: What's at Stake in the Current Debates?* eds. M. Husbands and D. J. Treier (Downers Grove/Leicester: InterVarsity/Apollos, 2004), 36-38.

[49] Some such understanding of the relation of works to judgment was already proposed by Wilckens, *Römer*, 1.142-46; Snodgrass, "Justification by Grace;" C. J. Roetzel, *Judgment in the Community: A Study of the Relationship Between Eschatology and Ecclesiology in Paul* (Leiden: Brill, 1972); K. P. Donfried, "Justification and Last Judgment in Paul," *Zeitschrift für die neutestamentliche Wissenschaft* 67 (1976), 90-110; R. Heiligenthal, *Werke als Zeichnen: Untersuchungen zur Bedeutung der menschlichen Taten im Frühjudentum, Neuen Testament und Frühchristentum*, Wissenschaftliche Untersuchungen zum Neuen Testament 2/9 (Tübingen: Mohr-Siebeck, 1983); L. Mattern, *Das Verständnis des Gerichtes bei Paulus*, Abhandlungen zur Theologie des Alten und Neuen Testaments 47 (Zürich: Zwingli, 1966); E. Synofzik, *Die Gerichts-und Vergeltungsaussagen bei Paulus: Eine traditions-geschichtliche Untersuchung*, Göttinger theologische Arbeiten 8 (Göttingen: Vandenhoeck & Ruprecht, 1977); J.-M. Cambier, "Le jugement de touts les hommes par Dieu seul, selon la vérité, dans Rom 2.1-3.20," *Zeitschrift für die neutestamentliche Wissenschaft* 66 (1975), 187-213; N. M. Watson, "Justified by Faith, Judged by Works—an Antinomy?" *New Testament Studies* 29 (1983), 209-21. Cf. more recently, McKnight, *New Vision*, 33-39.

[50] By way of qualification, Gathercole's charge that Dunn in particular has removed works from the agenda of last judgment is unfair, at least to a degree. In point of fact, Dunn acknowledges that the need actually to do the law was characteristic of historic Judaism (*Theology of Paul*, 135-36).

[51] Roetzel affirms that although Paul's judgment language shares the viewpoint of the OT, Apocalyptic, and rabbinic materials, he differs in that he places his materials in christological focus (*Judgment*, 90).

[52] Moore, *Judaism in the First Centuries of the Christian Era*. 3 vols. (Cambridge, MS: Harvard University Press, rep. 1966).

[53] Longenecker, *Paul*, 65-85.

[54] Ibid., 66-68. Note especially his assessment of "Nomistic Pharisaism" (ibid., 82-83).

[55] The translation "maintain" rather than "establish" for the verb *stēsai* is based on Jer 34 (LXX 41):18; Sir 11:20; 44:20; 45:23; 1 Macc 2:27). Particularly relevant in view of Paul's acknowledgment of Israel's zeal are Sir 45:23 (Phinehas "stood firm" [*stēnai*] when the people turned away) and 1 Macc 2:27 ("everyone who is zealous for the law and who maintains [*histōn*] the covenant, let him come after me"). This is Paul's real point: Israel is zealous to *maintain* "her own" (*tēn idian*) covenant righteousness and refuses to submit to God's latter-day embodiment of his righteousness in Christ.

[56] See my *Faith, Obedience*, 32-43, as seconded by J. A. Fitzmyer, *Romans*, Anchor Bible 33 (New York: Doubleday, 1993), 318. Wright similarly speaks of "Israel's idolatrous nationalism" (*Jesus and the Victory of God*, 462).

⁵⁷ T. C. Penner has admirably set James within an eschatological framework (*The Epistle of James and Eschatology: Re-reading an Ancient Christian Letter*, Journal for the Study of the New Testament: Supplement Series 121 [Sheffield: Sheffield Academic Press, 1996], esp. 121-213). However, Penner is wrong to think that in the milieu of Jewish tradition it is Paul who has deviated from the tradition (ibid., 68). While Rom 4:1-15 removes circumcision and Torah observance from the requirements of justification, 4:16-25 stresses none other than the persevering quality of Abraham's faith. Because the patriarch remained convinced of God's promise (v. 21), *"for this reason (dio)* it was reckoned to him as righteousness" (v. 22). Both James and Paul are occupied with Abraham's fidelity in testing situations, as supported by James' reference to "the perseverance of Job" in 5:11. See further J. B. Adamson, *James: The Man and His Message* (Grand Rapids: Eerdmans, 1989), 203-10, 266-307.

⁵⁸ Dunn, *Partings of the Ways*, 96-97.

⁵⁹ Ibid., 96.

⁶⁰ Ibid., 97.

⁶¹ As R. B. Gaffin maintains, the primary interest of biblical study is the interest of the text itself, namely, the history which the text reports and interprets. The concern of exegesis, then, is with what lies behind the text—the history of salvation. The discipline which seeks to correlate the findings of historical exegesis is biblical theology. Gaffin is certainly right that "this is an insight that the program of biblical hermeneutics needs to test and consider more carefully" ("The Place and Importance of Introduction to the New Testament," *The New Testament Student. Volume One: Studying the New Testament Today*, ed. J. H. Skilton [Nutley, NJ: Presbyterian & Reformed, 1974], 146). What is true of salvation history is likewise true of the place the NT occupies in the setting of the ancient world. See G. Osborne, *The Hermeneutical Spiral: A Comprehensive Introduction to Biblical Interpretation* (Downers Grove: InterVarsity, 1991), 21; J. Jeffers, *The Greco-Roman World of the New Testament Era: Exploring the Background of Early Christianity* (Downers Grove: InterVarsity, 1999), 293.

⁶² See my "The Biblical-Theological Method," *Exegetical Essays*, 1-15.

⁶³ Among many discussions, I refer simply to J. S. Feinberg (ed.), *Continuity and Discontinuity: Perspectives on the Relationship Between the Old and New Testaments. Essays in Honor of S. Lewis Johnson, Jr.* (Westchester, ILL: Crossway, 1988).

⁶⁴ See Garlington, *Galatians*, 148-49.

⁶⁵ Ibid., 240-41.

⁶⁶ See especially Wright, *Climax*; *New Testament and People of God*; *Jesus and the Victory of God*.

⁶⁷ See my "Role Reversal and Paul's Use of Scripture in Galatians 3.10-13," *Journal for the Study of the New Testament* 65 (1997), 101-04 (= *Exegetical Essays*, 228-31).

[68] McKnight, *New Vision*, 34.
[69] The phrase is that of M. Silva, "The Law and Christianity: Dunn's New Synthesis," *Westminster Theological Journal* 53 (1991), 341.
[70] In a personal communication from Professor Dunn.
[71] Gathercole, *Boasting*, 182-84, 187-88.
[72] Sanders, *Paul*, esp. 304, 320.

FAITH'S OBEDIENCE AND ISRAEL'S TRIUMPHANT KING: ROMANS 1:5 AGAINST ITS OLD TESTAMENT BACKDROP

1. Introduction

Paul's singular phrase "the obedience of faith" (Rom 1:5) appears at the pivotal point of the opening paragraph of Romans, which serves as a kind of "table of contents" for the entire epistle.[1] Traditionally, 1:16-17 has been looked upon as the letter's thematic statement. That is fair enough, as long as it is understood that these verses are, in point of fact, a recapitulation of the earlier announcement of Paul's intentions in 1:1-7. And the words that best summarize everything are: "the obedience of faith among all the nations for his name's sake." This is matched by the statement toward the end of Romans: Paul's desire to spread the gospel to lands beyond Rome (15:14-33). From these parallels we may deduce that Romans is bracketed on both ends by Paul's missionary concerns and ambitions.[2] If his preaching was meant to promote "the obedience of faith among all the nations" (1:5; 16:26), then he has been sent by Christ to "win obedience from the Gentiles, by word and deed" (15:18).

For this reason, J. D. G. Dunn is quite right: "To clarify what faith is and its importance to his gospel is one of Paul's chief objectives in this letter."[3] In order to appreciate the point, it will be necessary briefly to relate the importance of faith to a main undercurrent of Romans, namely, "to redraw the boundaries which marked out the people of God."[4] Whereas before to be a member of the covenant community was to live within the boundary set by the law, the eschatological people have assumed a new identity. And since there is now "no distinction" between Jew and Gentile (1:16-17; 2:11; 10:12), Paul endeavors in Romans, particularly in chapters 6-8 and 12-16, to expound the ethical and social responsibilities of this new corporate entity. With this end in view, the letter's opening paragraph draws upon concepts evocative of Israel's relationship to Yahweh and applies them to *all* the Romans, the called of Jesus Christ.[5] Again, the pivotal point of the introduction is v. 5: "A neat and fitting summary of his complete apologetic in Romans."[6]

In writing in the manner that he does, Paul portrays his mission as the instrument by which the risen Christ asserts his rule over the new people of God. W. A. Beardslee can say: "The apostle's preaching was not merely eschatological in its subject matter; it was itself a part of the eschatological drama. The apostle was called, not just to build a group of believers, but to take part in the work of God which is to culminate in a wholly new order of existence."[7] Anton Fridrichsen agrees: "When Paul in Romans introduces himself as a 'called apostle' he characterizes himself as an eschatological person. He is a man who has been appointed to a proper place and a peculiar task in the series of events to be accomplished in the final days of this world; those events whose central person is the Messiah, the Christ Jesus, crucified, risen, and returning to judgment and salvation."[8] This means that Paul's preaching forms an integral and indispensable part of the events of the end-times. It is through his proclamation of Christ that the new creation comes into being; and if he does not proclaim Christ, there is no new creation. No wonder he can say elsewhere: "Woe to me if I do not preach the gospel" (1 Cor 9:16).

All this is familiar. But even so, there is an extensive background to Rom 1:5 that has not been explored or even noticed by the commentators.[9] This milieu is provided by a number of passages that predict a king/son who would take the nations in captive obedience to himself. In the final chapter of my *Obedience of Faith*, I endeavored to explore some of the Jewish backdrop to the verse. However, there has never been a systematic presentation of those materials derived from Israel's Scriptures that bear on Paul's announcement that faith's obedience to King Jesus is now being proclaimed among the nations.

Because this essay is presented as a *donum* to Professor Norman Shepherd, it is only appropriate that its focus be that of the believer's obedience to Christ the King. Pauline scholars are in virtual agreement that "the obedience of faith" entails more than an obedience that consists in faith, one's believing reception of the gospel. Rather, "Faith does not mean intellectual consent to a proposition, but vital commitment to a program."[10] Or, as T. R. Schreiner puts it: "Paul never conceived of salvation taking root among the nations without a change of behavior. The gospel that takes hold of human beings changes them so that they become servants of righteousness. Such new behavior, however, has its roots in faith, in trusting God for the strength and power to live a new life."[11] The kingship of Christ, therefore, is far more than a theological theorem. Rather, the King issues a royal summons for the nations to comply with his will, and the only appropriate response is an obedience from the heart.

2. Romans 1:5 in the Opening of the Letter

Paul commences Romans by identifying himself as the called apostle of Jesus Christ, set apart for the gospel of God (v. 1). He then informs the readers that this gospel was promised beforehand through the prophets in the Holy Scriptures (v. 2). This is no incidental remark, because it will prove to be foundational to the way in which Paul uses the OT throughout the letter. Not only so, the fact that he grounds his gospel in the prophetic Scriptures means that the prophets of Israel provide the basic framework for interpreting Romans, as well as his preaching more broadly considered. That is to say, since the prophets are all about Israel's exile and return to the land, Paul's gospel is his announcement that, in Christ, the exile is now at an end and the captives have begun to return.[12] By his use of "gospel," then, Paul is the latter-day herald announcing that the new Israel has been delivered, not from Egypt, Babylon or any other human power but from the "present evil age" (Gal 1:4), and, as he will say so shockingly later in Romans, from the law! As such a herald, Paul follows in the footsteps of Jesus, who himself proclaimed that Isa 61:1-2, among others, was fulfilled in his preaching of the kingdom of God (Matt 11:5; Luke 4:17-21; 7:22). That there should be a deliverance above and beyond the original prophetic vision is confirmed by the fact that certain crucial features of the hoped-for release had not as yet been fulfilled. Most notably, Ezekiel's supramundane temple fails to be constructed, the Shekinah does not return to this temple, the Spirit is not poured out on the nation, and the new creation is not realized in all its splendor. But this is where the NT transposes all these anticipated blessings into the "higher octave" of salvation history and announces that they all have been fulfilled in Jesus of Nazareth, although a final and consummate phase of his accomplishment still awaits.

Next in his introduction, Paul announces that the gospel concerns God's Son. According to v. 3, this Son is a descendent of David ("according to the flesh"), which qualifies him to be Israel's king and Messiah (v. 3). "According to the flesh" is capable of various interpretations.[13] However, the phrase is perhaps best interpreted in light of 9:5 ("the Christ according to the flesh"), especially as compared with 9:3-4 ("my brothers," "my kinsmen according to the flesh" and "Israelites"). In other words, the reference is to Jesus' "fleshly" national and ancestral origins as an "Israelite." Thus, we might paraphrase "according to the flesh" in 1:3 as something like: "as to his national origins" (cf. 2 Tim 2:8: "Jesus Christ...of the seed of David"). At the forefront of "flesh" is just what Paul means by it in Rom 9:3-5, 6; 11:14 (Israel is "my flesh"); cf. 11:1-2. He is concerned in the opening paragraph of Romans to establish the groundwork of the whole letter. His point is that the subject of his gospel satisfies the requirements to be the Jewish Messiah and is, therefore, worthy of acceptance by Israel.

Verses 4-5 develop the notion of Jesus' kingship, the one who has been installed as "Son of God" on the throne of Israel. As background, Robert Jewett points to the royal decree of Ps 2:7, with its close analogues in the Aramaic section of Daniel.[14] Not only so, he became the Son of God "in power" when he was raised from the dead by the "Spirit of holiness" (cf. Ps 50:11; Isa 63:10). That is to say, his kingship entered into an even more powerful phase when he was raised "by the glory of the Father" (Rom 6:4) and exalted on high. Regarding Jesus' investiture with power, Otto Betz directs us to the conjunction of 1 Samuel 16 and 2 Samuel 5: David's anointment as king and his actual assumption of the role of kingship. "One need only think of David, the father of Jesus according to the flesh: he was chosen and anointed king at a very early age, but he had to wait a long time until he was raised to be king 'in power'." Jesus' kingship/messiahship thus fits into a Davidic typology. Moreover, in accord with the preaching of Peter in Acts 2:25-35, Jesus' resurrection is a "raising up" in a twofold sense: enthronement and raising from the dead. As foretold by Psalm 16, God would gloriously fulfill his promise and bring about the "raising" of the Messiah, not only as an enthronement but also as a resurrection from the dead.[15]

Paul thus issues the "royal decree" that God has vindicated his Son by raising him from the dead (cf. 1 Tim 3:16) and placing the Spirit upon him, in fulfillment of those prophetic passages that foretold the joint work of the Anointed and the Spirit (e.g., Isa 11:1-2; 42:1; 61:1; Mal 3:1-6; cf. Ezek 36:26-27; Joel 2:28). He is none other than the "Lord" who has commissioned Paul to promote "faith's obedience among all the nations for his name's sake." The actual phrase "the obedience of faith" (*hupakoē pisteōs*) is unique. No one before him ever used this combination of terms (though a kindred expression occurs in Acts 6:7: "a great many of the priests were *obedient to the faith*"). The idea is found frequently in Second Temple literature, but Paul was the first one to say it in so many words. I have argued elsewhere that Paul has in mind more than thing at the same time, i.e., both the obedience which *is* faith and the obedience that *results from* faith.[16] C. E. B. Cranfield puts it well: "The equivalence for Paul of faith in God and obedience to him may be illustrated again and again from this epistle. Paul's preaching is aimed at obtaining from his hearers true obedience to God, the essence of which is a responding to His message of good news and faith."[17] "So the scope of Paul's [missionary] work," writes Stephen Barton, "was not just evangelism with a view to initial conversion; it was also to do with building and establishing in the faith of Christ."[18]

It is just in this regard that the carefully chosen phrase "Spirit of holiness" (*pneuma hagiōsunēs*) in 1:4 comes into play. The promise of the Spirit as an "eschatological principle of obedience," as Barry Smith proposes, originates in the promise of Deut 30:6 that the hearts of the returned exiles will be circumcised, resulting in their obedience to the covenant. Later, Ezekiel will renew the same vision (11:19; 36:26, 27; cf. 37:14; 39:29; Jer 31:33; 32:39). The idea that God would spiritually transform his people in the last days, as Smith demonstrates, persists into the Second Temple period.[19] Drawing on *Jub.* 51:10-11 (1:20) and the Qumran texts of 4Q504 5:15-16; 1QS 4:21; 3:7-8; 9:3-4; 1QSb 1:1-2; 1QH^a 4:26; 8:15; 15:6-7; 4Q434-38, Smith insightfully concludes that "spirit of holiness" denotes a divinely granted disposition of obedience. As such, the phrase is synonymous with "the various expressions in the Hebrew Bible that describe the means by which Israel will be spiritually transformed at the eschaton."[20] Smith's observation on *Jubilees* pertains to the other texts too:

> The creation of a spirit of holiness is God's implanting of a disposition toward holiness in his people; similarly, purification is the removal of the disposition to sin. The result of God's creating a spirit of holiness for the Israelites and his purification of them is that the people will henceforth keep the commandments, never again turning away from God.[21]

So, it is hardly accidental that Paul should draw upon the very phrase "Spirit of holiness." In a context replete with eschatological references, it is none other than this Spirit who has raised Jesus from the dead but who, at the same time, has also raised Christian believers, according to Rom 6:4-11. Especially in conjunction with the ensuing verse, 1:5, "Spirit of holiness" as an "eschatological principle of obedience" virtually shouts out at us. What Jewish authors anticipated as a divine gift at the end of the age has, for Paul, been realized in Christ's resurrection and exaltation, as a result of which he has poured out his Spirit on all flesh (Joel 2:28-32; Acts 2:17-21; Rom 5:5; 1 John 2:20, 27).

3. Israel's Triumphant King in the Hebrew Scriptures

Genesis 49:8-10[22]

On his deathbed, the patriarch Jacob envisages the following for his son Judah:

Judah, your brothers shall praise you;
  your hand shall be on the neck of your enemies;
  your father's sons shall bow down before you.
Judah is a lion's whelp;
  from the prey, my son, you have gone up.
 He stooped down, he couched as a lion,
  and as a lioness; who dares rouse him up?
The scepter shall not depart from Judah,
  nor the ruler's staff from between his feet,
until he comes to whom it belongs;
  and to him shall be the obedience of the peoples.[23]

Here is the promise of the longevity of Judah's line: it will continue as the tribe of kingship up until and including the time when a final ruler will come to claim possession of what is rightfully his.[24] The kingly nature of a coming descendant of Judah is evident from the "scepter" and the "ruler's staff."[25] The disputed element is the phrase "to whom it belongs." Gordon Wenham surveys the various possibilities and opts for the translation: "until tribute is brought to him." As standing in parallel to "the obedience of the peoples," this rendering makes sense, especially in light of Ps 68:29; 76:10-12; Isa 18:7, all of which foretell that tribute that foreigners will bring their gifts up to Jerusalem to the king.[26]

But with all said and done, Gen 49:10, in both Hebrew and Greek, is sufficiently problematic that we will have to be content with the general idea that a royal descendant of Judah will head up the nations, especially given the LXX rendering.[27] What is more certain is that Gen 49:10 is considered to be the first messianic declaration of the patriarchal narratives. Indeed, when we connect Gen 49:10 with Gen 12:3; 15:5; 17:5-6; 18:18; 22:17-18; 28:14; 32:12; 35:11, this prospect of a coming ruler represents the zenith of a line of prediction concerning the universality of Abraham's progeny. Especially striking are 17:6, 16; 35:11, where kings are said to be the issue of Abraham, Sarah and Jacob.[28] The descendant of Judah, depicted by none other than Jacob himself in 49:10, is to become *the* conquering king who is identifiable with the seed (son) of Abraham (1 Chron 5:2; Gal 3:16) in his worldwide dominion over all the inhabitants of earth.[29] Therefore, Gen 49:10, in tandem with the other "kingship" passages in Genesis, richly informs our understanding of Rom 1:4-5: a king/son will assume the reins of government (Isa 9:6-7), not only of Israel but the entire world.

It is for this reason that the ruler is likened to a fierce lion that has seized its prey, returned to its den and there resides, daring anyone to challenge it. Elsewhere, similar imagery is applied to Israel (Num 23:24; 24:9; Deut 33:20, 22). Lions commonly were symbols of regal authority in the Middle East. "Historically," writes Wenham, "the military successes of King David from the tribe of Judah may be seen as the fulfillment of this blessing, which also give rise to the messianic title 'Lion of Judah'."[30] Yet readers of the NT are familiar with Rev 5:5: "Then one of the elders said to me, 'Weep not; lo, the Lion of the tribe of Judah, the Root of David, has conquered, so that he can open the scroll and its seven seals'." With the titles "Lion" and "Root," John combines Gen 49:9 and Isa 11:1, 10. According to Beale, the verb "conquer" serves as an introduction to both these OT titles and brings out their "conquering" significance, because "both concern the prophecy of a messianic figure who will overcome his enemy through judgment. Jesus fulfills these two prophecies."[31] So strikingly, Rev 5:6-14 proceeds to tell us how this one has overcome, namely, by his death and exaltation. What impresses one immediately is how very similar this combination of a conquering ruler, death and exaltation is to Rom 1:4-5.

Numbers 23:21-24

As with all the Balaam oracles, this second one starts out as a curse but ends up as a blessing upon Israel:

Behold, I received a command to bless:
  he has blessed, and I cannot revoke it.
He has not beheld misfortune in Jacob;
  nor has he seen trouble in Israel.
The Lord their God is with them,
  and the shout of a king is among them.
God brings them out of Egypt;

> they have as it were the horns of the wild ox.
> For there is no enchantment against Jacob,
>   no divination against Israel;
>   now it shall be said of Jacob and Israel,
>   "What has God wrought!"
> Behold, a people! As a lioness it rises up
>   and as a lion it lifts itself;
>   it does not lie down till it devours the prey,
>   and drinks the blood of the slain."

T. R. Ashley explains the thrust of this portion of the oracle: what Yahweh has said will be performed without fail, and what he has said is that Israel will be blessed. This contradicts Balak's image of God, whose motive in moving the site of the second oracle was to force God to change his blessing into a curse. Balaam thus rebukes Balak for his idea of God and informs him that his plan is a failure now: "No human—seer or otherwise—can contradict the utterance of the revealed will of Yahweh."[32] In nothing less than a *tour de force* manner, Balaam can actually proclaim that because of the Lord's design to bless Israel and bring her into the promised land, the nation is virtually trouble-free: no misfortune can be found among this people.

The victory of God over the Egyptian oppressors of his people is integral to this oracle: "God brings them out of Egypt; they have as it were the horns of the wild ox" (v. 22). The LXX, in J. W. Wevers' translation, reads: "The God who brought them (the people) out of Egypt is like the glory of the unicorn for him (i.e. Israel)." Wevers then comments, "What is meant by the simile is that the redeemer God is as resplendent as the fabled unicorn, understood as a beast celebrated for its ferocity and power. In other words, Israel's God is gloriously invincible."[33]

Israel's redemption from bondage is grounded in the kingship of Yahweh: "The Lord their God is with them, and the shout of a king is among them" (v. 21b). As Ashley again explains, here is the positive side of the reason why Yahweh had decided to bless Israel: God is present in the midst of his people. He translates the Hebrew as "rejoicing for a king." "This joyful shout is *for a king*, i.e., on account of the fact that Israel's true king is Yahweh (Exod 15:18; Deut 33:5; Judg 8:23; 1 Sam 8:7; 12:12; Isa 33:22), and that this divine king is not in a remote palace, but is in their very midst."[34] The relevance of the kingship of Yahweh in this text is that it forms a link in an intertextual chain stretching from Gen 49:10 to Mal 4:1-3 and culminating in Rom 1:5. For Paul, Israel's victorious king is none other than Jesus the Christ.

But there is more to the story. By the might of the warrior-king, the people themselves are celebrated as a lion/lioness, which "does not lie down till it devours the prey, and drinks the blood of the slain" (v. 24). As we have seen and will see immediately below, the figure of the lion originates with Gen 49:9 and its prophecy of the coming scion of Judah. Here the application of the image is to Israel. It is by virtue of her connection with this powerful one that the nation too takes on the characteristics of fierceness, power and might. Because Israel is both indwelt and empowered by Yahweh, she is invincible.

Numbers 24:17-19

Num 24:17-19 is a unwitting prophecy of a future Jewish ruler who would conquer the hostile powers of Moab and Edom and take them as his possessions:

I see him, but not now;
  I behold him, but not nigh:
a star shall come forth out of Jacob,
  and a scepter shall rise out of Israel;
  it shall crush the forehead of Moab,
  and break down all the sons of Sheth.
Edom shall be dispossessed,
  Seir also, his enemies, shall be dispossessed,
  while Israel does valiantly.

Balaam's fourth oracle proceeds from the desire of Balak to manipulate things to come. But as it turns out, this roadmap to the future is a far cry from Balak's intentions. In point of fact, an Israelite ruler is going to "crush the forehead of Moab," not the other way around! In Balaam's prophetic vision, this personage is likened to a star. Apart from this present text, the OT employs "star" only once as a royal symbol (Isa 14:12), although such a usage seems to have been common enough in the ancient Near Eastern context, including the Second Temple Jewish sources. Some of the NT references also presuppose the regal significance of "star" (Matt 2:2-10; Rev 22:16). The royal status of this individual is confirmed by the parallel term "scepter" (Gen 49:10; Psalm 45:6; Amos 1:5).[35]

The LXX departs from the MT with its rendering of v. 17: "I will point to him, but not now; I will bless him, but he draws not near: a star shall arise out of Jacob, a man shall spring out of Israel and shall crush the princes of Moab and shall spoil all the sons of Seth." This mention of a "man" matches the prior verse of Num 24:7: "There shall come a man out of his [Jacob's] seed, and he shall rule over many nations...."[36] Wevers remarks that the eschatological hopes of the people are now centered in an individual. Whether these hopes were meant to be realized in the reign of David or projected into the more distant future cannot be determined. In any event, he continues, "Such eschatological hopes did involve Jewish hopes in a future figure, not at all limited to Alexandrian Jews of the third century BCE."[37] The same pertains to the LXX of Isa 19:20, "a man who shall save them," which is apparently indebted to the LXX of Num 24:17b, and a direct line can be drawn from the one to the other.

G. K. Beale adds that the present passage itself is an echo of the earlier Gen 49:10, for at least four reasons. (1) There is the virtually verbatim wording of Num 24:9 and Gen 49:10: "He crouches, he lies down as a lion, and as a lion who dares rouse him?" (2) The use of "scepter" in Gen 49:10 matches that of Num 24:17. (3) Both the Genesis and Numbers texts identify their prophecies to be about the "latter days." (4) Both Genesis 49 and Numbers 24 explicitly refers to the "nations" as Israel's enemies who are to be defeated.[38] Like Gen 49:10, Num 24:17 (Isa 11:1, 10) is also taken up by Revelation (22:16): "I Jesus have sent my messenger to you with this testimony for the churches. I am the root and the offspring of David, the bright morning star." Along with Isa 11:10, there is here an allusion to Isa 60:1-3.

Deuteronomy 33:5, LXX

According to the LXX of Deut 33:5: "There shall be a ruler in the Beloved, when the rulers of the peoples are gathered together at one time with the tribes of Israel." The "Beloved," remarks Horbury, is Israel, and the LXX has Moses predict either the rule of God himself or an emperor-like ruler in the nation, a figure at the center and unity of Israel and the nations. At least, this is the most likely interpretation, whose probability is increased by its presence in *Tg. Neof.* Continues Horbury:

> The ruler to come would then naturally be identified with Balaam's star of Jacob in the latter days, lord over many nations, and with the final ruler whom the nations expect, according to the Blessing of Jacob. He is in

fact, as is most clear in the blessing of Jacob, the supreme Davidic king of the latter days.[39]

Horbury further explains that these oracles in their LXX form belong to the third century BC. Already at that time, they presuppose a developed messianic interpretation that gave rise to a chain of exegetical interconnections among these prophecies within the Pentateuch and also between the Pentateuch and the prophets. These LXX passages point to a consistent set of messianic hopes, constituting an expectation centered on a royal messiah that was sufficiently central and widespread among Jews of the third century to be included in the interpretation of the Pentateuch.[40]

2 Samuel 7; 1 Chronicles 17

Of obvious significance for Rom 1:3-5 is Yahweh's response to David's desire to build a house for him, resulting in the establishment of a covenant with David and his family. These texts from 2 Samuel and 1 Chronicles as a whole are significant for biblical theology generally and for the study of Davidic messianism in particular. However, our interests lie in a specific dimension of the promise to David, namely, peace as a result of conquest. According to 2 Sam 7:8-11 (as paralleled by 1 Chron 17:9-10):

> Now therefore thus you shall say to my servant David, Thus says the Lord of hosts, I took you from the pasture, from following the sheep, that you should be prince over my people Israel; and I have been with you wherever you went, and have cut off all your enemies from before you; and I will make for you a great name, like the name of the great ones of the earth. And I will appoint a place for my people Israel, and will plant them, that they may dwell in their own place, and be disturbed no more; and violent men shall afflict them no more, as formerly, from the time that I appointed judges over my people Israel; and *I will give you rest from all your enemies.*

The Lord reflects on David's vocation as a warrior and envisages the time when war would cease and the people would no longer suffer violence. In no uncertain terms, there will be rest (= peace) from all of David's enemies and those of his subjects.[41]

Verse 11 in particular echoes a number of passages in Joshua (1:13, 15; 11:23; 14:15; 21:44; 22:4; 23:1), according to which Israel and the land enjoyed rest after the conquest of Canaan. History will repeat itself, and the Lord will bring to pass a second conquest. The "planting" of Israel in the land is a metaphor for safety and security: never again will she be uprooted and removed.[42] The figure anticipates the prophets, who employ the same imagery in predicting the return from exile (e.g., Isa 60:21; 61:3; Jer 11:17; 24:6; 31:28; 32:41; 42:10; Ezek 17:22-23; 36:36; Amos 9:15).[43] All this will come to pass not in David's lifetime but in that of his son (2 Sam 7:12-13). Accordingly, the narrative of 1 Kings 1-10 represents a provisional fulfillment of Yahweh's pledge, when Solomon disposes of the last of David's enemies and introduces a period of unprecedented peace and prosperity. By way of a typological reading, therefore, Solomon prefigures a "divine warrior" who will defeat the enemies of God and his people, thereby becoming a "prince of peace" (Isa 9:6), whose reign as David's Son would know no end (Isa 9:7; Luke 1:32-33).[44]

The outstanding study of Peter Gentry examines 2 Samuel 7 as it relates to Isa 55:3.[45] Gentry's thesis is that "the sure mercies of David" are the acts of kindness performed by David, who serves a paradigm for Isaiah's future king. As such, the king's faithful acts of loyal love are none other than those of the Servant of Isaiah 53, whose offering of himself and whose resurrection enable him to bring to fulfillment the promises of Yahweh in the Davidic Covenant and is, at the same time, the basis for the new and everlasting covenant. This future king thus fulfills the roles required of the Israelite king by Deut 17:14-20 and 2 Samuel 7 by bringing the divine instruction, or Torah, to Israel and all the nations. He is, therefore, a leader and commander of the peoples and a covenant witness to the nations.

Psalm 2

Connected directly to 2 Samuel 7 is the Second Psalm's celebration of the coronation of David's son. That the royal son is to exercise hegemony over the nations is evident from the outset. The kings and rulers of the earth may have set themselves in opposition to Yahweh and his anointed, but their rebellion is futile and even laughable; it can only call forth the wrath of the real potentate of heaven and earth (vv. 1-6). All opposition to his purposes can only fail, because, he declares, "I have set my king on Zion, my holy hill." Then follows "the decree of the Lord" that his son is begotten this day and the nations are to be his heritage (vv. 7-9):

I will tell of the decree of the Lord:
He said to me, "You are my son,
today I have begotten you.
Ask of me, and I will make the nations your heritage,
and the ends of the earth your possession.
You shall break them with a rod of iron,
and dash them in pieces like a potter's vessel."

The "begetting" of the kingly son, in the Near Eastern milieu, has to do with his coronation and installation on the throne, not his actual birthday.[46] Even so, the metaphor is eloquent of a new beginning. As H-J Kraus describes it: "'You are my son, I myself have begotten you!' reveals itself as a creative word, one that originates a new existence. The chosen king is drawn to the side of God, he becomes the heir and representative of his rule."[47] With the ascension of the new monarch, a new state of affairs is inaugurated, one that, from now on, will bear his distinctive imprint. And this son is so honored by the Lord that all he need do is ask and the nations and the ends of the earth will become his. "Ask of me, and I will make..." recalls Yahweh's words to Solomon: "Ask what I should give you" (1 Kgs 3:5). His rule is likewise depicted in keeping with the Near Eastern setting; that is, it is an absolute sway that will brook no contradiction, and should insurrection arise, then he will deal with his enemies harshly, if not brutally. His weapon of choice is the "rod of iron," i.e., the royal scepter in the form of a staff or a short-handed mace.

Thereafter ensues the ultimatum that the kings of the earth must make their peace with this son (vv. 10-12). This is a picture of dominance and sovereignty: the Lord's anointed is to be obeyed without questioning. This stanza of the poem calls upon the rulers of the earth to show "good sense" in their response to the king's claim to sovereignty over them. Goldingay poses the question, How do they show such good sense by letting themselves be put right? There are three parallel answers to the question. For one, the rulers will serve him with reverence, though this does not come naturally to leaders. Second, they will submit to the Lord with pure hearts and an inward attitude corresponding to their outward words. Third, they will "rejoice with trembling." As Goldingay notes, the combination of joy and awe recurs in the twin exhortations of Ps 95:1-2, 6 and the twin descriptions of earth in Ps

97:1, 4.⁴⁸ Ps 100:1-2 similarly exhorts "all the earth" to "serve Yahweh with gladness." Psalm 2 thus affirms that service, reverence, joy and trembling go together, and that the nations are invited into this state of affairs.

Psalm 68:17-18

In this Psalm, God is portrayed once more as the divine warrior. The writer traces the victories of Yahweh from the exodus through the wilderness to the conquest of Canaan and finally his ascent to Zion. His exaltation is depicted graphically by vv. 17-18:

With mighty chariotry, twice ten thousand,
   thousands upon thousands,
   the Lord came from Sinai into the holy place.
Thou didst ascend the high mount,
   leading captives in thy train,
   and receiving gifts among men,
even among the rebellious, that the Lord God may dwell there.

The psalmist depicts God as the conqueror who descends from Sinai to subdue his enemies and make them part of his retinue as he ascends into the sanctuary of Sinai. The mention of chariotry finds it most relevant points of contact with Exodus 1-15, which refers ten times to Pharaoh's chariotry, and Judges 4-5, which mentions Sisera's chariotry seven times. "Both," writes Goldingay, "turn out to be spectacularly useless when Yhwh decides to Act."⁴⁹ As customary in the Near Eastern setting, Yahweh receives tribute from the defeated enemies, in recognition that he is the indeed the victorious king. Just whom historically the writer has in mind as Yahweh's enemies is not certain. Anderson suggests either the Canaanite kings (and their deities) who threatened the existence of God's people or, in a wider sense, all the forces that have opposed his rule.⁵⁰ It is of more than passing interest that Paul quotes this very passage in Eph 4:8, according to which the risen Christ bestows gifts on his servants.⁵¹

*Psalm 72:8-11*⁵²

Psalm 72, as Goldingay explains, is a prayer for the king and a promise regarding what will issue from the answer to the prayer. It is apparently a entreaty from the time of the monarchy when Israel had kings and needed this kind of appeal to be answered. More indirectly, the Psalm sets up prospects and warnings for kings and criteria for assessing them, and it functions as a piece of teaching that informs Israel on how to pray for its kings.[53] Within this prayer, vv. 8-11 beseech the Lord for the king's worldwide dominion and the conquest of his foes:

May he have dominion from sea to sea,
  and from the River to the ends of the earth!
May his foes bow down before him,
  and his enemies lick the dust!
May the kings of Tarshish and of the isles
  render him tribute,
 may the kings of Sheba and Seba
  bring gifts!
May all kings fall down before him,
  all nations serve him!

Marvin Tate adds that God is petitioned to make hostile, distant and powerful monarchs submit in service to the just and life-giving king of Israel: "His power has the effect of drawing together the rest of the world to serve him. Since he serves God, by implication he brings the nations to Yahweh's service as well."[54] This means that although the psalmist employs very "tough talk" in his petition that the king defeat his enemies, there is a benevolent end in view.[55] This is confirmed by the subsequent verses (12-14), which clarify that this king is not a bully but a deliverer and helper of the poor and needy. It is from the oppression of those who would injure and enslave his people that this royal person acts to subjugate his opponents. That Psalm 72 *in toto* echoes Genesis 49 is evident from the parallels elicited by de Hoop:[56]

Psalm 110

Psalm 110 is another royal Psalm. It is particularly akin to Psalm 2, inasmuch as both speak of the son of David's conquest of the nations.

The Lord says to my lord:
  "Sit at my right hand,
  till I make your enemies your footstool."
The Lord sends forth from Zion
  your mighty scepter.
  Rule in the midst of your foes (vv.1-2)!

And because of his prowess in war, continues the writer, "Your people will offer themselves freely on the day you lead your host upon the holy mountains" (v. 3), clearly reminiscent of Ps 68:18. Then, coming apparently out of the blue, this king is also declared to be a priest forever "after the order of Melchizedek (v. 4). Finally, there is the assurance to the king:

The Lord is at your right hand;
  he will shatter kings on the day of his wrath.
He will execute judgment among the nations,
  filling them with corpses;
he will shatter chiefs
  over the wide earth (vv. 5-6).

In typical fashion, the king will tolerate no rivals to his throne and sovereignty. And should there be a challenge to his power, then all the worse for the challengers!

Isaiah 9:1-7

In this famed oracle of the coming messianic king, the one who will cause the light of the new creation to shine upon those who formerly walked in darkness, vv. 4-5 take up the familiar figure of conquest:

For the yoke of his burden,
  and the staff for his shoulder,
  the rod of his oppressor,
  thou hast broken as on the day of Midian.
For every boot of the tramping warrior in battle tumult
  and every garment rolled in blood
  will be burned as fuel for the fire.

This declaration follows upon the encouragement of v. 3 that the Messiah will bestow joy on the nation. As J. N. Oswalt observes, instead of depopulation and dwindling away, the nation will swell, grow and become prosperous: "What is dealt with here are all the elemental fears of the people, and the prophet says that in place of fear there is joy."[57] At that point, vv. 4-5 proceed to state the immediate cause of the rejoicing, i.e., the militant activities of the king, whereby the deliverance is secured.

In pursuing his agenda of conquest, the Israelite king is going to remove the burdensome yoke and the rod of the oppressor. Oswalt notes that the Assyrian emperors delighted in reciting how they had imposed their heavy yokes upon captive peoples; and here Isaiah looks to the day when one mightier than the Assyrians of this world will break those yokes to pieces. God will end oppression by putting an end to the warfare upon which the oppression rests.[58] All this begins to be realized with the birth of a child, upon whose shoulders the kingdom of God ultimately will rest and whose reign will last forever (vv. 6-7). The irony of the situation is that the Lord will counter the temporary might and unrestrained hubris of the kings of the earth by raising up a child-deliverer (an echo of Isa 7:14).

Isaiah 11

On a par with Isaiah 9, chapter 11 of Isaiah is a celebrated anticipation of the coming scion of David. According to v. 1, "There shall come forth a shoot from the stump of Jesse, and a branch shall grow out of his roots." The house of David is here likened to a felled tree (cf. Amos 9:11). Yet from the tree's stump a sprout or twig begins to emerge (cf. Isa 4:2: "the branch of the Lord"). As consistent with Isaiah's overall imagery, the Messiah is depicted as "root out of dry ground," "despised and rejected of men" (Isa 53:2-3). That this personage should be called "a shoot from the stump of Jesse" identifies him with David, the son of Jesse. We recall that David himself was the youngest of Jesse's sons and, therefore, the least likely to be anointed as the king of Israel (1 Samuel 16). Nevertheless, from humble beginnings this "shoot from the stump of Jesse" will rise to become the ensign around whom all the nations will rally (vv. 10-12).

Verses 4-5, 13-16 evoke the image of the divine warrior who, equipped by the Spirit of the Lord (v. 2), will subdue formerly unruly nations. Consequently:

And his delight shall be in the fear of the Lord.
 He shall not judge by what his eyes see,
  or decide by what his ears hear;
 but with righteousness he shall judge the poor,
  and decide with equity for the meek of the earth;
 and he shall smite the earth with the rod of his mouth,
  and with the breath of his lips he shall slay the wicked.
Righteousness shall be the girdle of his waist,
 and faithfulness the girdle of his loins (vv. 3-5).

Cast in the role of a judge, this personage will come to the aid of the poor and the meek, when he smites the earth with the rod of his mouth (cf. Ps 2:9) and slays the wicked with the breath of his lips (as echoed by 2 Thess 2:8). As in the case of Ps 72:2-4, 12-14; Jer 21:12; 22:3, 16, Isaiah evokes the function of Hebrew judge, whose responsibility it was to help those in need. And as in Isa 9:1-7, the insurance of equity for the poor and meek hinges on the king/judge who subdues their enemies. Oswalt puts the question, How will the Lord put an end to oppression? The answer is: "God will not supplant oppression with greater oppression, nor will he replace warfare with warfare. Instead, he will do away with wars."[59] As the divine warrior, the weapons at his disposal are "righteousness" and "faithfulness." In keeping with the common Hebrew usage of parallelism, righteousness and faithfulness are tantamount to one another. In the prophets particularly, God's righteousness *is* his fidelity to save redeem Israel from exile. Or, put otherwise, his righteousness is his saving activity, one that is rooted in his faithfulness to the covenant.[60]

The effect of Messiah's military campaign is that there will be universal peace and security (vv. 6-9), a return to the bliss of the unfallen creation. Many passages in Isaiah hold forth this prospect, but one notable instance is Isaiah 32. The prophet foresees the time when a king, possessed of the Spirit of God, will reign in righteousness. The effect of his rule is stated in the most majestic terms: for the extent of the exile, Jerusalem will be desolate and inhabited by wild animals, that is:

until the Spirit is poured upon us from on high,
   and the wilderness becomes a fruitful field,
   and the fruitful field is deemed a forest.
Then justice will dwell in the wilderness,
   and righteousness abide in the fruitful field.
And *the effect of righteousness will be peace,*
   and the result of righteousness, quietness and trust for ever.
My people will abide in a peaceful habitation,
   in secure dwellings, and in quiet resting places (vv. 15-18).

What strikes the eye immediately is that Paul, in Rom 5:1, 5, echoes this very passage. According to v. 1, "being justified by faith we have peace with God." Paul follows the order of Isaiah: "the effect of righteousness will be peace, and the result of righteousness, quietness and trust forever." Likewise, v. 5 maintains that our hope will not expose us to (eschatological) shame, because God's love has been poured into our hearts through the Holy Spirit. In salvation-historical terms, Isaiah's prophecy is fulfilled on Pentecost with the effusion of the Spirit. This is why Paul takes up the language of Pentecost in v. 5 to assure all believers that they too have experienced Pentecostal grace with the outpouring of the same Spirit (cf. 1 John 2:20, 27). Therefore, Isaiah's king who reigns in righteousness is none other than Jesus the Spirit-endowed Messiah, who effects worldwide peace by means of his conquering might.

The remainder of the chapter (vv. 10-16) elaborates the reassembly of Israel, particularly in terms of the extension of her territory by the absorption of the other nations of the earth. This includes the conquest of ancient enemies such as Edom, Moab and Egypt. Center-stage in this capture of the nations is the "root of Jesse, who shall stand as an ensign to the peoples; him shall the nations seek, and his dwellings shall be glorious" (v. 10). In the day that the Lord extends his hand yet a second time to recover the remnant of his people, he "will raise a banner for the nations, and will assemble the outcasts of Israel, and gather the dispersed of Judah from the four corners of the earth" (v. 12).[61] Israel's King is to be the rallying point for all who come under his benevolent reign.

Isaiah 19:19-24

This is surely one of the most remarkable passages in the prophets, just because Isaiah engages in a redefinition of Israel that is virtually unmatched in the OT, if not breathtaking in proportions. In this oracle, not only will the worship of God be decentralized from Jerusalem, with an altar to the Lord in the midst of Egypt and a pillar to the Lord on its border, Egypt is depicted as the covenant people who "cry to the Lord because of oppressors." And when they do, "he will send them a savior, and will defend and deliver them." Here is a clear echo of Israel's cry for help to the Lord, *à la* Exod 2:23; 3:7, 9; Judg 3:9, 15; 4:3; 6:6, 7; 10:10, 12. Egypt, the former oppressor and captor, will be delivered when its enemies assail it—a striking instance of role reversal if there ever was one! Not only so, the Lord "will make himself known to the Egyptians; and the Egyptians will know the Lord in that day and worship with sacrifice and burnt offering, and they will make vows to the Lord and perform them."[62] Moreover, when they stray from Yahweh, he will smite and heal them until they return to him. And perhaps the most startling of all is: "In that day Israel will be the third with Egypt and Assyria, a blessing in the midst of the earth, whom the

Lord of hosts has blessed, saying, "Blessed be Egypt my people, and Assyria the work of my hands, and Israel my inheritance." Israel is now ranked alongside, not above, her most infamous former foes, though the Jewish people retain the preferential title of "inheritance" (cf. Deut 32:9).

Of special interest is that the LXX of v. 20 echoes its counterpart of Num 24:17b: "And it shall be for a sign to the Lord forever in the land of Egypt: for they will presently cry to the Lord because of those who afflict them, and he will send them *a man who will save them*; when he will judges he will save them." The last clause of the Hebrew reads: "a savior and a defender, and he will rescue them." The LXX, for its purposes, has chosen to merge the separate titles "savior" and "defender" into the one "man" who will save Israel when he judges.

Daniel 7:13-14

I saw in the night visions,
  and behold, with the clouds of heaven
    there came one like a son of man,
  and he came to the Ancient of Days
    and was presented before him.
And to him was given dominion
  and glory and kingdom,
    that all peoples, nations, and languages
    should serve him;
    his dominion is an everlasting dominion,
    which shall not pass away,
  and his kingdom one
    that shall not be destroyed.

Daniel's vision of a heavenly figure who descends to become the master of the nations is in complete conformity with all the other texts that have come in for consideration. That he is a regal personage follows from the terms "glory," "kingdom," "dominion" and the service of his subjects. Moreover, "glory" and the reference to the beasts in 7:12, 17, 19 evoke Adam, as confirmed by Ps 8:5-8. In writing of the creation of man, the Psalmist echoes the Genesis account:

Yet you have made him little less than God,
  and crowned him with glory and honor.
You hast given him dominion over the works of your hands;
  You have put all things under his feet,

all sheep and oxen,
  and also the beasts of the field,
the birds of the air, and the fish of the sea,
  whatever passes along the paths of the sea.

Correspondingly, Daniel's son of man possesses glory and honor and exercises dominion over the creation, including the various animals (Gen 1:24, 25-26, 28). He is a Jewish monarch who displaces the other kings and their empires (the four "beasts" of Babylon, Persia, Greece and Rome) and is served everlastingly by "all peoples, nations, and languages." In short, Dan 7:13-14 is a perfect match for Rom 1:5 (and is likewise the source of Rev 7:9).

Zechariah 9:9-10

Rejoice greatly, O daughter of Zion!
  Shout aloud, O daughter of Jerusalem!
Behold, your king comes to you;
  triumphant and victorious is he,
  humble and riding on an ass,
  on a colt the foal of an ass.
I will cut off the chariot from Ephraim
  and the war horse from Jerusalem;
and the battle bow shall be cut off,
  and he shall command peace to the nations;
his dominion shall be from sea to sea,
  and from the River to the ends of the earth.

Zechariah echoes the language of previous predictions of a coming combatant, who is, at the same time, a procurer of peace (Ps 72:1–11; 89:38–45; Isa 9:6–7; 11:1–5; Mic 5:2–4), all of which stem ultimately from Gen 49:10–11 via Psalm 72. The king is described with three Hebrew terms "righteous," "saved" and "humble" or "poor." (1) "Righteous" refers to the conduct of the king in accordance with his proper relationship with Yahweh and with his people. He is to keep his covenant with Yahweh (2 Sam 23:1–7). He is to rule his people in righteousness, which includes justice for the poor. Such action on the part of the king will result in rain (fertility) and peace (cf. Ps 72:1–7). (2) "Saved" does not mean primarily "possessing salvation," but refers to the act of being saved by Yahweh's action from some ordeal. It is the same word found in Ps 33:16–17: "A king is not saved by his great army; a warrior is not delivered by his great strength. The war horse is a vain hope for victory, and by its great might it cannot save." The idea is the same here as in Zech 9:9, except that the prophet is speaking of an eschatological king who will be saved by Yahweh. The thought is that the king will receive divine help and favor, so that whatever he does will prosper. He will keep covenant and rule righteously. (3) The third term is "humble" or "poor," which represents the Messiah as meek and lowly, not proud and boastful. There may be some connection here with the report of Moses' meekness (Num 12:3) and the suffering of Yahweh's servant (Isa 53:4).

Verse 10 contains three particularly notable motifs. (1) The new king will destroy every implement and semblance of war. Here, as elsewhere in the OT, the eschaton will be a time when wars will cease. The language is very much akin to Mic 5:10; Hos 2:18; Isa 2:4; Mic 4:3; Isa 9:5; Ps 46:9. (2) The new king will speak "peace" to the nations, in line with Isa 2:4 and Mic 4:3. "Peace" means not simply "blessing" or "wholeness" but the restoration of the creation, a return to Eden. The prophet sees the new king extending the blessings of Yahweh, which the psalmist reserved for Israel (Ps 72:7–11), to all the world. (3) The new king will rule from sea to sea and from the river to the ends of the earth (cf. Ps 72:8). Again, the assertion is made of the universal reign of Yahweh's king. Michael Fishbane argues effectively that Zech 9:9-10 is a throwback to Gen 49:10-11. For all its problems, Fishbane writes, the latter was understood messianically from early postbiblical times, i.e., as a royal expectation projected in terms of a future Davidic line.[63]

All in all, Zech 9:9-10 is but another instance of a divine warrior who will triumph over his enemies and those of his people, and, in the process, establish worldwide peace and prosperity, thus creating a "new Israel," or, as Paul terms it in Galatians, "the Israel of God" (Gal 6:16). The employment of this text in the "triumphal entry" of Christ into Jerusalem (Matt 21:1-11; Mark 11:1-10; Luke 19:28-40; John 12:12-15) is to the same effect.

Malachi 4:1-3 (Hebrew 3:19-21)

> For behold, the day comes, burning like an oven, when all the arrogant and all evildoers will be stubble; the day that comes shall burn them up, says the Lord of hosts, so that it will leave them neither root nor branch. But for you who fear my name the sun of righteousness shall rise, with healing in its wings. You shall go forth leaping like calves from the stall. And you shall tread

down the wicked, for they will be ashes under the soles of your feet, on the day when I act, says the Lord of hosts.

In line with Isa 4:2-6, Mal 1:3-4 envisages a day—*the* day of Yahweh—when the covenant community is going to be purged of its corruption, to the extent that the line of "the arrogant and all evildoers" will be obliterated for all time. The predicates "righteous and wicked" only occurs here in Malachi, but the contrast of those two groups is a major motif in the Psalms (e.g., 1, 37), Proverbs (e.g., 10:6, 7, 11, 16, 20, 24, 28, 30) and the prophets (e.g., Hab 1:4, 13; 2:4; 3:13). As we know by now, a righteous person in the OT was one who was faithful to his covenant relationships. The wicked, by contrast, were the enemies of the righteous, those who break their covenant and seek unlawful gain at the righteous person's expense. Consequently, when the "coming day" arrives, the wicked and evildoers will be burned like stubble and left in ashes without root or branch. But the ones who fear Yahweh's name will be warmed and healed by the rays of the sun of God's presence. Like calves confined to the stall, when they are released they will run and jump. They will be victorious over the wicked, their enemies.

Apart from the "coming day," another unique expression of Malachi's is "the sun of righteousness." Israel seemed to avoid references to the sun in her religious literature, perhaps because the sun was worshiped by the majority of her neighbors. Nevertheless, Ps 84:11 speaks of God as "a sun and shield;" and although "sun" does not appear in Ps 139:9; Isa 60:1, the thought of Yahweh being like the sun is present. As well, the rays of the sun must be behind the expression, "the Lord make his face to shine upon you" in the priestly blessing of Num 6:24–26. Consequently, "sun of righteousness" means that Yahweh's righteousness is like the rising sun that grants warmth, light and life to all God's creatures.

This passage is seen to be relevant to our concerns when it is linked to a prior text like Isa 9:1-2 and taken messianically, as Matthew (4:14-16) has done with the Isaianic oracle. C. F. Keil and F. Delitzsch relate that from Justin onward all the early commentators on Malachi understood "sun of righteousness" in christological terms: like Yahweh (Ps 84:11; Is 60:1), Christ is described as the rising sun.[64] The upshot would be that after the purging fires of judgment have done their work, the "sun of righteousness," i.e., the coming Israelite king, the embodiment of Yahweh's righteousness, will procure healing and everlasting joy.

Such a reading is very much in line with all of the texts considered above.

4. Reading Romans 1:5 Against Its Backdrop

As stated in the introduction, the scope of this study has been limited to those pre-Pauline messianic texts that have the most direct bearing on Rom 1:5. But even confining ourselves to the passages examined in this essay, there is an abundance of evidence that when Paul pens the words of Rom 1:5, he brings together a goodly number of OT materials concerning the coming Davidic king who would claim the nations as his possession. Each individual passage forms a part of the "big picture," whose climax is Paul's pronouncement that faith's obedience is to be rendered to Jesus, the Lord of the new covenant. Hermeneutically speaking, while space forbids any detailed reflection on Paul's use of the OT,[65] we may say with Peter Enns that Paul views the OT in "christotelic" terms. That is to say: "To read the Old Testament 'christotelically' is to read it *already knowing* that Christ is somehow the end to which the Old Testament story is heading."[66] Or, in other words, there is a "new covenant hermeneutic" that owes its origins to the pneumatic experiences of the early church.[67]

Given such a set of assumptions, Paul's echo of Gen 49:10 in Rom 1:5 is understandable enough. According to Beale, from the OT perspective it is a "mystery" that Genesis 49 and other texts could be speaking about voluntary obedience of Gentile enemies. "But now," he writes, "Paul sees this mysterious prophecy has begun fulfillment unexpectedly by Gentiles being taken into 'captive obedience' through trusting in the preaching about Christ."[68] Moreover, Beale suggests that Paul's "the obedience of faith among all the nations" could be a paraphrastic translation of the Hebrew of Gen 49:10: "to him is the obedience of the peoples." In like manner, he notes, *Gen. R.* 93.8 and 97 also understood the Hebrew of Gen 49:10 to refer to "the nations of the world," and *Gen. R.* 99.8 paraphrases with "all the nations."[69] To similar effect, the Targum to Genesis 49 yields a distinct messianic focus: "The ruler shall never depart from the House of Judah, nor the scribe from his children's children forevermore—until the Messiah comes, whose is the kingdom, and him shall the nations obey." Likewise, *Tg. Ps.-Jon.* renders as: "until the time when the Messianic King comes." And in *Gen R.* we find the paraphrase, "until tribute shall come to him," which is interpreted to mean that "all the nations of the world shall, in the future, bring a gift to [the]

Son of David." *T. Judah* also refers to the eschatological salvation of Israel and especially the Gentiles (24:5b; cf. Isa 11:10). Other documents combine the ideas of resurrection, Messiah and the Gentiles in their prophetic view, and certain rabbinic materials also link Gen 49:10 to OT Davidic texts, including Ps 2:7-9 and Dan 7:13-14. According to the Midrash on Ps 2:9: God, speaking to the Messiah, says: "If you ask for dominion over the nations, already they are your inheritance; if for the ends of the earth, already they are your possession."

Genesis 49, then, is the fountainhead of all the texts in the Hebrew Bible that anticipate a warrior-king who will exercise might on behalf of Israel, take her enemies captive and maintain hegemony over the other peoples. All the other passages accounted for in this study simply fall into line intertextually with the paradigm provided by Genesis 49. Yet as Paul reads and applies these passages to his mission, he transposes each into the "higher octave" of what God has done eschatologically in Christ. I would make particular mention of the LXX of Num 24:7, 17, as echoed in the LXX of Isa 19:20: Christ, for Paul, is the "man" who springs out of Israel to crush his enemies and rule the nations.[70] That he can portray Jesus as this divine warrior is evident from Eph 6:11-17 and 1 Thess 5:8 (cf. Matt 12:29; Luke 11:21-22), where he adapts and applies Isa 59:16-18. This picture fits easily and naturally into the fame of Rom 1:5, with its declaration that the risen Christ has taken the nations in captive obedience by virtue of his triumphal resurrection and exaltation.

That Paul would tie these eschatological themes into Christ's resurrection follows naturally enough from Psalms 2, 68 and 110. According to the first, the enthronement of David's son has come to pass with the exaltation of Jesus: he now occupies the throne of his father David (cf. Luke 1:32; 4Q246 2:1). It is he to whom the Lord says, "Ask of me, and I will make the nations your heritage, and the ends of the earth your possession." It is he who possess the regal authority by which he rules the nations "with a rod of iron." This is not a literal rod, of course, because Jesus' rule over the nations is best seen in the Roman Christians, who are far-famed for their faithful obedience to Jesus as Lord (Rom 1:8; 15:14; 16:19). Such obedience is not cringing and begrudging subservience but the willing and joyous service of the one who has been raised from the dead. Psalm 68 suits Paul's purposes in that the ascension of Yahweh on high provides a perfect model for Christ's resurrection/glorification/session at the right hand of God. In the Psalm, Yahweh's enemies are made part of his retinue, and as this imagery actually plays out in salvation history, it is believers, the former enemies of the Son of David and exalted Christ, who have now become his friends and servants by virtue of their reception of Paul's gospel. This is how the apostle effects the obedience of faith among all the nations for the sake of the name of Christ. Psalm 110 is of the same variety. In the NT, this Psalm is always quoted in connection with the exaltation of Christ, and Rom 1:4 is no exception. As the powerful Son of God, Jesus has ascended to the right hand of God and has entered into his regal authority, from which he will rule until all his enemies have been subdued (1 Cor 15:25-28). It is surely significant that Ps 110:3 declares: "Your people will offer themselves freely on the day you lead your host upon the holy mountains."

Paul's reading of Scripture, therefore, is both eschatological and christological, especially as he announces at the outset of Romans that his gospel is grounded in the prophetic Scriptures (1:2 with 16:26) and that Christ is the law's goal and termination (Rom 10:4; Gal 3:23-25).[71] Any lingering doubt is eliminated by Paul's assertion that faith's obedience is for the sake of the "name" of Christ. The notion of the name is derived from the declarations of Yahweh that Israel is called by his name, i.e., the nation is his particular possession. I have treated the matter elsewhere.[72] Suffice it to say here that by equating the name of Christ with Yahweh, Paul is saying in no uncertain terms that "all" the Roman Christians are the new, eschatological people of God, in fulfillment of such a prophetic text as Amos 9:11-12. In a metaphor akin to Isa 11:1, it is the "hut" of David (Amos 9:11) that is going to be rebuilt subsequent to the decline of his kingdom. In Amos' day, a dilapidated "shack" is what David's house had become, as contrasted to the palace he build for himself on his accession to the kingship (2 Sam 5:11). But David's fortunes are to be restored when the Lord acts to fulfill his promise of a new creation (Amos 9:13-15). It is not an actual house (dynasty) that is going to be (re)erected, but a "spiritual house" (new temple) will arise, with Christ as the cornerstone (Eph 2:19-22; 1 Pet 2:4-6; cf. Acts 7:47-50). He is the greater Son of David who has been raised in glory to extend his ancestor's kingdom to worldwide proportions. It was in the days of David and Solomon that the Israelite monarchy enjoyed its most extensive breadth. Yet even such supremacy pales in comparison to that of Jesus, who is to have dominion "from sea to sea" (Ps 72:8). Equally striking in Amos is the Lord's possession of "Edom and all the nations" who are called by his name. This aspect of Amos' prophecy would have stood out for

Paul, because it is particularly concerned to trumpet the name of Christ as he informs the Romans that they are the "called of Jesus Christ:" he is the Lord of his people, and they are his "possession" (Eph 1:14 = Exod 19:5).

The practical bottom line of this study is that kingship means just that—*kingship*. Against its backdrop, Paul's gospel by definition entails not simply belief in the existence of the "coming one" (Isa 26:21; 66:18; Hab 2:3-4 (LXX); Mal 3:1-2; Matt 3:11; Luke 7:18; Rom 5:13; Heb 10:37-38) but unconditional submission to his lordship, in other words, *the obedience of faith*. As straightforward (and Pauline) as this is, there remains, as Wright observes, an anxiety on the part of certain theologians that any stress on obedience creates the impression that "good moral works" take priority over "pure faith." However, he correctly dismisses any such anxiety as missing the point:

> When Paul thinks of Jesus as Lord, he thinks of himself as a slave and of the world as being called to obedience to Jesus' lordship. His apostolic commission is not to offer people a new religious option, but to summon them to allegiance to Jesus, which will mean abandoning their other loyalties. *The gospel issues a command, an imperial summons; the appropriate response is obedience.*[73]

In this all-important matter of the kingship of Christ and faith's obedience, it is Norman Shepherd who has been a pathfinder. Courageously and true to the biblical text, he has allowed Scripture to speak for itself and has not hesitated to go wherever it has led. It is only fitting, then, for him to have the last word:

> The good news of the gospel centers on the person and work of Jesus Christ and tells us what he has done to save us from the guilt and corruption of sin. The focal point of his mediatorial work for us is his death and resurrection. That is the gospel we find in the Gospels of Matthew, Mark, Luke, and John. The gospel calls us to look to Jesus Christ in faith, to turn away from sin in repentance, and to obey all that Jesus has commanded. Because of the regenerating and sanctifying work of the Holy Spirit, sinners can and do respond to this call. They believe in Jesus and walk according to his word. They trust and obey. They are forgiven and renewed. These are the righteous who will inherit the kingdom and enter into eternal life.[74]

[1] The textual problem of 16:25-27 is well-known, and scholarly opinion is expectedly diverse. C. E. B. Cranfield takes it to be a later editorial addition, but he ascribes it to an "orthodox source" and accounts for its presence "because its intrinsic merit commended it" (*A Critical and Exegetical Commentary on the Epistle to the Romans* [ICC; 2 vols.; Edinburgh: T & T Clark, 1979], 2.808-9). J. D. G. Dunn is likewise inclined to view it as a post-Pauline addition (*Romans* [WBC 38 a, b; 2 vols.; Dallas: Word, 1988], 2.913). Yet other scholars are open to the possibility of the text's authenticity: L. W. Hurtado, "The Doxology at the End of Romans," *New Testament Textual Criticism: Its Significance for Exegesis. Essays in Honour of Bruce M. Metzger* (eds. E. J. Epp and G. D. Fee; Oxford: Oxford University Press, 1981): 185-99; M. Bockmuehl, *Revelation and Mystery in Ancient Judaism and Pauline Christianity* (Grand Rapids: Eerdmans, 1990), 206; H. Gamble, *The Textual History of the Letter the Romans: A Study in Textual and Literary Criticism* (SD 42; Grand Rapids: Eerdmans, 1977), 129-32; B. M. Metzger, *A Textual Commentary on the Greek New Testament* (2nd ed.; Stuttgart: Deutsche Bibelgesellschaft, 2002), 470-73, 476-77). A convenient summary of the textual evidence is provided by R. J. Swanson, ed., *New Testament Greek Manuscripts: Variant Readings Arranged in Horizontal Lines Against Codex Vaticanus. Romans* (Wheaton: Tyndale House, 2001), 268-71. But even if editorial, the words *eis hupakoēn pisteōs* succinctly summarize Paul's intentions throughout the letter.

[2] The missionary outlook of the letter is demonstrated by P. Minear, *The Obedience of Faith: The Purposes of Paul in the Epistle to the Romans* (SBT 2/19; London: SCM, 1971); J. C. Miller, *The Obedience of Faith, the Eschatological People of God, and the Purpose of Romans* (SBLDS 177; Atlanta: Scholars Press, 2000); R. Jewett, "Romans," *The Cambridge Companion to St Paul* (ed. J. D. G. Dunn; Cambridge: Cambridge University Press, 2003): 91-104.

[3] Dunn, *Romans* (WBC 38 a, b; 2 vols.; Dallas: Word, 1988), 1.17.

[4] Dunn, "Romans 13:1-7—A Charter for Political Quietism?" *ExAud* 2 (1986), 61.

[5] See D. Garlington, *'The Obedience of Faith': A Pauline Phrase in Historical Context* (WUNT 2/38; Tübingen: Mohr Siebeck, 1991), 238-42.

[6] Dunn, *Romans*, 1.18. Commenting on Rom 15:18, Dunn remarks: "The recall of a key motif from 1:5 is no doubt deliberate since it ties together precisely a key theme of Jewish covenant self-awareness (obedience) and Paul's outreach to the Gentiles: it is precisely Paul's claim that the obligations of the covenant were being fulfilled in the faith response of the Gentiles" (ibid., 2.868).

[7] Beardslee, *Human Achievement and Divine Vocation in the Message of Paul* (SBT 1/31; London: SCM, 1961), 85. See as well the fine discussion of S. C. Barton, "Paul as Missionary and Pastor," *The Cambridge Companion to St Paul* (ed. J. D. G. Dunn; Cambridge: Cambridge University Press, 2003), 35-39.

[8] Fridrichsen, *The Apostle and His Message* (Uppsala: A.-B. Lundequistka, 1947), 3.

[9] In the recent *Commentary on the New Testament Use of the Old Testament* (eds. G. K. Beale and D. A. Carson; Grand Rapids: Baker, 2007), M. A. Seifrid makes no reference at all to the rich biblical precedents for Rom 1:1-7 as a whole. Similar oversights are committed by S. C. Keesmaat, "The Psalms in Romans and Galatians," *The Psalms in the New Testament* (eds. S. Moyise and M. J. J. Menken; London: Continuum, 2004): 139-61, and J. R. Wagner, "Isaiah in Romans and Galatians," *Isaiah in the New Testament* (eds. S. Moyise and M. J. J. Menken; London: Continuum, 2005): 117-32.

[10] J. D. Crossan and J. L. Reed, *In Search of Paul: How Jesus's Apostle Opposed Rome's Empire with God's Kingdom. A New Vision of Paul's Words and World* (San Francisco: HarperSanFrancisco, 2004), 385-86.

[11] Schreiner, *Romans* (Baker Exegetical Commentary on the New Testament 6; Grand Rapids: Baker, 1998), 815. Similar statements can be found in J. Murray, *The Epistle to the Romans* (2 vols.; NICNT; Grand Rapids: Eerdmans, 1959, 1965), 1.13-14; D. J. Moo, *The Epistle to the Romans* (NICNT; Grand Rapids: Eerdmans, 1996), 52-53; E. Lohse, *Der Brief an die Römer* (KEK; Göttingen: Vandenhoeck & Ruprecht, 2003), 68; G. N. Davies, *Faith and Obedience in Romans: A Study in Romans 1-4* (JSNTSup 39; Sheffield: Sheffield Academic Press, 1990), 28.

[12] N. T. Wright, *The New Testament and the People of God* (Christian Origins and the Question of God 1; Minneapolis: Fortress, 1991); id., *Jesus and the Victory of God* (Christian Origins and the Question of God 2; Minneapolis: Fortress, 1996); id., *The Challenge of Jesus: Rediscovering Who Jesus Was and Is* (Downers Grove: InterVarsity, 1999); id., *Paul: In Fresh Perspective* (Minneapolis: Fortress, 2005); J. D. Levenson, *Resurrection and the Restoration of Israel: The Ultimate Victory of the God of Life* (New Haven: Yale University Press, 2006; J. M. Scott, ed., *Exile: Old Testament, Jewish, and Christian Conceptions* (Supplements to the Journal for the Study of Judaism 56; Leiden: Brill, 1997); C. A. Evans, "Jesus and the Continuing Exile of Israel," *Jesus and the Restoration of Israel: A Critical Assessment of N. T. Wright's Jesus and the Victory of God* (ed. C. C. Newman; Downers Grove: InterVarsity, 1999): 77-100; B. Pitre, *Jesus, the Tribulation, and the End of the Exile: Restoration Eschatology and the Origin of the Atonement* (Grand Rapids: Baker, 2005); M. E. Fuller, *The Restoration of Israel: Israel's Re-gathering and the Fate of the Nations in Early Jewish Literature and Luke-Acts* (BZNW 138; Berlin: de Gruyter, 2006); R. Albertz, *Israel in Exile: The History and Literature of the Sixth Century B.C.E.* (SBL

Studies in Biblical Literature 3; Atlanta: Scholars Press, 2003); D. Garlington, "Covenantal Nomism and the Exile," *A Faith That Is Never Alone: A Response to the Faculty of Westminster Seminary California* (ed. P. A. Sandlin; La Grange, CA: Kerygma Press, 2007): 357-94.
[13] A convenient summary of opinion is provided by C. Anderson, "Romans 1:5 and the Occasion of the Letter: The Solution to the Two-Congregation Problem at Rome," *TrinJ* 14 (1993), 29-35.
[14] Jewett, *Romans: A Commentary* (Hermeneia; Minneapolis: Fortress, 2007), 104.
[15] Betz, *What Do We Know About Jesus?* (London: SCM, 1968), 98-100 (quotes from 99).
[16] D. Garlington, *Faith, Obedience, and Perseverance: Aspects of Paul's Letter to the Romans* (WUNT 79; Tübingen: Mohr Siebeck, 1994), 10-31.
[17] Cranfield, *A Critical and Exegetical Commentary on the Epistle to the Romans* (ICC; 2 vols.; Edinburgh: T & T Clark, 1979), 1.66.
[18] Barton, "Paul as Missionary and Pastor," 37-38.
[19] Smith, "'Spirit of Holiness' as Eschatological Principle of Obedience," *Christian Beginnings and the Dead Sea Scrolls* (eds. J. J. Collins and C.A. Evans; Grand Rapids: Baker Academic, 2006): 75-99.
[20] Smith, "Spirit of Holiness," 83, 97-98 (quote from 98). For some reason, Smith bypassed *T. Levi* 18:11, which, in its own context, bears the same significance as his chosen texts.
[21] Smith, "Spirit of Holiness," 78.
[22] The most comprehensive treatment of Genesis 49 to-date is the massive volume of R. de Hoop, *Genesis 49 in Its Literary and Historical Context* (*OtSt* 29; Leiden: Brill, 1999).
[23] Jacob's blessing of Judah and his other sons finds a parallel in Deuteronomy 33: Moses' farewell blessing of the tribes of Israel. Genesis 49 and Deuteronomy 33, in turn, gave rise to the Testament literature of the Second Temple period, most notably *The Testaments of the Twelve Patriarchs*.
[24] Judg 5:14 may be an echo of Gen 49:10. 4QpGen^{a-d} (= Gen4Q252-54a) has it that kings of David's line will never fail "until the Messiah of Righteousness comes, the Branch of David; for to him and to his seed has been given the Covenant of kingship of his people for everlasting generations, because he has kept [...] the Law with the members of the Community." Such is the understanding of several of the targums (see W. Horbury, *Jewish Messianism and the Cult of Christ* [London: SCM, 1998], 66, 93) and 4QBer: "*A ruler shall not depart from the tribe of Judah* while Israel has dominion, nor shall one who sits on the throne for David be cut off. For the staff is the covenant of kingship; the thousands of Israel are the feet, until the coming of the Messiah of righteousness, the branch of David, for to him and to his seed is given the covenant of the kingship of his people until the generations of eternity, because he kept the law with the men of the community." In an instance of bitter irony, Ezek 21:27 identifies the coming one as Nebuchadnezzar!

[25] See further G. Van Groningen, *Messianic Revelation in the Old Testament* (2 vols.; Eugene, OR: Wipf & Stock, rep. 1997), 1.172-73.

[26] Wenham, *Genesis* (WBC 1, 2; 2 vols.; Dallas: Word, 1987, 1994), 2.478. Wenham's proposal is seconded by de Hoop, *Genesis 49*, 129-38.

[27] A complete harmonization of the MT and the LXX of Gen 49:10 is not possible. The latter reads: "A ruler shall not fail from Judah, nor a prince from his loins, until there come the things stored up for him; and he is the expectation of the nations." However the problems are to be resolved on the linguistic level, J. W. Wevers' observation is to the point: "The Greek interprets the passage in the sense of a messianic hope to be rooted in the tribe of Judah" (*Notes on the Greek Text of Genesis* [SBLSCS 35; Atlanta: Scholars Press, 1993], 826). I would maintain the same for the Hebrew.

[28] Horbury passes on the Jewish traditions that Moses was considered to be the first Israelite king, on the basis of Deut 33:5, which could be translated "and he was a king in Jeshurun," and Exod 19:6 and 23:22 (LXX) (*Jewish Messianism*, 31, 49). The same is true of Philo, who reckoned Moses to be a "king, legislator, prophet and high priest" (*Praem.* 53-54; *Mos.* 1.149). See P. Borgen, "'There shall come forth a man:' Reflections on Messianic Ideas in Philo," *The Messiah: Developments in Earliest Judaism and Christianity* (ed. J. H. Charlesworth; The First Princeton Symposium on Judaism and Christian Origins; Minneapolis: Fortress, 1992), 342-46.

[29] See P. R. Williamson, *Abraham, Israel and the Nations: The Patriarchal Promise and its Covenantal Development in Genesis* (JSOTSup 315; Sheffield: Sheffield Academic Press, 2000), 262-67.

[30] Wenham, *Genesis*, 2.476.

[31] Beale, *The Book of Revelation* (NIGTC; Grand Rapids: Eerdmans, 1999), 349.

[32] Ashley, *The Book of Numbers* (NICOT; Grand Rapids: Eerdmans, 1993), 478.

[33] Wevers, *Notes on the Greek Text of Numbers* (SBLSCS 46; Atlanta: Scholars Press, 1998), 396.

[34] Ashley, *Numbers*, 479.

[35] "Scepter" and "star" carry over into Second Temple literature as kingly/messianic images. See J. J. Collins, *The Scepter and the Star: The Messiah of the Dead Sea Scrolls and Other Ancient Literature* (ABRL; New York: Doubleday, 1995).

[36] The Hebrew of this verse does not even resemble the Greek: "Water will flow from their buckets and their seed will have abundant water."

[37] Wevers, *Numbers*, 406.

[38] Beale, *John's Use of the Old Testament in Revelation* (JSNTSup 166; Sheffield: Sheffield Academic Press, 1998), 239-40, n. 244.

[39] Horbury, *Jewish Messianism*, 51. Wevers confirms that the LXX translator has in view a kind of *Moses Redidivus* (*Notes on the Greek Text of Deuteronomy* [SBLSCS 39; Atlanta: Scholars Press, 1995], 541).

[40] Horbury, *Jewish Messianism*, 51.
[41] The great Psalm of the Davidic covenant, Psalm 89, confirms this promise (vv. 22-23). "Peace" is the prophetic term for the restoration of the creation, once Israel returns to the land, when the whole earth will be a Garden of Eden. See my *An Exposition of Galatians: A Reading From the New Perspective* (3rd ed.; Eugene, OR: Wipf & Stock, 2007), 51-53.
[42] See further M. L. Strauss, *The Davidic Messiah in Luke-Acts: The Promise and Its Fulfillment in Lukan Christology* (JSNTSup 110; Sheffield: Sheffield Academic Press, 1995), 36-37.
[43] The figure of the plant corresponds to the fruitful field that Israel was to become upon return from captivity. In biblical-theological perspective, this is realized when believers in Christ bear "the fruit of the Spirit" (Gal 5:22-23). See Garlington, *Galatians*, 340-43; id., "Covenantal Nomism and the Exile," 363-66; and especially G. K. Beale, "The Old Testament Background of Paul's Reference to 'the Fruit of the Spirit' in Galatians 5:22," *BBR* 15 (2005): 1-38.
[44] On the figure of the divine warrior, see Levenson, *Resurrection and Restoration*, 201-16; T. Y. Neufeld, *Put on the Armour of God: The Divine Warrior from Isaiah to Ephesians* (JSNTSup 140; Sheffield: Sheffield Academic Press, 1997); T. G. Gombis, "Ephesians 2 as a Narrative of Divine Warfare," *JSNT* 26 (2004): 403-18.
[45] Gentry, "Rethinking the 'Sure Mercies of David' In Isaiah 55:3," *WTJ* 69 (2007): 279-304.
[46] See J. Goldingay, *Psalms. Volume 1: Psalms 1-41* (Grand Rapids: Baker Academic, 2006), 100.
[47] Kraus, *Psalms 1-59* (CC; Minneapolis: Fortress, 1988), 131. In this setting, it was taken for granted that the king was God's son. See J. H. Eaton, *Kingship and the Psalms* (SBT 2/32; London: SCM, 1976), 146-50. The king as God's son is commensurate with his role as God's image, i.e., the one who emulates behaviorally the Deity. The concept stems from Genesis 1-2. See the important discussions of Gentry, "Sure Mercies of David," 283-88; id., "Kingdom through Covenant: Humanity as the Divine Image," *Southern Baptist Journal of Theology* 12 (2008):16-42; W. R. Garr, *In His Own Image and Likeness: Humanity, Divinity, and Monotheism* (Culture and History of the Ancient Near East 15; Leiden: Brill, 2003), esp. 117-76; J. R. Middleton, *The Liberating Image: The Imago Dei in Genesis 1* (Grand Rapids: Brazos, 2005).
[48] Goldingay, *Psalms 1-41*, 102-3.
[49] Goldingay, *Psalms. Volume 2: Psalms 42-89* (Grand Rapids: Baker Academic, 2007), 325.
[50] Anderson, *Psalms*, 1.492.
[51] As explored in detail by W. H. Harris, *The Descent of Christ: Ephesians 4:7-11 and Traditional Hebrew Imagery* (Biblical Studies Library; Grand Rapids: Baker, 1996).
[52] On the Psalm as a whole and its influence on later literature, see C. C. Broyles, "The Redeeming King: Psalm 72's Contribution to the

Messianic Ideal," *Eschatology, Messianism, and the Dead Sea Scrolls* (eds. C. A. Evans and P. W. Flint; Studies in the Dead Sea Scrolls and Related Literature; Grand Rapids: Eerdmans, 1997): 23-40.
[53] Goldingay, *Psalms 42-89*, 381.
[54] Tate, *Psalms 51-100* (WBC 20; Dallas: Word, 1990), 224.
[55] See Goldingay, *Psalms 42-89*, 389-90; A. Weiser, *The Psalms: A Commentary* (OTL; Philadelphia: Westminster, 1962), 504. The sentiment of the Psalm, especially of v. 2, is taken up Jer 21:12; 22:3, 16 and thereafter expanded by 1QS 5:20-29.
[56] de Hoop, *Genesis 49*, 137-38 (translations his).
[57] Oswalt, *The Book of Isaiah* (NICOT; 2 vols.; Grand Rapids: Eerdmans, 1986, 1998), 1.241.
[58] Oswald, *Isaiah*, 1.243-44.
[59] Oswald, *Isaiah*, 1.244.
[60] See Garlington, *Galatians*, 142-49; id., *In Defense of the New Perspective on Paul: Essays and Reviews* (Eugene, OR: Wipf & Stock, 2005), 66-95; N. T. Wright, *What Saint Paul Really Said: Was Paul of Tarsus the Real Founder of Christianity?* (Grand Rapids: Eerdmans, 1997), 95-111.
[61] "Banner" occurs also in Isa 5:26; 13:2. In each instance, Yahweh raises the banner as a signal to the *nations*.
[62] "A more complete statement of the full mutual relation of Yahweh and Egypt cannot be imagined" (J. D. Watts, *Isaiah 1-33* [WBC 24; electronic version; Dallas: Word, 1985], 258).
[63] Fishbane, *Biblical Interpretation in Ancient Israel* (Oxford: Clarendon, 1985), 501-2.
[64] Keil/Delitzsch, *Commentary on the Old Testament* (10 vols.; Peabody: Hendrickson, rep. 2006), 10.662.
[65] Representative are: Beale/Carson, eds., *New Testament Use*; Keesmaat, "Psalms;" Wagner, "Isaiah;" G. K. Beale, ed., *The Right Doctrine from the Wrong Texts? Essays on the Use of the Old Testament in the New* (Grand Rapids: Baker, 1994); D. A. Carson and H. G. M. Williamson, eds., *It is Written: Scripture Citing Scripture. Essays in Honour of Barnabas Lindars* (Cambridge: Cambridge University Press, 1988); R. N. Longenecker, *Biblical Exegesis in the Apostolic Period* (2nd ed.; Grand Rapids: Eerdmans, 1999); R. B. Hays, *Echoes of Scripture in the Letters of Paul* (New Haven: Yale University Press, 1989); id., *The Conversion of the Imagination: Paul as Interpreter of Israel's Scripture* (Grand Rapids: Eerdmans, 2005); D.-A. Koch, *Die Schrift als Zeuge des Evangeliums: Untersuchungen zur Verwendung und zum Verständnis der Schrift bei Paulus* (BHT 69; Tübingen: Mohr Siebeck, 1986); C. A. Evans and J. A. Sanders, eds., *Paul and the Scriptures of Israel* (JSNTSup 83; Studies in Scripture in Early Judaism and Christianity 1; Sheffield: Sheffield Academic Press, 1993); C. D. Stanley, *Paul and the Language of Scripture: Citation Technique in the Pauline Epistles and Contemporary Literature* (SNTSMS 74; Cambridge: Cambridge

University Press, 1992); id., *Arguing with Scripture: The Rhetoric of Quotations in the Letters of Paul* (New York: T & T Clark International, 2004); R. E. Ciampa, *The Presence and Function of Scripture in Galatians 1 and 2* (WUNT 2/102; Tübingen: Mohr Siebeck, 1998); J. R. Wagner, *Heralds of the Good News: Isaiah and Paul in the Letter to the Romans* (Leiden: Brill, 2003); A. H. Wakefield, *Where to Live: The Hermeneutical Significance of Paul's Citations from Scripture in Galatians 3:1-14* (Academia Biblica 14; Atlanta: Scholars Press, 2003); F. Watson, *Paul and the Hermeneutics of Faith* (London: T & T Clark International, 2004); S. E. Porter, ed., *Hearing the Old Testament in the New Testament* (McMaster New Testament Studies; Grand Rapids: Eerdmans, 2006); B. W. Longenecker, ed., *Narrative Dynamics in Paul: A Critical Assessment* (Louisville: Westminster/John Knox, 2002); T. L. Brodie, D. R. MacDonald and S. E. Porter, eds., *The Intertextuality of the Epistles: Explorations of Theory and Practice* (Sheffield: Phoenix Press, 2008).

[66] Enns, *Inspiration and Incarnation: Evangelicals and the Problem of the Old Testament* (Grand Rapids: Baker, 2005), 154. We take note of the recent exchange between Enns and G. K. Beale in *Themelios*. Enns: "Response to Greg Beale," *Them* 32 (2007): 5-13. Beale: "Did Jesus and His Followers Preach the Right Doctrine From the Wrong Texts? An Examination of the Presuppositions of the Apostles' Exegetical Method," *Them* 14 (1989): 89-96; "Did Jesus and the Apostles Preach the Right Doctrine from the Wrong Texts? Revisiting the Debate Seventeen Years Later in the Light of Peter Enns' Book, *Inspiration and Incarnation*," *Them* 32 (2006): 18-43; "A Surrejoinder to Peter Enns on the Use of the Old Testament in the New," *Them* 32 (2007): 14-25. The gist of the debate pertains to whether Paul's employment of Scripture has organic roots in the original texts. Beale answers in the affirmative Longenecker's question, Can we reproduce apostolic exegesis (*Biblical Exegesis*, xxxiv-xxxix)? I agree, though I prefer to speak of "emulating" apostolic exegesis.

[67] S. McKnight, "Covenant and Spirit: The Origins of the New Covenant Hermeneutic," *The Holy Spirit and Christian Origins: Essays in Honor of James D. G. Dunn* (eds. G. N. Stanton, B. W. Longenecker and S. G. Barton; Grand Rapids: Eerdmans, 2004): 41-54.

[68] Beale, *John's Use*, 240.

[69] Beale, *John's Use*, 239.

[70] Cf. 1 Tim 2:5: "For there is one God, and there is one mediator between God and men, *the man Christ Jesus*." Ultimately, "the man" finds its origins in Adam, the first man.

[71] In the words of C. F. D. Moule, "The all-inclusiveness of Jesus Christ was the conviction that determined Paul's thinking and practice," because "Paul was caught in the explosion that was the person of Jesus" ("Jesus, Judaism, and Paul," *Tradition and Interpretation in the New Testament:*

Essays in Honor of E. Earle Ellis for His 60th Birthday [eds. G. F. Hawthorne and O. Betz; Grand Rapids: Eerdmans, 1987]), 50.

[72] Garlington, *Obedience of Faith*, 242-48.

[73] Wright, "Romans," *The New Interpreter's Bible* (12 vols.; Nashville: Abingdon, 2002), 10.420 (italics added). The conjunction of Phil 2:6-9 and 2:12-13 is particularly suggestive, i.e., the obedient one is to be obeyed. The Servant who was obedient unto death now seeks obedience from his faithful people.

[74] Shepherd, "Justification by Works in Reformed Theology," *Backbone of the Bible: Covenant in Contemporary Perspective* (ed. P. Andrew Sandlin; Nacogdoches, TX, 2004), 118-19. In the same volume, see further Shepherd, "Justification by Faith in Pauline Theology" (85-101). Shepherd's vision has been confirmed many times by other scholars. In a nutshell, faith's obedience is simply what is expected, given the nature of a biblical covenant. See recently S. J. Hafemann, "The Covenant Relationship," *Central Themes in Biblical Theology: Mapping Unity in Diversity* (eds. S. J. Hafemann and P. R. House; Grand Rapids: Baker Academic, 2007), 20-65.

"EVEN WE HAVE BELIEVED:"
GALATIANS 2:15-16 REVISITED

Paul's teaching on justification, as familiar as it is, continues to be scoured over and over again. Just when students of Paul think that the last word has been said on the subject, a new study appears shedding, or at least purporting to shed, new light on old texts and challenging our assumptions about those texts.[1] What occasions this essay is another look at the apostle's declaration of Gal 2:16 that *"even we (kai hēmeis) have believed in Christ Jesus, in order to be justified by faith in Christ, and not by works of the law...."* Because he is so insistent on the point, one is led to question why. What is there about the polemic of Galatians that compels Paul to underscore something that should have been taken for granted, namely, that Jewish believers are justified by the very same means as Gentiles? The answer to the question, I would propose, resides in Paul's challenge of one his opponents' most fundamental convictions: *the distinction between "saints" and "sinners."*[2]

1. The Immediate Setting in Galatians

Without retracing all of Paul's steps in Galatians 1 and 2, Gal 2:15-16 occurs within the subsection of 2:15-21, which acts as a summary of what has preceded, "Paul's Autobiography as Paradigm" (1:11-2:21), and a transition into the "Argument from Scripture and Salvation History" (3:1-4:31).[3] At first glance, the concluding verses of chap. 2 appear to be disjointed from what has immediately preceded. However, on closer inspection it is apparent that Paul does not in fact leave off talking about himself. Repeatedly in this coda to first major segment of the letter, he refers to himself, along with other like-minded Jewish Christians, either in the first person singular or plural or by means of the reflexive pronoun. The convictions at which he arrived about the vindication (justification) of the people of God were forged on the anvil of his own experience, as he made the painful transition from zealot persecutor of the church to proclaimer of the gospel.

The gist of his "autobiography as paradigm" is a plea to the Galatians that they are moving in the wrong direction.[4] That is to say, when Paul came to Christ, he ceased to be a "zealot" for the traditions of Israel (1:13-14). But, by contrast, his (mainly) Gentile readers are headed the opposite way: having come to Christ, they now want to become what Paul used to be! His design is actually stated later, in 4:12: "I plead with you, brothers, become like me, for I became like you." As Gaventa explains, "become like me" means that the Galatians are to imitate Paul "by rejecting all that threatens to remove them from an exclusive relationship to the gospel" (circumcision, etc.). Correspondingly, "for I became like you" means that "one reason for their imitation of Paul is that Paul has already rejected his zeal for the Law and the tradition."[5]

Not only does the paragraph bring to a close what has gone before, it also forms a transition into chaps. 3-4, in which Paul will expound in detail the salvation-historical grounding of his Christian certitude that Christ has ended the law, fulfilled the promise to Abraham and procured the gift of the Spirit for the reconstituted people of the new covenant. It is Paul's own experience of grace that represents *the climax of the story of Israel.*[6] As D. Lührmann quite rightly observes, these verses contain the theological essence of what Paul's conversion meant to him.[7] He and all believers have come into the inheritance promised to the patriarchs, as ensured by the giving of the law, whose function was to place a hedge around Israel until the coming of her King. And now that the King has come, the true seed of Abraham are those who have simply put their trust in Jesus. In all this, as J. L. Martyn writes, Paul's argument is more than a response to the opponents; it is also a "repreaching of the gospel."[8]

H. D. Betz maintains that 2:15-21 is the *propositio* of the letter, which, in his words, "sums up the *narratio's* material content" and "sets up the arguments to be discussed later in the *probatio*."[9] A number of interpreters who invoke Betz focus narrowly on vv. 16-17 and take *the theme* of Galatians to be justification by faith. A certain case can be made for this, because the ensuing chapters mention justification four times (3:8, 11, 24; 5:4). Nevertheless, 2:15-21 is more inclusive than justification, and as one keeps reading it becomes apparent that in terms of the sheer volume of ideas the real center of gravity of the letter's "theological" segment is the onset of the new age, the identity of the seed of Abraham, the gift of the Spirit, and liberation from the bondage of the law. In a nutshell, *Paul's concern is with the new age of the Spirit as inaugurated "in Christ" apart from the law.* Justification is a vital ingredient of the whole, but still essentially a subspecies of Paul's thought.[10]

2. "Jews by Birth"

As he builds up to the climactic statement that *"even we* have believed in Christ Jesus," Paul is very much concerned to remind his readers, in 2:15, that he and like-minded Jewish believers are "Jews by birth." The Greek noun translated "by birth" (*phusei*) appears in Rom 11:21, 24 in the sense of Israel being the "natural" branches, while the Gentiles are the "unnatural" (*para phusin*) branches. The Jews are marked out as the aboriginal people, by virtue of physical/national descent from Abraham, whereas the Gentiles are latecomers to the covenant. Jewishness, in other words, is determined by "nature" or birth. The same connotations are present in this verse. Paul speaks as any Jew of the period would have: there are Jews "by birth" as opposed to "sinners of the Gentiles" (see immediately below). Birth and lineage separate Jew from Gentile, and the covenant with Israel distinguishes "saint" from "sinner."

For the first time in the letter, Paul uses first person plural to denote Jewish Christians. In this particular case, Paul probably includes Peter and Barnabas (and James), notwithstanding their wavering in Antioch. He draws on the experience of Jewish believers, those who had been nurtured in Judaism and taught the word of God. The impact of vv. 15-16 is just this: *even we* (*kai hēmeis*) know that justification is not by "works of the law" but by "faith in Jesus Christ." In v. 16b, it is stated just this way: *"even we* have believed..."* (literal translation). By identifying himself and his associates as thoroughly Jewish believers, Paul disavows that the people from James are the legitimate heirs of Israel's hope. He would have us think very much in terms of "them and us." One might paraphrase vv. 15-16: "As distinct from *them*, the Judaizers and their followers, *we*, notwithstanding our Jewish heritage, know that a person is not justified by works of Torah but by faith in Christ; *even we*, who share the same historic biblical values as our opponents, have trusted in Christ for justification." Paul thus stands out against the inconsistency of Peter and Barnabas when they withdrew from the Gentiles (2:11-13).

"Gentile sinners" is a phrase that would have resonated in Jewish ears. As J. D. G. Dunn points out, in Jewish thought "sinners" meant preeminently "those whose lawless conduct marked them out as outside the covenant, destined for destruction and so not to be consorted with" (1 Sam 15:18; 24:28; Ps 1:1; 9:15-17; 37:34-36; 58:10; Prov 12:12-13; Sir 7:16; 9:11; 41:5-11).[11] As such, the term was synonymous with "Gentiles," who by definition were outside the covenant or "lawless" (Ps 9:15-17; 1 Macc 1:34; 2:44, 48; Tob 13:6; *Jub.* 23:23-24; 24:28 [cf. *Jub.* 22:16: "do not eat with them"]; *Pss. Sol.* 1:1; 2:1-2; 17:22-25; 4 Ezra 3:28-36; 4:23; cf. Matt 5:47; Luke 6:33).[12] Still more striking is the way in which the same term was used among the various Jewish factions. Members of one group would call themselves the "righteous," while outsiders were "sinners" (1 Macc 1:34; 2:44, 48; 1QH 2:8-12; 1QpHab 4:4-8; *Pss. Sol.* 4:8; 13:6-12; *1 Enoch* 5:4-7; 82:4-5).[13]

In so writing, Paul probably picks up on the very language employed by the Jerusalem delegation (2:12) to denote (denigrate) the uncircumcised Gentiles in Antioch.[14] This group apparently was invoking the word "sinners" to pressure the Galatians into becoming *really* "righteous" by coming under the yoke of the Torah, and in particular by practicing the dietary restrictions commanded by Moses. By using this phrase, Paul assumes the place of the "rank and file Jew" who looked upon the rest of the world "as outside the realm of God's covenant righteousness and sinful.... He looked out...from that perspective at the rest of humankind, echoing the dismissive attitude of that faithful member of the covenant people towards the non-Jews—'Gentile sinners'."[15] In short, from this vantage point, the "Gentile sinner" was "without hope" (Eph 2:12).[16] With a touch of irony, then, Paul gives his readers a glimpse of what the law-teachers really think of them. They are not acceptable as they are by faith alone, but rather must conform to rigid and outmoded notions of what constitutes righteousness.

3. "Even We Have Believed"

Verse 16 continues the sentence begun in v. 15 with the participle "knowing." NASB translates quite literally: "We are Jews by nature and not sinners from among the Gentiles; nevertheless knowing that a man is not justified by the works of the Law but through faith in Christ Jesus." NIV, by contrast, renders the participle as a finite verb and provides a somewhat smoother reading: "We who are Jews by birth and not 'Gentile sinners' know that a man is not justified by observing the law, but by faith in Jesus Christ."[17] Either way, Paul's point is that God's method of vindicating/justifying his latter-day people is matter well-known to every Jewish believer. According to B. Witherington, "he assumes it is the proper and normal view of Jewish Christians, in light of what they know and believe about the work of Christ."[18]

If the law-teachers in Galatia purport to represent the Jewish position on justification, Paul informs his readers that such is not the case. He and his company ("all the brothers with me," 1:2) have truly experienced God's justifying deed in Christ—and that apart from "the works of the law." In principle, this group includes James, Barnabas, and Peter. The latter two may have wavered briefly in Antioch, but in their right mind they would have been compelled to bear witness to the veracity of Paul's claim.

What is well-known to Paul and the others is that a person is not justified by works of the law but through faith in Jesus Christ. Each element of the proposition of v. 16a, "justified," "works of the law," and "faith in Jesus Christ" has become the object of intensive controversy in modern study. It will be possible only to summarize the most relevant data.

"Justified"

The characteristic Pauline verb articulating the justification of the people of God is *dikaioō*, translated traditionally as "justify" (Rom 2:13; 3:4, 20, 24, 26, 28, 30; 4:2, 5; 5:1; 6:7; 8:30, 33; 1 Cor 6:11; Gal 2:16, 17; 3:8, 11, 24; 5:4; Titus 3:7). The usage of this verb in the Greek OT, the matrix of Paul's own employment of it, is complex, especially when compared with the various Hebrew words underlying it. *Dikaioō* (like any other word) assumes different shades of meaning according to context.[19] Because of its occurrence in juridical settings, meanings like "justify," "vindicate," "acquit" stand out and provide a forensic framework within which to place Paul's doctrine of justification. Yet Paul's teaching on justification is more comprehensive than the verb *dikaioō*, because the idea of justification is linked to the concept of the righteousness of God in the OT. Strictly speaking, there is no independent doctrine of justification which is detachable from righteousness as a generic category. This means that the semantic range of *dikaioō* is broadened by its relation to the Hebrew/ covenantal concept of the "righteousness of God" (*dikaiosunē theou*). God's righteousness in the OT finds two points of contact with justification in Paul.

(1) There is the forensic/juridical setting of the Mosaic covenantal courtroom. The person who is vindicated and thus acquitted of all charges is declared to be "righteous" (Hebrew $ts^e ddiq$ = Greek *dikaios*) and then treated as such. Yet it is vital to remember that even in those instances in the LXX where *dikaioō* is strongly forensic, J. A. Ziesler reminds us that it is forensic in the

Hebrew sense, i.e., the verb signifies "restoration of the community or covenant relationship, and thus cannot be separated from the ethical altogether. The restoration is not merely to a standing, but to an existence in the relationship." As a result, "righteousness," in this scenario, has reference to a vindicated *existence* conferred on a person by a gracious God. "What this means is that men live together in freedom, possessing their civil rights in a good society. *It is not just a vindicated status, but a vindicated life.*"[20]

Therefore, the one of whom "justification" is predicated is regarded as "righteous," i.e., committed to the covenant and the God of the covenant in a household relationship. Likewise, E. Käsemann writes that in the OT and Judaism generally *dikaiosunē* has in view the relations of community members: "originally signifying trustworthiness in regard to the community, it came to mean the rehabilitated standing of a member of the community who had been acquitted of an offense against it."[21] J. Reumann concurs that righteousness/justice/justification terminology in the Hebrew scriptures is "action-oriented," not just "status" or "being" language, and "binds together forensic, ethical and other aspects in such a way that some sort of more unified ancient Near Eastern view can readily be presupposed."[22] In brief, it is the righteous person who is recognized in his/her true character and thus vindicated against all charges. Just how such a conception of "justification" can square with Paul's declaration that God justifies the *ungodly* (Rom 4:5) will be clarified below.

(2) The other point of contact between righteousness in the OT and Paul is the outlook on Israel's future as evidenced in the Prophets and several of the Psalms. The Prophets characteristically contemplate Israel's removal into Babylonian captivity because of her idolatry. Yet one day the nation is to return to her land when Yahweh acts in power to deliver her from bondage. At the time of this new exodus, the remnant of the people will enjoy the definitive forgiveness of sins, the restoration of the broken covenant, the glorious new creation, and vindication as those faithful to the Lord. It is Yahweh who vindicates the faithful from the charges of their enemies, who assume that he is unable to deliver his people and suppose that their faith in him is in vain. It is he who exonerates them, when, in the "eschatological courtroom," he judges their oppressors (Isa 10:5-19; Hab 2:2-20) and brings them back to the land from which they will never be uprooted again.[23]

It is in this context of promised deliverance that God is said to act righteously on behalf of his own. Especially striking is that in a number of key passages the terms "righteousness" and "salvation" (or "be justified") are placed in synonymous parallelism, e.g., Isa 45:8; 45:21-25; 46:13; 51:5–6, 8; 56:1; 59:17; 61:10; 62:1-2; 63:1; Ps 24:6; 51:14; 71:15–16; 98:1-3, 8-9 (LXX 97:2-3, 8-9); 4 Ezra 8:36, 39–40; CD 20:20; 1QS 11:11–15; *1 Enoch* 99:10. Noteworthy as well are Ps 35:27-28 (LXX 34:27-28); 72:1-4 (LXX 71:1-4, 7); 85:11-13 (LXX 84:12-14); 96:13 (LXX 95:13); Isa 9:7 (LXX 9:6); 11:1-2, 5; 45:8, 22-25; 51:5-6; 53:10-11; 61:11; Jer 23:5-6; Mal 4:2 (LXX 3:20).[24]

Several comments are in order. First, "righteousness" and "salvation" are synonymous, at least virtually so. The logic behind this is not difficult to discern. Righteousness by definition is God's fidelity to his people within the covenant bond.[25] As Wright expresses it, the phrase "the righteousness of God" to a reader of the LXX would have one obvious meaning: "God's own faithfulness to his promises, to the covenant." It is especially in Isaiah 40-55 that God's righteousness is that aspect of his character which compels him to save Israel, despite the nation's perversity and lostness. "God has made promises; Israel can trust those promises. God's righteousness is thus cognate with his trustworthiness on the one hand, and Israel's salvation on the other." He further notes that at the heart of the picture in Isaiah is the figure of the suffering servant through whom God's righteous purpose is finally accomplished.[26] Psalm 98 is likewise explicit that the revelation of God's righteousness to the nations is commensurate with the fact that he has remembered his lovingkindness and faithfulness to the house of Israel. Therefore, he demonstrates his fidelity when he springs into action to deliver Israel from her bondage (note that Psalm 98 is echoed in Rom 1:16-17, which likewise places in parallel "righteousness" and "salvation"). Thus, a formal definition of the Greek phrase *dikaiosunē theou* could be stated as: "God's faithfulness to his covenant with Israel, as a result of which he saves her from her exile in Babylon."[27]

Second, the return of Israel from exile *is* Israel's justification. The LXX of Isa 45:25 actually uses the verb *dikaioō*, translated "justified" by NASB. It is true that NIV renders the Hebrew of the verse as "found righteous" (*yitsddqu*). Yet the net value is the same: the people who return from exile are the vindicated ones whose righteousness is now made evident.

Third, the Hebrew of Isa 62:1-2 speaks of Israel's ("her") righteousness and salvation. However, the LXX has "my," referring to God, instead of "her." This may be accounted for by the textual tradition followed by the LXX at this point. Be that as it may, on the theological level there is no problem, because the blazing demonstration of Israel's righteousness and salvation is made possible only by the prior revelation of the Lord's righteousness/salvation.

These two interrelated branches of righteousness in the OT, of which Paul was heir, combine to inform us that justification, in his thought, is the vindication of the righteous, i.e., faithful people of God. In eschatological perspective, believers in Christ have been exonerated in the final assize and have been admitted into the privileges, responsibilities and fellowship of the covenant.[28] Given the parallel of "righteousness" and "salvation" in the Psalms and Prophets, and given especially the backdrop of captivity and return from exile, *dikaioō* in Paul means to "vindicate as the people of God" (when they return from exile). Historically, when the Lord caused Israel to return to the land, he vindicated the faithful remnant against the accusations of their enemies that they had rightly been taken into captivity, and that because of them Yahweh's name had been blasphemed among the nations (Isa 52:5; Rom 2:24). But in Paul, all this is transposed into the "higher octave" of what God has done in Christ at the turning of the ages— his own "eschatological courtroom." The actual enemy of believers, in Paul's apocalyptic world of thought, is not Babylon, but Satan.[29] He is the strong man who held them in the bondage of sin (Matt 12:29; Luke 11:21-22); he is "the accuser of our brothers, who accuses them before our God day and night" (Rev 12:10; cf. Rom 8:33-34a = Isa 50:7-9).

It is this cluster of ideas that is embodied by *dikaioō*. If God's righteousness is "his intervention in a saving act on behalf of his people," then the passive voice of the verb means "to be an object of the saving righteousness of God (so as to be well-pleasing to him at the judgment)."[30] When God in Christ intervenes to save his covenant partners, he plants them again in the newly created land, the new heavens and earth, never to be removed. This is "salvation" in the pregnant sense of the term: deliverance from evil and the bestowal of "peace" on a redeemed people (Rom 5:1 as it echoes Isa 32:15-18).[31]

In short, justification in Paul signals deliverance from exile and freedom from bondage, a leitmotif of Galatians (2:4-5; 3:23-29; 4:1-11, 21-31; 5:1-12, 13). One clear indication is the relationship of Rom 6:7 and 18. In the former verse, Paul writes that the one who has died "has been justified from sin" (*dedikaiōtai apo tēs hamartias*), with the latter verse providing the parallel: "liberated from sin" (*eleutherōthentes apo tēs hamartias*) (cf. Acts 13:38). The parallel is best preserved by rendering 6:7 as "freed from sin." Therefore, when Paul writes of justification, he characteristically has in mind the new exodus on which the latter-day people of God have embarked. Or, in other words, justification of necessity entails liberation from the bondage of sin.[32] Moreover, this saving righteousness is cosmic in its dimensions. At the end of the day, "the righteousness of God" is actively directed at the rescue of the creation (Käsemann). God's righteousness is his relation-restoring love.[33]

Within the setting of Paul's mission to the nations, justification functions to delineate just who are the latter-day people of God. In the eschatological new exodus that has been brought to pass in Christ, *it is Gentiles who are as much the vindicated people as Jews*, and this quite irrespective of Torah-loyalty, which is inclusive of, though not limited to, circumcision and the other traditional badges of Jewish self-identity. Therefore, justification is very much a covenantal term, speaking to the issue of the identity of the people of God.[34]

By way of qualification, however, I would join the chorus of those who have criticized Wright for driving a wedge between "justification" and "salvation," an apparent false dichotomy. E. P. Sanders is closer to the mark. Galatians has to do with entering the body of the saved: to belong to the new covenant *is* to be among the community of *the saved*.[35] Accordingly, justification does indeed tell us how to be saved, in that it depicts God's method of saving sinners—by faith in Christ, placing them in covenant standing with himself. If, then, justification is *by faith*, a procedure of salvation is prescribed: one enters the realm of salvation *by faith*.

By way of parallel to the outlook of Galatians, Rom 3:21-26 comes to mind. According to that passage, God, in his righteousness, has acted in Christ to remove the sin-barrier that stood between himself and an apostate humanity *in toto* (Rom 1:18-3:20). Jew and Greek alike are now the object of the saving fidelity of the God of Israel. Since all have sinned and fall short of the glory of God (Rom 3:23), all are now freely justified by his grace through the redemption which is in Christ Jesus (3:24). The covenant with Israel always envisaged a worldwide family.[36] But Israel, clinging to her own special status as the covenant bearer, has betrayed the purpose for which that covenant was made: "It is as though the postman were to imagine that all the letters in his bag were intended for him!"[37]

An important corollary is that the *center of gravity* of Paul's thought on justification is more the corporate body of Christ than the individual believer. As W. D. Davies writes:

> That there was such a personal dimension need not be denied, but it existed within and not separated from a communal and, indeed, a cosmic dimension. Paul's doctrine of justification by faith was not solely and not primarily oriented towards the individual but to the interpretation of the people of God. The justified man was "in Christ", which is a communal concept. And, necessarily because it was eschatological, the doctrine moved towards the salvation of the world, a new creation.[38]

Davies further points out that in both Galatians and Romans the discussion of justification by faith is immediately followed by that of the constitution of the people of God.[39] In the present context of Gal 2:15-16, *dikaioō* has to do specifically with the vindication/ restoration of Jews who have believed in Christ. No longer do they anticipate being vindicated at the last judgment by virtue of their loyalty to the God of Israel and his law; but rather eschatological vindication has taken place at the cross of Christ (v. 20), and "works of the law" are no longer relevant—this is a matter of common and well-established knowledge.

Finally, if it be asked, How can God justify the ungodly while being consistent with the practice of the Hebrew courtroom to acquit only the righteous? the answer quite simply is that those who were formerly ungodly in Adam have been made righteous in Christ. Here the perspective Phil 3:9 is much to the point. Paul speaks of a "righteousness from God" (*dikaiosunē ek theou*). It is God's own righteousness, defined as "covenant fidelity," that entails *the gift of righteousness*. In his own righteousness, God enables us to become what he is—righteous (2 Cor 5:21). His loyalty to his people consists in his conforming them to himself, so that he and they may live in uninterrupted covenant fellowship. God's righteousness has provided Christ as the propitiation for sins (Rom 3:21-26). In Adam all are guilty, but God has removed their guilt by means of the cross of Christ and thus can vindicate them as his faithful people. In these actions are embodied God's covenant faithfulness.

Without constructing a full-blown *ordo salutis*, there is a process whereby God justifies sinners. By the work of the Spirit, we are united with Christ and become God's righteousness in him (2 Cor 5:21); and it is by virtue of this relationship that God the judge pronounces us righteous and entitled to the full privileges of covenant membership. After all is said and done, Luther was right that the righteousness God requires is the righteousness he provides in Christ.

"Works of the Law"

As much debated as justification/righteousness is Paul's famous phrase "the works of the law."[40] Stated simply, "the works of the law" have reference to "the obligations laid upon the Israelites by virtue of their membership of Israel," whose purpose was "to show covenant members how to live within the covenant."[41] These are *covenant works*—"those regulations prescribed by the law which any good Jew would simply take for granted to describe what a good Jew did."[42] For this reason, "it would be virtually impossible to conceive of participation in God's covenant, and so in God's covenant righteousness, apart from these observances, these works of the law."[43] As such, the phrase articulates the whole duty (and privilege) of the Jew living under the Mosaic covenant. Martyn, then, wisely cautions that the word "works" can be misleading: "the expression simply summarizes the grand and complex activity of the Jew, who faithfully walks with God along the path God has opened up for him in the law."[44]

From one vantage point, "works of the law" encompassed the entirety of the Mosaic legislation, with no exceptions. From another, by Paul's day the phrase had taken on more specific connotations. Within the historical climate of Second Temple Judaism, especially from the time of the Maccabean revolt, key elements of the law had become the acid tests of loyalty to Judaism, now dubbed the "boundary markers" of Jewish self-identification (as placed in vogue by Dunn).[45] These were circumcision, food laws, purity laws, sabbath observance, and temple worship. These hardly exhausted the Jew's obligations under the law, but they did focus attention on crucial elements of his walk. This is so because it was precisely these components of the Torah which had come under attack during the Seleucid persecution of the Jews in the second century BC. Because of pagan "zeal against the law," "zeal for the (works of the) law" became the byword of the loyalists to the Jewish cause (1 Macc 2:26-27).[46]

In brief, writes R. B. Hays, "'works of the law' refer primarily to practices commanded by the law (circumcision, dietary laws, sabbath observance) that distinctively mark Jewish ethnic identity; *these symbolize comprehensive obedience to the law's covenant obligations.*"[47] As Hays is careful to state, works of the law are not confined to the "boundary markers." Rather, it is the "boundary markers" that in the historical setting served to focus the faithful Israelite's commitment to the entire revealed will of God.[48] These were the "litmus paper" tests of fidelity. Accordingly, Witherington can say that by his use of the phrase Paul opposes "obedience to the Mosaic Law and seeking to be part of the community that relates to God on the basis of the Mosaic covenant." This is objectionable because "the Mosaic Law and obedience to it is not, in Paul's view, how one got into Christ, how one stays in Christ, or how one goes on in Christ. It is no longer what defines and delimits who the people of God are and how they ought to live and behave."[49]

In arriving at such a conception of "works of the law," recent scholarship has concentrated on the historical setting in which these words assume their significance. Apart from the general atmosphere of zeal for the law and the desire on the part of Israelites to maintain their distinctive covenant identity, especially noteworthy is the occurrence of strikingly similar phrases in the DSS (1QS 5:21, 23; 6:18; 4QFlor 1:7; cf. 1QH 1:26; 4:31; CD 13:11).[50] Among the Scrolls, 4QMMT is particularly intriguing because its very title is, as normally translated, "*Some of the Works of the Torah*" (*miqsat maasē ha-torah*). This writing has been called a "halakic letter," in which a representative of the sect (perhaps "The Teacher of Righteousness") airs his grievances about "the state of the nation" to the religious/political establishment in Jerusalem.[51] The letter contains an exhortation for its readers to follow the example of the godly kings of Israel and a warning that they will incur the curses of Deuteronomy if they do not reconsider their own beliefs and practices *vis-à-vis* the demands of the law. If the readers do mend their ways, it will be "reckoned to them as righteousness." It is in this setting that "works of the Torah" articulates the community's own standard of covenant life. The members of the sect thus define themselves in relation to other Jews by their distinctive "walk" (*halakah*) in the ways of Yahweh.

In the present context of Galatians 2, the phrase "works of the law" serves to pinpoint the dispute with the Judaizers. When Peter withdrew from table fellowship with Gentile believers (2:11-13),[52] he effectively sent the message that they must submit to the law in order to be acceptable to God. Paul counters this false impression by the emphatic assertion that "*we* know" that works of the law have become irrelevant as far as justification is concerned. At one time, the Jewish faithful directed their trust toward Yahweh, believing that he would vindicate those who maintained their allegiance to him, as that allegiance was expressed by remaining within the Torah.

Crucial here is an appreciation of the centrality of the Torah in Israel's self-consciousness of being the chosen people. It is the book of Deuteronomy that gives the classic statement of the role of the Torah in the life of the people. The heart of the book (chaps. 5-28) consists of a restatement of the covenant made at Sinai. Deut 29:1 sums up the whole of that block of material: "These are the words of the covenant which the Lord commanded Moses to make with the sons of Israel in the land of Moab, besides the covenant which He had made with them at Horeb" (NASB). Throughout the book, the emphasis of covenant life is sustained and reinforced in numerous restatements of the promise (and warnings): "this do and live" (Deut 4:1, 10, 40; 5:29-33; 6:1-2, 18, 24; 7:12-13). This promise does not originate in Deuteronomy, because Lev 18:5 had already said: "So you shall keep My statutes and My judgments, by which a man may live if he does them; I am the Lord" (NASB).

But with the turning of the ages, as Paul will clarify especially in 3:23-25, the law has served its purpose in salvation history, namely, to lead Israel to Christ. From this point onward, to cling to the Torah is nothing less than idolatry (4:8-9), because such zeal for the law obscures one's view of the Christ and the actual nature of his work, making the law, rather than Christ, the "Jewish gateway to salvation."[53]

> This is why faith in Christ and "works of the law" are opposites: one cannot opt for Christ's system *and* Moses' system at the same time because they are mutually exclusive options for salvation. Either one believes in Christ or one chooses to commit oneself to the law. One cannot live under both systems without destroying one or the other's integrity.[54]

Paul, then, asserts that justification is not "from ("out of") works of the law" (*ex ergōn nomou*). Even excellent scholars like Betz and McKnight translate this phrase as: "*on the basis of* the works of the Torah." Betz's particular rationale is that Paul's Greek phrase is a "theological abbreviation" for the longer proposition that the works of the law form the "basis" of salvation in the Jewish schema.[55] The problem, however, is twofold. One, a certain amount of presuppositional work goes into this reading, i.e., presuppositions regarding the character of first-century Judaism and Paul's response to it. Two, such a paraphrase is linguistically unnecessary. I would argue that Paul's Greek is not an abbreviation for something longer but a full statement that makes perfectly good sense on its own terms. In point of fact, Paul consistently uses prepositions that denote origin (*ek*), sphere (*en*) and agency (*dia*). He avows that justification does not originate from or find its location within the parameters of the ancient covenant people; rather, it comes "through (*dia*) faith in Jesus Christ." Paul thus seeks to be justified "in Christ" (2:17), not "in the law." C. H. Cosgrove confirms that Paul characteristically construes "justify" (*dikaioō*) with prepositions indicating instrumentality, not evidential basis.[56] In his words: "The question never becomes whether one can be justified *on the basis of* the law or works but remains always whether one can be justified in the sphere of the law."[57]

"Faith in Jesus Christ"

"Works of the Torah" have given way to "faith in Jesus Christ." The Greek phrase traditionally translated "faith in Jesus Christ" (*pistis Iēsou Christou*) has itself been the subject of a great deal of investigation in recent times. The growing consensus is that Paul has in view the covenant faithfulness of Christ himself (taking the genitive case of *Iēsou Christou* as subjective genitive).[58] This reading is attractive in many ways; and it is undoubtedly true that the NT does represent Jesus as the man of faith, especially in the Gospel temptation narratives and the Letter to the Hebrews. Nevertheless, because the phrase is so disputed, it seems unwise to build an entire position on it alone, as though a single phrase could bear that much semantic freight.[59]

Without championing the traditional translation for the sake of tradition, Paul's language is best taken as our faith which is directed *specifically and exclusively* to Jesus the Christ.[60] In grammatical categories, the genitive case could be called adjectival genitive, i.e., that part of the phrase literally translated "of Jesus Christ" defines in some manner the character of the "faith" which is placed in him. A. J. Hultgren appropriately renders the whole phrase as "Christic faith."[61] That is to say, the faith which was once directed to the God of Israel now finds its object in Jesus the Christ.

It is surely significant that Paul nowhere provides a formal definition of faith, simply because he presupposes the meaning found in the OT and Jewish tradition. What is distinctive about his teaching on faith is its *christological focus*. With the advent of Jesus the Messiah, the only legitimate faith is that which finds its repose in him, the one who is "the end of the law" (Rom 10:4). At one time, faith assumed a nationalistic bias and was meaningless apart from the devotion of the believing Israelite to the Torah, the expression of God's covenant will for his people. But now that the "dividing wall of hostility" (Eph 2:15) has come down in Christ, faith latches specifically onto this one who has accepted all the nations without distinction (Rom 1:1-7; 15:7; Eph 2:17; Acts 2:39).

This reading that Christ both defines faith and is the object of faith is confirmed by the second clause of v. 16: "even we have believed in Christ Jesus" (the first two clauses of the verse could be looked upon as a kind of synonymous parallelism), and v. 20b: Paul lives by "faith in the Son of God," where *tou huiou tou theou* is clearly objective genitive.

As a working definition of faith, McKnight's is as good as any: faith is "the initial and continual response of trust in, and obedience to, Christ by a person for the purpose of acceptance with God."[62] The Greek word for "faith" in the NT (*pistis*) corresponds to the Hebrew word for "faith" in the OT (*'emunah*), which always signifies faith in and faithfulness to God.[63] As the godly Israelite was to trust in Yahweh for life and salvation, the Christian has directed his faith(fulness) to Christ. Faith as such is not redefined; in essence, its OT meaning is preserved. But Paul has in view a faith which is detached from Jewish "covenantal nomism," meaning that one "gets in" the people of God by faith alone; and once in, one "stays in" the covenant relationship by virtue of the same faith, which is no longer attached to the "works of Torah." Henceforth, according to v. 16d, "by works of the law no flesh shall be justified." Therefore, the Reformation stress on *sola fide* captures the heart of Paul's missionary theology.

The sum of this crucial and pivotal statement of v. 16a, with all its complications and disputed components, is that Jewish

Christians ("even we") are fully convinced that with the onset of the eschaton, Christ, not the law, is the "gateway" to salvation. Faith is to be specifically directed to him, the Lord of the new covenant, and such trust has displaced commitment to the Torah as the emblem of faithfulness to Yahweh. The only conclusion could be that "a person is not justified by (from) works of the law *but only* (*ean mē*) through faith in Jesus Christ."

The remainder of v. 16 is a buttressing and further unpacking of the complex proposition of its first clause. Paul restates emphatically that "*even we* have believed in Christ Jesus in order to be justified by faith in Christ and not by (out of) works of the law." In light of everything said above, his meaning is clear enough. Yet to substantiate his claim, Paul feels compelled to add: "because by (out of) works of the law no flesh will be justified." These words (as those of Rom 3:20) are an echo of Ps 143:2: "And do not enter into judgment with Your servant, For in Your sight no man living is righteous" (NASB). As T. George informs us, Psalm 143 is a prayer to God for deliverance from the enemy. As he notes, the rescue envisioned there depends entirely on God's faithfulness and righteousness (which are virtually one and the same): "For your name's sake, O LORD, preserve my life; in your righteousness, bring me out of trouble." (v. 11). George appropriately concludes: "Thus rather than merely snatching a prooftext to support his predetermined conclusion, Paul had in mind the motif of unilateral rescue and divine deliverance that pervades the entire Psalm."[64]

In light of the above discussion of justification and righteousness, Paul's citation of this text is entirely understandable, because justification by definition entails Israel's deliverance from her enemies. Psalm 143 thus recalls the deliverance from exile motif associated with God's righteousness when he intervenes on the behalf of his oppressed people. The specific verse alluded to by Paul, comments A. A. Anderson, is rather unique in a lament: instead of hinting at his own righteousness and protesting innocence, the Psalmist recognizes that all humans are sinful in the sight of God.[65] In humility and with a sense of realism, David confesses that in his heart of hearts he is no better than his enemies. For this reason, he pleads with God not to "enter into judgment" with him. This means, according to Anderson: "do not subject me to a strict examination in which my human insignificance and sinfulness would become painfully obvious; rather judge between your servant and his persecutors.... If the standard were certain absolute principles, then no one would be righteous before God."⁶⁶ David shrinks from such an examination because "no one living is righteous before you."⁶⁷

In the Psalms, righteousness is, on the one side, measured just in terms of one's commitment to the covenant bond as expressed by the observance of the law.⁶⁸ In this regard, David can say: "The Lord has rewarded me according to my righteousness; According to the cleanness of my hands He has recompensed me" (Ps 18:20 [NASB]); and "I have done justice and righteousness; Do not leave me to my oppressors" (Ps 119:121 [NASB]). But the other side of the coin is highlighted by Ps 143:2: left to themselves and unaided by grace, the righteous could never stand in judgment before the God of the universe. "If *no one* could claim to be sinless or just before God, that included members of the covenant people."⁶⁹

The appropriateness of Psalm 143 to make this point goes without saying, especially as compared with Paul's employment of David's penitential confession of Ps 32:1-2 in Rom 4:7-8. By underscoring the factor of human sinfulness, he stresses that justification hinges on divine enabling; one must be possessed of a righteousness that comes from God, because, in the words of Isa 64:6, our inherent "righteousness" is nothing but "filthy rags" (note especially the context here: God's sovereign power is exercised in a new exodus to deliver Israel from captivity). The law by itself cannot provide what it demands; not that the law is deficient, but it has become "weak through the flesh" (Rom 8:3), i.e., human idolatry and moral inability. Thus it is that the Lord himself—the Lord Jesus Christ—must become the righteousness of his people (2 Cor 5:21 = Isa 61:10; Jer 23:6; 33:16).

It must be said that in terms of historical realism no right-minded Jew of Paul's day would have denied the verities of sin and the necessity of a righteousness that comes from God, as sufficiently illustrated by the penitential prayer tradition and the Qumran Scrolls (e.g., 1QS 11:1-3, 5, 11-12, 13-15; 1QH 4:30-33; 7:30-31; 13:17).⁷⁰ So, to understand Paul's evocation of Psalm 143, we must take notice of his whole train of thought, as this comes to the fore in his adaptation, not exact quotation, of the Psalm (more momentarily). His concern is not for justification in the abstract but specifically a justification of "flesh" that would come by "works of the law." However cognizant the Jew would have been of sin and the need of divine righteousness, he would have been just as quick to insist that the law, God's preeminent means of grace, was given to rectify the multitude of evils caused by Adam's sin. But not so for Paul. According to his teaching elsewhere, the law works wrath (Rom 4:15) and increases the trespass (Rom 5:20), so that the Mosaic period as a whole could be summarized as an era of condemnation (2 Corinthians 3). The law was never intended to justify; it was, rather, a pointer to Christ (3:23-24).

Paul thus counters the notion that the law was given to reverse the curse. In pressing law-observance on Gentile Christians, the Judaizers thought that it was the law itself, under God, which provided righteousness and life. God, to be sure, is the ultimate source of both; but the channel of blessing is the Torah (e.g., Sir 17:11; 45:5; Bar 3:9; 4:1; cf. 4 Ezra 7:127-31; 14:22, 29, 30, 34; *Pss. Sol.* 14:2-3; Ps.-Philo 23:10, all building on Lev 18:5; Deut 4:1, 10, 40; 5:29-33; 6:1-2, 18, 24; 7:12-13). There was no thought of a Christ who bestows his own righteousness on the people—and certainly not apart from the law. Very unlike Paul (Gal 3:23-25; Rom 10:4), for them Jesus the Messiah was but a servant of the Torah, not its goal and reason for existence.[71]

It is in this theological and pastoral climate that Paul is bold enough to modify the actual wording of Ps 143:2 (LXX 142:2). Where the Psalmist said: "no *living being* will be justified *before you*," Paul rephrases: "*by works of the law no flesh* will be justified." There are two obvious differences between the original wording of the Psalm and Paul's reworking of it. One is the insertion of "works of the law" and the deletion of "before you." "Works of the law" articulated the Israelite's responsibilities within the covenant and served to set the standard of his commitment to Yahweh. It was by remaining within the parameters of the Torah that one could be assured of a favorable verdict at the last judgment.

The other alteration is the substitution of "flesh" for "living being." "Flesh" (Hebrew *basar*; Greek *sarx*) is common enough in the OT and LXX as a designation of the human being, especially from the vantage point of the finitude, weakness, and corruptibility of the human race (e.g., Gen 6:12; Isa 31:3; cf. Sir 31:1; 1QH 15:21). But "flesh" in Galatians also bears connotations of the "old creation" in which the Judaizers continue to live and in which they are compelling the Galatians to reside as well.[72] Both components together, "works of the law" and "flesh," are an index to the Jewish/Judaistic position on justification. It is just "flesh" that will, according to such an ideology, be justified "by works of the law."

It is over against these taken-for-granted points of orthodoxy on the part of his Jewish rivals that Paul avows "no flesh" can be justified/vindicated "by works of the law."

> ...in speaking of "all flesh" Paul has in view primarily and precisely those who think their acceptability to God and standing before God does depend on their physical descent from Abraham, their national identity as Jews. It is precisely this attitude, which puts too much stress on fleshly relationships and fleshly rites, precisely this attitude which Paul excoriates in his parting shot in 6.12-13—"they want to make a good showing in the flesh...they want to glory in your flesh."[73]

Dunn further observes that with Psalm 143 more sharply defined in terms of physical and national identification, the addition of "from works of the law" is merely a further clarification of "flesh," because the works of the law in this letter, as epitomized by circumcision and the like, are primarily acts of the flesh.[74] Flesh, for this reason, was high on the Judaizers' agenda. Carter adds that Paul's substitution of "flesh" for "living being" anticipates the eschatological distinction between flesh and Spirit that he will draw at the end of the letter. Sinfulness is not defined in terms of Gentiles who disregard the Jewish law; instead, Paul's use of "flesh" defines sin in terms of universal participation in the present evil age (1:4). "Those whose existence is determined by flesh rather than by Spirit are [on] the wrong side of the eschatological boundary and so cannot be justified by works of Jewish Torah."[75] It is by means of his reworked version of Ps 143:2 that Paul both nails down his premise of v. 16a and paves the way for 3:10-13, in which he will audaciously assert that the Jewish teachers and their committed followers are under the curse of the law just because of their (idolatrous) attachment to the flesh = law.[76]

In Gal 2:16, Paul thus redraws the boundaries that serve to demarcate the people of God. As the whole of Galatians bears witness, believers' new point of reference is not the Torah, but Christ and the Spirit, as they both have created a new community of love.[77] Carter is right that, according to Paul, the Jewish people themselves (and, I would add, the Jewish Christian missionaries) are on the outside. In thinking that the key to a right relation to God is a matter of observing the law, they are "simply trying the wrong door." As he continues, Paul's position is radical indeed, because "the law and its observance were central to the Jewish symbolic universe, fundamental to their identification of themselves as having been elected to be God's covenant people."[78]

4. Conclusions

It is none other than the time-honored distinction, in Jewish thinking, between "Jews by birth" and "Gentile sinners" that calls for Paul's emphatic assertion that "*even we*" Jewish believers have been justified by no other means than faith alone in Christ Jesus. The "saints,"[79] no less than the "sinners," have come to the realization that the story of Israel has reached its climax in Christ. That being the case, Torah-fidelity is no longer the path to (eschatological) salvation. In this regard, the gist of Paul's polemic in Galatians can be summed up in the "no distinction" motif of Romans (2:11; 3:22; 10:12). If anything, such an appraisal of Christ and the law in relation to the vindication of the people of God is what most radically distinguishes Pauline Christianity from the Judaistic variety—for Paul, the "sinners" are now the "saints!" Actually, such a conclusion is not so shocking, given the way that Paul, by means of "hermeneutical jujitsu," employs the tactic of role reversal in Gal 3:10-13 and 4:21-31. By the time he is through, his opponents are, no less, apostates from Yahweh and latter-day Ishmaelites![80]

Apart from the central thesis of this essay, the above exposition serves to confirm the growing trend in Pauline research respecting the character of justification. That there is a forensic/juridical dimension to the doctrine is not to be doubted; indeed, it is substantiated from the OT data. Nevertheless, there is more to it than that. Given that the courtroom is that of the Hebrew covenant, not the Greco-Roman or modern hall of justice, the pronouncement of justification *"is not just a vindicated status, but a vindicated life."*[81] I hasten to add that the "vindicated life" is not by any stretch of the imagination to be construed as a "justification by decency."[82] Rather, the vindication is that of the returning righteous remnant of Israel, who are "justified" because of their fidelity to the Lord and his covenant. From the eschatological vantage point, it is Jesus who is now the Lord of the New Covenant—it is to him that the Christian's allegiance is due, the one who has broken down the "dividing wall of hostility" (Eph 2:11-22) between Israel and the nations. It is *in him* that believers have become the righteousness of God (2 Cor 5:21); they have been exonerated in the great assize and have been admitted into the privileges, responsibilities, and fellowship of the new covenant.

In a nutshell, justification in Paul signals deliverance from exile and freedom from bondage. Therefore, when Paul writes of justification, he characteristically has in mind the new exodus on which the latter-day people of God have embarked.[83] Moreover, this saving righteousness is cosmic in its dimensions. In the Prophets, the return of the exiles corresponds to the recreation of all things.[84] At the end of the day, this means that "the righteousness of God" is actively directed at the rescue of the creation (Käsemann). God's righteousness is his relation-restoring love, and justification is his act to liberate his creatures from corruption and return the cosmos to its pristine condition.[85]

None of this is to suggest that the standing of the individual before God is to be relegated to a footnote in the divine purpose. But it is to say that the corporate character of the "Israel of God" (Gal 6:16) is at least as important as its individual makeup, if indeed not more so. Wright in particular has been criticized for stressing the corporate to the virtual exclusion of the individual. But notwithstanding the partial validity of such a critique, at least Wright and others have endeavored to redress the balance in favor of an appreciation of justification in its *heilsgeschichtlich* dimensions.

---

[1] Recent developments are surveyed by S. Westerholm, *Perspectives Old and New on Paul: The "Lutheran" Paul and His Critics* (Grand Rapids: Eerdmans, 2004), 3-258; P. T. O'Brien, "Justification in Paul and Some Crucial Issues of the Last Two Decades," *Right With God: Justification in the Bible and the World*, ed. D. A. Carson (London/Grand Rapids: Paternoster/Baker, 1992), 69-95; C. G. Kruse, *Paul, the Law, and Justification* (Peabody: Hendrickson, 1996), 27-53.

[2] I am proceeding along traditional lines that Paul's antagonists were "Jewish Christian missionaries," whose conception of the place of the law in the messianic age differed from that of Paul. The thesis of M. D. Nanos, *The Irony of Galatians: Paul's Letter in First-Century Context* (Minneapolis: Fortress, 2002), that the "Influencers," as he calls them, were representatives of local synagogues attempting to win the Gentile Galatians to non-Christian Judaism is intriguing but hardly convincing. While respecting Nanos' position, A. A. Das rightly concludes that the "they group" in the letter is comprised of Jewish Christians in the Galatians' midst, not non-Christian Jews (*Paul and the Jews* [Peabody: Hendrickson, 2003], 17-29).

[3] The major component of 1:11-2:21, an unusual passage in Paul's letters, is "Pauline autobiography;" that is, Paul writes about himself principally to present an example to his converts and to provide contrastive models between his ministry and that of his rivals. See J. H. Schütz, *Paul and the Anatomy of Apostolic Authority*, Society for New Testament Studies Monograph Series 26 (Cambridge: Cambridge University Press, 1975), 128-58; G. Lyons, *Pauline Autobiography: Toward a New*

Understanding, Society of Biblical Literature Dissertation Series 73 (Atlanta: Scholars Press, 1985); B. Dodd, *Paul's Paradigmatic 'I': Personal Example as Literary Structure,* Journal for the Study of the New Testament: Supplement Series 177 (Sheffield: Sheffield Academic Press, 1999); M. V. Hubbard, *New Creation in Paul's Letters and Thought,* Society for New Testament Studies Monograph Series 119 (Cambridge: Cambridge University Press, 2002), 191-99; cf. W. P. de Boer, *The Imitation of Paul: An Exegetical Study* (Kampen: Kok, 1962). B. Fiore shows that Paul's promotion of himself as an example falls into line with Greco-Roman precedents ("Paul, Exemplification, and Imitation," *Paul in the Greco-Roman World: A Handbook,* ed. J. Paul Sampley [Harrisburg: Trinity Press International, 2003], 228-37). Such self-exemplification, therefore, would probably not have come as a surprise to his Galatian readers or have been offensive to them. In Gal 1:11-2:21, as B. R. Gaventa puts it, "Paul presents himself as an example of the working of the gospel" ("Galatians 1 and 2: Autobiography as Paradigm," *Novum Testamentum* 28 [1986], 313). Cf. J. D. G. Dunn, "Paul's Conversion—A Light to Twentieth Century Disputes," *Evangelium, Schriftauslegung, Kirche: Festschrift für Peter Stuhlmacher zum 65. Geburtstag,* eds. J. Adna, S. J. Hafemann and O. Hofius (Göttingen: Vandenhoeck & Ruprecht, 1997), 88-90. Such is Paul's "biography of reversal" (Schütz, *Anatomy,* 133).

[4] The "wrong direction" motif reemerges quite prominently in 3:1-3. The Galatians, having begun in the age of Spirit, now want to be perfected in the flesh, i.e., the era of the flesh (the law). They are so "foolish" because their quest for perfection is anachronistic: they are going in the wrong direction; they want to reverse the plan of the ages! See my *An Exposition of Galatians: A New Perspective/Reformational Reading.* 2nd ed. (Eugene, OR: Wipf & Stock, 2004), 152.

[5] Gaventa, "Autobiography as Paradigm," 321.

[6] As M. J. Gorman writes, Paul responds to the Galatian crisis by telling a series of stories—"Stories about himself, about Christ, about the Galatians and their experience of the Spirit, about God, about the Law, about biblical characters like Abraham and Hagar and Sarah, and about life together.... These stories all serve his main purpose of dissuading the Gentile Galatians from being circumcised" (*Apostle of the Crucified Lord: A Theological Introduction to Paul and His Letters* [Grand Rapids: Eerdmans, 2004], 192). That Paul's gospel, and that of the NT generally, purports to be the story of Israel reaching its climactic point is demonstrated brilliantly by N. T. Wright, *The Climax of the Covenant: Christ and the Law in Pauline Theology* (Minneapolis: Fortress, 1991); id., *The New Testament and the People of God,* Christian Origins and the Question of God 1 (Minneapolis: Fortress, 1991); id., *Jesus and the Victory of God,* Christian Origins and the Question of God 2 (Minneapolis: Fortress, 1996); id., *What Saint Paul Really Said: Was*

Paul of Tarsus the Real Founder of Christianity? (Grand Rapids: Eerdmans, 1997).
[7] Lührmann, *Galatians*, Continental Commentary (Minneapolis: Fortress, 1992), 46.
[8] Martyn, *Galatians*, Anchor Bible 33a (New York: Doubleday, 1997), 247.
[9] Betz, *Galatians: A Commentary on Paul's Letter to the Churches in Galatia*, Hermeneia (Philadelphia: Fortress, 1979), 114.
[10] Representative literature on justification includes: Wright, *Saint Paul*, 113-33; Martyn, *Galatians*, 264-75; G. Howard, *Paul: Crisis in Galatia: A Study in Early Christian Theology*, Society for New Testament Studies Monograph Series 35. 2nd ed. (Cambridge: Cambridge University Press, 1979), 46-65; V. M. Smiles, *The Gospel and the Law in Galatia: Paul's Response to Jewish-Christian Separationism and the Threat of Galatian Apostasy* (Collegeville: Glazier, 1998), 133-46; M. J. Gorman, *Cruciformity: Paul's Narrative Spirituality of the Cross* (Grand Rapids: Eerdmans, 2001), 122-46; A. McGrath, *Studies in Doctrine* (Grand Rapids: Zondervan, 1997), 355-480; id., *Dictionary of Paul and His Letters*, eds. G. F. Hawthorne, R. P. Martin and D. G. Reid (Downers Grove: InterVarsity, 1993), 517-23; M. A. Seifrid, *Justification By Faith: The Origin and Development of A Central Pauline Theme*, Novum Testamentum Supplements 68 (Leiden: Brill, 1992); id., *Christ, Our Righteousness: Paul's Theology of Justification*, New Studies in Biblical Theology 9 (Downers Grove: Apollos, 2000); D. Garlington, *Exegetical Essays*. 3rd ed. (Eugene, OR: Wipf & Stock, 2003), 285-99.
[11] Dunn, *The Epistle to the Galatians*, Black's New Testament Commentary 9 (Peabody: Hendrickson, 1993), 133.
[12] The Greek terms alternate between *anomoi* and *paranomoi*.
[13] "Righteous" = *dikaioi*; "sinners" = *hamartōloi*.
[14] Although there are limitations to the method, any interpretation of Galatians inevitably resorts to a certain amount of "mirror reading" of the text. See J. M. G. Barclay, *Obeying the Truth: A Study of Paul's Ethics in Galatians*, Studies of the New Testament and Its World (Edinburgh: T. & T. Clark, 1988), 37-45; id., "Mirror Reading a Polemical Letter: Galatians as a Test Case," *Journal for the Study of the New Testament* 31 (1987), 73-93, rep. in *The Pauline Writings*, The Biblical Seminar 34, eds. S. E. Porter and C. A. Evans (Sheffield: Sheffield Academic Press, 1995), 247-67. Such mirror reading was anticipated by C. K. Barrett, *Essays on Paul* (London: SPCK, 1982), 154-70.
[15] Dunn, *Galatians*, 133. On the "sinners," see Dunn, *Jesus, Paul, and the Law: Studies in Mark and Galatians* (Louisville: Westminster/John Knox, 1990), 71-77, 150-51; id., *The Partings of the Ways: Between Christianity and Judaism and Their Significance for the Character of Christianity* (Philadelphia: Trinity Press International, 1991), 102-7; id., *Jesus Remembered*, Christianity in the Making 1 (Grand Rapids: Eerdmans, 2003), 526-32; D. Garlington, *'The Obedience of Faith': A*

Pauline Phrase in Historical Context, Wissenschaftliche Untersuchungen zum Neuen Testament 2/38 (Tübingen: Mohr-Siebeck, 1991), 49-55, 95-98; and at length M. Winninge, *Sinners and the Righteous: A Comparative Study of the Psalms of Solomon and Paul's Letters*, Coniectanea biblica, New Testament 26 (Stockholm: Almqvist & Wiksell, 1995).

[16] 2 Macc 6:12-17 states the position of at least one author with regard to the sinfulness of Jews in contrast to Gentiles. The sins of the nations are punished with a view to destruction, while Jewish sinners are merely disciplined.

[17] On the construction, see R. N. Longenecker, *Galatians*, Word Biblical Commentary 41 (Dallas: Word, 1990), 83.

[18] Witherington, *Grace in Galatia: A Commentary on Paul's Letter to the Galatians* (Grand Rapids: Eerdmans, 1998), 173.

[19] See my *Exegetical Essays*, 285-87, 297-99.

[20] Ziesler, *The Meaning of Righteousness in Paul: A Linguistic and Theological Enquiry*, Society for New Testament Studies Monograph Series 20 (Cambridge: Cambridge University Press, 1972), 20, 25 (italics mine). See also Gorman, *Cruciformity*, 142-43.

[21] Käsemann, "'The Righteousness of God' in Paul," *New Testament Questions of Today* (Philadelphia: Fortress, 1969), 172.

[22] Reumann, *Righteousness in the New Testament: "Justification" in the United States Lutheran-Roman Catholic Dialogue, with Responses by Joseph A. Fitzmyer and Jerome D. Quinn* (Philadelphia: Fortress, 1982), 16.

[23] Cf. Wright, *Saint Paul*, 33-34.

[24] See the further assemblage of passages by R. H. Gundry, "The Nonimputation of Christ's Righteousness," *Justification: What's at Stake in the Current Debates?* eds. M. Husbands and D. J. Treier (Downers Grove/Leicester: InterVarsity/Apollos, 2004), 36-38.

[25] Recently, M. Seifrid has attempted to distance righteousness from covenant and place it more in proximity to the concept of creation ("Righteousness Language in the Hebrew Scriptures and Early Judaism," *Justification and Variegated Nomism. Volume 1: The Complexities of Second Temple Judaism*, eds. D. A. Carson, P. T. O'Brien and M. A. Seifrid [Grand Rapids: Baker, 2001], 415-42). In my response, I have argued that Seifrid's bifurcation of covenant and creation is a false one and that righteousness still finds its proper definition within the parameters of the covenant.

[26] Wright, *Saint Paul*, 96.

[27] Ibid., 96-97.

[28] Cf. Gorman, *Apostle*, 201.

[29] As a definition of Apocalyptic, that of F. M. Cross is as good as any (*The Ancient Library of Qumran*. 3rd. ed. [Sheffield: Sheffield Academic Press, 1995], 69, n. 3). Modern scholarship has increasingly come to recognize that in Paul generally, and Galatians in particular, there is a

decided apocalyptic element. The movement is chronicled by R. B. Matlock, *Unveiling the Apocalyptic Paul: Paul's Interpreters and the Rhetoric of Criticism*, Journal for the Study of the New Testament: Supplement Series 127 (Sheffield: Sheffield Academic Press, 1996). Handy overviews are provided by Gorman, *Apostle*, 21-23; Das, *Paul and the Jews*, 34-36. At more length, see J. C. Beker, *Paul the Apostle: The Triumph of God in Life and Thought* (Philadelphia: Fortress, 1980). As for Galatians specifically, see Martyn, *Galatians*, 97-105; id., "Apocalyptic Antinomies in Paul's Letter to the Galatians," *New Testament Studies* 31 (1985), 410-24, now reprinted in *Theological Issues in the Letters of Paul* (Nashville: Abingdon, 1997), 111-123; J. D. G. Dunn, *The Theology of Paul's Letter to the Galatians* (New Testament Theology; Cambridge: Cambridge University Press, 1993), 46-52; R. G. Hall, "Arguing like an Apocalypse: Galatians and Ancient *Topos* outside the Greco-Roman Rhetorical Tradition," *New Testament Studies* 42 (1996), 434-53; M. De Boer, "Paul's Quotation of Isaiah 54.1 in Galatians 4.27," *New Testament Studies* 50 (2004), 370-89.

[30] S. Motyer, "Righteousness by Faith in the New Testament," *Here We Stand: Justification by Faith Today* (London: Hodder & Stoughton, 1986), 48.

[31] See D. Garlington, *Faith, Obedience, and Perseverance: Aspects of Paul's Letter to the Romans*, Wissenschaftliche Untersuchungen zum Neuen Testament 79 (Tübingen: Mohr-Siebeck, 1994), 75-76.

[32] Among the commentators on Romans, see especially J. Murray, *The Epistle to the Romans*, New International Commentary on the New Testament. 2 vols. (Grand Rapids: Eerdmans, 1959, 1965), 1.222; T. R. Schreiner, *Romans*, Baker Exegetical Commentary on the New Testament (Grand Rapids: Baker, 1998), 319. Surprisingly neglected is Murray's "Definitive Sanctification," *Collected Writings of John Murray*. 4 vols. (Edinburgh: Banner of Truth, 1977), 2.277-84.

[33] K. L. Onesti and M. T. Brauch, *Dictionary of Paul and His Letters*, eds. G. F. Hawthorne, R. P. Martin and D. G. Reid (Downers Grove: InterVarsity, 1993), 836-37; M. Barth, *Justification: Pauline Texts Interpreted in Light of the Old and New Testaments* (Grand Rapids: Eerdmans, 1971), 17, 74-82.

[34] See W. J. Dumbrell, "Justification in Paul: A Covenantal Perspective," *Reformed Theological Review* 51 (1992), 91-101.

[35] Sanders, *Paul, the Law, and the Jewish People* (Philadelphia: Fortress, 1983), 45-46. See further my *Galatians*, 6-7.

[36] Wright, *Climax of the Covenant*, 162-68.

[37] Wright, *Saint Paul*, 108.

[38] Davies, "Paul: From the Jewish Point of View," *The Cambridge History of Judaism. Volume Three: The Early Roman Period*, eds. W. Horbury, W. D. Davies and J. Sturdy (Cambridge: Cambridge University Press, 1999), 715-16.

[39] Ibid., 716. Cf. C. B. Cousar, *Galatians*, Interpretation (Louisville: John Knox, 1982), 56-58.
[40] On the interpretations, see T. N. Schreiner, *Dictionary of Paul and His Letters*, eds. G. F. Hawthorne, R. P. Martin and D. G. Reid (Downers Grove: InterVarsity, 1993), 975-79.
[41] Dunn, *Galatians*, 135-36.
[42] Dunn, *Jesus, Paul*, 194. H. Schlier shows that in some literature "works of the law" appear as "works of the commandments," or in rabbinic traditions simply as "works." These "works" constitute the "law of the Lord" as over against the "law of Beliar" (*Der Brief an die Galater*, Kritisch-exegetischer Kommentar über das Neue Testament. 5th ed. [Göttingen: Vandenhoeck & Ruprecht, 1971], 91-92). This would tend to confirm that when Paul uses the word "works" by itself, he employs it as shorthand for the longer phrase "works of the law."
[43] Dunn, *Jesus, Paul*, 193.
[44] Martyn, *Galatians*, 261.
[45] Dunn, *Jesus, Paul*, e.g., 192, 194. See at length E. J. Christiansen, *The Covenant in Judaism and Paul: A Study of Ritual Boundaries as Identity Markers*, Arbeiten zur Geschichte des antiken Judentums und des Urchristentums 27 (Leiden: Brill, 1995).
[46] M. Hengel, *The Zealots: Investigations into the Jewish Freedom Movement in the Period from Herod I until 70 A. D.* (Edinburgh: T. & T. Clark, 1989), 146-228.
[47] Hays, *The HarperCollins Study Bible: New Revised Standard Version*, eds. W. A. Meeks, et al. (New York: HarperCollins, 1993), 2185 (italics mine). Cf. J. D. G. Dunn, *The Theology of Paul the Apostle* (Grand Rapids: Eerdmans, 1998), 354-59; J. A. Ziesler, *The Epistle to the Galatians*, Epworth Commentaries (London: Epworth, 1992), 25-26. According to Sanders, "There is...something which is common to circumcision, Sabbath, and food laws, and which sets them off from other laws; they created a social distinction between Jews and other races in the Greco-Roman world" (*Paul, the Law*, 102).
[48] This being so, the thunder is taken out of A. A. Das' attempt to impute to Dunn a notion of "works of the law" that would restrict the scope of the phrase to the "boundary markers" (*Paul, the Law, and the Covenant* [Peabody: Hendrickson, 2001], 155-60). Das perpetuates a common misrepresentation of Dunn's position. No wonder, Dunn justifiably issues a note of protest in *Theology of Paul*, 358, n. 97.
[49] Witherington, *Grace*, 172. To the same effect are Ziesler, *Galatians*, 26; S. McKnight, *Galatians*, NIV Application Commentary (Grand Rapids: Zondervan, 1995), 119-21; G. W. Hansen, *Galatians*, IVP New Testament Commentary Series 9 (Downers Grove: InterVarsity, 1994), 69-70.
[50] M. Winger's attempt to eliminate 4QFlor 1:7 from consideration is not at all convincing (*By What Law? The Meaning of Nomos in the Letters of Paul*, Society of Biblical Literature Dissertation Series 128 [Atlanta:

Scholars Press, 1992], 135). Not only G. Vermes' translation of the passage (quoted by Winger) but that of F. G. Martinez renders: "And he commanded to build for himself a temple of man, to offer him in it, before him, the works of the law" (*The Dead Sea Scrolls Translated: The Qumran Texts in English* [Leiden: Brill, 1994], 136). Here, "the works of the law" are tantamount to the community's sacrifice as placed upon the altar of the temple. The application to Paul is hardly speculative, as Winger claims, but indicates that the sect's covenantal duty was regarded in sacrificial terms, an idea very much relevant to Paul. Moreover, contra Winger, this is not the only occurrence of the phrase *maasē ha-torah* in the Scrolls (as cited above). The subsequent publication of 4QMMT (unavailable to Winger) simply nails down the case.

[51] On 4QMMT, see Das, *Paul and the Jews*, 41, n. 61; Dunn, *Theology of Paul*, 357-58; id., "4QMMT and Galatians," *New Testament Studies* 43 (1997), 147-53; N. T. Wright, "Justification and Eschatology in Paul and Qumran: Romans and 4QMMT," *History and Exegesis: New Testament Essays in Honor of Dr. E. Earle Ellis on His 80th Birthday*. ed. Sang-Won (Aaron) Son. New York/London: T & T Clark, 2006, 104-32; R. E. Ciampa, *The Presence and Function of Scripture in Galatians 1 and 2*, Wissenschaftliche Untersuchungen zum Neuen Testament 2/102 (Tübingen: Mohr-Siebeck, 1998), 186-91; C. M. Pate, *Communities of the Last Days: The Dead Sea Scrolls, the New Testament and the Story of Israel* (Downers Grove: InterVarsity, 2000), 47-48, 58-61; M. Abegg, "4QMMT, Paul, and 'Works of the Law,'" *The Bible at Qumran: Text, Shape, and Interpretation*, ed. P. Flint. Studies in the Dead Sea Scrolls and Related Literature (Grand Rapids: Eerdmans, 2001), 203-16; J. Kampen and M. J. Bernstein (eds.), *Reading 4QMMT: New Perspectives on Qumran Law and History*, Society of Biblical Literature Seminar Series 2 (Atlanta: Scholars Press, 1996). The entire text with commentary is in E. Qimron and J. Strugnell (eds.), *Discoveries in the Judean Desert X. Qumran Cave 4. V: Miqsat Maase Ha-Torah* (Oxford: Clarendon, 1994).

[52] On the significance of table fellowship and Peter's separation from the Gentiles, see my *Galatians*, 113-14.

[53] H. Räisänen, *Paul and the Law*, Wissenschaftliche Untersuchungen zum Neuen Testament 29 (Tübingen: Mohr-Siebeck, 1983), 177-91. I have explored the Torah-idolatry motif in *Faith, Obedience, and Perseverance*, 32-43; *Galatians*, 198-202.

[54] McKnight, *Galatians*, 122.

[55] Betz, *Galatians*, 116.

[56] Cosgrove, "Justification in Paul: A Linguistic and Theological Reflection," *Journal of Biblical Literature* 106 (1987), esp. 654-61. The one place where Paul apparently speaks of "basis" is Phil 3:9: "the righteousness of God based on faith" (*tēn ek theou dikaiosunēn epi tē pistei*). But even here, apart from the fact that *dikaioō* is absent from the

text, the contrast is with a righteousness that is not "*of* the law" (*ek nomou*) but "*through* faith in Christ" (*dia pisteōs Christou*).

[57] Cosgrove, "Justification in Paul," 662.

[58] As represented, e.g., by R. B. Hays, *The Faith of Jesus Christ: An Investigation of the Narrative Substructure of Galatians 3:1-4:11*, The Biblical Resource Series. 2nd ed. (Grand Rapids: Eerdmans, 2002); M. D. Hooker, "*PISTIS CHRISTOU*," *New Testament Studies* 35 (1989), 321-42. B. W. Longenecker, *The Triumph of Abraham's God: The Transformation of Identity in Galatians* (Nashville: Abingdon, 1998), 95-107; I. G. Wallis, *The Faith of Jesus Christ in Early Christian Traditions*, Society for New Testament Studies Monograph Series 84 (Cambridge: Cambridge University Press, 1995); S. A. Cummins, *Paul and the Crucified Christ in Antioch: Maccabean Martyrdom and Galatians 1 and 2*, Society for New Testament Studies Monograph Series 114 (Cambridge: Cambridge University Press, 2001), 198-206; P. Foster, "The First Contribution to the *Pistis Christou* Debate: A Study of Ephesians 3.12," *Journal for the Study of the New Testament* 85 (2002), 75-96.

[59] See the discussions of Dunn, "Once More, *PISTIS CHRISTOU*," *Pauline Theology. Volume IV: Looking Back, Pressing On*, Society of Biblical Literature Seminar Series 4, eds. E. E. Johnson and D. M. Hay (Atlanta: Scholars Press, 1997), 61-81. C. E. B. Cranfield, "On the *Pistis Christou* Question," *On Romans and Other New Testament Essays* (Edinburgh: T. & T. Clark, 1998), 81-97; T. L. Carter, *Paul and the Power of Sin: Redefining 'Beyond the Pale'*, Society for New Testament Studies Monograph Series 115 (Cambridge: Cambridge University Press, 2002), 98, n. 55. Debates back and forth are in Johnson/Hay (eds.), *Pauline Theology*, 33-92.

[60] Cf. F. Mußner, *Der Galaterbrief*, Herders theologischer Kommentar zum Neuen Testament 9. 4th ed. (Freiburg: Herder, 1981), 171.

[61] Hultgren, "The *Pistis Christou* Formulation in Paul," *Novum Testamentum* 22 (1980), 257, 259-60.

[62] McKnight, *Galatians*, 121.

[63] See E. Perry, "The Meaning of *'emunah* in the Old Testament," *Journal of Bible and Religion* 21 (1953), 252-56; H. Wildberger, *Theological Lexicon of the Old Testament*, eds. E. Jenni, et al. 3 vols. (Peabody: Hendrickson, 1997), 1.147-51; A. Jepsen, *Theological Dictionary of the Old Testament*, eds. G. J. Botterweck and H. Ringgren. 13 vols. (Grand Rapids: Eerdmans, 1974-), 1.316-20; D. Garlington, *'The Obedience of Faith': A Pauline Phrase in Historical Context*, Wissenschaftliche Untersuchungen zum Neuen Testament 2/38 (Tübingen: Mohr-Siebeck, 1991), 10-11. *Emunah* is likewise predicated of Yahweh in his faithfulness to Israel.

[64] George, *Galatians*, New American Commentary 30 (Nashville: Broadman and Holman, 1994), 191.

[65] Anderson, *The Book of Psalms*, New Century Bible. 2 vols. (Grand Rapids: Eerdmans, 1972), 2.926.
[66] Ibid., 2.926-27.
[67] A. Weiser adds: "As he faces God in prayer his sinfulness dawns on him; at the same time he comes to realize that God would be quite justified in 'entering into judgment with him'. He visualizes his sinfulness within the larger context of the universal sinfulness of mankind and so recognizes its ultimate seriousness as a failure before God that is inherent in man's nature and therefore cannot be overcome by his own efforts.... And when he bases his petition that God may not enter into judgment with him on the argument that no man living is righteous before him, then this statement is not meant as an excuse which by pointing to the others who are subject to the same condemnation seeks to reduce his own guilt and responsibility. On the contrary, he discerns in the fact that all men are in bondage to sin and are unable to free themselves from it by their own efforts (cf. vv. 8, 10) the utter seriousness and power of sin; he realizes that this is his own personal situation in which but one way is left open to him: to give himself wholly up to the grace of God. This is why he does not even make the slightest attempt, which we frequently encounter elsewhere, to protest his innocence and look for a legal claim that might justify his petition. As he utters his petition, which includes the confession of sin, he comes before God as a suppliant, not as one who makes demands on him" (*The Psalms: A Commentary*, Old Testament Library [Philadelphia: Westminster, 1962], 819).
[68] See H. J. Kraus, *Theology of the Psalms* (Minneapolis: Augsburg, 1986), 154-62.
[69] Dunn, *Galatians*, 140.
[70] On the penitential prayer tradition, see R. A. Werline, *Penitential Prayer in Second Temple Judaism: The Development of a Religious Institution*, Society of Biblical Literature Early Judaism and Its Literature 13 (Atlanta: Scholars Press, 1998); J. H. Newman, *Praying by the Book: The Scripturalization of Prayer in Second Temple Judaism*, Society of Biblical Literature Early Judaism and Its Literature 14 (Atlanta: Scholars Press, 1999); M. J. Boda, *Praying the Tradition: The Origin and Use of Tradition in Nehemiah 9*, Beihefte zur *Zeitschrift für die alttestamentliche Wissenschaft* 277 (Berlin: de Gruyter, 1999), as summarized in Boda's "Praying the Tradition: The Origin and Use of Tradition in Nehemiah 9," *Tyndale Bulletin* 48 (1997), 179-83. A bibliography of penitential prayer can be accessed at: http://divinity.mcmaster.ca/boda/prayer/index.html.
[71] See Martyn, *Galatians*, 124-25.
[72] Garlington, *Galatians*, 152, 241, 257-58.
[73] Dunn, *Jesus, Paul*, 199.
[74] Ibid., 199-200.
[75] Carter, *Paul*, 101.

[76] See my "Role Reversal and Paul's Use of Scripture in Galatians 3.10-13," *Journal for the Study of the New Testament* 65 (1997), 85-121 (= *Exegetical Essays*, 213-47).
[77] Cf. my "Burden Bearing and the Recovery of Offending Christians (Galatians 6:1-5)," *Trinity Journal* ns 12 (1991), 151-83 (= *Exegetical Essays*, 249-84).
[78] Carter, *Paul*, 101.
[79] Paul alludes to the "saints" of the OT in Gal 1:2. See my *Galatians*, 37-38.
[80] "Hermeneutical jujitsu" is R. B. Hays' phrase (*Echoes of Scripture in the Letters of Paul* [New Haven: Yale University Press, 1989], 112). On the role reversal motifs of 3:1-13 and 4:21-31, see respectively my "Role Reversal" and *Galatians*, 212-28.
[81] Ziesler, *Righteousness in Paul*, 142-43.
[82] F. F. Bruce, *The Spreading Flame: The Rise and Progress of Christianity from its First Beginnings to the Conversion of the English* (Exeter: Paternoster, 1958), 336, writing of the soteriology of Pelagius.
[83] Apart from the various volumes of Wright, the return from exile motif has been canvassed by M. Knibb, "The Exile in the Literature of the Intertestamental Period," *Heythrop Journal* 17 (1976), 253-72; id., "Exile in the Damascus Document," *Journal for the Study of the Old Testament* 25 (1983), 99-117; J. M. Scott, "Paul's Use of the Deuteronomic Tradition," *Journal of Biblical Literature* 112 (1993), 645-65; id., "'For As Many as Are of Works of the Law Are under a Curse' (Galatians 3.10)," *Paul and the Scriptures of Israel* (eds. C. A. Evans and J. A. Sanders; Journal for the Study of the New Testament: Supplement Series 83. Studies in Scripture in Early Judaism and Christianity 1. (Sheffield: Sheffield Academic Press, 1993), 187-221; id., (ed.), *Exile: Old Testament, Jewish, and Christian Conceptions*, Journal for the Study of Judaism: Supplement Series 56 (Leiden: Brill, 1997); Pate, *Communities*; id., *The Reverse of the Curse: Paul, Wisdom, and the Law*, Wissenschaftliche Untersuchungen zum Neuen Testament 2/114 (Tübingen: Mohr-Siebeck, 2000); C. A. Evans, "Jesus and the Continuing Exile of Israel," *Jesus and the Restoration of Israel: A Critical Assessment of N. T. Wright's Jesus and the Victory of God*, ed. C. C. Newman (Downers Grove: InterVarsity, 1999), 77-100.

The degree to which Second Temple Jews were aware of a continuing exile is disputed, especially as the textual evidence is not uniform (e.g., Bar 4:36-37; 5:5-9 versus Jdt 4:1-5; 5:17-19; Josephus *Ant.* 4.8.46 §344; 10.7.3 §§112-13; 11.1.1 §§1-4). For references pertaining to the debate, see Das *Paul*, 153-55; id., *Paul and the Jews*, 38. In any event, whether Paul's contemporaries were aware of a continuing exile or not, effectively the nation was still in bondage until the appearance of another Moses who would lead them on a new exodus of redemption. As far as Galatians is concerned, the exile has in fact been reversed with the liberation of the people of God from the bondage of the law. Das may be right that Paul's opponents considered the exile to be at an end because of Israel's devotion to the law since the return from Babylon. But so ironically, the nation's rejection of Jesus the Messiah has brought about a *new exile* for the majority of the Jewish people (*Paul and the Jews*, 38, n. 55).

[84] E.g., Isa 2:2-4; 25:6-12; 26:19; 35; 60; 65:17-25; Ezekiel 36-37. This hope for the end-time was taken up and intensified by the Jewish apocalyptic movement, e.g., *Jubilees* (passim) *Joseph and Aseneth* (passim); 4 Ezra 7:50, 113; *2 Apoc. Bar.* 31:5; *1 Enoch* 91:15-17. See respectively Hubbard, *Creation*, 11-25, 26-76.

[85] Hubbard's study has yielded the conclusion that new creation is on Paul's mind from the earliest stages of Galatians and forms its culminating point at the end of the letter (6:15) (*New Creation*, 191-232). In a very real sense, new creation is what Galatians is about. The root of the matter is that this new creation assumes a different shape than the old: the former things that used to identify the community of faith have now given way to the age of the Spirit.

ROLE REVERSAL AND PAUL'S USE OF SCRIPTURE IN GALATIANS 3:10-13

1. Introduction

It is but a truism that Paul's use of the OT is a perennial puzzlement to many of his interpreters. Among the most pondered passages in his letters is Gal 3:10-13, with its employment respectively of Deut 27:26; Hab 2:4; Lev 18:5; and Deut 21:23. On one level, the agenda of this segment of Galatians is clear enough. In order to support his contention that "those who are of works of the law are under a curse" (v. 10a), Paul selects two passages (Deut 27:26; 21:23) which predicate cursing of a class of individuals, with two others sandwiched in between which counterbalance cursing with life (Hab 2:4; Lev 18:5).[1] These several pronouncements of "the law and the prophets" are proof positive to Paul that his critics in Galatia are cursed by God and that only those who heed his gospel are blessed.

On another lever, however, the inner workings of his tack have been the source of rather intense headaches for exegetes. The problem, in brief, resides not in the original intention of these texts, but in Paul's application of them to his Jewish opponents, including the members of the Galatian churches who were inclined to listen to them. Particularly problematic is the reasoning of 3:10, which appears to be self-contradictory. As C. D. Stanley explains, this verse, at least at first glance, presents a genuine conundrum: "Whereas Paul's own statement [of 3:10a] appears to pronounce a "curse" upon anyone who would attempt to live by the Jewish Torah, the biblical text to which he appeals [Deut 27:26, in 3:10b] clearly affirms the opposite: its "curse" falls not on those who *do* the Law, but on those who *fail* to do it."[2]

Therefore, while elements of the passage are straightforward enough, what remains contested is the rationale behind the apostle's conviction that his adversaries are under the curse of the Torah, and how precisely the texts chosen by him support his accusation. Moreover, an additional complication arises out of the proposition of v. 13 that Christ, assuming the place of the incorrigible son of Deuteronomy 21, "delivered us from the curse of the law, having become a curse for us." In what sense could the Messiah, for Paul, have actually been considered the "glutton and drunkard" of Deut 21:20 who would not obey the voice of his parents?

In attempting to resolve these problems, the present essay argues a twofold thesis. (1) Gal 3:10-13, Paul's cursing of his opponents, is rooted in Gal 2:17-18, according to which the apostle tacitly identifies this group as "ministers of sin" and "transgressors," who seek to thwart the eschatological purposes of God in Christ. They are no less than apostates and enemies of God; it is upon them that the curse of the law justly falls.[3] Therefore, as intensely ironic as it may seem, the people most loyal to and zealous for the Torah are condemned by none other than the Torah itself as covenant-breakers. (2) The OT passages adduced by him subserve his relegation of the opponents to the status of the enemies of God. Appropriately so, because each passage, especially as viewed in context, speaks to the issues of apostasy and perseverance.

2. Ministerial Role Reversal as a Result of the Christ-Event

Without retracing all of Paul's steps up to 3:10, a crucial turning point in the argument comes at 2:11, where he begins to recount the incident at Antioch. As B. R. Gaventa observes, Paul here shifts from the confirmation of his apostolate and gospel to his challenge to Cephas, a "pillar" of the Jerusalem church. As she notes, Paul's language reflects the intensity of his challenge to Jerusalem, as evidenced especially by 2:11, 13, 14.[4] Especially important for our purposes, Gaventa further observes that in the remainder of chap. 2 Paul insists again on the singularity of his gospel and prepares for the argument regarding the law and Christ in chaps. 3-4. However, the clash with Peter, the account of which effectively extends through 2:21, also looks backward as being the final stage of Paul's autobiographical narrative commencing with 1:10. The purpose of this narrative, Paul's "biography of reversal," is to communicate a personal word to the Galatians. That is to say, when Paul became a believer in Jesus, he ceased to be a "zealot" for the traditions of Israel.[5] This is a message Paul was convinced his readers needed to take to heart, because having become believers in Jesus themselves, they want to become "zealots" for these very traditions. This is why he pleads with them later: "Become as I am, because I have become as you" (4:12).

Hence, assuming that Paul's agenda in Galatians is both unified and specific, we may deduce that the citations of 3:10-13 must bear some relation to the choice Paul places before his readers: zeal for the law or zeal for Christ. Deut 27:26; Hab 2:4; Lev 18:5; Deut 21:23 are thus placed in service to support the course of action recommended by Paul—the decision for Christ. Therefore, his employment of these passages grows out of the sharpened polemic which leads up to and flows out of the incident at Antioch and cannot be properly understood apart from the battle lines drawn on that occasion.

In addition to this general theological thrust of 1:1-2:21, in which the "zeal" motif occupies the foreground, Paul's attack takes a decidedly personal turn when he relates the clash between Cephas and himself. For him, the core issue had to do with "the truth of the gospel" (2:5, 14), i.e., whether uncircumcised and non-kosher Gentiles could be admitted to table fellowship and thus be recognized as the people of God. As Paul saw it, Peter's "hypocrisy" resided in his inconsistency: the one who himself lived "as a Gentile" was attempting to compel Gentiles "to live as Jews" in order to be acceptable to the God of Israel.[6] Yet he does not let the matter rest there. Beginning with v. 15, he brings himself and other Jewish Christians into the fray by appealing to their common outlook. In his words: "We ourselves, who are Jews by birth," have come to understand that our vindication as the people of God is not "from works of the law" but "from faith in Jesus Christ" (v. 16). In vv. 15-16, two factors stand out.

One is the stress on the first person plural, indicated by the emphatic "we" at the beginning of 2:15. This is the first of several instances in which the first person plural is used to denote Jewish Christians of the Pauline sort, who had been nurtured in Judaism and taught the Torah. The impact of "we" is thus: *even we* know that justification is not "from works of the law" but rather "from faith in Jesus Christ." In v. 16b, it is stated just this way: "*Even we* have believed." Moreover, Paul stresses the ethnic factor by speaking of this group as any Jew of the period would have: they are "Jews by birth (*phusei*), not Gentile sinners." By way of cross-reference, in Rom 11:21, 24, *phusei* designates Israel as the "natural" branches, while the Gentiles are the "unnatural" (*para phusin*) branches. "Jews by birth" (nature) is thus a way of designating Jews as the aboriginal people and the Gentiles as late-comers to the covenant. It is by drawing the lines between himself and his associates, on the one side, and "the men from James), on the other, that Paul would have us think very much in terms of "them and us." One might paraphrase: "As distinct from *them*, the Judaizers and their followers, *we*, notwithstanding our Jewish heritage, know that a person is not justified by works of Torah, but by faith in Christ; *even we*, who share the same historic biblical values as our opponents, have trusted in Christ for justification."

The second factor is the identity of the phrases "works of the law" and "faith in Jesus Christ." Without rehashing the continuing debate on the two, the position herein assumed is that "works of the law" are tantamount to "covenantal nomism" (E. P. Sanders, J. D. G. Dunn) or "nomistic service" (E. Lohmeyer, J. B. Tyson), and that "faith in Jesus Christ" is "Christic faith," i.e., faith directed specifically to Jesus of Nazareth as Israel's Messiah.[7] It is both the renunciation of "works" and the espousal of "Christic faith" which demarcate the Pauline camp from the Judaizers. Whereas the latter insist on qualifying Jesus' messiahship in terms of the Torah, the former are equally adamant that Christ does away with the law and, therefore, with the distinctions which once divided Jew and Gentile. Accordingly, the core issue of the Galatian letter can be reduced to a basic choice: Christ or the Torah.[8]

Gal 2:17 enters the picture with its continued stress on the experience of Jewish Christians of the Pauline party (as brought to the fore especially by "even we" at the end of the second clause). Having stated their abandonment of the law in favor of the Christ of his gospel, Paul now poses a rhetorical question, intended, presumably, to ward off an objection from the Judaizers' side. Paul's interlocutor, it appears, thinks that a justification which bypasses the Torah turns a Jew into a "Gentile sinner," thus making Christ a "a minister (promoter) of sin." This comes as no surprise given that the circumcision party, if anything, would have sought adamantly to preserve the separated status of the people of God, and particularly the integrity of the Messiah. Accordingly, "sinners" here means what it does in so many places in Jewish literature, namely, those outside the covenant.[9] More specifically, "those outside the covenant" are Gentiles (as opposed to apostate Jews); and the precise combination of words "sinners of the Gentiles" is very much in line with contemporary Jewish usage, i.e., Gentiles were "sinners" by definition. So, from the Judaizers' point of view, to seek to be justified in *Paul's Christ* meant the abandonment of God's age-old standard of righteousness, which for them was nothing short of forsaking the covenant and becoming as pagans. To them, the conclusion was inevitable: *Paul's Jesus* is nothing but a promoter of apostasy.

Paul's comeback is introduced by his customary "by no means," followed (in v. 18) by a response to the accusation brought against him. His reply entails a role reversal: it is precisely in rebuilding the things which he tore down, the Torah, that he would become a "transgressor" or apostate, not the other way around. That is to say, were he to insist on the segregated status of the ancient people as insured by the law (e.g., Num 23:9; *Ep. Arist.* 139-42; *Jub.* 22:16), *then* he would transgress with respect to God's eschatological purpose in Christ, *then* he would be found unfaithful to the one who was destined to be the goal (*telos*) of the law (Rom 10:4; Gal 3:23-26). "Transgressor" thus assumes a new meaning in light of the Christ-event. The term used to mean one who forsook the law; but now it means to embrace the law, i.e., as being a necessary complement to the "in Christ" experience.

It is this ideology, I want to argue, which opens up Paul's use of the Scriptures in 3:10-13. If fidelity and infidelity have been redefined eschatologically with respect to God's purposes in Christ, ministerial role reversal has *ipso facto* occurred. Now that "the faith" has come (Gal 3:23), it is Paul who promotes genuine fidelity to God's (new) covenant, not the Judaizers. The latter actually foster unfaithfulness, because although they champion Jesus as Israel's Messiah, the Torah for them remains indispensable as the Jewish gateway to salvation. In this, they have repudiated the Christ of Paul's proclamation, who has abolished for all time the very peculiarities of the law.

The remainder of Paul's reflection on the incident at Antioch (vv. 19-21) serves to buttress his proposition that a new way of looking at things has come about as a result of the Christ-event. According to v. 19a, Paul is now dead to the law. Indeed, it was the law itself which brought about his demise; the law, as it were, became the instrument of its own cessation in Paul's believing experience. The parallel is Rom 7:7-13. The logic of that passage is that even though the law per se is not sin, it was, nevertheless, by the law's instrumentality that he came to recognize his own idolatry. Paul, then, represents himself as the example of one who was placed under the discipline of the law and "shut up to sin" (Gal 3:22) in order that he might find Christ. In other words, he applies the macrocosm of this salvation-historical principle to the microcosm of his own experience (note again the emphatic "I" (*egō*) at the beginning of Gal 2:19, which corresponds to "we" and "even we" in the previous verses); he is the voice of those Jewish Christians who have "died to the law;" in him the law has revealed sin and increased the trespass; he is an Israelite in whom the law has achieved its long-range redemptive purpose.

2:20 extends Paul's reply to the Judaizers by elaborating his new life *in Christ*. The verse can be read as Paul's response to the

Jewish conviction that possession of the law *eo ipso* insures life (e.g., Deut 4:1, 10, 40; 5:29-33; 6:1-2, 18, 24; 7:12-13; Sir 17:11; 45:5; Bar 3:9; 4:1; cf. 4 Ezra 14:30; *Pss. Sol.* 14:2). The repeated emphatic "I" of v. 20 approximates, in the parlance of psychology, the human "ego." It is no longer Paul's "ego" which controls the direction of his life and allegiances, but Christ. From now on, the crucified Messiah, the Christ of the cross, is the master of Paul's fate and the captain of his soul. Therefore, his whole existence "in the flesh" is "by faith in the Son of God." No longer does his faith necessitate zeal for the law, but is now focused solely on the Christ who, on the tree, brought an end to the Torah.

The reversal of zeal motif thus emerges once again from 1:11-2:10, corresponding to the ministerial role reversal theme of 2:11-21. And more than anything else, it is the death of the Messiah on the cross which highlights in such dramatic fashion the redirection of Paul's zeal. Yet it was such an identification with Jesus, the outcast of Israel, that the opponents could not tolerate. Effectively, they would not come "outside the camp" and suffer *as Jesus had suffered*, bearing the reproach of a reprobate. Because they feared reprisal from their compatriots, as directed toward Jesus first and Paul later, they would not stop preaching circumcision for the sake of Christ's *cross* (Gal 6:11), the implement of his banishment from the community of Israel. Paul, by contrast, turned from circumcision to embrace persecution for the sake of the cross (Gal 5:11; 6:17). In his case, zeal has been redefined, thereby making the term central in the debate with the Judaizers. Consequently, as R. G. Hammerton-Kelly observes, Galatians must be placed within the context of the larger struggle among the Jews of the late second temple period over what constituted a proper zeal for God.[10]

2:21 is intended to head off another objection from the opponents, namely, that Paul's gospel nullifies the grace of God. "Nullify" (*atheteō*) means to render the covenant inoperative. It is an expected term inasmuch as "grace" (*charis*) is Yahweh's covenant love for Israel. Thus, in nullifying the grace of God, as the charge went, Paul was accused of making shipwreck the covenant relationship itself. However, this is precisely what Paul disclaims, because, in his words, "if righteousness is through the law, then Christ died to no purpose." The wording shifts from "grace" to "righteousness" because "righteousness" is the outcome of "grace." If Yahweh's "grace" is his self-giving to his people in his election and sustenance of them, then Israel's expected response is "righteousness," her compliance with the standards of the covenant, in keeping with the relationship established at Sinai. Righteousness, in short, speaks of Israel's covenant standing, i.e., the exercise of her privileges and obligations under the law.

This being so, Paul's logic is clear enough: if the old state of affairs simply continues into this era, then the death of Christ is to "no purpose." His underlying assumption (not shared by the Judaizers) is that Christ's death was designed specifically to usher in the new age by setting aside the Torah in its existing form. If we ask, How could Paul reason in such an *a priori* manner?, the answer is that he is still appealing to the experience of certain Jewish Christians who know that righteousness comes by way of Christ alone, "apart from the law" (Rom 3:20). The implication is that the Judaizers are nothing but "false brethren" (Gal 2:4; cf. Phil 3:2-3). He is just as explicit in 2 Corinthians. According to 2 Cor 11:13-14, this same basic group is branded as "false apostles;" it is from such "unbelievers" that the Corinthians were to segregate themselves (6:14-7:1).

3. The Age of the Spirit versus the Age of the Flesh

The so-called *probatio* section of Galatians commences with Paul's astonishment that his readers are so eager to follow the lead of his antagonists (3:1-5). One reason for his dismay is the manner in which Christ was preached to them, i.e., as *crucified*. Given that the Judaizers were deeply embarrassed by the notion of a crucified Messiah—"a blasphemous contradiction in terms"[11]—there must be more than a touch of irony to Paul's castigation. In other words, the cross, in which he glories (6:14), actually possesses an attractiveness about it, because, according to 2:19-20, the cross is the place where the Son of God displayed his love. Thus, in turning away from the Christ of the cross, the Galatians were in the process of rejecting God's love for them. The second reason is the Galatians' experience of the Spirit: did it come "from works of the law" (*ex ergōn nomou*) or "from the hearing of faith" (*ex akoēs pisteōs*)? Obviously, it was the latter. However, their lack of discernment (cf. Luke 24:25) was such that they were confused about the direction of salvation history. They had forgotten that they began "in the Spirit," i.e., in the historical era of the Spirit's advent, in which they were enabled to perform miraculous works. Paul, then, found it necessary to remind them that the continual stream of the Spirit commenced at "the ends of the ages" (1 Cor 10:11), which, for him, meant liberation from the era of the Torah (2 Corinthians 3).

The operative words of v. 3b are the eschatological verbs "begin" (*enarchomai*) and "perfect" (*epiteleō*). The former marks the inception of the Galatians' Christianity "in the Spirit" at the turning of the ages,[12] and "perfect" ("complete") is eschatological in the forward looking sense inasmuch as it contemplates the consummation of the process of perfection begun with the advent of Christ and the Spirit (cf. Phil 1:6; Heb 6:1). The problem, however, is that the readers wanted to be "perfected" "in the flesh." "Flesh," in this place, by way of contrast with "Spirit," is not "the sinful nature" or "human effort" (as per NIV); it is, rather, the *era* of the flesh, i.e., the old covenant/old creation. If it be asked why the former aeon is called "flesh," the answer may reside in the fact that the Torah ministered largely to that dimension of human nature. Consequently, the flesh was high on the Judaizers' agenda.[13] Thus, the question of v. 3 is pointedly historical in its thrust. No wonder, the Galatians are "foolish." Their quest for perfection is anachronistic: they are going in the wrong direction; they want to reverse the plan of the ages!

It is Paul's insistence on a chronologically consistent eschatology, interestingly enough, which accounts for the addition of Abraham to the equation in vv. 6-9. While some of its details are exegetically debatable, the gist of the section is clear enough: the patriarch is invoked as one who was characterized by "the hearing of faith," not "the works of the law."[14] Simply put, Abraham belongs to "us," "they of faith" (*hoi ek pisteōs*), not to "them," (*hoi ek nomou*). In principle, the progenitor of the Jewish race, to whom the gospel was "preached beforehand" (v. 8), finds his proper identification in the age of the Spirit, not the age of the flesh, even though he lived in the pre-eschatological era. To adapt an observation of T. L. Donaldson's, the link between Abraham and "those of faith" seems to have been constructed without any reference to Israel at all.[15] Therefore, Abraham is in the same arena as the Gentiles, of whom righteousness can be predicated in spite of their own uncircumcision and non-observance of the Torah. This becomes all the more ironic as one considers that Abraham, *prima facie*, was the perfect model for the Jewish missionaries: it was he who converted from paganism to the true God and his law.

It is just the un-Jewishness of Paul's use of Abraham which provides the bridge into his cursing of his opponents; that is, in the salvation-historical purposes of God, the paradigm of eschatological justification is provided not by the Torah, but by Abraham, who had nothing to do with the Torah. Thus, the

Judaizers are actually at variance with the experience of their hero and model. In their endeavor to maintain the law as the standard of righteousness, they have chosen to remain on the wrong side of the eschatological divide, so that instead of being like Abraham, they have become very unlike him. Since righteousness, in Paul's view, is now defined by *his* gospel (Rom 2:16; 16:25), these people have disqualified themselves from being the seed of Abraham because they are aligned with the "flesh."[16] And as vv. 10-13 will argue, they have actually become God's enemies (cf. Rom 11:28) and are for that reason subject to the law's curse.

4. The Scriptures and the Apostasy of the Judaizers

As Paul, in 3:10-13, turns directly to the "curse of the law," the "curse" is placed conspicuously in contrast to the "blessing" of Abraham. (Below, in vv. 13-14, the order is reversed: the curse of the law turns into the blessing of Abraham). In his schema, "blessing" belongs to the eras of Abraham and the Sprit, while the age of the Torah is epitomized as "curse." So far, it has been intimated that the Judaizers are under the curse because they have, for all practical purposes, self-consciously chosen to remain in the age of the law, thus opposing God's eschatological designs in Christ. As Betz puts it, the logic behind Paul's words is simply that exclusion from blessing equals curse; and the "men of the Torah" are excluded from blessing because they regard the observation of the law as a condition for salvation.[17]

But while these ideas, I believe, are present in 3:1-9, they are, more or less, subliminal. It is Paul's use of the OT in 3:10-13 which elevates his underlying intentions from mere impressions to an articulated tactic in his dealings with his antagonists. In attempting to come to terms with the mentality underlying Paul's use of the Bible, we shall first probe each passage in its own context and thereafter attempt to fit these prominent portions of Israel's Scriptures into the theological and polemical program of Gal 3:10-13.

The Quotations in Their Original Contexts

Deuteronomy 27:26

As Paul begins to unfold his agenda, v. 10a is connected with the foregoing verses by means of its first use of the conjunction "for" (*gar*). The conjunction is causal strictly speaking: those who are "from works of the law," or, according to v. 11, "in the law," are not "blessed with Abraham;" they are "under a curse" just because they have severed their connections with the patriarch by virtue of their preference for the Mosaic period. The second "for" of the verse (10b) introduces the first of the OT quotations, Deut 27:26, which is intended to prop up the allegation that "those who are of works of the law" are under a curse.[18] In other words, the "law people" are cursed by none other than the law itself, the very law to which they are unswervingly loyal and to which they look as the paradigm of Jesus' messiahship and God's will for his covenant partners. One cannot help but wonder if in nomenclature "those who are of works of the law" corresponds to "the men of the community" of 1QS 5:1 and "the men of the law" of 4QS 1:1. If so, the identity of the group is the more readily discernible: they are the people devoted to the standards of the covenant.

Deuteronomy 27:1-30:20 is devoted to the renewal of the covenant. It opens with the initial exhortation for Israel to keep the commandments (27:1-14), passes into the twelve curses of Mt. Ebal (27:15-26) and thereafter into the blessings for obedience (28:1-14) and the curses for disobedience (28:15-68), followed by a reiterated admonition to keep the covenant (29:1-15), as accompanied by another restatement of the punishments for forsaking the bond with Yahweh (29:16-29). Finally, there is a prophecy of Israel's inevitable banishment and restoration (30:1-10), although Moses pleads with Israel to choose life rather than death, especially as the commandment is performable given its proximity to her (30:11-20). This whole section of Deuteronomy is appropriately summarized by Wright: "Deuteronomy 27-30 is all about exile and restoration, understood as covenant judgment and covenant renewal."[19] Hence, the overall impression left by these several chapters is that fidelity or the absence thereof to Yahweh and his covenant are of paramount importance, because life and death, blessing and cursing, respectively hinge on the decision which Israel will make.

Chap. 27 is occupied with various social misdeeds and the resultant curses. The centre of gravity of the materials is idolatry (v. 15). Indeed, because of its pivotal position in the structure of the chapter, one receives the impression that idolatry is the fountainhead of the vices enumerated in vv. 16-26. The pattern is only to be expected, because forsaking Yahweh opens the floodgates to all kinds of sins. Accordingly, the whole of this recitation of curses is summarized by its final item: "Cursed be he who does not confirm the words of this law by doing them" (v. 26). Thus, idolatry and its attendant evils are avoided by "doing" the law. In the mind of the author(s), the root issue was faithfulness to Yahweh, as exemplified by obedience to his laws; conversely, the one who is devoted to idols cannot help but incur the curses kept in store for disobedience.

V. 26, as Peter Craigie remarks, has a summary and all-inclusive nature: it describes the person who does not render the positive action which obedience to the law demanded. "There is a sense," he says, "in which the previous eleven curses are only examples, the twelfth curse making it quite clear that any action that does not *elevate the words of this law* brings an offender under the curse of God." To this extent Craigie is correct. However, his ensuing comment is wide of the mark: "the reach of the law is so all-pervasive that man cannot claim justification before God on the basis of 'works of the law'."[20] Apart from pressing the familiar theological category, "on the basis of works of the law," which is out of keeping with Paul's own choice of words, Craigie makes two other mistakes. One is a failure to recognize that Deut 27:15-26 revolves around *idolatry*, with its resultant problems. The cursed one, "who does not confirm the words of this law by doing them," is not merely the one who falls short at various points, but the apostate and idolater. The "reach of the law" is not perfect compliance with its demands, or anything approaching it, but fidelity to the God who graciously gave it to Israel. The other mistake is a failure to realize that the law is in fact performable. Obedience to the Torah in the Hebrew Scriptures themselves (as distinct from later theologies) is never portrayed as an unobtainable goal. Rather, according to Deut 30:11-20, it is a thing within Israel's grasp ("this commandment...is not too hard for you, neither is it far off," v. 11). One is able to say this because, again, "keeping the law," "obedience," and such expressions, speak of perseverance, not sinless perfection.[21]

The operative word of Deut 27:26 is "remain," as complemented by "do" (the latter is parallel to and defined by the former). The LXX, an adaptation of which is quoted by Paul, reads (as translated): "cursed is every man who does not remain in all the words of this law to do them." The underlying Hebrew of the verb "remain" (*emmenō*) is one which literally means "to uphold" (*yakim*) the words of the Torah. One might have expected the LXX dress of *yakim* to be a form of *histēmi*. In fact, Paul himself seems to be aware of the appropriateness of this verb, when, in Rom 3:31, he writes, "we uphold the law" (*nomon histomen*). On my reading, this means "we uphold the [eschatological] purpose for which the law was given." We shall see momentarily that there is an appropriateness to the verb here chosen (*emmenō*), one which evidently appealed to Paul. Nevertheless, the force of *yakim* is not to be overlooked: the Israelite was to "uphold" or "support" "the words of this law," which were given to regulate the relationship between Yahweh and his people. In so doing, one would honor one's prior faith-commitment to Yahweh. The same note of allegiance to (or renewal of) the covenant is sounded by the hiphil stem of the verb *qum* in, e.g., 2 Kgs 23:3, 24. By way of further illustration, 1 Sam 15:11, 13; Jer 35:15, 16 present us with a study in contrast: as over against those who have broken faith with the Lord, there are individuals who have "upheld" the Torah. At heart, then, the point of Deut 27:26 is: "Cursed be anyone who is fundamentally disloyal to the law—anyone who does not, by his actions, show that he is on the side of the law and anxious to 'make the law stand'."[22]

That the LXX chose *emmenō* for *yakim* is understandable, given that the verb "has the meaning of remaining within a specified territory."[23] Its selection may reflect the climate in which portions of the translation took place, i.e., the necessity of persevering in "the holy covenant" (1 Macc 1:15) in the face of the Hellenistic onslaught. Elsewhere, *emmenō* likewise means "persevere in" (Sir 2:10; 6:20; 11:21 [in parallel to *pisteuō*]; 1 Macc 10:26, 27; Philo, *Cong.* 125; Josephus, *Ag. Ap.* 2.257; cf. Num 23:19).[24] Furthermore, in other crucial passages in Deuteronomy, the kindred *menō en*, as it reproduces $d^e baq\ b^e$, denotes dedication to Yahweh and continuance in his ways (e.g., 11:22; 13:4; 30:20; cf. Josh 22:5; 23:8-11). In these verses, the phrase stands in parallel with the synonymous expressions "keeping the commandments" and "loving Yahweh." Not surprisingly, the idea of "remaining"/"abiding"/"cleaving" is taken up by later Jewish literature. Ben Sira, for example, more than once correlates cleaving to God with obedience (e.g., Sir 11:22; 13:4; 30:20). To cleave (*dabaq*) to God entails dispositions such as love, fear and faith, virtues commended by the scribe throughout his book. The usage carries over into the NT in such passages as John 15:1-11, according to which the disciples must "abide in" (*menō en*).

Habakkuk 2:4

Having confronted his opponents with a text threatening apostasy with the wrath of God, in v. 11, Paul turns to the other side of the coin, to a prophetic passage calling to mind Yahweh's vindication of his faithful people, who are "blessed" rather than "cursed." Hab 2:4 is introduced as providing the reason why it is obvious that "in the law no one will be justified before God. "In the law" is the functional equivalent of "those who are of works of the law" in the previous verse. Accordingly, for Paul it is evident that those who remain "in the law," the Judaizers and those like them, cannot be "justified before God," simply because "the righteous will live by faith," the implication being that these people do not belong to the company of the righteous who will live because of their faith(fulness).

Hab 2:4 represents an outstanding instance of God's intervention to save his people (his "righteousness"). In context, the prophet is confronted with the impending invasion of the holy land by the Chaldeans. The fact that a nation far more sinful than Israel should be the instrument of her judgment occasions a crisis of faith on Habakkuk's part. In the face of his pleas, God answers that in time he will punish the Chaldeans for their iniquity. In the meantime, however, the righteous of Israel will "live," i.e., by their fidelity to the covenant they will survive the enemy invasion and return to their own land. Such is the original meaning of "the righteous will live by his faith(fulness)". The focus is not on how one becomes righteous; but rather, the righteousness of the covenant is presupposed.[25] And Yahweh's assurance to the prophet is just that the righteous person will live through the judgment and ultimately be vindicated ("justified") "faith his faith(fulness)." The basic and really simple point, then, is that in the original setting it is the faith(fulness) of the righteous Israelite which will ensure his deliverance: when the judgment falls, it is reliance on the Lord himself which will see him through. Hence, Paul's Greek ought to be rendered: "the righteous shall live by [out of] his faith(fulness)."[26]

But faith(fulness) directed toward God could never be abstracted from the Israelite's commitment to the Torah. Indeed, the ensuing context affirms this. After the assurance that the righteous shall live by his faith(fulness) (*emunah*), Hab 2:5-17 immediately lodges a bitter complaint against the unrighteous, who have forsaken the law in various regards. This rehearsal of vices eventuates in the root cause of all ungodliness—idolatry (vv. 18-

19).²⁷ Instead of giving heed to the idol, a "dumb stone," the whole earth is to keep silence in the presence of Yahweh, who is in his holy temple (v. 20).

Again, Paul quite consciously draws on a passage from the Jewish Scriptures which speaks directly to the issue of perseverance over against apostasy. In this particular case, he chooses one which has as its *Sitz im Leben* a crisis of faith in the history of Israel. As was to become the order of the day during the Greek and Roman periods, the preexilic people of God are forced to decide for Yahweh, despite a pagan presence pummeling them with brute violence. In view of such a daunting prospect, Habakkuk ponders the question later to be raised by Jewish Apocalyptic: Is Yahweh able to deliver his people and bring just retribution on their enemies? The answer is that in spite of all, those who continue to trust in him will, by virtue of that faith(fulness), survive the devastation. Accordingly, the return of the faithful remnant to the land will be their "justification," i.e., their vindication as the righteous people of God.

Leviticus 18:5

In v. 12, Paul returns to the books of Moses, again to shore up a thesis. This time the thesis is: "the law is not of faith; rather, the one who does them will live by [in] them."²⁸ The link with Hab 2:4 is provided by "life," as signaled by "will live" in both verses. The choice of words, "the law is not of faith," is certainly terse, but is explicable given Paul's propensity for prepositions of origin and sphere (*ek* and *en*). To say that the law is "not of faith" is to affirm that the law and faith belong to distinctly different historical realms: the former does not occupy the same turf in the salvation-historical continuum as the latter. It is true that Paul propounds a certain juxtaposition of believing and doing, which we shall examine below. Nevertheless, it is a juxtaposition grounded in historical factors.

The section of Leviticus commencing with 17:1 and extending through 27:34 could be termed: "maintaining the covenant with a holy God." A wide variety of topics is covered, but the centre of gravity is that of preserving the integrity of the covenant by means of the various provisions of the Torah. Chapter 18 in particular focuses on sexual matters. Given the equation of adultery with idolatry in ancient Judaism,²⁹ one is not surprised to find discussions of it in this portion of the book (cf. 20:10-21). In other words, fidelity in marital relations is a picture of Israel's devotion to her "husband," Yahweh.

As a kind of heading to chap. 18, recalling the preamble to the Decalogue, v. 2 sounds the oft-repeated note of Leviticus: "Say to the people of Israel, I am the Lord your God." These words signal both Yahweh's ownership of Israel and her peculiar privilege to have him as her God. Immediately thereafter, in vv. 3-4, Yahweh distinguishes his people from Egypt, from which they came, and Canaan, to which they are going. These peoples have their "statutes," but Israel is not to do them; it is, rather, Yahweh's "ordinances" and "statutes" which she is to "walk in." The notion of "walking" in itself is eloquent of perseverance; it is tantamount to "doing" and "keeping" the Torah (vv. 4-5).[30] (It was, of course, the Israelite's "walk" in the ways of Yahweh which inspired the rabbinic category of *halakah*.) Hence, Yahweh's fundamental admonition to his people is that they are to repudiate the statues and, therefore, the gods of Egypt and Canaan and cleave to him alone. It is none other than the marriage-like alliance between God and Israel which is epitomized by the climactic statement of v. 5: "You shall therefore keep my statutes and my ordinances, by doing which a man shall live: I am the Lord." Israel's loyalty to Yahweh as the Lord of the covenant is thus embodied in her diligence to observe the Torah, thereby insuring the integrity and continuance of the community.

The two components of 18:5 are "do" and "live." "Do" is clarified by the immediate context, inasmuch as it stands in parallel to "keeping" the commandments and "walking" in them. The point is hardly that of earning anything (with the unspoken assumption that no one actually can earn life by keeping the law). It is, instead, perseverance in the standards set by Yahweh's covenant, as opposed to giving heed to the "statutes" of the Egyptians and the Canaanites. When one "does" the law, one acknowledges that Yahweh is one's God and that his will alone determines the norms of covenantal life, in contrast to the licentious deities of the outside world, who permit the "abominations" prohibited by 18:6-30. To "do the law," in short, is to be "obedient," i.e., to remain faithful to the God who called his people out of bondage.

"Live" is likewise qualified by the covenant setting. On this basis, it is arguable that the life in question is not eschatological or eternal as such. Gordon Wenham, for example, maintains that life of Lev 18:5 is physical and earthly, even though such a life is a happy one, in which a person enjoys God's bounty of health, children, friends and prosperity (cf. Lev 26:3-13; Deut 28:1-14;

30:11-20; Neh 9:29; Ezek 20:11).[31] It is to be conceded to Wenham and others that "live" does indeed mean primarily "to go on living" in the land, especially in view of Ezekiel 20, the first "commentary" on Lev 18:5. Even so, we must reckon with the fact that in certain strands of Jewish interpretation the eschatological dimension is very much present. For example, 1QS 4:6-8 makes "everlasting blessing and eternal joy in life without end" the extension of "long life" and "fruitfulness" here and now (cf. Dan 12:2; Wis 2:23 [passim]; 2 Macc 7:9; 4 Macc 15:3; 17:12). Conversely, reserved for those who follow "the spirit of falsehood" (the apostates) are a multitude of plagues now and "everlasting damnation," "eternal torment" and "endless disgrace" hereafter (1QS 4:12-14). Likewise, *Tg. Ps-J.* and *Tg. Onq.* to Lev 18:5 both posit everlasting life as the reward of doing the Torah (cf. Luke 10:25). Indeed, such an eschatological slant on the life of Lev 18:5 would have played readily into Paul's hands, as he transposes the life of the Torah into eternal life in Christ.[32]

In sum, Lev 18:5 is the OT's classic statement of "covenantal nomism." The verse is "a typical expression of what Israel saw as its obligation and promise under the covenant;" it is an expression of how first-century Jews would have understood righteousness, i.e., "life within the covenant, "covenantal nomism," the pattern of religion and life which marked out the righteous, the people of the covenant."[33] Therefore, one continues to live within the covenant relationship by compliance with its terms, i.e., by "doing the law" or perseverance.[34] It is life as the outcome of law-observance which doubtlessly gave rise to the expressions "the law of life" (Sir 17:11; 45:5) and "the commandments of life" (Bar 3:9; 4:1; cf. *Pss. Sol.* 14:2; 1QS 4:6-8; *Ep. Arist.* 127; 4 Ezra 14:30; Philo, *Cong.* 86-87).[35] These commandments are no less than the very embodiment of Israel's wisdom: "All who hold her fast will live, and those who forsake her will die" (Bar 4:1).

Deuteronomy 21:23

The final text is a return to the curse, specifically the punishment meted out to the reprobate son, who would not "obey the voice of his parents." However, after v. 12, the Judaizers drop out of sight and the application of the curse is now to Christ, who "redeemed us from the curse of the law, having become a curse for us" (v. 13).

Deuteronomy 21 is composed of a set of disparate laws relating to murder, war and family affairs. While there appears to be no unifying element to the chapter as such, vv. 18-23 form a fairly well-defined pericope: the death of the son (vv. 18-21) and his subsequent treatment (vv. 22-23). That the son is "stubborn" and "rebellious" is instructive in itself, because these are terms characteristic of Israel's resistance of and apostasy from Yahweh's lordship in the wilderness and afterwards. Thus, while the son's behavior was in the first instance confined to a household, its implicit threat would be against the security and continuity of the covenant community at large. His deportment is all the more grievous because of its specific nature, i.e., disobedience to parents, which, according to Deut 27:16, *ipso facto* incurs Yahweh's curse. He is further characterized as "a glutton and a drunkard," an index to the kind of life led by one who has rejected not only his parents but Yahweh as his God (cf. Prov 23:20). In light of Matt 11:19; Luke 7:34, "glutton and drunkard" may have become a stereotyped idiom for "apostate" by the first century. But be that as it may, "glutton and drunkard" is juxtaposed to "obey," which throughout Jewish literature uniformly signals covenant fidelity.

After the evil had been purged from Israel by the death of this man (v. 21), the corpse was to be hanged on a "tree" or "wooden post" as an example to others (cf. Num 25:4; Josh 10:26-27; 2 Sam 21:6-9). This is not crucifixion as such, simply because the person was affixed to the tree after death.[36] Moreover, the body was to be buried on the same day as the capital punishment, not left to suffer the further degradation of being consumed by scavengers. Even so, the hanged man was nothing less than "the curse of God," whose severity of punishment was reserved for individuals who had cursed God and in turn must incur his curse (cf. Job 2:9). The issue was not that of infringing this or that peculiarity of the Torah, but rather the repudiation of Yahweh himself, along with his chosen people. This is why the hanged man suffered "a formal and terminal separation from the community of God's people."[37] As we shall see, it is Paul's casting of Jesus in the role of the apostate of Deuteronomy 21 which illumines to no small degree his *modus operandi* in Gal 3:10-13.

The Quotations in the Fabric of Paul's Theological and Polemical Agenda

The Historical Direction of Paul's Thought

Paul is concerned to delineate two arenas or spheres in which one might choose to dwell: the old age with the Torah at stage centre, or the new age with Christ occupying the forefront. This impression is again confirmed by the prepositions employed in our text, but more especially by 3:1-6, which establishes Paul's governing perspective as old age vs. new age along a time-line of salvation history. Paul thus envisions a context of existence in which a person lives: one may belong either to the old or the new, but not both at the same time. One might say that his prime concern is eschatology; but it is an eschatology determinative of soteriology. In other words, salvation hinges on being on the correct side of the eschatological divide, of being "in Christ," not "in the law."

That his thought unfolds in linear/historical terms has at least one important corollary. Time-honored terminology such as "reliance on works of law" or the "basis" of justification, etc., is wide of the mark as far as Paul's own argument is concerned.[38] Particularly given the broader scope of his soteriology, his overriding agenda is to establish that it is "in Christ," in the "new covenant" and "in the Spirit" that one becomes the righteousness of God and escapes the "dispensation of death" (2 Cor 3:4-18) that was the Torah. In a nutshell, the heart of Paul's soteriology is that one becomes and then remains a faithful member of the covenant people by virtue of being "in Christ" vs. being "in the law." The focus, in other words, is on the complex of the person of Jesus and his work within the new era, not on a transactional "basis." One might say that lying at the heart of Paul's theology is, to coin a phrase, his "christological eschatology."

If these comments are at all insightful, the texts adduced by Paul have as their primary function the delineation of one age from the other. On the one side, there is the era of the Torah. Those who cling to it are cursed because their allegiance is to the wrong epoch of salvation history. Not only has their eschatology resulted in their own undoing, their guilt is aggravated by their zeal to win others to their cause. The "cursing" passages (Deut 21:23; 27:26), then, have peculiar applicability to the Judaizers. The very texts to which they probably appealed to encourage Gentiles to embrace the law have been turned against them by Paul. On the other side is the era of the Spirit and the accomplishment of God's salvific designs in Jesus of Nazareth, the crucified Messiah. It is only the people who are "of faith in Jesus Christ" in the specifically Pauline sense (not "of works of the law" or "in the law") who can partake of the life proffered by Hab 2:4 and Lev 18:5. In keeping with Paul's use of the figure of Abraham in Gal 3:6-9, the "life" of these texts is accessible only as one is committed unreservedly to the new age. The "life" texts, therefore, demarcate the era of "the hearing of faith" from that of "works of the law."

The Juxtaposition of Believing and Doing

Virtually every commentator recognizes that Paul, in some way or the other, plays off believing and doing, especially in the statements of vv. 11-12. But in what sense are the two set in opposition? The majority of scholars assume that they are mutually exclusive by the nature of the case: "faith" by definition excludes "works," and vice versa. However, in historical perspective, any dichotomy between believing and doing in the Jewish schema is simply off base: Judaism was and is as much a "faith system" as Christianity. In attempting to untangle the inner workings of Paul's reasoning, we are helped by the recognition that he purposely distinguishes entities which are indistinguishable in the Hebrew Scriptures themselves. In a manner resembling Rom 2:13, where a wedge is driven between "hearing" and "doing" (a thing unthinkable to the Jewish mind), he intentionally pits one component of covenant life against another. In so doing, he presses the notion that there is another kind of "doing the law" than the Mosaic variety, one which corresponds to the "obedience of faith" (Rom 1:5) which has been revealed eschatologically "apart from the law" (Rom 1:17; 3:21).[39] The inseparability of faith and obedience in the Hebrew Bible is still intact, but both have been refocused on Jesus, the crucified Messiah.

It is true that v. 12 poses a problem. Its proposition, "the law is not of faith," is buttressed by the words of Lev 18:5: "the one who does them [the statutes] will live by [in] them." On the usual reading, Paul is taken to mean that "the law has nothing to do with faith" in this sense: whereas the law required performance, the gospel enjoins only faith. As the argument goes, anyone who would be justified "on the basis of works" must reckon seriously with what the Torah itself says: "the one who does them will live by [in] them." However, this more or less traditional interpretation falters for two reasons. (1) "Doing the law," according to the context of Lev 18:5, is not "performance", but the exercise of faith within the parameters of the covenant. (2) Neither the Bible nor later Jewish theology recognizes a distinction between doing and believing: they are the two sides of the same coin.[40]

This means that the resolution of the problem must be sought along the lines of the historical character of Paul's argument. His is not a topical discussion of faith and works, but an epochal delineation of the respective places of law and faith in salvation history. We are to think of two historical eras, meaning that the law, the period of the disciplinarian, cannot arise "from faith," the period of maturity (3:23-25), simply because of the chronological impossibility of the procedure (again, 3:1-5). Even if, for the sake of argument, "of faith," encapsulates a "faith-principle," the faith in question is specifically "faith in Jesus Christ" (2:16) and "the faith" which have now come to displace the era of the *paidagōgos* (3:23-25), which possessed its own kind of "faith-principle." Still, What is the precise relationship of the two clauses of v. 12?

If our analysis is correct that the law and (Christian) faith belong to distinct historical eras, then we may answer by paraphrasing v. 12: "the law and faith may occupy separate historical compartments, *nevertheless (all')*, the Torah's own standard of fidelity remains intact" ("he who does them will live by them"). Now, however, the call for faithfulness has been projected into the present eschatological context, whereby "doing the law" is redefined as faith(fulness) directed to *the Christ of Paul's gospel*. As regards the Judaizers, this principle of life as a result of adherence to the Torah does not apply, because they have failed to observe the law in its overall salvific design, i.e., to lead Israel to Christ (3:23-25). In short, they live in the wrong age and will not relinquish the law in favor of a law-free gospel as procured by the death of the Messiah "on the tree." Herein resides their apostasy.

The Key Issue: Perseverance vs. Apostasy, Not Sinless Perfection

The Judaizers are not under the curse because they have failed to keep the law "perfectly," but because they have proven defective in the central matter: fidelity to the God of Israel. It is in this originally intended sense of Deut 27:26 that the opponents are cursed: they have not persevered "in all things written in the book of the law, to do them."[41] J. M. Scott maintains, rightly in my view, that Paul's use of Deut 27:26 is grounded in the Deuteronomic theology more broadly speaking. For the apostle, this verse does not represent a "retrograde voice of legalism" for the simple reason that he assumes the Deuteronomic perspective so prevalent in Second Temple literature, as reflected in the penitential prayer of Dan 9:1-19 and parallel passages. The impact of this theology as implemented by Paul is that the divine judgment begun in 587 continues on Israel and that the Jewish people remain in exile until the present day. In this regard, the tack of Gal 3:10 resembles the employment of Isa 52:5 in Rom 2:24.[42] All this makes extraordinarily good sense in light of the thesis herein proposed: Paul would envision the on-going exile to be the product of Israel's latter-day "apostasy," consisting in her unflagging zeal for the Torah and the national life. The representatives of this "eschatological apostasy" in Galatia are the circumcision party.

Proof positive to Paul that the opponents are apostate is their lack of love. According to 5:14, "the whole law is fulfilled in one word: 'You shall love your neighbor as yourself'." The appeal to Lev 19:18 implies that the Judaizers sustain an apostate-like relationship to the covenant, because lying at the core of the covenant is the Israelite's love for Yahweh and neighbor (cf. Deut 30:16; Matt 22:36-40). Because they have engendered "biting and devouring," "provoking one another," and "envy of one another" (5:15, 26) on the part of their followers, the opponents have disqualified themselves from being the people of God. The Judaizers do not keep "the whole law" (5:14), because they have disregarded its sum and substance, its very *raison d'être*.[43] The relation between love and the covenant is confirmed by Deut 30:16, which correlates loving God with walking in his ways and keeping his commandments.

Paul's Underlying Presupposition

Paul, in keeping with his custom, uses the Bible in his pursuit of a theological agenda; and, as ever, agendas imply goals and their underlying tactics. In plain language, Paul works with presuppositions. Among interpreters, the most commonly supposed assumption on Paul's part (his unexpressed premise) is that the law demands a quantitative obedience which, by virtue of human sinfulness, is impossible to render. The necessary corollary of this position is that Paul insisted on perfect obedience to the law. This approach, to my mind, has been successfully rebuffed by several scholars.[44] Nevertheless, I believe that Paul does assume something, namely, what has been established by the preceding portion of Galatians: the Judaizers have become "ministers of sin" and "transgressors" because of their preaching of "another gospel." Therefore, the apostasy/perseverance texts of Deut 27:26; Hab 2:4; Lev 18:5; Deut 21:23 are directly applicable to them by virtue of role reversal.

It is just in this regard that Paul's quotation of Hab 2:4 in particular assumes significance. The opponents, understandably, were adamant that faith(fulness) was inconceivable apart from the Torah; only such faith(fulness) would stand one in good stead at the last judgment. 1QpHab 8:1-3 provides a famous illustration.[45] Paul, however, has detached faith(fulness) from its specifically Mosaic setting: faith(fulness) is still required, but its object is no longer the Torah (including some such figure as the Teacher of Righteousness).[46] In a word, he shifts the focus of "faith" away from the law onto the person of Christ, the new object of faith. It is by virtue of this adjustment that Hab 2:4 can "prove" for Paul that the righteousness of God is now revealed "apart from the law" (3:21). To be sure, the Judaism of his day uniformly made God the object of faith (e.g., 1 Macc 2:59, 61; cf. 4:9-11); but it is likewise true that reliance on the law was the indispensable expression of one's faith in God (e.g., 1 Macc 2:64; Sir 32:24-33:3). It would be a fair assessment to say that for Judaism generally God and the Torah were the twofold object of faith: to believe in the one was *ipso facto* to believe in the other. But over against such a conviction, Paul makes God *in Christ* the focal point of faith(fulness) with no further qualification. From now on, one is able to "get in" and "stay in" the covenant by virtue of a faith(fulness) detachable from a Mosaic standard.

This being so, the totality of the Mosaic era had only one goal: to point to Jesus (Gal 3:23-25; Rom 10:4). In the case before us, Paul draws on a typology of the last judgment potentially discoverable in Habakkuk and the other prophets (i.e., the Babylonian captivity and return to the land) and applies it to the level of the antitype. That is to say, God's righteousness as his saving action has taken place in Christ. Therefore, the eschatological revelation of "the righteousness of God" no longer takes account of the Mosaic context of the same righteousness. Accordingly, Hab 2:4, for Paul, is definitive because it is the fulfillment in Jesus which clarifies the long-range intentions of God. As ever, the difference between Paul and his opponents is his conception of this particular Messiah as the end-product of the Scriptures.

Justification

Paul is quite sure that no one will be justified before God in the law" (v. 11), just because "the righteous will live by faith" (Hab 2:4). The question, naturally, is: How does Hab 2:4 establish Paul's proposition? Given that the prophet commends faith(fulness) as the ideal for all who would embrace the Sinai covenant, the passage seems to support the Judaizers rather than Paul (as all the other texts drawn on in 3:10-13). In a nutshell, the answer resides in alterations resulting from the Christ-event.

In Habakkuk, the life of the righteous person was coextensive with his vindication ("justification") as a member of the loyal remnant who would return from captivity (e.g., Isa 10:21-22 and many prophetic passages). In a very real sense, it was just "in the law" that the people of God expected to be vindicated. Nevertheless, as in Rom 1:17, Paul detaches faith(fulness) from its Mosaic setting and predicates faith(fulness) of the believer in Christ—quite irrespective of the Torah—now that the righteousness of God has been revealed in the gospel to "*all*" who believe" (Rom 1:16; 3:21, etc.). It is the "eschatological now" which marks the divide between the age of the "flesh" and the age of the "Spirit" (Gal 3:3) and has refocused faith on a new object. Whereas faith(fulness) was once directed to Yahweh, who chose to keep his people distinct from the nations, from now on it is placed in the Christ of Paul's gospel who has received all without distinction. Henceforth faith is pointedly "faith in Jesus Christ" (= "by faith in the Son of God" [2:20])—"Christic faith." Therefore, the Judaizers are not the "righteous" who "live," because their faith is anachronistic, rooted, as it is, in the wrong covenant. Their sort of faith is exercised by "those who are of works of the law," not by the people who are "of faith" and "in the Spirit."

All this suggests rather forcefully that role reversal is very much operative in the justification discussion of Galatians. To their consternation, no doubt, the opponents are informed that the rules have changed. They, who only would have expected to be vindicated "in the law" as the appropriate arena and expression of their faith, are now told that they are excluded from the community of salvation: they are no longer the "righteous" who live " by [of] faith;" hey cannot be justified while they remain as they are; they are "under the curse" by definition. To be sure, such ideas would have appeared entirely far-fetched to the opponents, not to mention their chagrin at Paul's use of the Scriptures to back up his claims. Even so, Paul is insistent that the eschatological justification/ vindication/restoration of the new "Israel of God" (Gal 6:16) entails a reassessment of the prevailing understanding of who the "righteous" are and the conditions under which they may expect to be justified.

Paul's Christology

Apart from Paul's penchant for role reversal, his christology must have been a factor in his assessment of his competitors, a christology which engendered a radically different conception than theirs of the role of the law and "the obedience of faith" in the messianic age. It was, once more, Paul's "christological eschatology" which was the deciding factor. One might ascribe a similar awe-inspiring vision of Christ to the opponents, especially as they must have been impressed by his resurrection and the advent of the Spirit on Pentecost. But it was Paul's peculiar conception of Jesus and his work which most radically drew the line of demarcation between himself and the Jewish Christian missionaries.

In rather stark discontinuity with so many Jewish convictions regarding the eternity of the Torah (e.g., Bar 4:1; Wis 18:4), the law, for Paul, was intended only to be provisional, a "disciplinarian to Christ," whose purpose was to keep Israel separate from the nations *until the coming of (the) faith* (Gal 3:23-25). It is, in other words, the Pauline "in Christ" experience which has rendered all previous distinctions null and void, so that now there can be neither Jew nor Greek in him (Gal 3:28). Thus, however valid the law may have been for its time, "*now* the righteousness of God has been revealed apart from the law" (Rom 3:21).

Role Reversal and the Judaizers

At the risk of some repetition, a further word should be appended to the phenomenon of role reversal, which more than any other factor discloses Paul's use of the OT in Gal 3:10-13. While modern readers may marvel, as many of his Jewish contemporaries must have, at Paul's seemingly quixotic treatment of these passages, I would argue that it is understandable enough given not only certain broad assumptions, but in particular the agenda pursued up to 3:10-13(14). It is in the "reversal of zeal" and "ministerial role reversal" motifs of Gal 1:1-3:9 that one finds the groundwork laid for the apostle's remarkable application of cursing and blessing texts to the Judaizers. With the passing of the tutelage of the Torah (3:23-25), faith has been redirected to a crucified Messiah, who has inaugurated the age of the Spirit and has expanded the boundaries of the covenant community. But the Judaizers, in their unabated zeal for the Torah, are excluded from life and blessing. They belong to the wrong era and, consequently, their faith is misdirected. More than that, in desiring to keep intact the things which have now been torn down in Christ (2:18), they have become the latter-day "transgressors" and "promoters of sin." It is they who now promote defection from Yahweh; they have transgressed with respect to God's eschatological purpose in Christ and have proven unfaithful to the one who was destined to be the goal (*telos*) of the law. Therefore, it is they, who are "of the law" and "in the law," who incur the eschatological curse pronounced by the Torah itself against apostates.

It is Paul's opinion of his opponents that both explains and is confirmed by the allegory of Gal 4:21-31. C. K. Barrett once observed that as the underlying story of Gen 21:8-14 stands, it supports the Judaizers' position rather than Paul's. Indeed, as in the case of Gen 15:6, the incident was probably put in play by the Judaizers to further their missionary program, and for that reason was take up by Paul as well, only with his own spin.[47] In a remarkable instance of what R. B. Hays calls "hermeneutical jujitsu,"[48] I would argue that Paul turns the tables on the opponents just in terms of his theology of role reversal. The reason why Gen 21:8-14 can fit his purposes is that the Judaizers are now considered to be the children of Ishmael, not Isaac; it is they, not the uncircumcised Galatians, who are to be cast out as foreigners to the covenant; it is they who are "sinners of the Gentiles;" it is they who are born of the slave woman, "according to the flesh" (4:22-25, 29, 30-31)!

It takes little historical imagination to be convinced that the Judaizers did not conceive of themselves in such terms. Quite the contrary, from their vantage point, they had indeed entered the new age and viewed themselves as "Jewish Christian missionaries" who were attempting to extend the reign of Messiah Jesus to the nations. But as Paul saw things, they believed too much in their conviction that the Messiah would preserve an unmodified Torah and Jewish societal values. From his perspective, they were *for all practical purposes* still in the preeschatological era. At best, Paul might have thought them confused about the character of the messianic age; or at worst, which seems to have been his actual assessment of them, they were perverting the plan of salvation by not recognizing that the Torah was destined to pass away in Christ. The "cash value" of their ("other") gospel, accordingly, was that Gentiles were excluded from the covenant until such time as they became "honorary Jews." For Paul, this was unconscionable, because it distorted "the truth of the gospel" (2:5, 14) beyond recognition.

There would appear to be a certain resemblance between the Jewish Christian missionaries and the Qumran sect. According to 4QMMT C12-20, it is none other than the blessings and cursings of Deuteronomy which are said to have been fulfilled in the events contemporary with the community; that is, the priestly establishment in Jerusalem is currently under the curse because of its defection from the Torah (cf. 1QS 2:5-18; 5:7b-20). After so saying, the writer of the letter encourages his readers to consider the godly kings of Israel, who feared the Torah and were seekers of it (vv. 23-25). And it was just because of his concern for their welfare that he and his group sent them "some of the precepts of the Torah according to our decision," so that they might be delivered from "the plans of evil and the devices of Belial" (vv. 27, 28).[49] In like manner, the Judaizers were motivated by a sincere desire for the blessing of the Gentiles and their avoidance of the curse of the law; and it would seem that their care grew out of the same zeal for the purity of the Torah as author of 4QMMT (and 1QS) and his determination to preserve the integrity of the believing.

The Ultimate Role Reversal

It is none other than Jesus' own relation to the old and new communities respectively that brings us to consider *the ultimate role reversal—the cursing of the Messiah by the Torah*. By definition, the Davidic king was the representative of Yahweh and the embodiment of his righteousness. Yet as startling as it must have been, Paul consigns his Messiah to the curse which befell the apostate of Deut 21:23 (cf. Matt 11:19; Luke 7:34).[50] Dunn thinks it plausible that Deut 21:23 was used in Jewish sectarian polemic against the early Christian claim that the crucified Jesus was Messiah. If so, he continues, Paul's ingenuity is shown by the fact that he does not dispute the charge, but turns it to his own ends:

"For him the crucial factor was that the curse denoted a status outside the covenant, 'expelled from the people of God'." Because the cursed criminal was a defilement of the land of inheritance, the curses of Deuteronomy 27 and 28 not only involved the withdrawal of covenant blessing, but climax in being put outside the promised land to live among Gentiles. "To affirm that the crucified Jesus was cursed by God, therefore, was tantamount to saying that he had been put outside the covenant, outside the people of God." By implication, then, the resurrection, God's vindication of his Son (Rom 1:4; 1 Tim 3:16), signified "God's acceptance of the 'outsider,' the cursed law-breaker, the *Gentile sinner*."[51]

It is the death of Jesus within the framework of covenant curse and renewal (*à la* Deuteronomy 27-30) which J. M. Scott and N. T. Wright have most helpfully applied to our passage. As Wright phrases it, Gal 3:13 in particular is not an isolated explanation of the cross or a proof text for justification by faith, or anything so atomistic. It is, rather, in his words, "the sharp expression of a theme which occupies Paul throughout the chapter: the fact that in the cross of Jesus, the Messiah, the curse of exile itself reached its height, and was dealt with once and for all, so that the blessing of covenant renewal might flow out the other side, as God always intended." The interpretation gains in plausibility by the observation that at least some Jews of Paul's era believed that Israel was still under the curse of the exile inasmuch as the prophecies of her restoration had not been fulfilled in the expected manner. Paul thus views the cross of Jesus as the climax of the covenant curses and the commencement of Israel's restoration. In this capacity, Jesus is Israel's "redeeming representative." "He *is* Israel, going down to death under the curse of the law, and going through that curse to the new covenant life beyond."[52]

This insight tallies with Paul's stated purpose of the Messiah's condemnation by the law: to redeem others from the Torah's curse (3:13). The verb "redeemed" (*exagorazō*) is chosen because of its biblical associations with the liberation of slaves. Two acts of liberation in the OT particularly stand out. One is the exodus from Egypt, "the house of bondage." The other is new exodus from Babylon, as anticipated by the Prophets. The typological potential of this concept, of course, is exploited by the NT generally and not least by Paul. However, in Galatians, Paul is driving at something very specific, namely, the "new bondage" is that of the Torah. The motif emerges clearly enough from the ensuing train of thought: (1) 3:23-25 likens life under the law to the constraints imposed by a disciplinarian; (2) 4:4 has in view the redemption of "those under the law," an especially novel idea, since, in historical perspective, "those under the law" would have been free from (Egyptian) bondage by the nature of the case (cf. John 8:33); (3) 4:8-9 equates devotion to the Sinai covenant with the bondage of pagan idolatry.[53] Role reversal, then, promotes further role reversal and irony is compounded by irony: the Messiah is treated by Israel as an outcast and thus brings the curses of Deuteronomy to a climax; but in the process, he liberates his new people from the "bondage" which still curses the Judaizers and potentially their admirers.

The beneficiaries of Christ's redemption are "us." In keeping with Paul's use of personal pronouns throughout the present context, "us" refers to that group of Jewish Christians whose main representative is the apostle himself, the erstwhile "zealot" turned proclaimer of the gospel.[54] This is the company which has come to recognize that Jesus is the terminus of the law, and that to remain "under law" would be an egregious contradiction to Yahweh's design to displace the Torah with him. It is they, by virtue of their experience of the Spirit (3:3-5; 5:16-26; 6:1), who have left the era of the "flesh," "the elements of the world" (4:3), in order to enter the "new creation" (Gal 6:15; 2 Cor 5:17). Had they remained as they were, they would have incurred the same "curse of the law" as their Jewish compatriots, who have rejected Yahweh's Anointed (cf. Acts 4:24-28). And as far as Paul is concerned, the Jewish Christian missionaries are no better off than their non-Christian counterparts, because their outlook on Jesus of Nazareth is not discernibly different. The parallel to 3:13 is 4:4-7: the one "born under the law" redeems those "under the law," i.e., Jews who have entered into their true (eschatological) sonship by virtue of the combined work of Christ and the Spirit. Paul's immediate focus, then, is on the "Jews by birth" (2:15). But if even they have come to recognize that Christ is the end of the law and the deliverer from bondage, then the Gentile Galatians must as well. Otherwise, they will be subject to the same condemnation as their Judaizing mentors.

But not only was Jesus "born under the law" to "redeem those under the law," he had to be cursed by the law "in order that the blessing of Abraham might come upon the Gentiles, that we might receive the promise of the Spirit through (the) faith" (3:14). The force of 3:14 is that Gentile Christians are equally blessed with Jewish Christians, who have received the prophetic promise of the Spirit. This is very much in keeping with the centre of gravity of

Paul's teaching on the death of Christ, i.e., the cross has broken down the boundary of the law in order to procure the blessing of Abraham for all. Moreover, in their prophetic contexts, "the promise of the Spirit" is normally associated with the new exodus motif. Hence, the liberation of the latter-day exodus is applied by Paul to the eschatological "Israel of God" (6:16), which knows no ethnic or cultural distinctions: Jew and Gentile equally are the redeemed "sons of God" who cry "Abba, Father" (4:4-7). In so doing, Paul joins a chorus of Jewish tradition regarding the future inclusion of the Gentiles. The difference, however, is that he announces that such expectations have been realized already in the cross-event.[55]

5. Summary and Conclusions

We have argued that the key to Gal 3:10-13 resides in an ideology of role reversal, whereby, in light of the Christ-event and the presence of the eschatological Spirit, fidelity to the God of Israel has been redefined. At one time, to cling tenaciously to the law was the *sine qua non* of fidelity to Yahweh. However, given that Jesus the Messiah, for Paul, has abrogated the Torah, and considering that the Galatian believers received the Spirit by "the hearing of faith," not "works of the law," Zealot-like devotion to the law is now considered by the apostle to be the sin of sins—apostasy, consisting in infidelity to the salvific plan of God for "the ends of the ages" (1 Cor 10:11).

The passage contains two pivotal words: "life" and "curse." "Life" is the reward of the righteous Israelite's faith(fulness). In the first instance, this life is continued blessing in the land, including health, prosperity, family and friends, etc. In the larger perspective, however, life is expanded to include "eternal life," particularly as Paul regards "life" to be the extension to others of the resurrection life of Christ. Correspondingly, "curse" is to be defined as the death penalty reserved for the renegade to the covenant. Such a one was not permitted to live in the land, the place of God's blessing, and could not, therefore, attain to the life of the age to come. The curse was, most pointedly, "the curse of the law." While this phrase is open to interpretation, it would be a fair assessment to say that "the curse of the Law is the curse which the Law brings and which, in this sense, the Law itself is."[56] Both life and cursing (death) combine to form a complex whole, and both carry clear covenantal overtones: "'life' is the chief blessing of the covenant, as death is its chief curse."[57] Both are developed with respect to the opponents in Galatia: they must bear the curse of exclusion from the bliss of the age to come.

As regards Paul's invocation of the cursing passages in particular, Deut 21:23; 27:26 correspond to his own curse of Gal 1:8-9, which could be rendered: "Cursed be any man who is fundamentally disloyal to the gospel."[58] There is, one might say, not only "the curse of the law," but as well "the curse of the gospel," a curse pronounced against those who would revert to the law. So ironically, the curse of the gospel is the eschatological curse of the law imposed on those who prefer it over the Christ of Paul's proclamation.[59] But the Judaizers are not only cursed by Paul's gospel as apostates, they are, as it were, "ministers of sin" (2:17). They not merely reject this gospel, but actively promote defection from it to their "other gospel." They, in other words, are in the same class as an angel who might conceivably preach such a gospel and who are for that reason accursed. Their "apostasy" is further evident by their lack of love toward those who will not conform to their strictures. In so responding, they have eviscerated the covenant.

It is role reversal resulting from the eschatological situation which opens an avenue of understanding to the problem posed at the beginning of this essay, i.e., whereas Gal 3:10a pronounces a curse upon anyone who would attempt to live by the Torah, the biblical text to which Paul appeals, Deut 27:26, affirms just the opposite: the curse falls not on those who do the Law, but on those who *fail* to do it (Gal 3:10b). Our explanation is that there is an irony involved in Paul's assertion and its biblical support. That is to say, in their very keeping of the law, the opponents have not kept it, because they have not "upheld" it in its eschatological design, i.e., to point Israel to Jesus of Nazareth as the one who has done away with the barriers of separation between nations. Their "infidelity" thus consists in their retention of a Torah which *ipso facto* was nationalistically restrictive.[60] To state it yet another way, it is because the opponents retain their identity as Jews of the Mosaic stripe that they have failed to "do the law;" it is because they are "in the law" and "of works of the law" that they are condemned by the Torah's curse. Therefore, given Paul's set of assumptions, Deut 27:26 can be placed in service because doing the law is now tantamount to not doing the law. Since the turning of the ages, to live by the law is a failure to keep the law! In a word, the opponents are apostates in a newly (re)defined eschatological sense.

It is from the vantage point of eschatological role reversal that Paul's actual use of the Bible pays dividends for the exegete. The frequent assumption is that he lifts words from the OT in order to provide proof texts for pet doctrines, all the while disregarding their original setting. However, without rehearsing the debate respecting the bearing of context on the NT's use of the Scriptures,[61] Paul, I would submit, is indeed cognizant of the original intention of the passages adduced in Gal 3:10-13; and the more one takes this intention into account, the more light is shed on his purposes in appealing to the biblical texts in the first place. While many of Paul's readers have called into question his handling of the Scriptures, it does possess its own kind of internal consistency, one which, in his estimation, was consonant with the story of Israel and supplied him with materials to articulate his conviction that cursing and blessing are apportioned according to one's stance toward Jesus of Nazareth.[62] And as scholarship continues its quest for new light on Paul's use of the OT, the phenomenon of role reversal in his letters is one well-worthy of further exploration.

---

[1] Gal 3:10-13 would thus appear to be a chiasmus:
A Curse (Deut 27:26)
  B Life (Hab 2:4)
  B Life (Lev 18:5)
A Curse (Deut 21:23)
[2] C. D. Stanley, "'Under a Curse': A Fresh Reading of Galatians 3.10-14," *New Testament Studies* 36 (1990), 481. Cf. M.-J. Lagrange, *Saint Paul: Épitre aux Galates*, Etudes Bibliques (Paris: Gabalda, 1950, 69); D. Lührmann, *Galatians*, Continental Commentary (Minneapolis: Fortress, 1992), 60-61. It was actually Luther who first noticed the problem.
[3] F. F. Bruce touches on this approach with his recognition that Paul's argument is "very much *ad hominem*" (*The Epistle to the Galatians: A Commentary on the Greek Text*, New International Greek Testament Commentary [Grand Rapids: Eerdmans, 1982], 162). Bruce, however, does not develop the idea or follow through with it consistently. Similarly, H. D. Betz anticipates this investigation by pointing out that the conclusion of 3:10—the "men of the Torah" are under a curse—is contained already in the *propositio* of 2:15-21 (*Galatians: A Commentary on Paul's Letter to the Churches in Galatia*, Hermeneia [Philadelphia: Fortress, 1979], 144). Other studies approximating the present attempt to explain this difficult passage are: J. D. G. Dunn, *Jesus, Paul, and the Law: Studies in Mark and Galatians* (Louisville: Westminster/John Knox, 1990), 215-41; J. P. Braswell, "'The Blessing of Abraham' Versus 'The Curse of the Law'": Another Look at Gal 3:10-13," *Westminster*

Theological Journal 53 (1991), 73-91; N. T. Wright, *The Climax of the Covenant: Christ and the Law in Pauline Theology* (Minneapolis: Fortress, 1991), 137-56; J. M. Scott, "Paul's Use of the Deuteronomic Tradition," *Journal of Biblical Literature* 112 (1993), 645-65; id., "'For As Many as Are of Works of the Law Are under a Curse' (Galatians 3.10)," *Paul and the Scriptures of Israel*, eds. C. A. Evans and J. A. Sanders. Journal for the Study of the New Testament Supplement Series 83. Studies in Scripture in Early Judaism and Christianity 1 (Sheffield: Sheffield Academic Press, 1993), 187-221. The contexts of the cursing passages have been explored in brief by F. F. Bruce, "The Curse of the Law," *Paul and Paulinism: Essays in Honour of C. K. Barrett*, eds. M. D. Hooker and S. G. Wilson (London: SPCK, 1982), 27-36. Bruce recognizes that the issue in these cursing texts is that of perseverance vs. apostasy.

[4] B. R. Gaventa, "Galatians 1 and 2: Autobiography as Paradigm," *Novum Testamentum* 28 (1986), 317.

[5] Ibid., 314-19.

[6] On "live as a Jew," see Dunn, *Jesus, Paul*, 145-50, 154-55.

[7] A. J. Hultgren, "The *Pistis Christou* Formulation in Paul," *Novum Testamentum* 22 (1980), 248-63. The phrase of this verse is matched in 2:20 by "in faith in the Son of God." In both cases, the genitives are best taken as "adjectival."

[8] T. D. Gordon, "The Problem at Galatia," *Interpretation* 41 (1987), 32-43.

[9] Dunn, *Jesus, Paul*, 61-88.

[10] R. G. Hammerton-Kelly, "Sacred Violence and the Curse of the Law (Galatians 3.13): The Death of Christ as a Sacrificial Travesty," *New Testament Studies* 36 (1990), 102.

[11] Bruce, *Galatians*, 166.

[12] In 3b, "now," in all probability, is to be construed with "having begun in the Spirit" rather than with what follows. The reason for thinking so is that "now" in Paul is characteristically eschatological, signifying the onset of the new age (e.g., Rom 3:31; 5:10; 6:22; 7:6, 17; 8:1). Thus, the Galatians have begun *now*, in the era of the end-time manifestation of God's "grace" (5:5; cf. John 1:17).

[13] J. H. Neyrey, *Paul, in Other Words: A Cultural Reading of His Letters* (Louisville: Westminster/John Knox, 1990), 159.

[14] See S. K. Williams, "Justification and the Spirit in Galatians," *Journal for the Study of the New Testament* 29 (1987), 91-100. C. K. Barrett suggests that Paul takes up the passage quoted by the opponents (Gen 15:6) and attempts to refute their exegesis ("The Allegory of Abraham, Sarah, and Hagar in the Argument of Galatians," *Essays on Paul* [London: SPCK, 1982], 159). In all probability, each of the texts quoted in 3:10-13 was forwarded by the opponents.

[15] T. L. Donaldson, "The 'Curse of the Law' and the Inclusion of the

Gentiles: Galatians 3.13-14," *New Testament Studies* 32 (1986), 101.

[16] In this letter, to be "under a curse" is synonymous with being in the old age. It is equivalent to "under sin," (3:22), "under law" (3:23), "under guardian and stewards" (4:2), and "under the elements of the world" (4:3). See further L. Belleville, "'Under Law': Structural Analysis and the Pauline Concept of Law in Galatians 3.21-4.11," *Journal for the Study of the New Testament* 26 (1986), 53-78.

[17] Betz, *Galatians*, 144.

[18] Throughout this essay, translations such as "of [from] works of the law" or "of [from] faith," etc., reflect the "partisan *ek*" of Paul's Greek. That is to say, to be "of" or "from" an entity is to belong to it. As BDAG (296) explain, "In these cases the idea of belonging, the partisan use, often completely overshadows that of origin." The upshot is that for Paul it is all-important to belong to the right group: either the "law-party" or the "faith-in-Jesus Christ-party." An essay on this partisan use of *ek* is now in the works.

[19] Wright, *Climax*, 140 (italics deleted). Wright's overall thesis that covenant theology lies behind Paul's use of the Scriptures is undoubtedly correct.

[20] P. Craigie, *The Book of Deuteronomy*, New International Commentary on the Old Testament (Grand Rapids: Eerdmans, 1976), 334.

[21] *If* there is any emphasis on "all" (only in the LXX), it is qualitative, not quantitative. Israel was not free to pick and choose from the variety of the commandments: each one had its peculiar importance. It is in this sense that Paul can write in Gal 5:3 that everyone who receives circumcision is bound to keep *the whole law*. Ironically enough, the Judaizers do not keep "the whole law" because of the absence of love on their part (5:14). Note how in Deut 30:16 loving God is correlated with walking in his ways and keeping his commandments.

[22] J. Bligh, *Galatians: A Discussion of St. Paul's Epistle*, Householder Commentaries 1 (London: St. Paul, 1970), 257.

[23] H. Schlier, *Der Brief an die Galater*, Kritisch-exegetischer Kommentar über das Neue Testament. 5th ed. (Göttingen: Vandenhoeck & Ruprecht, 1971), 132.

[24] See also BDAG, 322-23. J. W. Wevers confirms that although *menō* plus *en* does not display the transitive nature of the Hebrew construction of Deut 27:26, the Greek rendering "to abide by" or "persist in" is not far removed from the sense of the original "cause to stand," "establish," "uphold" (*Notes on the Greek Text of Deuteronomy*, Society of Biblical Literature Septuagint and Cognate Studies 39 [Atlanta: Scholars, 1995], 425).

[25] As acknowledged by H. N. Ridderbos: "The question is not how a man shall become righteous, but how the righteous (the pious) shall *live*, in the full and deep sense of an unafraid and unthreatened life" (*The Epistle of Paul to the Churches of Galatia*, New International Commentary on the New Testament [Grand Rapids: Eerdmans, 1953], 124). Ridderbos, in

fact, consistently recognizes the original thrust of each of the OT passages placed in service by Paul. By contrast, Ridderbos' successor on Galatians, R. Y. K. Fung, has argued elaborately for "he who is righteous by faith" as the most appropriate sense of the Hebrew and Greek versions of Hab 2:4 (*The Epistle to the Galatians*, New International Commentary on the New Testament [Grand Rapids: Eerdmans, 1988], 143-45). However, Ridderbos is right: the prophet has in view the behavior of the already righteous person. The same was conceded by J. B. Lightfoot (*St. Paul's Epistle to the Galatians* [London: MacMillan, 1865], 138).

26 The LXX's own "the righteous will live by faith of [in] me" is normally taken to be a reference to Yahweh's own fidelity, by which the righteous person will live. However, in Greek terms, *mou* could just as well be "objective genitive," i.e., the faith(fulness) of "the righteous person" (*ho dikaios*) has God as its object. Either way, there is no reason to believe that Paul has departed from the original sense of the text (cf. Schlier, *Galater*, 133). Why Paul omits the personal pronoun "of me" (*mou*) is adequately explained by F. Mußner. According to Mußner, Paul is not interested in the *mou* because of his christological interpretation of Habakkuk; that is, whereas *mou* concentrates on Yahweh, Paul wishes to shift attention to Jesus. It is in his christological application of the prophet that the life of Hab 2:4 has special reference to "life in Christ" (Gal 2:2) (*Der Galaterbrief*, Herders theologischer Kommentar zum Neuen Testament 9 [Freiburg: Herder, 1981], 227). In any event, only the Greek is problematic. The Hebrew unambiguously reads "his faith(fulness)," designating the person's own faith(fulness).

27 Cf. how 1QS 4:9-11 attributes all kinds of vices to "the spirit of perversity," which corresponds to the idolatrous frame of mind decried by 1QS 2:11-12; 2:26-3:2.

28 Why Paul omits "man" (*anthrōpos*) from the LXX of Lev 18:5 is uncertain and probably should not materially affect our understanding of his intentions. In any event, it does not follow that he sees this text as devoid of the principle of faith. R. N. Longenecker thinks that Paul may have deleted *anthrōpos* in order to remove Lev 18:5 from the category of the rabbinic texts which play on the term (i.e., as indicating generic humanity), so as to bring *law-keeping Gentiles* within its purview (*Galatians* [WBC 41; Dallas: Word, 1990], 121). One can understand how this idea would have played readily into the Judaizers' hands. But even if this tradition was alive in Paul's day, it is a *non sequitur* that "doing" would have been divorced from "believing," as Longenecker seems to assume.

29 See D. Garlington, *'The Obedience of Faith': A Pauline Phrase in Historical Context*, Wissenschaftliche Untersuchungen zum Neuen Testament 2/38 (Tübingen: Mohr-Siebeck, 1991), 186-91 (esp. 190-91).

30 Note how in Deut 10:12 "walk" is combined with other synonymous expressions: "And now, Israel, what does the Lord your God require of

you, but to *fear* the Lord your God, to *walk* in all his ways, to *love*, to *serve* the Lord your God with all your heart and with all your soul." According to Deut 13:4, instead of listening to false prophets, the people are to *walk after the Lord their God, fear* him, *keep* his commandments and *obey* his voice. Cf. Bar 4:2; 3:14, and contrast Jer 11:8; Sir 2:12-14; Wis 6:4; Tob 1:2; 14:2; Bar 1:17-19; 2:10; 3:12-13; 2 Macc 6:1; 11:25; 3 Macc 3:4; 4 Macc 2:8, 23.

[31] G. J. Wenham, *The Book of Leviticus*, New International Commentary of the Old Testament (Grand Rapids: Eerdmans, 1979), 253. J. E. Hartley agrees that life here means that "Israel will have a secure, healthy life with sufficient goods in the promised land as God's people" (*Leviticus*, Word Biblical Commentary 4 [Dallas: Word, 1992], 293).

[32] It is on this note that Galatians virtually commences (1:1): Jesus' resurrection inaugurates the eternal messianic age, corresponding, as it does, to the oracles concerning the captivity and restoration of Israel, the nation's own death and resurrection (e.g., Isa 26:19; Ezek 37:1-14; Hos 6:1-2).

[33] J. D. G. Dunn, *Romans*, Word Biblical Commentary 38 a, b. 2 vols. (Dallas: Word, 1988), 2.601.

[34] The expression "the doers of the law" in Rom 2:13 is modeled on Lev 18:5 and like statements. The same phrase crops up in 1 Macc 2:67, where it designates loyalist Jews who would be vindicated against the Gentiles by divine justice. Significant also are 1QpHab 7:11; 8:1; 12:4-5. See D. Garlington, *Faith, Obedience, and Perseverance: Aspects of Paul's Letter to the Romans*, Wissenschaftliche Untersuchungen zum Neuen Testament 79 (Tübingen: Mohr-Siebeck, 1994), 67-71.

[35] See further C. H. Cosgrove, *The Cross and the Spirit: A Study in the Argumentation and Theology of Galatians* (Macon: Mercer University Press, 1988), 90-91.

[36] In time, crucifixion came to be regarded in some circles as fulfilling Deut 21:22-23. Especially striking is 11QTemple 64:6-13, a halakic interpretation of Deut 21:22-23, which explicitly equates crucifixion with Yahweh's curse against *traitors to Israel*. In a similar vein, 4QpNah 5-8 possibly alludes to Deut 21:22 in its notice that "the lion of wrath" (Alexander Jannaeus) introduced into Palestine the practice of hanging "living men, which was never done before in Israel." J. A. Fitzmyer ("Crucifixion in Ancient Palestine, Qumran Literature, and the New Testament," *Catholic Biblical Quarterly* 40 [1978], 498-507; id. "Paul and the Dead Sea Scrolls," *The Dead Sea Scrolls After Fifty Years: A Comprehensive Assessment*, eds. P. W. Flint and J. C. Vanderkam. 2 vols. [Leiden: Brill, 1998-99], 2.607-9), in agreement with Y. Yadin (*The Temple Scroll*. 3 vols. [Jerusalem: Israel Exploration Society, 1983], 1.373-79), accepts the linkage of the two passages from the Scrolls and concludes that crucifixion was in fact practiced by some Jews to execute criminals—and both passages seek to justify this method of capital punishment by an application of Deut 21:22-23. See additionally Bruce,

"Curse," 31-32; M. Wilcox, "'Upon the Tree'—Deut 21:22-23 in the New Testament," *Journal of Biblical Literature* 96 (1977), 88-90; O. Betz, "Jesus and the Temple Scroll," *Jesus and the Dead Sea Scrolls*, ed. J. H. Charlesworth (New York: Doubleday, 1992), 81-85); J. Zias and J. H. Charlesworth, "Crucifixion: Archaeology, Jesus, and the Dead Sea Scrolls," ibid., 277-79.

[37] Craigie, *Deuteronomy*, 286.

[38] As is true of Paul's usage generally, the phrases "of works of the law," "in the law," and "under law" (3:23; 4:4, 21) in Galatians (and elsewhere) have to do with the sphere in which the opponents and their followers choose to dwell, i.e., in the era of the Torah, not the age of the Spirit. As far as justification in particular is concerned, C. H. Cosgrove has shown that Paul characteristically construes the verb *dikaioō* with prepositions indicating instrumentality, not evidential basis ("Justification in Paul: A Linguistic and Theological Reflection," *Journal of Biblical Literature* 106 [1987], esp. 654-61). In his words: "The question never becomes whether one can be justified *on the basis of* the law or works but remains always whether one can be justified in the sphere of the law" (ibid., 662).

[39] Garlington, *Faith, Obedience*, 59.

[40] The bulk of my *Obedience* is devoted to this proposition.

[41] The various interpretations of Paul's use of Deut 27:26 are summarized by Betz, *Galatians*, 145-46; Stanley, "Curse," 482-86; Scott, "Galatians 3.10," 188-94.

[42] Scott, "Galatians 3.10," 194-213; id., "Deuteronomic Tradition," 657-58.

[43] See D. Garlington, "Burden Bearing and the Recovery of Offending Christians (Galatians 6:1-5)," *TrinJ* ns 12 (1991), 151-83.

[44] J. D. G. Dunn, *The Epistle to the Galatians* (BNTC; Peabody: Hendrickson, 1993), 171; id., *Jesus, Paul*, 226; S. McKnight, *Galatians* (NIV Application Commentary; Grand Rapids: Eerdmans, 1995), 154-55; Wright, *Climax*, 144-45; G. Howard, *Paul: Crisis in Galatia*, Society for New Testament Studies Monograph Series 35. 2nd ed. (Cambridge: Cambridge University Press, 1990), 51-54.

[45] Longenecker (*Galatians*, 119) notes that *Exod. R.* 23.5 couples Hab 2:4 with Gen 15:6, as it makes the point that the former summarizes the whole Torah in one principle: faithfulness rewarded by faith (cf. *Mid. Ps.* 17A.25 and *b. Mak.* 24a). The linkage of the two is appropriate, because both have to do with the perseverance of faith.

[46] Paul thus agrees and disagrees with the Jewish interpretation of Hab 2:4 at the same time (see Betz, *Galatians*, 147): fidelity is still the order of the day, but it is now to Christ, not the Torah. On Paul's "eschatological" use of Hab 2:4, see K. Kertelge, *"Rechtfertigung" bei Paulus: Studien zur Struktur und zum Bedeutungsgehalt des paulinischen Rechtfertigungsbegriffs*, Neutestamentliche Abhandlungen 3. 2nd ed. (Münster: Aschendorff, 1967), 89-95.

[47] Barrett, "Allegory," 162. Cf. Longenecker, *Galatians*, 199; Hammerton-Kelly, "Sacred Violence," 108.
[48] R. B. Hays, *Echoes of Scripture in the Letters of Paul* (New Haven: Yale University Press, 1989), 112.
[49] On 4QMMT, see M. Abegg, "4QMMT, Paul, and 'Works of the Law,'" in *The Bible at Qumran: Text, Shape, and Interpretation*, ed. P. Flint. Studies in the Dead Sea Scrolls and Related Literature (Grand Rapids: Eerdmans, 2001), 203-16; J. D. G. Dunn, "4QMMT and Galatians," *New Testament Studies* 43 (1997), 147-53; J. Kampen and M. J. Bernstein, eds., *Reading 4QMMT: New Perspectives on Qumran Law and History*, Society of Biblical Literature Seminar Series 2 (Atlanta: Scholars Press, 1996); E. Qimron and J. Strugnell, eds., *Discoveries in the Judean Desert X. Qumran Cave 4. V: Miqsat Maase Ha-Torah* (Oxford: Clarendon, 1994).
[50] It is true that Paul's adaptation of the LXX of Deut 21:23, "cursed is everyone who hangs on a tree," omits the words "by God." This is frequently said to reflect Paul's reluctance to assert directly that Jesus was cursed by God. However, Fitzmyer points out that the same omission occurs in 4QpNah 3-4 i 8, which uses Deut 21:23 similarly to Paul ("Crucifixion," 512). See also Wilcox, "Tree," 87. There is another modification of the LXX, which C. D. Stanley thinks implies that the curse had already fallen on the victim prior to his hanging on the tree. To Paul this was unacceptable because it had to be that Christ was cursed *on the tree* (*Paul and the Language of Scripture: Citation Technique in the Pauline Epistles and Contemporary Literature*, Society for New Testament Studies Monograph Series 74 [Cambridge: Cambridge University Press, 1992], 246). However, this seems unlikely. See rightly B. Lindars, *New Testament Apologetic: The Doctrinal Significance of the Old Testament Quotations* (London: SCM, 1961), 233. Lindars cites *Sanh.* 6:4, where Deut 21:23 is quoted and discussed: "None is hanged save the blasphemer and the idolater." "The man," comments Lindars, "is not accursed because he has been hung, but hung because he is already accursed on account of his crime." Lindars then notes that Jesus, in the gospels, was condemned before the cross
[51] Dunn, *Galatians*, 178 (italics mine).
[52] Wright, *Climax*, 141, 151-52 (italics his). See the discussions of ibid., 141-56; Scott, "Galatians 3.10," 217-221.
[53] See my *Faith, Obedience*, 39-40; N. J. Calvert, "Abraham and Idolatry: Paul's Comparison of Obedience to the Law with Idolatry in Galatians 4.1-10," *Paul and the Scriptures of Israel*, eds. C. A. Evans and J. A. Sanders. Journal for the Study of the New Testament Supplement Series 83. Studies in Scripture in Early Judaism and Christianity 1 (Sheffield: Sheffield Academic Press, 1993), 222-37.
[54] In support, see Wright, *Climax*, 143-44, 154. For a summary of opinion, see Donaldson, "Curse," 95-99 (Donaldson himself opts for the position herein taken).

[55] Donaldson, "Curse," 99-100.
[56] Betz, *Galatians*, 149 (quoting Schlier).
[57] Wright, *Climax*, 149.
[58] Bligh, *Galatians*, 257.
[59] Paul's "curse" (*anathema*) is thus equivalent to Hebrew *herem*, sacred cursing (e.g., Lev 27:28-29; Deut 7:26; 30:7; Josh 6:17-18; 7:1, 11-13). From his perspective, those who "pervert the gospel of Christ" (1:7) ought to receive the same treatment as that meted out to Christ by their non-Christian Jewish compatriots. In their case, however, the curse is that of the new covenant. Paul picks up on the language of the Torah, but his application is within the framework of his gospel.
[60] Cf. Dunn, *Jesus, Paul*, 228-30.
[61] See the collection of essays in G. K. Beale (ed.), *The Right Doctrine from the Wrong Texts? Essays on the Use of the Old Testament in the New* (Grand Rapids: Baker, 1994), 137-309.
[62] Cf. Wright, *Climax*, 140, 144, 155; Hays, *Echoes*; E. E. Ellis, *Paul's Use of the Old Testament* (Edinburgh: Oliver & Boyd, 1957), 126-39, 147-48; R. N. Longenecker, *Biblical Exegesis in the Apostolic Period* (Grand Rapids: Eerdmans, 1975), 121; M. Noth, "'For All Who Rely on Works of the Law are Under a Curse'," *The Laws in the Pentateuch and Other Studies* (London: SCM, 1966), 118-31; D.- A. Koch, *Die Schrift als Zeuge des Evangeliums: Untersuchungen zur Verwendung und zum Verständnis der Schrift bei Paulus*, Beiträge zur historischen Theologie 69 (Tübingen: Mohr-Siebeck, 1986), 338-40, 347-50; C. A Evans and J. A. Sanders, eds., *Paul and the Scriptures of Israel*, Journal for the Study of the New Testament Supplement Series 83. Studies in Scripture in Early Judaism and Christianity 1 (Sheffield: Sheffield Academic Press, 1993).

IMPUTATION OR UNION WITH CHRIST?
A RESPONSE TO JOHN PIPER

1. Introduction

Recent days have seen the publication of a new study from John Piper, *Counted Righteous in Christ: Should We Abandon the Imputation of Christ's Righteousness?* (Wheaton: Crossway, 2002). According to one reader, Dr. Piper's book is "certainly the most solid defense of the imputed righteousness of Christ since the work of John Murray fifty years ago" (John Frame, from the back cover). This book emerges from vigorous contemporary debate over the cardinal issues of imputation, justification and righteousness, and represents a reaffirmation of the traditional Protestant position on these questions.

It must be clarified from the outset that this response to Piper's book represents a kind of "mediating" position. Not that the purpose is to bridge a gap simply for the sake of being a "peacemaker," but rather that the baby is not to be thrown out with the bath water. That is to say, the *intention* of the doctrine of imputation is not to be disputed: *our righteousness comes from Christ and is for that reason an "alien righteousness."* However, it is a question of modality. The prophets anticipate the day when the Lord himself will become our righteousness (Isa 61:10; Jer 23:6; 33:16), corresponding to the time when none other than his Servant will make many righteous (Isaiah 53:11). But how precisely does this transpire? It is the contention of this paper that the free gift of righteousness comes our way by virtue of *union with Christ*, not imputation as classically defined.[1]

The design of this study is to engage Piper's exegetical/ theological arguments. The introductory material pertaining to the setting in family, church, culture and nations is really not in dispute. Every Christian would agree that justification by faith is vital for the preservation and well-being of each. But in their own way, these remarks tellingly bring to the fore a central issue in Piper's presentation. Throughout his book, Piper assumes that justification by faith and imputation are tantamount to each other, as though the former could not exist apart from the latter. So, it is well from the outset of this response to go on record that justification by faith as such is not in contention, only the mechanics of how justification "works." Likewise, that the righteousness of Christ becomes our possession by faith alone is taken for granted, and indeed defended, in the following pages.

Given, then, our common faith in Christ and the efficacy of his blood and righteousness, we are obliged, even in the climate of heated debate, to be ever vigilant to maintain the apostolic mandate to the church: "I therefore, a prisoner for the Lord, beg you to lead a life worthy of the calling to which you have been called, *with all lowliness and meekness, with patience, forbearing one another in love, eager to maintain the unity of the Spirit in the bond of peace*" (Eph 4:1-3).

Procedurally, I have chosen to follow Piper's own outline. His arguments are normally summarized in detail and sometimes with lengthy quotations, in order to let him speak for himself as much as possible. Then, in some cases following the summaries and in others intertwined with them, I have sought to provide what response is possible within the parameters allotted.

2. Sketch of Piper's Argument

The launching pad of Piper's book is an article by Robert Gundry (see 44), who is taken as a leading representative of "the challenge to historic Protestant teaching."[2] According to Piper, Gundry's revision of the Protestant schema of justification can be summarized under four heads (47-48).

> (1) Our "faith is reckoned as righteousness" in the sense that our righteousness "consists of faith even though faith is not itself a work." In other words, faith, instead of receiving the imputed righteousness of Christ, is itself our righteousness by God's decision to impute it to be so.
>
> (2) Justification does not involve any positive imputation of divine righteousness (neither God's nor Christ's) to believers.
>
> (3) God's righteousness is his "salvific activity in a covenantal framework" as opposed to imputation in a "bookkeeping framework." This salvific activity, called "justification," includes what has traditionally been called "sanctification": justification "has to do with liberation from sin's mastery."

(4) The doctrine that Christ's righteousness is imputed to believing sinners needs to be abandoned as unbiblical.

In Piper's "Exegetical Response to the Challenge," appeal is made to the standard Pauline texts which are supposed to contain the doctrine of imputation. Piper is particularly concerned to deny that justification is in any sense a liberation from sin. In his view, such a understanding of texts like Rom 6:6-7 results in a confusion of justification and sanctification. As much at stake as anything is a methodology of reading Pauline texts. In particular, Piper objects to a "controlling biblical-theological paradigm" ("new paradigm") which, he believes, is too "vague and general" and fails to do justice to passages in Paul. Piper is afraid that this approach "bears all the marks of a widespread scholarly paradigm that exerts a controlling effect on the exegesis of the texts that do not clearly support it" (70).

3. Piper's Exegetical Presentation and Response

The evidence that the righteousness imputed to us is external and not our faith

The primary passage educed in support of this proposition is Rom 4:1-11. Verse 3 of chapter 4 quotes Gen 15:6. As translated by Piper, the latter passage reads: "Abraham believed God, and *it was credited* to him for righteousness" (italics his). The mainstay of the argument from Romans 4 is the translation of the Greek verb *logizomai* as "reckoned," "counted" or "imputed." Thus, given such a translation of Paul's Greek, it follows for Piper that righteousness becomes the possession of the believer by virtue of imputation.

However, the problem resides precisely in the translation and, consequently, the interpretation of *logizomai*. It is true that members of this basic family of words can mean "credit/charge to one's account" (e.g., Phlm 18 [*ellogeō*]), and *logizomai* itself is used by Paul in the sense of "keep a record of" (1 Cor 13:5). The LSJ classical Greek lexicon cites a couple of instances in which it bears the sense of "set down to one's account," although these are isolated instances and do not occupy any place of prominence in the verb's semantic range.[3] However, a glance at the BAGD Lexicon informs one that in biblical Greek *logizomai* characteristically means things like "reckon," "calculate," "count," "take into account," "evaluate," "estimate," "think about," "consider," "think," "be of the opinion," "look upon as" (as do LSJ).[4]

Given such established and common usages, it is striking that Piper overlooks the fact that the most proximate occurrence of *logizomai* to Romans 4 is Rom 3:28, where the verb can hardly be translated "impute" or "credit." Rather, Paul "considers" or "concludes" that one is justified by faith apart from the works of the law (cf. the same usage in Rom 6:11). Indeed, this strategic employment of *logizomai* provides a very natural lead-in to chapter 4, which almost immediately quotes Gen 15:6.

It is true that BAGD translate *logizomai* in Rom 4:4, 5, 6, 9, 11, 22 as "place to one's account" or "credit." The editors do so because these verses, they correctly note, are taken after Gen 15:6. Yet it is just Gen 15:6, *rightly understood*, that provides the linguistic and conceptual background to Romans 4. What the exegete must "reckon with" is that *logizomai* is not an isolated entry in a lexicon, but rather part of an idiom that is Hebrew in origin.

In quoting the LXX of Gen 15:6, Paul draws upon the phrase *logizomai eis* ("*it was reckoned* to him *as* righteousness"). The language of the LXX, in turn, is based on the underlying Hebrew phrase *hashab l^e* . This idiom is common enough in the OT as meaning "to consider a thing to be true."[5] As such, the Hebrew and Greek phrases at stake are best translated as "reckon," not "credit" or "impute." Piper seems to use all three more or less synonymously; but in fact they are not. Dictionaries such as *The American Heritage Dictionary* and *Merriam Webster* assign to "reckon" meanings like "to count or compute" or "to consider as being; regard as," the latter being more relevant for the present purposes.

In short, the point of Gen 15:6, as taken up by Romans 4, is that Abraham was regarded as a righteous, that is, covenant keeping, person when he continued to place his trust in God's promise of a seed.[6] This correlation of fidelity to God and the reckoning of righteousness was alive in the Jewish consciousness of the Second Temple period. According to 1 Macc 2:52, "Was not Abraham found faithful when tested, and *it was reckoned to him as righteousness*?"

Having quoted Gen 15:6, with its full phraseology, "*it was reckoned* to him *as* righteousness," Paul, in good midrashic fashion, singles out key words from the text, in particular "righteousness" and "reckon." In vv. 4, 5, 6, 9, 11, 22, he reiterates that righteousness "is reckoned to" individuals. As observable in Paul's writing, shorthand expressions can serve as stand-ins for a longer string of words. The most conspicuous example is Paul's substitution of "works" for "works of the law." In the instances before us, "righteousness" is placed in the passive voice with the indirect object in the dative case. Thus, instead of wording that renders more literally the Hebrew text of Gen 15:6, Paul streamlines his diction into a more recognizable Greek idiom.[7]

But in every case, the point is the same: individuals are considered to be righteous.[8] In context, Paul is driving home the argument that righteousness does not hinge on circumcision and devotion to Israel's Torah. Abraham in particular is singled out, among other reasons, because he was vindicated (justified) as a righteous person before circumcision and the advent of the law. The argument gains in impact in light of the standard Jewish dogma that the patriarch kept none other than the law of Moses before Sinai (Sir 44:20; *2 Apoc. Bar.* 57:2; CD 3:2).[9]

Piper picks up on the common understanding that Rom 4:4-5 is cast in terms of a commercial transaction. Verse 4, anyway, is capable of such an interpretation, since *logizomai* can use used in the sense of "calculating" a wage. It may well be that Paul here pauses to draw on an analogy from the business world, because, in terms of contractual relationships, *logizomai* can mean a reckoning of payment for work done.[10]

Nevertheless, the control factor over Paul's choice of words is Gen 15:6. While 4:4 may be a reflection on a well-known principle of business practice, 4:5 returns to the idiom of *logizomai eis*: the believer's faith is considered to be his righteousness. Paul's thought is grounded in the sphere of the Hebrew covenant, according to which individuals are thought to be faithful when they place their confidence in the God of Israel and give concrete expression to their faith by obedience to his commands.[11] The radical thing in Paul, however, is that peoples of all kinds can be looked upon as obediently faithful quite apart from Torah observance and Jewish ethnic identity. It is those who simply place their trust in Jesus who truly walk in Abraham's footsteps, making the patriarch the father of circumcised and uncircumcised alike (Rom 4:12).

It is just such an appraisal of the reckoning of righteousness that opens up the intention of Rom 4:6: *because of its object*, faith, and faith alone, is accepted in the place of allegiance to the law of Moses, including, most prominently, the various boundary markers of Jewish identity. In strict terms, faith is *reckoned as* righteousness; that is, our faith in Christ is looked upon as tantamount to righteousness in its quintessential meaning—conformity to the will of God—because *in Christ* we have become God's very righteousness (2 Cor 5:21).

Again, we must read Paul in light of his Jewish context and the polemics of the Roman letter. To his Jewish compatriots, righteousness was inconceivable apart from the Torah, so much so that one document can actually coin the phrase, "*the righteousness of the law of God*" (*T. Da*n 6:11).[12] Given, additionally, that faith in Paul is specifically trust in Jesus of Nazareth as Israel's Messiah, the impact of Romans 4 is that righteousness is no longer to be assessed in terms of one's relation to the law, but rather by one's relation to Jesus the Christ. His purpose, then, is to argue that Abraham's (and our) faith is considered to be covenant fidelity, with no further qualifications and requirements.

To my mind at least, this interpretation is bolstered by a consideration of the alternative. On Piper's construction, faith is "credited/imputed for righteousness" (55). However, this introduces at least a *prima facie* confusion. Surely, the heart of Piper's argument is that righteousness is imputed or credited to the believer in the act of faith. This being so, in what sense can faith meaningfully be "imputed?" If righteousness is imputed by faith, then how can faith itself be imputed? It would seem that Piper has arrived at a double imputation, that of righteousness and of faith. This would appear to be a muddling of ideas, particularly as everywhere in the NT faith is predicated as the response of the human being himself/herself to the gospel. To be sure, faith is the gift of God, but to speak of the imputation of faith makes for an odd combination of terms. By contrast, if faith is *reckoned/considered to be* righteousness, the difficulty disappears.

Excursus: Does Righteousness Consist of Faith?

Piper takes issue with Gundry's formulation, "It is our faith, not Christ's righteousness, that is credited to us as righteousness" (quoted on 59, n. 6; 122). Who is right? First notice the following tabulation of passages in Romans 4:

v. 4: the wage is reckoned (calculated) according to grace;
v. 5: faith is reckoned as righteousness;

v. 6: God reckons righteousness apart from works, the Lord does not reckon sin;
v. 9: Abraham's faith is reckoned as righteousness;
v. 11: righteousness reckoned to all believers;
v. 22: Abraham's faith is reckoned as righteousness.

It is readily evident that both faith and righteousness are the objects of "reckoning:" faith is considered to be righteousness; righteousness is considered to exist apart from works; all believers are looked upon as being righteous (righteousness is reckoned to them).

Nevertheless, in a certain qualified sense, one may say that righteousness does consist of faith. But a formulation of the matter must be carefully nuanced. Strictly speaking, righteousness is, by definition, conformity to the covenant relationship; it *consists of* a faithful obedience to the Lord whose will is enshrined in the covenant. Yet the beginning of "faithfulness" is "faith." In keeping with the Hebrew term *'emunah*, the Greek noun translated "faith," *pistis*, is two-sided: faith and faithfulness.[13] Given this set of data, righteousness does consist of *pistis* in the expansive sense of *'emunah*, that is, covenant conformity. At the same time, however, as Piper correctly observes from Rom 10:10, *pistis* as initial trust in Christ has righteousness as its goal, that is, righteousness as covenant standing. In one sense, faith leads to righteousness; and in another, faith consists in righteousness.

It is simply a fact of church history that there has never been uniformity on the relation of faith to righteousness. In a paper entitled "John Wesley: Spiritual Empiricist," D. A. Adams remarks that as far back as Luther's controversy with Rome, the point of friction lay in respective understandings of how justification was applied.[14] It is in the question, "How is the sinner accounted righteous before God?" that the various doctrines of justification diverge.

He notes that the Augsburg Confession confronts this issue specifically. According to the Confession: "Also they [the churches] teach that men cannot be justified [obtain forgiveness of sins and righteousness] before God by their own powers, merits, or works; but are justified freely [of grace] for Christ's sake through faith, when they believe that they are received into favor, and their sins forgiven for Christ's sake who by his death hath satisfied for our sin. This faith doth God impute for righteousness before him."

Adams continues that, in the Lutheran conception, faith is not only the means to justification, but also in some way is the substance of that justification. The sinner is made just, not initially by the removal of sin, but by the infusion of faith. This is why Luther can talk about being *simul justus et peccator*, "at once righteous and a sinner." Sin remains; but because of faith, God, in grace, does not impute it to us. Faith is an inward righteousness (*justitia interior*), which is awakened by God and which heals the malady of the soul and makes man righteous. Everyone who believes in Christ is righteous, not yet fully in reality, but in hope. It is this theology which the Augsburg confession reflects when it states: "This faith doth God impute for righteousness before him." Faith seems to be equated with the righteousness that comes of justification. Faith is accepted by God instead of righteousness. Wesley, in contrast, perceives faith differently: rather than being the substance of righteousness, faith is the means to righteousness.

Adams then proceeds to demonstrate how the Westminster Confession formulated its doctrine of imputation in direct reaction to Augsburg. In this light, I would ask, Which is the more "orthodox:" Augsburg or Westminster? Since theologians of such standing have been at odds over this question for centuries, I would plead that it is unnecessary—at the very least—to take Gundry to task for his equation of faith with righteousness. He would appear to be in rather good (Lutheran!) company.

As confirming evidence of his exposition of Romans 4, Piper cites Rom 10:10 and Phil 3:8-9. As to the former, Piper is quite right that faith has righteousness as its goal. I would add that the verse is structured in terms of the familiar Already/Not Yet schema of salvation inaugurated and salvation consummated. Our initial faith in Christ results in righteousness as our covenant standing. Then, from the stance of covenant loyalty, we confess Christ, a confession that has as its terminal point eschatological salvation (Rom 1:17; cf. Rom 5:9-10).[15]

By contrast, Piper's treatment of Phil 3:8-9 is less adequate. He simply assumes that the "righteousness from God" is by way of imputation. In so doing, he has overlooked the most obvious factor of the text, namely, *union with Christ*: Paul desires to be *found in him*, not having a righteousness of his own as derived from the law. The locus of God's righteousness is now Christ, not the Torah.

Thereafter, Piper refers to Rom 3:28, whose wording is quite similar to Rom 4:5, 6. Given his understanding of the "crediting" of righteousness in Romans 4, he draws the conclusion that justification by faith, spoken of in 3:28, must be in terms of imputation. Yet, another reading of Romans 4 will result in a different take on 3:28, namely, that faith justifies because we are united to Christ and are "found in him" (Phil 3:9). While this identification is not explicit in Rom 3:28, it will become so in 5:12-19, and 8:1-11 (the mutual indwelling of believers in Christ and in the Spirit, and vice versa).

To be sure, Rom 3:27-31 serves as lead-in to Romans 4 and paves the way for the discussion of that chapter. But we must not overlook the obvious: this concluding paragraph of chapter 3 is devoted to the proposition that Jew and Gentile are now equal in the eyes of God.[16] The great effect of justification by faith is that boasting is now excluded.[17] It is precisely on this note that chapter four commences. Thus, the mainstay of the argument of Romans 4 is that all who walk in the footsteps of Abraham are "reckoned," that is, considered to be his seed, quite apart from circumcision and the Torah. Paul's purpose is not to articulate a dogma of imputation, but to demonstrate that faith is the great equalizer of nations.

The external righteousness credited to us is God's

Under this heading, Piper first gives consideration to the flow of thought from Rom 3:20 to 4:6. This phase of the argument is essentially presuppositional. By referring back to 3:20 and onward, the set of assumptions derived from the earlier part of his book provides the conceptual framework for asserting that the verses leading up to 4:6 provide "strong contextual evidence...that Paul conceived of justification in terms of an imputation of external righteousness..." (67). Methodologically, however, it would have been preferable to do things the other way around, by tracing the context forward instead of backward. Imputation is simply not mentioned in 3:21-26, and one has to assume its presence in order to find it.

In actuality, the argument from context can be seen to yield rather different results. Rom 3:21-26 can be termed, "The Eschatological Revelation of the Righteousness of God." At the head of the section stands 3:21 ("But now the righteousness of God has been revealed apart from the law, although the law and the prophets bear witness to it"). This declaration is, in fact, a recapitulation of 1:16-17, but with the addition of the important phrase, "but now." This "eschatological now" marks the turn of the ages (Rom 5:9; 7:6; 16:26; Eph 2:12-13; Col 1:26-27; 2 Tim 1:9-10; Heb 9:26). "Now" is the period of the definitive fulfillment of the prophetic Scriptures, the "fullness of time," in which God has sent forth his son (Gal 4:4), or, in terms of 2 Cor 6:2, it is the "acceptable time," the "day of salvation."

There is a dramatic and climactic quality to these words as they form the contrast to everything that has gone before in 1:18-3:20, but especially 3:19-20. In those verses in particular, Paul drew his conclusion that the "works of the law" cannot justify because they were never intended to justify; the law's purpose was to reveal sin. He maintains this over against Israel's misunderstanding of the law. For her, the law in its unmodified Mosaic form was meant to be eternal. For Paul, however, the law was only a means to an end, namely, to reveal sin and direct people to the righteousness which is through faith *in Jesus Christ*.

This is not the place to provide anything like a full commentary on this portion of Romans. Suffice it to say that as a throwback to 1:16-17, "righteousness" and "justification" in 3:21-31 are to be understood in terms of Paul's thematic statement of the letter: the revelation of the righteousness of God.[18] In point of fact, 1:16-17 itself is a restatement of 1:5: the obedience of faith among all the nations for the sake of the name of Christ.[19] Inasmuch as Paul commences and concludes Romans by rooting his christological gospel in the prophetic Scriptures (1:2; 16:26; cf. 3:21),[20] we are not surprised that the conception of righteousness found in 1:17 is none other than that of the Prophets (and the Psalms) themselves. The parallel between "salvation" and "righteousness" in 1:16-17 is particularly to be noted. According to some prominent prophecies of Israel's return from exile, these two theologically charged terms stand in synonymous parallelism.[21] "Righteousness," according to these texts, *is* "salvation" (= deliverance from exile). Accordingly, justification in Paul has to do with a new exodus on which the latter-day people of God have embarked.[22]

It is especially to be observed that the wording of Rom 1:17 is dictated by Ps 98:2, 9 (LXX 97:2, 9): "The Lord has made known his salvation; before the nations he has revealed his righteousness.... For he comes to judge the earth; he will judge the world in righteousness and the peoples with uprightness." In Paul's mind also must have been such Psalm texts as 9:8; 96:13. God's righteousness, therefore, is to be revealed to *the nations* and no longer restricted to Israel. The Psalmist, as alluded to by Paul, declares that the Gentiles as well as Israel are to be the recipients of the Lord's saving deed; both without distinction are to be regarded as Yahweh's special possession (Exod 19:5 = Eph 1:14; 1 Pet 2:9). Furthermore, Paul's quotation of Hab 2:4, a conspicuous instance of Yahweh's saving deed, simply buttresses the point.[23]

To cut to the chase, "righteousness" *in these passages*, and, consequently, in Rom 1:17; 3:21, 22, 25 (26) is not what Piper calls "external righteousness" (= the active obedience of Christ), but rather God's saving activity on behalf of Israel, when he releases the people from bondage and plants them again in the land never to be moved.[24] This is not to rule out righteousness as an attribute of God. Indeed, it is just the "righteous," covenant keeping, God who springs into action to redeem his people from slavery and graciously renew the covenant with them. Therefore, as the bridge into Romans 4, Rom 3:21-31 (as informed by 1:16-17) argues against "the imputation of external righteousness" and in favor of a salvation-historical reading of Paul, whereby the apostle's intention is seen to be that of announcing the availability of God's saving activity to *all who believe* (1:16; 3:22), because *there is no distinction* (3:22; 10:12). If the exile has been turned in Israel's favor, then this latter-day Israel is constituted of Gentile and Jew indiscriminately.[25] The identity of the redeemed people of God is no longer determined by the Jewish Torah, because God's righteousness has been revealed to the nations (in fulfillment of Ps 98:2, 9) *"apart from the law"* (3:21).

None of this is meant to abstract God's righteousness as saving activity from the work (obedience) of Christ. But it is to say that this salvation-historical reading of the text necessitates a paradigm shift away from the old *loci*-type of discussion of righteousness/justification to an awareness that Paul represents Christ as the bringer of a new creation and a new exodus, the liberator from the bondage of sin and defilement. It is only by "biting the bullet" and making the paradigm shift that we can recover the original *dynamic* of the biblical doctrine of justification.

For further buttressing evidence, Piper cites 2 Cor 5:21. In support of Piper *vis-à-vis* Gundry, I would maintain that God's righteousness is not to be distinguished from Christ's righteousness. For all practical purposes, they are one and the same, especially in light of Paul's affirmation of two verses earlier that *God was in Christ* reconciling the world to himself (5:19). On the other hand, it would appear to me that Gundry's handling of this text is not as "vague" as Piper would have us believe (68). Indeed, Gundry is precisely on the mark by his notice that "Paul uses the language of union, reconciliation, being made, and becoming rather than the language of imputation" (ibid.).

Piper rejoins that the question is not about "mere explicitness" of language, but about "the *reality* revealed through language" (ibid.). This, of course, involves a certain amount of question begging. He seeks to justify that imputation is the reality embedded in this verse by an appeal to the other side of the coin: Christ being made "sin" for us. His reasoning here is essentially circular. He assumes that Christ became sin by virtue of the imputation of our sins to him; therefore, it is not arbitrary or unnatural, he thinks, to understand God's righteousness in terms of imputation as well. In fairness, the verb *logizomai* does occur in the immediate context (v. 19), translated by Piper as "*not imputing their trespasses to them.*" As noted above, the sense of *logizomai* as "set down to one's account" does occur in isolated instances (in classical Greek). However, it certainly is not the usual meaning, and it would appear that Piper presses it here (and elsewhere) in the interests of the thesis pursued in his book.

R. P. Martin's rendering, on the other hand, is much better: "*not charging* their trespasses against them," so as to hold the trespassers themselves accountable. He further notes that "reckon something to someone" (*logizesthai tini ti*) is a characteristic of Pauline soteriology and its idioms. He then correctly makes cross reference to Ps 32:2: "Happy is the man to whom Yahweh *does not reckon* sin."[26] V. P. Furnish likewise translates as "*not charging their trespasses to them,*" in the strongly forensic sense, and also picks up the allusion to Ps 32:2. He cites as well 2 Sam 19:19 (Shimei pleading with David): "Let now my Lord not charge me with transgression."[27] L. Belleville comments to the same effect: "To 'count against them' (*logizomenos autois*) in the world of commerce referred to calculating the amount of a debt.... Today we might think of charges on a credit card for which we are held legally responsible. Here it means not posting debts to our account that should be rightfully ours."[28] Cf. 1 Cor 13:5: loves does not "keep a record of evil" (*ou logizetai to kakon*).

Therefore, instead of having to bear the consequences of our trespasses ourselves, Paul, by a use of *the abstract for the concrete*, declares Christ to be a "sinner" who has taken accountability for our sins. It is certainly conceivable that Jesus became "sin" by virtue of the imputation of our trespasses to him; and on the theological level this is hardly an objectionable idea.

More to the point exegetically is the consideration that the notions of "sin" and "sinner," in biblical/Jewish thought, pertain largely to the realm of apostasy.[29] For Christ to be made "sin," or more concretely, a "sinner," is a way of saying that he was subjected to "the curse of the law," when he "became a curse for us" (Gal 3:13). Gal 3:13 is a fitting analogy to the present text in that Paul consigns the Messiah to the curse which befell the apostate of Deut 21:23.[30] The ultimate irony, then, is that the Christ, the one who knew (experienced) no sin, was treated as though he were one well-acquainted with sin. And more, by propounding the notion of a crucified Messiah, Paul forwards what F. F. Bruce calls a "blasphemous contradiction in terms."[31] What is at stake in 2 Cor 5:21, therefore, is not imputation, but what M. D. Hooker has termed "interchange in Christ."[32] That is to say, an exchange has taken place on the cross: Christ and we have switched places. He became what we were—sin—and we have become what he is—the very embodiment of God's righteousness.

Justification is not liberation from sin's mastery

At this stage of the book, methodological issues are raised. In brief, Piper registers his objections to "a controlling biblical-theological paradigm" for exegesis. To quote him:

> One of the troubling things about this "developing standard in biblical theological circles" is that it is generally expressed in the same vague and general ways that make systematic categories so annoying to exegetes. In other words, it bears all the marks of a widespread scholarly paradigm that exerts a controlling effect on the exegesis of texts that do not clearly support it (70, citing Gundry).

Piper then proceeds to complain that this "new paradigm" (73) "is so broad and vague ('salvific activity') that almost anything God does can be included in it—even punitive judgment, if the punishment is seen as judgment on the enemies of God's people and thus 'salvific' for the elect" (70).

By way of reply, it is a misnomer—and a very misleading one too—to call the biblical-theological approach to exegesis "broad and vague" just because it brings the panorama of redemptive history to bear on individual texts. The method seeks to be holistic, not atomistic (the tendency of the systematic-theological approach), in its appraisal of biblical passages. If the Bible is the "book of the acts of God,"[33] then God has acted supremely in Jesus Christ to bring to fulfillment the story of Israel.[34] If Jesus is the hope of Israel, one would simply expect that the Lord's workings with the ancient people would provide the most natural entrée into his latter-day speaking by his Son (Heb 1:2).

This being so, as R. B. Gaffin maintains, the primary interest of biblical study is the interest of the text itself, namely, the history which the text reports and interprets. The concern of exegesis, then, is with what lies behind the text—the history of salvation. The discipline which seeks to correlate the findings of historical exegesis is biblical theology. Gaffin is certainly right that "this is an insight that the program of biblical hermeneutics needs to test and consider more carefully."[35]

In the concrete, all this means that the context of Paul's pronouncements about justification, righteousness, redemption, etc., is none other than the prophetic Scriptures of Israel, in which his very gospel is anchored (Rom 1:2; 3:21; 16:26; Eph 3:4-6). It is hardly "broad and vague" to set Paul's "carefully-worded statements about justification" (71) within the panorama of the magnificent manner in which God has prepared the ground for the final revelation of his righteousness. It is, after all, just "the law and the prophets" that bear witness to the eschatological revelation of the righteousness of God (Rom 3:21). Consequently, Piper is guilty of rather egregious question begging in his allegation that this "widespread scholarly paradigm...exerts a controlling effect on the exegesis of texts that do not clearly support it" (70).

The "cash value" of Piper's aversion to the "new paradigm" is his resistance of justification as a liberation from sin. In part, his disinclination to think of justification in such terms is due to a certain understanding of the Greek verb *dikaioō*, traditionally translated as "justify" or "declare righteous." According to Piper, *dikaioō* consistently means "justify" in the declarative sense, not "purify" in the transformational sense (71). In so writing, he is particularly concerned not to merge "justification" and "sanctification."

In fairness once more, he realizes that it is not as though the one has nothing to do with the other:

> In a profound sense God's justifying act is "salvific" and is foundational and preparatory for all of God's subsequent sanctifying work by which we are liberated from sin's mastery. So the two works of God (justification and sanctification) are closely connected, and in the broadest sense justification "has to do with" liberation from sin's mastery. It "has to do with" it in the sense that justification gives the foundation of a right standing before God, through the imputation of divine righteousness, which is then followed by the blessings that come to a justified sinner, including the liberating, sanctifying work of God's Spirit (71).

After so saying, Piper takes on Gundry again. According to the latter (commenting on Rom 3:24-26), redemption means liberation from slavery. Therefore, "justification," for Gundry, "does not have to do with an exchange of our sins for the righteousness of Christ; rather, it has to do with liberation from sin's mastery" (71). In taking a stance over against such a conception of justification, Piper, again, is partially correct. In view of 2 Cor 5:21, an exchange or "interchange" has indeed taken place between Christ and the believer (see above). To this degree, Gundry has at least overstated his case by disallowing any sense in which Christ and we have "switched places." Certainly, the most natural way to understand prophetic passages such as Isa 61:10; Jer 23:6; 33:16 is in terms of the Lord Jesus becoming the righteousness of his people.

That said, Gundry is still right that redemption is indeed liberation from slavery and pertains especially to the release of Israel from Egyptian and later Babylonian bondage.[36] In brief, redemption has to do with the motif of new exodus/return from exile.[37] To my mind at least, to speak of God's justifying act as "salvific," as Piper does (71), opens the door to a more comprehensive understanding of justification than just the forensic declaration that the sinner has now been acquitted of all charges. Certainly, it does mean this much, and the primary forensic thrust of justification is not to be minimized. However, "salvific," within the scope of biblical thought, is never merely "getting over the hump" of the broken law of God which stands as a witness against one. "Salvation," rather, is two-sided. As Cranfield explains, the negative content of salvation is indicated in Rom 5:9: "it is salvation from the final eschatological wrath of God." But there is a positive side as well: "it is the restoration of the *doxa* [glory] which sinful men lack."[38] In order to be consistent with this definition, it must follow that a "salvific" justification entails no less than a return to the integrity of unfallen Adam before his apostasy from God the Creator.

In this light, P. Stuhlmacher's conclusion, as quoted by Piper, is difficult to resist: "the dogmatic distinction…between a justification which is first only reckoned legally (forensic-imputed) and a justification which is creatively at work (effective) is…an unbiblical abstraction."[39] Furthermore, as a biblical theologian, Stuhlmacher is sensitive to the fact that "in the Old Testament, in the early Jewish tradition, and in the NT, God's righteousness thus means the salvific activity of God the creator and judge, who creates for those concerned righteousness and well-being."[40] In fact, the sequel to this last statement is worth quoting at length.

> In this way Paul made the expression "the righteousness of God" the center of the gospel in that, together with the Christians before and beside him, he spoke of God's salvific activity for the sinful world in and through Christ and related God's righteousness strictly to faith. Through faith in Jesus Christ as redeemer and Lord, every individual Jew and Gentile obtains a positive share in the work of the one, just God who brings forth through Jesus Christ peace, salvation, and deliverance for Israel, the Gentile nations, and the (nonhuman) creation. For Paul and his apocalyptic view of history and creation, the final judgment of the entire world is soon approaching. To obtain a share in God's righteousness by virtue of faith means to be acquitted of all guilt and to be accepted in the new world of God in which death (and with it all distress) will be overcome (cf. Rom 8:18ff.; 1 Cor 15:50ff.). But in Paul's gospel this righteousness of God is already being revealed before the beginning of the day of judgment and made possible for those who believe.[41]

Against this broad biblical backdrop, Gundry is not wrong to infer from Rom 3:24 that justification entails liberation from the mastery of sin. At the very least, we can say with J. A. Ziesler that "the use of this image [redemption] reminds us that though the focus of the passage is on acceptance/justification, and so on the removal of guilt, the idea of release from slavery is also present."[42] Yet we can go even further by paying attention to Paul's exact wording: it is *through the redemption* in Christ Jesus that all are justified. The commentators all seize on the theological import of "redemption" without giving the preposition "through" (*dia*) due consideration.[43] Yet Paul's language is clear enough: in strict terms, *justification transpires by means of redemption.* Since Paul was not encumbered by an *ordo salutis*, he could reverse what to us moderns is the proper order—*first* justification and *then* deliverance from sin![44] But what, at first sight, might strike us as being odd makes perfectly good sense given the sequence of events in the Prophets: *first* the people are delivered from captivity and *thereupon* are "justified" or vindicated as the faithful remnant returned from exile.[45]

Even apart from this exegetical datum, on the theological level is it simply true that where justification is found deliverance is as well; the one is incomplete without the other. If, in our theology, justification is meant to eventuate in liberation from sin's mastery (= "sanctification"), it would indeed seem like an unbiblical abstraction to place the two, as it were, in hermetically sealed containers. There must always be an ebb and flow, a give and take, between the two. As the saying goes, "the model has to breathe."

For the next number of pages (73-79), Piper pursues the question of how the "new paradigm" mishandles, in his view, the teaching on justification in Rom 6:6-7. He correctly notes that v. 7 provides the rationale for v. 6. That is to say, the reality of our death to sin is predicated on the basis of our having been "justified from sin" The question is, then: *How* does v. 7 ground v. 6? "Does it ground it by saying that when you die with Christ you are freed from sinning? Or does it ground verse 6 by saying that when you die with Christ, you are freed from the guilt and condemnation of sin—that is, that you are justified and acquitted from sin and now have a right standing with God" (75)?

Having posed the issue in these terms, Piper again chastises Gundry for assuming that "justification from sin" means liberation from sin's mastery (75). In pressing his hard-and-fast distinction between justification and liberation, Piper allows that the former may refer to the "indispensable foundation" of the latter: "It may be that justification—as declaration of freedom from guilt and condemnation—is that without which we could not even get started in the battle against sin's dominion" (75-76).

By way of parallel, he cites Acts 13:39, where likewise the phrase "justified from" appears. In light of the preceding verse, it is inferred that the phrase cannot mean "liberated from," but rather "acquitted from" or "forgiven for." Thus, Rom 6:7 is likely to have this meaning. "If so," he writes, "the point of verse 7 would be to give not a definition but a *ground* for the ethical transformation of verse 6. The ground for no longer being enslaved to sin (v. 6) is our justified standing with God (v. 7)" (76 [italics his]).

In contrast to the "new paradigm," Piper continues by advancing another way of reading Rom 6:6-7. He begins by reiterating the conviction that the verb *dikaioō* is incapable of meaning "liberate" and must, therefore, bear the meaning it "always has," that is, "declare righteous." Not unexpectedly, then, it is argued that "God's imputed righteousness, and our right standing with God, over against our sin (Rom 6:7) is the clear and distinct and necessary ground for sanctification—our liberation from sin (v. 6, 'no longer enslaved to sin')" (77).

Next, Piper contends that the very presence of the questions, "Are we to continue in sin that grace may increase?" (Rom 6:1), and "Shall we sin because we are not under law but under grace?" (Rom 6:15), is a "powerful indication that justification does not include liberation from the mastery of sin." "For if it did, these questions would not plausibly arise. If Paul had just spent three chapters teaching that justification means God's powerful salvific activity in liberating people from the mastery of sin, why would the question arise: So shall we sin that grace may abound" (ibid.)?

In Piper's opinion, what gives some measure of plausibility to these rhetorical questions of Rom 6:1 and 6:15 is the teaching of Romans 3-5 that "justification is emphatically not liberation from the mastery of sin;" it does not include sanctification. Such is precisely what creates the need for Paul to write Romans 6-8: to show why God's imputing his own righteousness to us by faith apart from works does not result in lawlessness, but in fact necessarily leads to righteous living. Therefore, Piper avers, we are not at all encouraged to blur the relationship between sanctification and justification that Paul preserves in Rom 6:6-7: justification is the necessary and prior basis of sanctification (77-78).

This subsection of the book is rounded off with the proposal that sin enslaves by its guilt, resulting in hopelessness and despair. The remedy to sin's guilt is justification as legal acquittal from sin, and the declaration of our righteousness before God grounds the possibility of liberation from slavery to sin. "In wakening hope for acceptance with God by faith alone, it creates the very possibility and foundation for fighting against the bondage of sin that enslaves us" (78-79).

Without anything like a comprehensive reply, I would like to touch on the salient points of Piper's presentation.

(1) First of all, there is the matter of the verb *dikaioō*. Traditional translations of this verb have been guilty of reductionism, as though the verb always and only means "declare righteous." A survey of the extant Greek literature argues quite otherwise. In point of fact, *dikaioō* is not an easy verb to translate. As is true of any Greek word, there is no one English equivalent to cover its every usage;[46] its overall significance is determined by the cluster of ideas stemming from the OT and Paul's use of it in specific contexts. I refer simply to my previous study of the term.[47] The only real point to be made here is that the semantic range of *dikaioō* is broad enough to cover liberation from sin as well as declarative justification.[48]

(2) Second, in Rom 6:7, Paul speaks specifically of being "justified from sin." Not unexpectedly, commentators are divided on the precise import of this conjunction of terms, just because of its rarity in the literature. Besides Acts 13:39, Dunn points to two other (non-canonical) occurrences of *dikaioō* followed by the preposition *apo* ("from"): Sir 26:29: "A merchant can hardly keep from wrongdoing, and a tradesman will not be *declared innocent of sin*;" and *T. Sim.* 6:1: "See, I have told you everything, so that I might be *exonerated with regard to* sin." Dunn then paraphrases the verse as "declared free from (responsibility in relation to) sin."[49] In this light, Piper's translation, "acquitted from" or "forgiven for," is not to be ruled out of court. The resultant English is somewhat awkward, but then so is any attempt to render Paul's Greek quite literally.[50]

D. J. Moo, in contrast to Dunn and Piper, takes "justified from sin" to mean "set free from [the power of] sin."[51] Some such wording does have the advantage of smoothing out the problem of translation, while fitting quite naturally into the conceptual framework of Rom 6:1-7:6 as a whole, which is entirely devoted to the proposition that the believer has been delivered from the clutches of sin. The point only gains in strength if this text is placed against its natural backdrop of exile and return—the redemption of Israel (see below).

Moo, however, points to two further occurrences of *dikaioō* as construed with *apo*: Matt 11:19 = Luke 7:35, noting, however, that in these texts *dikaioō* means to "vindicate."[52] Without developing the idea at all, Moo perhaps has hit on something. I would contend that "justify" and "vindicate" are synonymous, at least virtually.[53] In biblical-theological perspective, the justification of the people of God is their vindication when they return to the land and resume their privileged position within the covenant. Thus, "vindicate from sin" would make fine sense as meaning that we have been absolved with regard to the charges of sin.

Perhaps the solution lies in a combination of ideas. The possibility exists that Paul has telescoped his language, so as to compact at least two ideas into one set of words. That is to say, his meaning could be: "the one who has died has been justified/vindicated, so that he has been freed from sin." In this case, the more usual sense of *dikaioō* could be retained, with, nonetheless, the stress falling on justification in its liberating effects. It would not be unlike Paul to compress complementary and overlapping ideas into a streamlined construction (the most famous of which is "the righteousness of God," not to mention "the obedience of faith").

If we ask what in this context would account for Paul's peculiar turn of phrase, the answer is readily at hand, in Rom 6:17-18: "But thanks be to God that you, having once been slaves of sin, have become obedient from the heart to the form of teaching to which you were entrusted, and that you, *having been set free from sin*, have become slaves of righteousness" (NRSV). In this parallel (neglected by Piper), we have a clue to the unusual and almost unprecedented locution, "justify from."

To pick up from my earlier study of justification, the motif of liberation from a captive power is entirely explicable within the cadre of the righteousness of God as his saving activity to redeem Israel from her oppressors. As Wright explains, in the setting of the Prophets, God is the judge. Israel comes before him to plead her case against the wicked pagans who are oppressing her. She longs for her case to come to court, for God to hear it, and, in his own righteousness, to deliver her from her enemies. She longs, that is, to be justified, acquitted, vindicated. And because the God who is the judge is also her covenant God, she pleads with him; be faithful to your covenant! Vindicate me in your righteousness![54]

> In Paul, all this is transposed into the "higher octave" of what God has done in Christ at the turning of the ages—his own "eschatological courtroom." The actual enemy of believers is not Babylon (or Egypt) but Satan himself. He is the strong man who held them in the bondage of sin (Matthew 12:29; Luke 11:21-22); he is

"the accuser of our brothers, who accuses them before our God day and night" (Revelation 12:10; cf. Romans 8:33-34a). It is this cluster of ideas which is embodied by *dikaioō*. If God's righteousness is "his intervention in a saving act on behalf of his people," then the passive voice of the verb means "to be an object of the saving righteousness of God (so as to be well-pleasing to him at the judgment)."[55] When God in Christ intervenes to save his covenant partners, he plants them again in the newly created land, the new heavens and earth, never to be removed. This is "salvation" in the pregnant sense of the term: deliverance from evil and the bestowal of "peace" on a redeemed people. In short, justification in Paul signals deliverance from exile and freedom from bondage (one of the key motifs of Galatians). One of the clearest indications is the relationship of Romans 6:7 and 18. In the former verse, *dikaioō* is literally translated "justified from sin." As such, it forms a parallelism with the verb "liberated from sin" (*eleutheroō*) in 6:18. The parallel is best preserved by rendering 6:7 as "freed from sin." Therefore, when Paul writes of justification, he characteristically has in mind the new exodus on which the latter-day people of God have embarked. Moreover, this saving righteousness is cosmic in its dimensions. At the end of the day, "the righteousness of God" is actively directed at the rescue of the creation.[56]

Schreiner's exposition of Rom 6:7 is very much in accord with the one represented herein. According to Schreiner, the verb "justified" (*dedikaiōtai*, here in the perfect tense) is not merely forensic in v. 7, as is clear from the way the entire proposition of v. 7 relates to v. 6. The argument, he writes, seems to be that *righteousness necessarily involves freedom from the power of sin*.

> This point is crucial for Paul's argument. Justification cannot be separated from sanctification.... Only those who have died with Christ are righteous and thereby are enabled to conquer the mastery of sin. Many commentators have struggled with the use of *dedikaiōtai* in a context in which power over sin is the theme because they invariably limit justification to being declared righteous. The use of the verb in this context, however, suggests that *righteousness is more than forensic in Paul. Those who are in a right relation to God have also been dramatically changed; they have*

also been made righteous. This is confirmed by the language of being enslaved to righteousness (cf. 6:18, 20, 22); believers have been transformed by the Spirit (cf. 2 Corinthians 3:8-9)....[57]

Some may be surprised that John Murray comes remarkably close to the understanding of Rom 6:7 advocated by the proponents of the "new paradigm." Far from sharply bifurcating justification and freedom from sin, Murray proposes the following:

> "Justified from sin" will have to bear the forensic meaning in view of the forensic import of the word "justify". But since the context deals with deliverance from the power of sin the thought is, no doubt, that of being "quit" of sin. The decisive breach with the reigning power of sin is viewed after the analogy of the kind of dismissal which a judge gives when an arraigned person is justified. Sin has no further claim upon the person who is thus vindicated. This judicial aspect from which deliverance from the power of sin is to be viewed needs to be appreciated. It shows that the forensic is present not only in justification but also in that which lies at the basis of sanctification. A judgment is executed upon the power of sin in the death of Christ (cf. John 12:31) and deliverance from this power on the part of the believer arises from the efficacy of this judgment. This also prepares us for the interpretation of the forensic terms which Paul uses later in 8:1, 3, namely, "condemnation" and "condemned", and shows that *these terms may likewise point to that which Christ once for all wrought in reference to the power of sin (8:3) and to our deliverance from this power in virtue of the judgment executed upon it in Jesus' cross* (8:1).[58]

At the end of the day, whatever we make precisely of the expression "justify from" on the semantic plane, on the conceptual level the intention is clear enough: *dikaioō* is the functional equivalent of *eleutheroō*. In the act of justification, we have been "set free from" sin, in both its legal and behavioral effects, and have become enslaved to righteousness.[59] *Dikaioō* is thus seen to be flexible enough to overlap with *eleutheroō*.

Acts 13:38-39 presents us with the same ambiguity as Rom 6:17, and commentators are divided along the same lines as before. C. K. Barrett is of the opinion that *dikaioō* followed by *apo* does not bear its "usual Pauline forensic sense," but rather means something like "release from."[60] B. Witherington rightly remarks that the language of justification and faith in Christ echoes the basic Pauline message, but in the sense that "Jesus sets one free from all sins."[61] Schrenk too takes the verb to signify liberation.[62] On the other hand, F. F. Bruce thinks that *dikaioō* is "justify" and should not have its force "weakened" by the rendering "be freed."[63] J. A. Fitzmyer agrees.[64]

Once more, we may opt for one understanding or the other, or it may be, as suggested above, that Paul's language is telescoped, so as to include both justification and liberation (I would add that the translation "freed from" is hardly a "weakened sense," as in Bruce's estimation). In any event, that v. 38 makes reference to the forgiveness of sins hardly clinches Piper's exclusive translations of "acquitted from" or "forgiven for." If we are forgiven, we are, by definition, no longer in bondage to sin. Moreover, in the setting of the Hebrew covenant (remember, Paul is here speaking to Jews), forgiveness is always with a view to restoration to covenant privileges and responsibilities. It is vital to recall that even in those instances in the LXX where *dikaioō* is strongly forensic, Ziesler reminds us that it is forensic in the *Hebrew* sense, that is, the verb signifies "restoration of the community or covenant relationship, and thus cannot be separated from the ethical altogether. The restoration is not merely to a standing, but to an existence in the relationship."[65]

(3) Third, there is Piper's contention that if Paul had just spent three chapters teaching that justification means God's powerful salvific activity in liberating people from the mastery of sin, why would the question arise: "So shall we sin that grace may abound?" The most obvious rejoinder is that Paul is forced to deal with a *misunderstanding* of his teaching up to this point in Romans. As Dunn notes, the question of Rom 6:1 arises because the previous teaching is controversial.[66] In particular, in 5:20-21, Paul has had the temerity to claim that *Christ, not the Torah, is the source of life*.

Various Jewish sources voice the conviction that the law in of itself would insure life. Ben Sira uses the actual phrase "the law of life" (Sir 17:11; 45:5), while the author of Bar commends to his readers "the commandments of life" (Bar 3:9). These commandments are no less than the very embodiment of Israel's wisdom: "All who hold her fast will live, and those who forsake her will die" (Bar 4:1; see also *4 Ezra* 14:30; *Pss Sol.* 14:2; cf. *4 Ezra* 7:129). Hand in hand went the equally strong conviction that the law was eternal and unchangeable (e.g., Sir 24:9, 33; Bar 4:1; *Jub.* 16:29; 31:32; 32:10, 15, 21-26, 28; 33:10; Wis 18:4; *T. Naph.* 3:1-2; *4 Ezra* 9:26-37).

In the face of these traditions, Paul's stance is altogether conspicuous. For one thing, the verb "come in alongside" (*pareisēlthen*), in v. 20, implies that the law is not eternal: its entrance onto the stage of history was occasioned only by the advent of sin (5:12). More startling yet is the law's actual function—to intensify the problem created by Adam, that is, to cause sin to reign in death. "Trespass" and "sin" are retained from the foregoing discussion in Romans 5, signifying that Adam's apostasy has not, as supposed, been rectified by the Torah, because it preeminently is the stimulus of "trespass" and "sin." The nation of Israel preferred to view the law as God's definitive answer to sin rather than only a means to an end, that is, as preparation for the "coming one" (v. 14), whose act of obedience would put an end to sin forever. In Paul's mind, therefore, Israel's "sin" has abounded all the more because of her misunderstanding and misapplication of the Torah.

Hence, the specific point of dispute pertains to the place and function of the law in the new creation. To the Jewish mind, the law functioned as an identity marker and a boundary, reinforcing Israel's distinctiveness and separation from the nations. As *Jub.* 22:16 not so delicately puts it: "Separate yourself from the Gentiles, and do not eat with them, and do not perform deeds like theirs. And do not become associates of theirs. Because their deeds are defiled, and all of their ways are contaminated and despicable, and abominable." *Ep. Arist.* (139, 142) expresses the same conviction in terms which reinforce this sociological function of the law:

> In his wisdom the legislator...surrounded us with unbroken palisades and iron walls to prevent our mixing with any of the other peoples in any matter.... So, to prevent our being perverted by contact with others or by mixing with bad influences, he hedges us in on all sides with strict observances connected with meat and drink and touch and hearing and sight, after the manner of the law.

Note particularly how the author links observance of the food laws with protection from defiling contact ("bad influences") with outsiders. What entered the mouth, as prescribed by Moses, had scrupulously to be monitored, otherwise the flood gates to pagan immorality would be flung wide open (contrast Mark 7:14-23). Consistent with this consciousness of separation by the "fence" of the Torah is the appraisal of others as outsiders: these were the "lawless" and the "sinners," that is, either pagans who never were within the pale of the law or apostate Jews. It is just this desire to live within the law, to be marked off from the "lawless" and the "sinner," which became in time a dominant concern in the factionalism of the period from the Maccabees to the emergence of rabbinic Judaism.

In this light, Paul's Jewish objector draws what to him is the logical consequence of the apostle's pronouncements in the last paragraph of Romans 5. If life can be obtained through some other source than the Torah, then it follows that *God has removed his safeguard against sin*: Why not, then, sin that grace may abound? Paul's interlocutor thus charges that antinomianism is the logical product of his theology. Accordingly, Paul's rejoinder is that far from opening the doors to sin, new creation life in Christ means yielding one's members to righteousness, not sin. What counts is union with Christ (6:5-11), not an ongoing relationship with the law.

As an indication that Paul has in fact taught liberation from sin prior to Romans 6, I would submit Rom 5:18, with its phrase "the justification of life (*dikaiōsis zoēs*)." It is just the concept of life that forms one of the linchpins connecting Romans 5 and 6. The former chapter concludes on this note (5:21, as preceded by vv. 17-18), and the latter virtually commences with the same theme (6:4-11).

"Life" may be taken as the "eternal life" (Rom 2:7) of "the age to come," the restoration of the Creator/creature relationship enjoyed in Eden. In keeping with the apocalyptic outlook generally, "life" in Paul is eschatological and protological at the same time: the end is a return to the beginning. Yet what is the relation of "justification" to "life?" I would propose that inasmuch as Paul's use of the Greek genitive case (in this case, "of life") frequently ignores established conventions, it is plausible to see the present instance as a mingling of various types of genitive: qualitative, result, direction and epexegetical. But whatever grammatical tags are applied, F. J. Leenhardt's comments are particularly relevant. The phrase "justification of life" speaks of "a justification which introduces us to divine life;" and given the close connection of present and future eschatological life in Paul, "justification of life" "suggest equally the idea of a justification which is here and now realized in a life which concretely practises righteousness, as will shortly be said (6:11, 13, 16, 18, 19, 22, 23). It will be noted that Christ's obedience of which our text speaks becomes also the believer's obedience, an obedience which leads to the practise of righteousness (6:16)."[67]

If, then, our justification is one that has resulted in life, and we have been raised with Christ and have become partakers of the life of the age to come, *ipso facto* we have been liberated from sin. Rom 6:1-7:6 is but the unpacking of the implications of "life."

In addition to everything else, Piper's reasoning can be turned against him. A similar objection to Paul's theology is raised in Rom 6:15: "Are we to sin because we are not under law but under grace?" Are we to assume that Paul had not taught such a thing in Romans 3-5 just because some opponent is barking up the wrong tree? In principle, he certainly has instructed us that we are not under law but under grace. See 3:21-31; 4:13-14; 5:12-21 (where the law is placed in the old Adamic era of sin and condemnation, which era we have exited because of the obedience of Christ on our behalf).

(4) In the fourth place, the caveat that we must not blur the relationship between justification and sanctification rests on the underlying *ordo salutis* (order of salvation) that forms a significant substratum of Piper's book. We will return to this in the concluding reflections. Suffice it to say here that the grid provided by an *ordo salutis* necessitates a rigid distinction between the two, because, on this construction, justification and sanctification refer to two distinct entities. However, a different approach, a *historia salutis* (history of salvation), will yield different results. If justification is conceived of as the entry into the covenant relationship, then it marks the point at which our "definitive sanctification," to use John Murray's phrase, commences.[68] Rather than "blurring" the justification/sanctification distinction, I would prefer to speak in terms of the mutual interpenetration of the concepts, as illustrated by overlapping circles.[69]

In this regard, Brad Young very helpfully calls to mind that Paul's thinking is Jewish in character, a telling point when it comes to comprehending and unpacking his universe of discourse.

> As a Jewish theologian, Paul pursues a conceptual approach to his teachings. His thought processes are not linear but circular. His theological concepts are interactive. Indeed, they are connected one with another in continuous motion. Paul's keen intellect works

quickly. The apostle understands God and his great love for all humanity as a vibrant whole. One concept belongs to a complex of interactive ideas. Each term he uses to communicate his thought is clustered with other interactive concepts concerning God's relationship to people.... When the contours of Pauline thought are considered in a cycle of interactive concepts rather than in a straight line where each new idea supersedes and eliminates the previous one, the apostle's conceptual approach to God is given fresh vigor. It is a Jewish way of thinking.[70]

Consequently, what might appear to the Western mind as a "blurring" of ideas is actually, in the Jewish mindset, what Young calls "a cycle of interactive concepts." The hermeneutical impact of this observation is apparent enough: modern interpreters must be prepared to undergo a paradigm shift to this Jewish way of thinking in order to enter the thought processes of the apostle, and indeed of the biblical writers generally.

(5) Fifth, one can agree that sin enslaves by its guilt, resulting in hopelessness and despair, and that the remedy to sin's guilt is justification as legal acquittal from sin and the declaration of our righteousness before God. This much is certain. Nevertheless, the reason why people experience the *guilt* of sin is because of their *practice* of sin. Accordingly, the guilt of sin decreases both because of forensic justification and the ability imparted by the same justification to yield our members as implements of righteousness (Rom 6:19). To this end, we are to "reckon" or "consider" (*logizomai*) ourselves dead to sin and alive to God in Christ (Rom 6:11).

After all is said and done, one may argue, and argue well, on the basis of Rom 6:7 (and Acts 13:38) for a forensic justification. The problem with Piper's particular construction, however, is twofold. One, he has to assume that such a justification is made possible only by means of imputation, because the term and the concept nowhere appear in Romans 6. Granted, he makes his assumption on the basis of Romans 4; but, of course, a different reading of Romans 4 will remove the foundation of that supposition. Two, Piper's bifurcation of justification and freedom from sin is a false dichotomy that results, in Stuhlmacher's words, in "an unbiblical abstraction."[71]

Piper's final bit of supporting evidence that (in his view) justification is not liberation from sin's mastery is the flow of thought in Rom 8:3-4. The argument again is from cause to effect:

justification results in sanctification. It is doubtful that anyone would disagree with this, given that sanctification, as defined by Piper, is "progressive." I would only qualify that against the backdrop of Romans 6, as illumined by Murray's study, there is a "definitive" quality to sanctification, one that coincides with justification. In any event, Rom 8:3-4 says nothing about imputation.

Piper's conclusion to this entire subsection of the book is that the "assault" on the historic distinction between justification and sanctification is unsuccessful. He finds no exegetical warrant for allowing the "vague and general designation" of the righteousness of God as "salvific activity" to lead us away from the traditional understanding of justification as the imputation of divine righteousness. Accordingly, Piper sees no exegetical warrant for construing justification so as to include liberation from sin's mastery. Gundry's arguments in particular, says Piper, "do not overthrow the traditional Protestant understanding of Scripture that finds in justification the imputation of divine righteousness and a clear and necessary distinction between this act and God's subsequent and necessary work of sanctification" (80).

Our response can be brief. (1) God's righteousness as "salvific activity" is hardly "vague and general." On the contrary, it is as concrete as any concept could be, taking its place squarely within the continuum of salvation history. All one needs do is read Paul against the backdrop of the Prophets of Israel, who so graphically and *concretely* depict the time when Yahweh would spring into action to terminate the exile and plant his people again in the land. (2) As for myself, there is in fact copious exegetical warrant for construing justification in such a way as to include liberation from sin's mastery, and such exegetical considerations have been presented above. (3) It is not the purpose of this paper to "overthrow" anything, but to submit that the inflexible justification/sanctification model, at the very least, is in need of qualification. It is too schematized and too "scholastic" to allow for the dynamic, not to say dramatic, character of what God has done in Christ to effect a new creation out of the chaos of sin. (4) The most conspicuous shortcoming of this division of the book is the given that justification must transpire by means of imputation and by no other means. I can only say that there is no exegetical warrant for such an assumption.

Is the divine righteousness that is imputed to believers the righteousness of Christ?

In this penultimate segment of the book, Dr. Piper adduces passages in support of his proposal that the righteousness imputed to the believer is specifically that *of Christ*.

2 Corinthians 5:21 and Philippians 3:9

Piper revisits these two passages to which appeal has been made before. As to the former, he does concede that this text does not say explicitly that Christ's righteousness is imputed to believers. "But," he adds, "it does say that believers, because they are 'in Christ,' become God's righteousness the way Christ was made sin as a sinless person" (82). Precisely! Paul points us to the "in Christ" experience as the source of our righteousness.

The problem is that Piper thinks it necessary to resort to imputation to explain the "mechanics" of how we have become the righteousness of God. The same is true of Charles Hodge and G. E. Ladd, both quoted by Piper (81-83). All three are quite right that it is *Christ's righteousness* that has been made ours. Yet apparently for the sake "doctrinal explicitness" and "systemization" (81, n. 26) it is not sufficient to stick with the actual import of Paul's words. Rather, it is thought that only imputation will explain how such a text as this "ticks." I would submit otherwise: *union with Christ is the modality of our becoming "the righteousness of God."*

As 2 Cor 5:21, Phil 3:9 has been addressed above. The point we endeavored to press from this verse is actually affirmed by Piper (84).

> Notice that the righteousness Paul counts on having "from God" is pursued with a longing to "be found in Christ." The righteousness that he has is his because he is "found in Christ." This use of "In Christ" is positional. In Christ by faith is the place where God's righteousness counts as our own. Thus "being found in Christ" is the way to "have a righteousness not my own."

However, an otherwise excellent comment is marred by the follow-up remark: "True, this does not say explicitly that Christ's righteousness is imputed to us, but along with the other evidence presented here that is *a natural implication of this verse*" (ibid. [italics mine]). It is just the "natural implication" that is at issue. It seems to me far simpler and exegetically more straightforward just to stay with the Pauline language. Everything is explained by his doctrine of union with Christ, and one need look no further for a rationale or elucidation. Apart from the factor of imputation, the passage from Calvin quoted by Piper (ibid., n. 30) says it all:

> Therefore, that joining together of Head and members, that indwelling of Christ in our heart—in short, that mystical union—are accorded by us the highest degree of importance, so that Christ, having been made ours, makes us sharers with him in the gifts with which he has been endowed. We do not, therefore, contemplate him outside ourselves from afar in order that his righteousness may be imputed to us but because we put on Christ and are engrafted into his body—in short, because, he deigns to make us one with him. For this reason, we glory that we have fellowship of righteousness with him.[72]

1 Corinthians 1:30

Piper is correct, *vis-à-vis* Gundry, to insist that our union with Christ is what connects us with divine righteousness. The quotation from C. K. Barrett is apropos (85-86):

> The root of the thought is forensic: man is arraigned in God's court, and is unable to satisfy the judge unless righteousness, which he cannot himself produce, is given to him.... Christ himself becomes righteousness for him (2 Cor. 5:21), and God the judge views him not as he is in himself but in Christ.[73]

Piper then reacts to the criticism that he has simply assumed the presence of imputation in this passage. In order to provide our own response, we must hear him in his own words (86-87):

> One may object that Christ's becoming sanctification for us is not an imputed reality but rather is worked in us; so why should we assume that Christ's becoming righteousness for us refers to an imputed righteousness? In answer, I don't *assume* it. Instead I note that the other passages that connect righteousness with being "in Christ" have to do with justification (Galatians

> 2:17) and speak of a righteousness that is "not our own" (Philippians 3:9) and that "we become the righteousness of God" in the same way Christ became sin, that is, by imputation (2 Corinthians 5:21). Then I observe that there is no reason to think that Christ must "become" for us righteousness exactly the same way he becomes wisdom and sanctification and redemption. This is not said or implied.
>
> In fact, it is plausible to see a natural progression in the four realities that Christ is for us. In our union with Christ he becomes "wisdom" for us in overcoming the blinding and deadening ignorance that keeps us from seeing the glory of the cross (1 Corinthians 1:24). Then he becomes righteousness for us in overcoming our guilt and condemnation (Romans 8:1). Then he becomes sanctification for us in overcoming our corruption and pollution (1 Corinthians 1:2; Ephesians 2:10). Finally, he becomes redemption for us in overcoming, in the resurrection, all the miseries, pain, futility, and death of this age (Romans 8:23). There is no reason to force this text to mean that Christ becomes all these things for us in exactly the same way, namely, by imputation. He may become each of these things for us as each reality requires.

In reply, first of all, it would be unfair to charge that Piper engages in bare presuppositionalism with regard to 1 Cor 1:30, without recourse to other passages that, in his view, teach imputation. To be sure, there are other texts that connect righteousness with being "in Christ," that have to do with justification as a righteousness "not our own," and that teach that "we become the righteousness of God" in the same way Christ became "sin." My only response is that these other passages, taken on their own terms, do not in fact speak of imputation (as I read them, of course).

Second, the point is taken that there is no reason to think that Christ must, at least in the abstract, "become" for us righteousness in exactly the same way that he becomes wisdom, sanctification and redemption. The problem, however, is that it has to be established that Paul does in fact contemplate righteousness in essentially different terms than these three categories.

I would argue that the *prima facie* impact of 1 Cor 1:30 is just that *union with Christ* is the source for all these blessings, with no discernible differentiation between them as pertains to modality or mechanics. Literally translated, Paul's Greek reads: "of him [God] you are *in Christ Jesus*, who became for us wisdom from God, and righteousness and sanctification and redemption." I would submit that an unbiased reading of the text yields the conclusion that Paul is affirming that Christ has become wisdom, sanctification and redemption in precisely the same manner as he has become righteousness for us. If so, then Wright is not off-base at all to maintain that if we take 1 Cor 1:30 as a textual basis for imputed righteousness, then "we must also be prepared to talk of the imputed wisdom of Christ; the imputed sanctification of Christ; and the imputed redemption of Christ."[74]

In the third place, Piper would seem to have constructed his own sort of *ordo salutis* on the basis of 1 Cor 1:30, as though Paul were following a schematized progression of salvific realities. That such a "natural progression" is present is not immediately evident, and certainly the commentators do not point to any particular order in Paul's choice of terms. That Paul is not thinking in *ordo salutis* terms is confirmed by the parallel statement in 1 Cor 6:11: "But you were washed, you were sanctified, you were justified in the name of the Lord Jesus Christ and in the Spirit of our God." Here, washing and sanctification precede justification, unthinkable in terms of an *ordo salutis*. Commenting on this text, G. R. Beasley-Murray can say that the "sanctification" by the Spirit and "justification" by the Lord Jesus occurred at the same time—it is a once-for-all consecration Paul has in mind, not a process.[75] In like manner, the "sanctification" of 1 Cor 1:30 makes perfectly good sense when viewed as "definitive," not "progressive" (as understood by Piper). "Sanctification," then, would correspond to the "righteousness" (covenant conformity) Christ became for us when we were incorporated into him.[76]

In sum, the evidence educed from these passages by Piper clearly confirms that the righteousness of God is none other than the righteousness of Christ. Nevertheless, it has not been established that *imputation* is the means by which Christ's righteousness becomes ours. As throughout, my contention is that Christ has become our righteousness by virtue of union with himself, plain and simple.

Romans 10:4

Apart from certain differences owing to my "New Perspective" reading of this verse, I must agree with Piper that Israel's problem was her failure to recognize Christ as the goal (*telos*) of the law, and that God's righteousness is now localized *in Christ* rather than the Torah. However, it is equally conspicuous that Rom 10:4 is silent about any notion of imputation. Piper is sensitive to this, and his appeal takes the following form:

> If one allows for biblical reflection and comparison and synthesis and a desire to penetrate to reality behind words (as with, for example, the biblical doctrines of the Trinity, the two natures of Christ, or the substitutionary atonement), then the doctrine of the imputation of Christ's righteousness is not an artificial construct of systematic theologians but is demanded by the relevant texts (90).

Certainly, anyone who believes in the unity of Scripture and its inspiration will want to engage in reflection, comparison and synthesis for the purpose of a penetrating analysis of the text. However, I would prefer to say that instead of realities "behind words," there are realities *embedded* in words. Granted, we may have to dig deep to uncover these embedded realities by none other than reflection, comparison and synthesis. Nevertheless, there must be the presence of *such words* that serve as symbols of or signposts to underlying realities (referents). The Trinity, the two natures of Christ and substitutionary atonement, I would say, are not appropriate analogies to imputation, simply because there is a preponderance of words that allow for the construction of a theology of each. Not so, I would argue, in the case of imputation: the pertinent words are simply not extant in the NT.

Romans 5:12-19

Now ensues a lengthy defense of imputation based on Rom 5:12-19. Again, it will be possible only to address the most salient aspects of Piper's argument.[77]

The reasoning deployed is that of analogy: just as Adam's sin was imputed to his posterity, so also the righteousness of Christ has been imputed to all who are in him. As Piper states: "The basis of our justification before God is a divine righteousness that comes to us in a way analogous to the way Adam's sin came to us. As we were in him and share in his sin, so we are in Christ and share in his righteousness" (93).

Foundational to this more or less traditional Reformed interpretation of "original sin" is the belief that verses 13-14 of Romans 5 have to do not with individual sins committed by the race of Adam, but Adam's own trespass which has now been credited to the account of all who are descended from him. According to Piper (94):

> Now what is the implication that Paul wants us to see? He wants us to see that universal human death was not owing to individual sins against the Mosaic Law, but to man's sinning in Adam. That is what he is trying to clarify. Verse 12, at the end, says that death spread to all "because all sinned." So Paul argues and clarifies: But people died even though their own individual lawbreaking was not the reason for dying; their individual sins weren't counted. The reason all died is because all sinned in Adam. Adam's sin was imputed to them.

Piper concedes that v. 14 could be read in another way than in terms of the imputation of Adam's sin. Those over whom death reigned from Adam to Moses could have been guilty: (1) of violating individual commands given before Moses; (2) of violating the law written on he heart (Rom 2:15). However, he rejects these possibilities, citing, in part, the case of the infants who died as the result of "the imputation of Adam's sin."

Piper qualifies that his argument does not hinge on infants being in view, but he defends the interpretation contextually in terms of Paul's perceived purpose for focusing on the period between Adam and Moses. For one thing, there is what he calls the way in which Paul "in general and loosely" points to solidarity with Adam in his transgression as the cause of everyone's death, not their own transgressions. Second, there is the "specific and strict" argument that relates to the legal implication of people dying as punishment in a time period that had no explicit laws specifying death penalties.

It is the second of these purposes, says Piper, that commands Paul's attention. "Paul is primarily concerned in Rom 5:12-21 concerned to show the *legal*, not the moral, triumph of grace over the *legal*, not moral, problem of sin" (99). As buttressing evidence, he cites the presence of the term "condemnation" in 5:16, which is taken to be (only) the legal consequence of death. The bottom line, then, of Piper's understanding of Rom 5:13-14 is that "death is not first, and most deeply, owing to our own individual sinning, but to our being connected with Adam in such a way that his sin really made us guilty and liable to condemnation" (100).

On the basis of all the above, Piper, as expected, draws the parallel between the imputation of Adam's sin and the imputation of Christ's righteousness (101-3):

> The parallel here is this: The judicial consequences of Adam's sin are experienced by all his people not on the basis of their doing sins like he did, but on the basis of their being in him and his sin being imputed to them. As soon as that becomes clear in Paul's argument—just at this point—he brings in Christ as the parallel. The point is to make clear what the focus of the parallel is: The judicial consequences of Christ's righteousness are experienced by all his people not on the basis of their doing righteous deeds like he did, but on the basis of their being in and his righteousness being imputed to them....
> So the problem of the human race is not most deeply that everybody does various kinds of sins. Those sins are real, they are huge, they are enough to condemn us, and they do indeed play a role in our condemnation. But the deepest problem is that behind all our depravity and all our guilt and all our sinning there is a deep mysterious connection with Adam, whose sin became our sin and whose judgment became our judgment. And the Savior from this condition and this damage is a Savior who stands in Adam's place as a kind of second Adam (or "the last Adam," 1 Corinthians 15:45). By his obedience he undoes what Adam did. By his obedience he fulfilled what Adam failed to do. In Adam all men were appointed (*katestathēsan*) "sinners," but all who are in Christ are appointed (*katastathēsontai*) "righteous" (5:19). In Adam all received condemnation; in Christ all receive justification (5:18).

The next phase of Piper's exposition is the contrast between Adam and Christ in Rom 5:15-17. Paul's aim, says Piper, is "to magnify the grace and sufficiency of the justification that comes through Christ for sinners" (103). Verse 15 strikes the contrast in terms of Adam's transgression as over against Christ's righteousness, which is understood as a gift. "The implication is that although Adam's transgression brought death to many, Christ's righteousness, as a free gift, abounded... for many" (104).

Verse 16 continues the contrast. From this verse, Piper deduces three things. (1) As the counterpart to "condemnation," justification is a declaration of righteousness, not liberation from sinning. (2) The judgment that resulted in condemnation is the counting of Adam's sin as our sin, on the basis of our union with Adam. (3) The foundation (basis) for justification is the free gift of Christ's righteousness.

Verse 17 then give another reason why the free gift is not like the effect of Adam's sin, but totally outstrips this one-to-one correspondence of the type and the antitype. "Paul's point is that the triumph of God's grace and gift of righteousness will not simply replace the reign of death with the reign of life, but rather "much more" will make *believers reign in life* like kings in the presence of our Father forever and ever" (106).

As all commentators acknowledge, vv. 18-19 of Romans 5 complete the comparison begun by Paul in v. 12 but immediately broken off by vv. 13-14. Piper now focuses on these verses. The main point of v. 18 is that justification happens to all who are connected to Christ, in the same manner that condemnation happened to those who were connected to Adam. Adam acted sinfully, and because we were connected to him, we are condemned in him. Christ acted righteously, and because we are connected to Christ we are justified in Christ. Adam's sin is counted as ours. Christ's "act of righteousness" is counted as ours.

Verse 19 supports this by making the same point in another way: through the disobedience of Adam many were made sinners, and through the obedience of Christ many will be made righteous. Paul here becomes more specific in explaining how Adam's sin brings condemnation and how Christ's righteousness brings justification. The fulcrum of the argument is the verb translated by NASB (and others) as "made" (*kathistēmi*). Piper favors the rendering of "appointed" because it is consistent with the doctrine of imputation. That is to say, many are "appointed" sinners or righteous by virtue of either Adam's sin or Christ's righteousness. In both cases, the stress falls not on personal transgressions or acts of righteousness, but on our connection with Adam or Christ respectively.

The treatment of Rom 5:12-19 is rounded off by a detailed defense of Christ's "one act of righteousness" as his life of obedience, as contra Gundry, who limits it to his death. In my estimation, each of Piper's arguments is well-taken. As Cranfield maintains, Christ's "one act of righteousness" (*dikaiōma*) is not just his death, but his obedient life as a whole: "His loving God with all His heart and soul and mind and strength, and His neighbour with complete sincerity, which is the righteous conduct which God's law requires."[78]

An adequate exegesis of Rom 5:12-19, with all its grammatical and theological complexities, would require a volume in itself.[79] So, our response must be limited to the actual points raised by Piper from the passage, which we shall take section by section.

Romans 5:12

To begin, there can hardly be any disagreement as to the basic analogical nature of Paul's argument: just as the work of Adam resulted in condemnation and death, so also the work of Christ has resulted in righteousness and life. The question, of course, pertains to whether these divergent effects are due to imputation or some other factor. The bedrock of Piper's particular reading of Romans 5 is the proposition that "universal human death was not owing to individual sins against the Mosaic Law, but to man's sinning in Adam.... The reason all died is because all sinned in Adam. Adam's sin was imputed to them" (94).

This more or less traditional Reformed interpretation of Rom 5:12 rests on the words of its last clause, frequently translated "all sinned" (*pantes hēmarton*), in the English simple past tense. That is to say, sin entered the world, and death through sin, because "all sinned" *in Adam*; that is, Adam's sin, by means of imputation, was made the personal responsibility of every human being descended from him and Eve. This view of "all sinned" was spearheaded by Augustine, who was influenced by the Vulgate's translation of the Greek words *eph' hō* in 5:12c (normally translated into English as "because") as *in quo*, that is, "in whom," namely, Adam. From that point onward, it was customarily assumed that Paul was asserting the dogma of "original sin" as formulated by later Roman Catholic (and Protestant) thought.

More contemporary exegetes who have rejected the Vulgate's rendering of *eph' hō* still latch onto the aorist tense of the verb "sinned" (*hēmarton*). L. Morris, for example, is quite sure that the tense has to point to "one act in the past"—the sin of Adam.[80] Yet in order to maintain such a once-for-all point of reference for "all sinned," that is, the sin of Adam in the Garden of Eden, it is necessary to bypass or at to least minimize the significance of *the very same combination of words* in Rom 3:23: "all have sinned (*pantes hēmarton*) and come short of the glory of God," Paul's epitome of the entire history of human apostasy and idolatry.

In turn, Rom 3:23 glances back to 3:9: Paul's indictment that Jew and Gentile alike are under sin," the bottom line to the foregoing discussion of mankind's rebellion against its Creator. In fact, 3:23 itself is a summary of 1:18-3:20—Paul's "covenant lawsuit" against the "sin" of the human race in Adam—in which Adam/creation motifs occupied a place of some prominence.[81] With the willing compliance of the first man, the agenda of creation was sabotaged by Satan, and all who bear Adam's likeness continue his resistance to the Creator and thus fall perpetually short of the divine image. Humanity (including Israel) in Adam is idolatrous (apostate) by definition: all his progeny bear his image in that they are born in a condition of estrangement from God (cf. Ps 51:5), with an inbuilt disposition to serve the creature rather than the Creator.

Hence, Rom 3:23, as it distills the charge of 1:18-3:20 that all are "under sin," sheds a considerable amount of light on Rom 5:12. In both cases, the words "all have sinned" are to be taken in the same sense, that is, death has spread to all because all *have sinned*, that is, all *have apostatized*, because of their union with Adam. Thus interpreted, the aorist in each instance is "constative" (summary) and is to be translated by the English present perfect tense.[82]

The point of these observations is to say that a mainstay of the argument for imputation is removed if Rom 5:12c has reference to personal and individual sin. But, then, how do we understand the immediately following verses?

Romans 5:13-14

In these verses, Paul provides a rationale for the proposition of v. 12: even in the period from Adam to Moses death reigned over those who did not sin "in the "likeness of Adam's trespass." With an apparent glance back to 4:15 ("where there is no law there is no transgression"), the reasoning seems to be that the generations of people between these two men must have violated some law. But what law? If our interpretation is correct that the sinning in 5:12 is not Adam's exclusively, then precisely which law has been broken, so as to account for sin and death?

As is true more than once in 5:12-19, Paul's logic is not made explicit, leaving us to discern his intentions from the broader setting of Romans. In one regard, his justification of v. 12 is a statement of the obvious, that is, the reality of death from Adam to Moses; yet, in another, he appears to beg the question, namely, the existence of a law antecedent to that delivered to Israel at the time of the exodus. However, in keeping with his procedure in Romans to bypass the Torah and return to creation, Paul is best understood as here building on presuppositions already established in 2:14-15. That is to say, by virtue of bearing the image of God, all humans are in possession of the law written on the heart, whose function was to regulate the aboriginal (creation) covenant, as seen by its present-day function of linking mankind to its Maker, in conjunction with the co-witness of the conscience (cf. 1:32). Death, therefore, was universal in the pre-Mosaic period because of the repudiation of *this* law, not the Torah. We are thus taken back to 1:18 in that the rejection of the law written on the heart is tantamount to the suppression of the knowledge of God.

It is thus explicable that there were those who died, even though they did not sin "in the likeness of Adam's transgression" (*epi tō homoiōmati tēs parabaseōs Adam*). As in 8:3, the noun *homoiōma* here means an "exact likeness."[83] We might say that Adam's descendants did not willfully rebuff a clearly revealed command (the normal meaning of "trespass" [*parabasis*] in Paul), as Israel was later to do. But more to the point, "the likeness of Adam's trespass" indicates that they did not do *precisely* what Adam did, that is, eat a piece of forbidden fruit in the Garden of Eden as an act of willful rebellion. Even so, they die because their sin in principle is an act of apostasy from Yahweh. In suppressing the knowledge of God inscribed on the heart (1:18-23), humanity in the first Adam has rejected God himself and, as a result, suffers the fate of Adam. It is especially noteworthy that Adam and Eve ate from "the tree of the knowledge of good and evil." "Good" and "evil" mean not so much "right" and "wrong" as *the* good of acknowledging God the Creator and *the* evil of renouncing him (see especially Deut 30:15; Isa 7:15; Rom 2:7-10; 7:13-20; 15:2; 16:19; 1 Cor 10:6-7).

In opposition to this appeal to "the law written on the heart," Piper cites the death of infants in the time-frame from Adam to Moses. Attention is frequently called to the fact that "those who did not sin after the likeness of Adam's trespass" (v. 14) are to be equated with the "all" who "sinned" (v. 12). This, of course, is correct. However, the most pertinent thing we can say is that a large substratum of the Roman letter is formed by the proposition that there is "no distinction" between Jew and Gentile. It is to this end that Paul uses the adjective "all" some 73 times in the epistle. A case in point is 3:23-24: all have sinned, and yet all are justified through the redemption in Christ. The focus here, as in 5:12c, is not so much quantitative as qualitative.[84] "All," in other words, has reference to the Jew/Gentile divide that has now been demolished in Christ. Therefore, in 5:14, Paul's sights are not set on infants or the mentally deficient. His argument is that Israel, as much as the Gentiles, is "in Adam" and repeats his sin.[85]

That Paul should single out the period from Adam to Moses makes most sense when viewed against the backdrop of his dialogue with Israel in 5:12-19.[86] Having stated his thesis that universal sin and death are the effect of one man's disobedience, Paul, in vv. 13-14, seems compelled to defend what he has written. Very noticeable, remarks Dunn, is the speed with which Paul's thought reverts to the law—a further indication that *it* was the chief point of tension between Paul the Christian and the traditional emphases of Judaism.[87] In particular, v. 12 would have appeared to the Jewish mind to contain a puzzling proposition. Given Paul's consistent denial of the existence of the law before Sinai, How could there have been sin strictly speaking, since, ostensibly, there was no law according to which sin could be reckoned? Sin, after all, for Judaism was measured in relation to *the Torah*. It is this which Paul now seeks to clarify.

His explanation glances back at 4:15b, "where there is no law there is no transgression," where these words are appended to the statement of the previous part of the verse, "for the law works wrath." By claiming, in 5:12, that "all" have sinned, Paul has implied that they have rejected God's law and have, therefore, been the recipients of wrath (death). This, of course, raises a historical problem: if the law (of Moses) works wrath, and if sin is not reckoned apart from the law, How could there have been sin and death before Sinai?

For a sizable segment of Judaism anyway, the answer was obvious: the Torah has existed from the dawn of history, and the nations are exposed to wrath because they have spurned the eternal Torah. As early as Ben Sira (2nd century BC) this idea is in evidence: Abraham himself kept none other than the law (of Moses) during a time of testing (Sir 44:20). Afterward, the author of *Jubilees* would make the same claim (24:11; cf. 23:10), as does a later rabbinic text (*Kidd.* 4:4). Even more striking in *Jubilees* is the preexistence of the law on "heavenly tablets," "the eternal books always before the Lord" (16:29; 31:32; 32:10, 15, 21-26, 28; 33:10; 39:7). The eternity of the law is likewise the conviction of Sir 24:9, 33; Bar 4:1; Wis 18:4; *T. Naph.* 3:1-2.[88]

In rather stark contrast, Paul allows that there was an era prior to and distinguishable from that of the Torah (v. 13a). A law has been spurned, a law which functions similarly to the law which "works wrath." However, it is not the law of the Sinai covenant, as in 4:15; it is, rather, some law in existence before the birth of Israel's nationhood, which effectively eliminates the grounds for Israel's boasting in the Torah; it is none other than this law, preceding the Torah, which produced death in the period from Adam to Moses (v. 14). Vv. 13-14, therefore, can be plausibly interpreted as the apostle's denial of a recognized tenet of Jewish theology. For him there was a period during which the Torah as such was not in existence but in which, nevertheless, "death reigned." In turn, this would be a tacit rebuff of the perspective of Sir 10:19, according to which the non-Jewish segment of the human race is unworthy of honor because it has transgressed the commandments. In other words, the Gentiles, from Paul's vantage point, are not deserving of death because they have violated *the Torah*. He thus appeals to the existence of this pre-Mosaic law as a great leveler of the human race. In the words of 3:23: "*All* have sinned."

Apart from some such historical reading of Paul's text, Piper's explanation leaves us at a loss as to why he would single out the period *from Adam to Moses*. Why do solidarity with Adam and the legal consequences of sin pertain especially to *this period* as opposed to any other? The answer is not clear.

Romans 5:15-17

Of the three points Piper deduces from these verses, two are in dispute, because we quite agree that the foundation for justification is the free gift of *Christ's righteousness*.

For one, in keeping with overall thesis of this book, the claim is made that as the counterpart to "condemnation," justification is a declaration of righteousness, not liberation from sinning. It is to be granted that in Romans 5 Paul does not speak of liberation as such; that discussion is left for 6:1-7:4. Nevertheless, he has paved the way for this subsequent teaching by his assertion of the union of the believer with Christ the Last Adam, the one who has created a new race of beings in his own image. We have exchanged the headship of Adam for the headship of Christ. By definition, we have been liberated from "sin" in the sense of the old Adamic existence of idolatry and apostasy.

In this regard, an exegetical issue is raised by the word translated "justification" (*dikaiōma*) in v. 16. This rendering is simply taken for granted by Piper and others. However, the same term occurs in v. 18, where it is normally rendered "act of righteousness." Protestant exegesis has tended to assume that the usage in v. 18 is distinct from that in v. 16, where it is taken to be "justification," set within a strictly forensic frame. However, apart from assigning a different sense to the term than it bears in v. 18 (with no particular hint from Paul), the interpretation is flawed in not taking sufficiently into account the Hebraic/covenantal backdrop of the *dik-* family of words.[89] What is in view in v. 16 is not merely a declaration and a resultant status, but a commitment to a relationship, evidenced by the holiness of the covenant and a determination to persevere in it. It is such a wholehearted devotion to the Creator/creature relationship, in v. 16, which is the effect of God's free grace in Christ. The conclusion is reinforced by the recollection that underlying Rom 5:1 is Isaiah 32, Israel's restoration to the covenant, the result of which is "peace" (*shalōm*).

Therefore, at stake in Rom 5:12-19 is not simply a legal standing, but an entire new existence (new creation): we have been enabled to be obedient by virtue of our union with the Obedient One himself, the Last Adam.[90] Correspondingly, "condemnation" is not merely a judicial pronouncement, but a state of estrangement that can do none other than produce death in the all-embracing sense. For this reason, it is better to speak of *original death* rather than original sin.[91]

This reading of Romans 5 has been defended by me elsewhere.[92] If I may just quote the conclusion of that study:

> The obedience of Christ, according to Romans 5, is specifically his fidelity to God the Creator and his perseverance in the course set before him by his Father. Christ thus plays out the role originally assigned to Adam as the progenitor of the human race: he is the actual *eikōn tou theou* [image of God], the one who projects onto the field of space and time the likeness of the invisible God (Colossians 1:15). It is he who is obedient, where another son of God, Israel, failed, whose history can be characterized by Paul in 2 Corinthians 3:7, 9 as an era of condemnation and death.
>
> Paul, however, does not contemplate the obedience of Christ as an end in itself, because it is *through* the one man that obedience has been disseminated *to* all. At heart, human obedience is the acceptance of one's identity as the image of God and the consequent obligation of creaturely service. The obedience of the

> Christian is thus the antipode of his former disobedience, his rejection of Creator/creature distinction. In short, the believer has been delivered from the slavery of his former existence (Romans 6:15-23; 8:2; Ephesians 2:1-3) and enabled to persevere in the faith-commitment incumbent originally on the first Adam.[93]

Piper's other point from Rom 5:15-17 is that the judgment that resulted in condemnation is the counting of Adam's sin as our sin, on the basis of our union with Adam. That man outside of Christ in union with Adam is to be granted, but the first part of the proposition is to be challenged, in that Piper attributes condemnation to the imputation of Adam's sin.

Without going into any real detail, the interpretation favored by me is essentially that of Calvin and Cranfield, with some modification.[94] It usually comes as a surprise to students in the Reformed tradition that Calvin did not follow the lead of Augustine by holding to the imputation of Adam's sin.[95] Cranfield follows suit when he interprets "all sinned" in 5:12 in terms of the "the fruit of the desperate moral debility and corruption which resulted from man's primal transgression and which all succeeding generations of mankind have inherited."[96]

Very much in line with Calvin and Cranfield, I would suggest, nonetheless, a certain refinement. It is not to be overlooked that in Romans 5 the apostle's thought is steeped in the creation. Thus, while it is probable that Paul envisages humanity in Adam as inheriting a "sinful nature," the most relevant thing we can say is that *man in Adam enters the world devoid of the Spirit*. With George Smeaton, we may conceive of Adam as "the temple of the Holy Spirit."[97] Therefore, when Adam fell, he forfeited the presence of the Spirit, so that all his descendants emerge from the womb bereft of the Spirit's influence. As formed in the likeness of "the man of dust" (1 Cor 15:49), man in Adam, in Paul's words elsewhere, is a "natural man" (*psuchikos anthrōpos*) (1 Cor 2:13), possessing, in his fallenness, a "reprobate mind" (Rom 1:28).

Vis-à-vis Cranfield and others, it is to be conceded that the present context directly concerns man's immediate involvement in Adam's sin and death, not moral corruption as such. This is why I would emphasize that "sin," in the first instance, is not so much "depravity" as a (damnation-) historical state introduced by Adam. Human failing is a reality; yet, in perspective, it is but the by-product of the apostasy bequeathed by Adam, whose hallmark is the absence of the Spirit. Again thinking in salvation-historical terms, confirmation is had by Paul's teaching that the impartation of the Spirit is a new creation: in becoming the renewed image of God, humankind "in Christ" is again indwelt by the Spirit. We might say that whereas the first Adam forfeited the Spirit, the last Adam, in his role as life-giver, restores the Spirit (1 Cor 15:45).

Most deeply, then, our sin-problem is not due to the imputed guilt of Adam, but rather to our apostasy as a consequence our birth "in Adam," devoid of the Spirit.

Romans 5:18-19

The only matter to be addressed is that of the verb *kathistēmi*, translated by Piper as "appoint;" that is, humans are "appointed" either "sinners" or "righteous" by virtue of imputation, either that of Adam's sin or of Christ's righteousness. Murray opts for a similar rendering of "constitute."[98] The translation of words in individual contexts always depends on interpretation. Piper's translation thus suits his appraisal of Rom 5:12-19 as a whole, along with the doctrine of imputation he sees in other Pauline texts. Yet Cranfield proposes that *kathistēmi*, in the passive voice, may have been chosen by Paul as the true passive equivalent of the verb *ginomai* ("become"). If so, his point is simply that "all" have "become" either sinners or righteous, depending on their relationship to Adam or Christ respectively.[99]

The relationship between Christ's "blood and righteousness"

Under this heading, Piper revisits the verb *dikaioō* (with cross reference to the previously canvassed "imputation" passages in Paul), maintaining that it does not mean "forgive." Forgiveness, he writes, means to be found guilty and then not have the guilt reckoned to one, but let go. "So we should be careful that we not assume justification and forgiveness are identical" (115).

Thereafter, he considers the usage of Psalm 32 in Romans 4. Contrary to those interpreters who take justification and forgiveness in 4:7-8 to be virtually synonymous, Piper reasons that such is not the case. He is concerned that we not assume that justification means only forgiveness of sins. When Paul speaks of being justified by Christ's blood, "we have no warrant for *equating* the totality of justification with sin-bearing, sin-removing work of Christ or with forgiveness" (118-19 [italics his]).

One may grant that justification is not exhausted by sin-removal and forgiveness. Yet, apart from Rom 4:7-8, justification and forgiveness are brought into very close proximity in Rom 3:24-25. Whether semantically "identical" or not, justification and forgiveness coincide and, for all practical purposes, address the same issue: *reconciliation to God*.[100] Piper's attempt to distinguish them so sharply in 4:7-8 involves a certain degree of mental gymnastics. The fact that Paul singles out "blessing" from the quotation of Psalm 32 hardly proves his point, since the "blessing" in question is embodied precisely in words like "forgiven" and "covered."

The attempt to fine-tune the relationship of the various soteriological categories, such as making forgiveness the "constitutive element" of justification, so as to distance the former from the latter, reprises the old analytical, systematizing approach that attributes to Paul a methodology and set of assumptions that are conspicuously absent from his text. To a biblical theologian anyway, such over-refinement is practically pointless. It is surely striking that the Augsburg Confession (quoted above) equates the verb "justified" with "obtain forgiveness of sins and righteousness."

4. Concluding Reflections

If anything, this response to Piper's book has yielded areas of overlap and agreement and areas of tension and disagreement. In bringing this study to a conclusion, I want, first of all, to call attention to the agreement. We are in accord that the righteousness of the Christian believer comes from Christ and Christ alone. In fulfillment of Isa 61:10; Jer 23:6; 33:16, the eschatological Israel has been endowed with the robe of the Lord's own righteousness. Although it is disputed that the modality of this endowment is imputation, we affirm without hesitation that it is "*in him*" (2 Cor 5:21) and by virtue of his person and work that we have become God's own righteousness. After all is said and done, Luther was right that the righteousness God requires is the righteousness he provides in Christ.

Such a conclusion naturally raises a couple of questions. If we are in accord on such a basic issue, then what is the debate all about? If it is only a matter of modality, then why is dialogue even necessary? These are fair questions, and they deserve fair answers.

(1) For one thing, stress on union with Christ rather than imputation places christology, rather than soteriology, at the

forefront of Paul's theology (and that of the NT generally). The showcase of the apostle's thought is *not* justification, as time-honored as that notion is in Reformation theology. It is, rather, union with Christ or the "in Christ" experience. From this vantage point, Col 1:18 exhibits the very life blood of Paul's preaching—that *in all things he may have the preeminence*. One most certainly agrees with Piper that the glory of Christ is the most precious reality in the universe (14); and it is precisely Paul's doctrine of union with Christ that underscores this, because the focus is on *Christ himself*, not most prominently a transaction performed by him. Of all the great mottoes of the Reformation, the most outstanding and important is *solus Christus*.

Hand in hand with the preeminence of the person of Christ is that union with him bespeaks a personal (covenant) relationship that is obscured when legal and transactional matters are give as much prominence as they are in traditional Reformed thought. "Imputation" is the transferal of a commodity from one person to another; but "union" means that we take up residence, as it were, within the sphere of the other's existence. I would particularly press the point, since throughout Piper's book justification by faith is equated with imputation, as though there could no other mode of justification than imputation.[101]

More than anything else, the NT, and Paul in particular, would have us know that the most supreme of Christ's benefits is *Christ himself*. Our life is hid with God in Christ (Col 3:3). Indeed, in two very telling passages, Paul moves, as it were, from the greater to the lesser: from Christ to his benefits: "For you have died, and your life is hid with Christ in God. When Christ who is our life appears, then you also will appear with him in glory" (Col 3:3-4); and "our commonwealth is in heaven, and from it we await a Savior, the Lord Jesus Christ, who will change our lowly body to be like his glorious body, by the power which enables him even to subject all things to himself" (Phil 3:20-21). Paul's order is all important: *first* the savior and *then* the glorious redemption of the body.

(2) In the second place, the debate is necessary (and healthy) because it is vital to have *biblical* notions of the "righteousness of God." Because of its emphasis on the transactional character of the work of Christ, Protestantism has unduly constricted righteousness to its legal and forensic dimension. That this dimension exists, and is even primary, is not to be disputed. Nevertheless, it is my opinion—one that has been formulated over a period of some thirty years now—that the time has come to stop letting the

conflict with Rome dictate the agenda of exegesis and allow Pauline texts such as Rom 2:1-16 speak to us in their intended meaning and with all their power. If it is "the doers of the law who will be justified" (2:13), then Paul means just that.[102]

These conclusions are hardly the place to debate the merits or demerits of the *ordo salutis*. Suffice it to say that Reformed scholars such as A. A. Hoekema and R. B. Gaffin have subjected it to careful scrutiny and have found it wanting.[103] When it comes to the relation of justification and sanctification in particular, I would simply reiterate what I have said elsewhere.[104] No support can be found for distinguishing between the righteousness of the beginning and the righteousness of the end, between the "righteousness of faith" and the "righteousness of life." Further, "justification" and (definitive) "sanctification" coincide, provided that the former is defined as the power of Christ taking over our life, so that justification is seen to be coextensive with new creation. Consequently, what is customarily termed "sanctification" is actually the extension of "justification," or, better, "rightwising."[105]

(3) Third, all of the above brings me to say that my main disagreement with Piper has to do with his insistence that justification has nothing to do with liberation from sin. To reiterate from above, justification and righteousness pertain to our conformity to God's covenant, not simply a forensic status. Granted, the former is the consequence of the latter, and the two are not to be reversed. Even so, it is justification that introduces us to the (new) covenant, and in the context and environment of the covenant we begin to live out the righteousness of God.[106] In a nutshell, justification is transformation.[107]

Like many Protestant exegetes, Piper has restricted the verb *dikaioō* to "declare righteous." In my view, however, the overall best shorthand translation of *dikaioō* is "vindicate." The verb gives voice to a declaration, but a declaration resultant from an activity (God's saving righteousness). This declaration also opens the way into the life of the covenant, because the one acquitted in the Hebrew courtroom resumes his/her responsibilities and privileges within the community. When Israel is vindicated at the time of release from exile, the new covenant is established, and peace is the result of the nation's renewed righteousness (Isa 32:16-17 = Rom 5:1).

These two perspectives combine to inform us that *dikaioō*, in the active voice, is "to righteous," "to rightwise," "to place in the right" or "to save" in the comprehensive sense. In the passive, it is "to be an object of the saving righteousness of God (so as to be well-pleasing to him at the judgment)."[108] As Martyn puts it, the subject Paul addresses in his use of *dikaioō* is that of God's *making right what has gone wrong*.[109] Alistair McGrath points the whole nicely: *dikaioō* "denotes God's powerful, cosmic and universal action in effecting a change in the situation between sinful humanity and God, by which God is able to acquit and vindicate believers, setting them in a right and faithful relation to himself."[110] My plea would be that instead of "counted righteous in Christ," we are "made righteous in Christ."[111]

(4) Fourth, exegetical methodology is, in its own right, a notable issue. We are grateful to Dr. Piper for the exegetical approach he has taken to the subject of imputation. If the doctrine is to be established, it must be on the basis of texts. Yet it is just the assumptions underlying our respective attempts at exegesis that have surfaced in this interchange. Particularly troubling is Piper's repudiation, or at least deprecation, of a biblical-theological framework of interpretation, called by him the "new paradigm." As I read him, his preference is for a systematic theological/confessional entrée into the Pauline passages.[112]

Reformed people have resisted the word "new" at least since the time of Spurgeon's famous dictum that anything new in theology cannot be true. A case in point is the knee jerk reaction of many to the "New Perspective on Paul" in his relation to Second Temple Judaism. However, I would call attention to another famous dictum, that of one of Spurgeon's theological forebears, the Puritan pastor, John Robinson. According to Robinson, new light is always breaking forth from the Word of God; and it is in that spirit that I would maintain that a great deal of light has been shed on the Word of God since the inception of the biblical theological movement. Some conservatives remain suspicious of biblical theology as a discipline because of its roots in the Enlightenment.[113] Yet it is none other than biblical theology, or a salvation-historical methodology, that has given rise to numerous insights that would have remained in obscurity otherwise. As pioneered by the likes of Geerhardus Vos, and furthered by evangelicals such as Herman Ridderbos and George Ladd, biblical theology has been one of the gifts of God to the modern church.[114]

In the words of Vos, we may say that the Bible is "a historical book full of dramatic interest." To quote the whole passage: "Biblical theology [a branch of exegetical theology] imparts new life and freshness to the truth by showing it to us in its original historic setting. The Bible is not a dogmatic handbook but a historical book full of dramatic interest. Familiarity with the history of revelation will enable us to utilize all this dramatic interest."[115] Accordingly, the doctrines of justification and the righteousness of God take on a new life and a new excitement when viewed against the backdrop of God's determination to remain true to his covenant in delivering his people from the house of bondage. His righteousness *is* his saving activity when he springs into action to defend, save and vindicate his own. Yet so much of this dynamic is lost with the *loci, ordo salutis*, systematizing approach. The Scriptures thus appraised are indeed reduced to a "dogmatic handbook."

In closing, it must be placed beyond all doubt that imputation as a concept is hardly objectionable: what evangelical could, at least with any degree of consistency, protest the notion that Christ has become our righteousness in the gospel? But as pertains to a strict doctrine of imputation, exegesis of texts must be the deciding factor. It has been the contention of this paper that exegesis will steer us away from imputation to union with Christ.

It is just because fidelity to the text is of utmost importance that I must stress that the contemporary resistance to traditional notions of imputation is not an "attack" (as claimed by Wayne Grudem, on the back cover of the book); nor is it an "assault," as Piper himself maintains (80). Quite the contrary, it is an endeavor to hear the text speak on its own terms within its own context. It is particularly disturbing that Dr. Piper (70, n. 16) equates the proponents of the "new paradigm" with those who "erode truth and clarity," who "practice cunning" and "tamper with the Word of God" (2 Cor 4:2). One hopes that he does not mean this literally, because later in 2 Corinthians, Paul says of these people: "such men are false apostles, deceitful workmen, masquerading as apostles of Christ. And no wonder, for Satan himself masquerades as an angel of light. It is not surprising, then, if his servants masquerade as servants of righteousness" (2 Cor 11:13-15a). Is such language really applicable to those who take another view of imputation?!

In the spirit of "iron sharpening iron," it is hoped that this interaction will begin to bring "Beroeans" together in a mutual quest for understanding "the mind of Christ."

---

[1] A definitive work on union with Christ in English is yet to be written. For the time-being, see the excellent introductions of J. D. G. Dunn, *The Theology of Paul of Paul the Apostle* (Grand Rapids: Eerdmans, 1998),

390-412 (see 390, n. 1, for literature); H. N. Ridderbos, *Paul: An Outline of His Theology* (Grand Rapids: Eerdmans, 1975), 57-64; D. J. Moo, *The Epistle to the Romans*, New International Commentary on the New Testament (Grand Rapids: Eerdmans, 1996), 391-95.

[2] Documented by Piper as appearing in *Books and Culture*, January/February 2001 and March/April 2001. The choice of Gundry as a representative of "the challenge to historic Protestant teaching" is understandable enough and makes for a convenient foil. However, it is ultimately reductionistic because there are so many variations on the theme, especially considering that "the challenge" is becoming very widespread indeed.

[3] H. G. Liddell, R. Scott and H. S. Jones, *A Greek-English Lexicon* (Oxford: Clarendon, 1968), 1055.

[4] W. Baur, W. F. Arndt, F. W. Gingrich and F. W. Danker, *A Greek-English Lexicon of the New Testament and Other Early Christian Literature*. 2nd ed. (Chicago: University of Chicago Press, 1979), 475-76.

[5] The passages that have a direct bearing on Gen 15:6 are those which are generally translated "regard as" or "reckon," whereby the verb, to quote G. Von Rad, gives voice to "a process of thought which results in a value-judgment, but in which *this value-judgment is related not to the speaker but to the value of an object*" ("Faith Reckoned as Righteousness," *The Problem of the Hexateuch and Other Essays* [London: SCM, 1984], 125-26). To phrase it otherwise, a thing is considered to be acceptable not because of a predisposition in the one making the judgment, but because the object commends itself by its inherent qualities. See Lev 7:11-18; 17:1-9; Num 18:25-32; 2 Sam 19:20; Prov 27:14; and especially Ps 106:31, the only other place in the OT that replicates Gen 15:6: "it was reckoned to him [Phinehas] as righteousness." In the case of Phinehas, it was hardly a matter of imputation, but the declaration that this man was considered to be faithful to Yahweh's covenant. A bit ironically, the passages adduced by O. P. Robertson, as cited by Piper (57, n. 4), support a "non-imputational" reading of *logizomai* (Gen 31:15; Num 18:27).

[6] See the stimulating exposition of Abraham's pilgrimage of faith in W. Brueggemann, *Genesis*, Interpretation (Atlanta: John Knox, 1982).

[7] Actually, the Hebrew original of Gen 15:6 is in the active, not passive, voice. The text reads literally: "He [God] reckoned it to him [Abraham] as righteousness."

[8] The same applies to the non-reckoning of sin to David in Paul's quotation of Ps 32:2. A. A. Anderson remarks that vv. 1-2 of the Psalm exhibit three different terms for sin, which are matched by three different expressions describing the ways of God in dealing with transgression. The third phrase, "to reckon no iniquity," says Anderson, "seems to imply that God *no longer considers* the repentant man a sinner" (*The Book of Psalms*, New Century Bible. 2 vols. [Grand Rapids: Eerdmans, 1972], 1.31-32 [italics mine]). He refers as well to 2 Sam 19:19 and considers the possibility that Ps 32:2 contains an allusion to release from a debt.

[9] See further T. R. Schreiner, *Romans*, Baker Exegetical Commentary on the New Testament (Grand Rapids: Baker, 1998), 215-17.
[10] J. D. G. Dunn, *Romans*, Word Biblical Commentary 38 A, B. 2 vols. (Dallas: Word, 1988), 1.203.
[11] Inasmuch as the backdrop for Paul is the covenant with Israel, the "working" of Rom 4:4 is most naturally understood as "covenantal nomism," to use the phrase placed in vogue by E. P. Sanders (*Paul and Palestinian Judaism: A Comparison of Patterns of Religion* [Philadelphia: Fortress, 1977], 75, 420, 422, 544). In following this "covenantal nomism" model, it is not to be denied that in Rom 4:4-5 Paul challenges a works-principle in Judaism. Yet the ensuing context (vv. 9-12) supports the contention that Paul's concern is not with a merit theology, but with the works of covenant loyalty subsequent to circumcision (cf. Gal 5:3). That "the one who works" receives a "wage" (v. 4) is not a particular problem, because the "wage" in question is eternal life bestowed at the end of this age on those who remain faithful to Yahweh, whose will is enshrined in the Torah. Qualitatively, the Jewish position is no different than that embodied in the parable of Matt 20:1-16: the workers in the vineyard receive the wage of their labor, that is, the eschatological kingdom of God as preached by Jesus. Hence, the works envisaged by Romans 4 (and other passages) are just those demanded by the Torah; they accompany faith and eventuate in the life of the age to come. To be sure, works *are* a condition of "staying in" the covenant. Yet "staying in" is not "getting in." Israel's works are but its response to Yahweh's saving grace: they are tantamount to *perseverance*, not "works-righteousness legalism."
[12] See my *'The Obedience of Faith': A Pauline Phrase in Historical Context*, Wissenschaftliche Untersuchungen zum Neuen Testament 2/38 (Tübingen: Mohr-Siebeck, 1991), 232-253, 258-59.
[13] Garlington, *Obedience of Faith*, 10-11 (with other literature). I would submit that the revelation of the righteousness of God "from faith to faith" (Rom 1:17) can be understood along these lines. No doubt, the precise significance Paul's Greek phrase *ek pisteōs eis pistin* is widely disputed. However, in keeping with the basic idiom *ek... eis...* (e.g., Ps 83:8 [LXX]; 2 Cor 3:18), and the parallel of Rom 1:5 with 1:17, it is not farfetched to take it as a declaration of the multi-functional character of faith in its initial, intermediate and ultimate phases. The Christian life commences with trust in Christ (faith) and eventuates in faithfulness to him.
[14] Adams, "John Wesley: Spiritual Empiricist," unpublished seminar paper, University of Western Ontario, 1992. The paper can be accessed online at www.tbs.edu/documents.htm.
[15] Scholars point out that Rom 1:17 is actually a confessional formula, corresponding to Mark 8:38; Luke 9:26 as compared with Matt 10:32-33; Luke 12:8-9. P. Stuhlmacher and O. Michel were the first to draw attention to this. Both note that in positive terms Paul could have said "I

confess the gospel." See Stuhlmacher, *Gottes Gerechtigkeit bei Paulus*, Forschungen zur Religion und Literatur des Alten und Neuen Testaments 87 (Göttingen: Vandenhoeck & Ruprecht, 1966), 78; Michel, *Der Brief an die Römer*, Kritisch-exegetischer Kommentar über das Neue Testament. 14th ed. (Göttingen: Vandenhoeck & Ruprecht, 1978), 86.

[16] It is frequently noted that Rom 3:29 ("Or is God the God of Jews only? Is he not the God of Gentiles also?") is an allusion to the *Shema* of Deut 6:4: the oneness of the God of Israel. In Judaism, the confession "God is one" was the hallmark of Jewish distinctiveness (see V. H. Neufeld, *The Earliest Christian Confessions*, New Testament Tools and Studies 5 [Grand Rapids: Eerdmans, 1963], 34-41). Paul, of course, agrees that the God of Israel is the sole God. However, he infers that the oneness of God, as reflected by the *Shema*, is an indication of the oneness of the human race. This, he says, has a direct bearing on justification: "since God is one, who will justify the circumcised by faith and the uncircumcised through faith." He takes the "God is one" confession of Judaism and makes it serve the interests of Gentile equality with Israel, not exclusion from her, just as in Rom 2:14-15 the Decalogue, possessed by Jew and Gentile alike, serves the same function (J. M. Bassler, *Divine Impartiality: Paul and a Theological Axiom*, Society of Biblical Literature Dissertation Series 59 [Chico: Scholars Press, 1982], 141-52).

[17] S. J. Gathercole has demonstrated that Israel's boasting pertains to her confidence before God and her distinctiveness from other nations (*Where is Boasting? Early Jewish Soteriology and Paul's Response in Romans 1-5* [Grand Rapids: Eerdmans, 2002]). To be sure, Gathercole has demonstrated that boasting is grounded in actual performance of the law. Even so, it is not necessary to place a "legalistic" construction on the obedience in question.

[18] Such is the thesis of A. Schlatter's commentary, *Romans: The Righteousness of God* (Peabody: Hendrickson, 1995), and propounded more recently by A. K. Grieb, *The Story of Romans: A Narrative of God's Righteousness* (Louisville: Westminster/John Knox, 2002).

[19] See Garlington, *Obedience of Faith*, 232-253.

[20] N. T. Wright correctly stresses that throughout Romans Paul's gospel is christologically conditioned ("The Messiah and the People of God: A Study in Pauline Theology with Particular Reference to the Argument of the Epistle to the Romans." D. Phil. Thesis, Oxford University, 1980). This means that the apostle depicts *his* gospel as the culmination of *the* gospel of the Hebrew Scriptures (Isa 40:9; 41:27; 52:7; 61:1-2; Joel 3:5 [LXX]; Ps 67:12 [LXX]).

[21] See Isa 45:22-25; 51:5-6; 62:1-2; Ps 98:2-3, 8-9 (LXX 97:2-3, 8-9). Noteworthy as well are Ps 35:27-28 (LXX 34:27-28); 72:1-4 (LXX 71:1-4, 7); 85:11-13 (LXX 84:12-14); 96:13 (LXX 95:13); Isa 9:7 (LXX 9:6); 11:1-2, 5; 45:8, 22-25; 51:5-6; 53:10-11; 61:11; Jer 23:5-6; Mal 4:2 (LXX 3:20).

[22] Standing behind Rom 5:1 is Isa 32:1-18, particularly vv. 15-18. See my

Faith, Obedience, and Perseverance: Aspects of Paul's Letter to the Romans, Wissenschaftliche Untersuchungen zum Neuen Testament 79 (Tübingen: Mohr-Siebeck, 1994), 75-76.

[23] See my *An Exposition of Galatians: A New Perspective/Reformational Reading*. 2nd ed. (Eugene, OR: Wipf & Stock, 2004), 161.

[24] To be sure, righteousness in Paul has been understood variously. See the handy compendium provided by N. T. Wright, *What Saint Paul Really Said: Was Paul of Tarsus the Real Founder of Christianity?* (Grand Rapids: Eerdmans, 1997), 101.

[25] The notion of a new exodus is hardly new to biblical scholars. However, in recent days, the return from exile motif is beginning to receive the attention it deserves. See throughout N. T. Wright, *The New Testament and the People of God*, Christian Origins and the Question of God 1 (Minneapolis: Fortress, 1991); id., *Jesus and the Victory of God*, Christian Origins and the Question of God 2 (Minneapolis: Fortress, 1996); id., *The Climax of the Covenant: Christ and the Law in Pauline Theology* (Minneapolis: Fortress, 1991), 137-56; J. M. Scott (editor), *Exile: Old Testament, Jewish, and Christian Conceptions*, Journal for the Study of Judaism: Supplements 56 (Leiden: Brill, 1997); C. M. Pate, *Communities of the Last Days: The Dead Sea Scrolls, the New Testament and the Story of Israel* (Downers Grove: InterVarsity, 2000); id., *The Reverse of the Curse: Paul, Wisdom, and the Law*, Wissenschaftliche Untersuchungen zum Neuen Testament 2/114 (Tübingen: Mohr-Siebeck, 2000).

[26] Martin, *2 Corinthians*, Word Biblical Commentary 40 (Waco: Word, 1986), 154. See n. 8 above.

[27] Furnish, *II Corinthians*, Anchor Bible 32A (Garden City: Doubleday, 1984), 319. E.-B. Allo similarly renders: "not counting their misdeeds against them" ("ne leur comptant point leurs fautes") (*Saint Paul: Seconde Épître aux Corinthiens*, Etudes Bibliques [Paris: Gabalda, 1937], 169).

[28] Belleville, *2 Corinthians*, IVP New Testament Commentary Series (Downers Grove: InterVarsity, 1996), 156. Piper's translation, "imputing trespasses," is essentially incongruous, since sin is already our possession: it does not have to be imputed.

[29] On "sin" and "sinners," see J. D. G. Dunn, *Jesus, Paul, and the Law: Studies in Mark and Galatians* (Louisville: Westminster/John Knox Press, 1990), 71-77, 150-51; id., *The Partings of the Ways: Between Christianity and Judaism and Their Significance for the Character of Christianity* (Philadelphia: Trinity Press International, 1991), 102-7; M. Winninge, *Sinners and the Righteous: A Comparative Study of the Psalms of Solomon and Paul's Letters*, Coniectanea biblica, New Testament 26 (Stockholm: Almqvist & Wiksell, 1995); Garlington, *Obedience of Faith*, 49-55, 95-98; id., *Faith, Obedience, and Perseverance*, 89-95.

[30] See my *Galatians*, 165-66.

[31] Bruce, *Commentary on Galatians*, New International Greek Testament Commentary (Grand Rapids: Eerdmans, 1982), 166.

[32] Hooker, "Interchange in Christ," *Journal of Theological Studies* 22 (1971), 349-59.

[33] As per G. E. Wright and R. H. Fuller, *The Book of the Acts of God: Christian Scholarship Interprets the Bible* (London: Duckworth, 1957).

[34] See throughout Wright's *Jesus and the Victory of God*.

[35] Gaffin, "The Place and Importance of Introduction to the New Testament," *The New Testament Student. Volume One: Studying the New Testament Today*, ed. J. H. Skilton (Presbyterian & Reformed, 1974), 146. What is true of salvation history is likewise true of the place the New Testament occupies in the setting of the ancient world. See G. Osborne, *The Hermeneutical Spiral: A Comprehensive Introduction to Biblical Interpretation* (Downers Grove: InterVarsity, 1991), 21; J. Jeffers, *The Greco-Roman World of the New Testament Era: Exploring the Background of Early Christianity* (Downers Grove: InterVarsity, 1999), 293.

[36] See, among many, D. Hill, *Greek Words and Hebrew Meanings: Studies in the Semantics of Soteriological Terms*, Society for New Testament Studies Monograph Series 5 (Cambridge: Cambridge University Press, 1967), 49-66; L. Morris, *The Apostolic Preaching of the Cross*. 3rd ed. (Grand Rapids: Eerdmans, 1965), 18-29; id., *Dictionary of Paul and His Letters*, eds. G. F. Hawthorne, R. P. Martin and D. G. Reid (Downers Grove: InterVarsity, 1993), 784-85; R. L. Hubbard, *New Dictionary of Biblical Theology*, ed. T. Desmond, et al. (Downers Grove: InterVarsity, 2000), 716-18; B. Byrne, *Romans*, Sacra Pagina 6 (Collegeville: Liturgical Press, 1996), 131-32. In a footnote on "redemption" (73, n. 20), Piper agrees with Morris that the "essential meaning" of the word is "ransoming" rather than "deliverance" (Morris, *Apostolic Preaching*, 41). Given the exodus and new exodus context of the word (and concept), this is unlikely. But even if it were true, the payment of a ransom is always to the end that a release take place.

[37] "That Paul should use *apolutrōsis* ["redemption"] in a sense in which several *lutron*-words are used in the LXX would be natural enough, and natural too for him to see a parallel between the act of liberation accomplished by God in Christ and the act of liberation by which God had set His people free from slavery in Egypt" (C. E. B. Cranfield, *A Critical and Exegetical Commentary on the Epistle to the Romans*, International Critical Commentary. 2 vols. [Edinburgh: T. & T. Clark, 1975, 1979], 1.206, n. 3).

[38] Cranfield, *Romans*, 1.89.

[39] Stuhlmacher, *Paul's Letter to the Romans: A Commentary* (Louisville: Westminster/John Knox, 1994), 63-64.

[40] Ibid., 31 (quoted by Piper, 72).

[41] Ibid.

[42] Ziesler, *Paul's Letter to the Romans*, PTI New Testament

Commentaries (London: SCM, 1989), 111.
[43] The same preposition features prominently in the discussion of Rom 5:12-19: it is *through* the two men respectively, Adam and Christ, that sin entered the world and then later was rectified.
[44] Note the similar procedure in Gal 4:6: it is *because we are sons* that God has sent the Spirit of his Son into our hearts.
[45] The passages that explicitly affirm the Lord's intention to bestow righteousness on his people, Isa 61:10; Jer 23:6; 33:16, occur in the setting of return from exile. Additionally, Isaiah 32, the background to Rom 5:1, prophecies to the same effect: righteousness, resulting in peace, is the effect of the new creation attending Israel's reoccupation of the land.
[46] See E. P. Sanders, *Paul, the Law, and the Jewish People* (Philadelphia: Fortress, 1983), 13-14, n. 18; J. L. Martyn, *Galatians*, Anchor Bible 33A (New York: Doubleday, 1997), 249-50.
[47] Garlington, "A Study of Justification by Faith," *Reformation and Revival Journal* 11 (2002), 55-58, 68-70. The article is reprinted in my *Exegetical Essays*, 285-99.
[48] Still valuable is the study of J. A. Ziesler, *The Meaning of Righteousness in Paul: A Linguistic and Theological Enquiry*, Society for New Testament Studies Monograph Series 20 (Cambridge: Cambridge University Press, 1972), 52-58. Ziesler shows that *dikaioō* in the LXX is largely forensic, but forensic in the wider Hebrew sense as including the relational element of the covenant. Moreover, the verb can broaden so as to mean "be righteous." A similar range of meanings is demonstrated by G. Schrenk, "*dikaioō*," *Theological Dictionary of the New Testament*, eds. G. Kittel and G. Friedrich. 10 vols. (Grand Rapids: Eerdmans, 1964-76), 2.211-19 (including "liberate from" in Acts 13:3; Rom 6:7).
[49] Dunn, *Romans*, 1.320.
[50] In accord with Piper are Cranfield, *Romans*, 1.311, n. 1; J. A. Fitzmyer, *Romans*, Anchor Bible 33 (New York: Doubleday, 1993), 437.
[51] Moo, *Romans*, 377.
[52] Ibid., n. 129.
[53] See my "Justification by Faith," 55-58 (passim); *Galatians*, 103-8; *Faith, Obedience, and Perseverance*, 56-71.
[54] Wright, *Saint Paul*, 98-99.
[55] S. Motyer, "Righteousness by Faith in the New Testament," *Here We Stand: Justification by Faith Today* (London: Hodder & Stoughton, 1986), 48.
[56] Garlington, "Justification by Faith," 62-63. See additionally Motyer, "Righteousness," 55; E. Käsemann, "'The Righteousness of God' in Paul," *New Testament Questions of Today* (Philadelphia: Fortress, 1969), 168-82.
[57] Schreiner, *Romans*, 319 (italics mine). Schreiner refers as well to Ziesler, *Romans*, 161; Byrne, *Romans*, 194, 202; Stuhlmacher, *Gerechtigkeit*, 75-76. I would add Stuhlmacher, *Romans*, 92. It is

regrettable that Schreiner later changed his mind (*Paul: Apostle of God's Glory in* Christ: *A Pauline Theology* [Downers Grove: Apollos, 2001], 189-217). He was right the first time!

[58] Murray, *The Epistle to the Romans*, New International Commentary on the New Testament. 2 vols. (Grand Rapids: Eerdmans, 1959, 1965), 1.222 (italics mine).

[59] See further Schrenk, "*dikaioō*," 218.

[60] Barrett, *The Acts of the Apostles*, International Critical Commentary. 2 vols. (Edinburgh: T. & T. Clark, 1998), 1.650.

[61] Witherington, *The Acts of the Apostles: A Socio-Rhetorical Commentary* (Grand Rapids: Eerdmans, 1998), 413-14.

[62] Schrenk, "*dikaioō*," 218.

[63] Bruce, *The Acts of the Apostles: The Greek Text with Introduction and Commentary*. 3rd ed. (Grand Rapids: Eerdmans, 1990), 312.

[64] Fitzmyer, *The Acts of the Apostles*, Anchor Bible 31 (New York: Doubleday, 1998), 518.

[65] Ziesler, *Righteousness*, 20. See also M. J. Gorman, *Cruciformity: Paul's Narrative Spirituality of the Cross* (Grand Rapids: Eerdmans, 2001), 142-43.

[66] Dunn, *Romans*, 1.306.

[67] Leenhardt, *The Epistle to the Romans* (Cleveland: World, 1961), 148.

[68] See Murray's surprisingly neglected essay, "Definitive Sanctification," *Collected Writings of John Murray*. 4 vols. (Edinburgh: Banner of Truth, 1977), 2.277-84.

[69] Cf. my *Faith, Obedience, and Perseverance*, 151-61.

[70] Young, *Paul the Jewish Theologian: A Pharisee among Christians, Jews, and Gentiles* (Peabody: Hendrickson, 1997), 40-41, 42.

[71] Stuhlmacher, *Romans*, 63-64.

[72] Calvin, *Institutes of The Christian Religion*, ed. J. T. McNeill; trans. F. L. Battles (Philadelphia: Westminster, 1960), 3.11.10. See further C. B. Carpenter, "A Question of Union with Christ? Calvin and Trent on justification," *Westminster Theological Journal* 64 (2002), 363-386.

[73] Barrett, *A Commentary on the First Epistle to the Corinthians*, Harper's New Testament Commentaries (New York: Harper and Row, 1968), 60.

[74] Wright, *Saint Paul*, 123.

[75] Beasley-Murray, *Baptism in the New Testament* (London: MacMillan, 1962), 164-65.

[76] G. D. Fee, in my estimation, artificially stresses the forensic side of *dikaiosunē* at the expense of the ethical (*The First Epistle to the Corinthians*, New International Commentary on the New Testament [Grand Rapids: Eerdmans, 1987], 86).

[77] See my own treatment of this passage in *Faith, Obedience, and Perseverance*, 79-109.

[78] Cranfield, *Romans*, 1.289; cf. Leenhardt, *Romans*, 146.

[79] The problems of the passage and the history of interpretation are

canvassed by J. Murray, *The Imputation of Adam's Sin* (Nutley, NJ: Presbyterian & Reformed, 1977); C. E. B. Cranfield, "On Some of the Problems of the Interpretation of Romans 5.12," *Scottish Journal of Theology* 22 (1969), 324-41; S. L. Johnson, "Romans 5:12—An Exercise in Exegesis and Theology," *New Dimensions in New Testament Study*, eds. R. N. Longenecker and M. C. Tenny (Grand Rapids: Zondervan, 1974), 298-316; G. P. Hutchinson, *The Problem of Original Sin in American Presbyterian Theology* (Philadelphia: Presbyterian & Reformed, 1972).
[80] Morris, *The Epistle to the Romans* (Grand Rapids: Eerdmans, 1988), 231.
[81] See Garlington, *Faith, Obedience, and Perseverance*, 34-37; M. D. Hooker, "Adam in Romans I," *New Testament Studies* 6 (1959-60), 297-306; D. J. W. Milne, "Genesis 3 in the Letter to the Romans," *Reformed Theological Review* 39 (1980), 10-18.
[82] In agreement with A. J. M. Wedderburn, this interpretation of "sin" (*hamartanō*) is supported by the fact that Paul normally uses the verb with regard to responsible and personal sinning, particularly in the Romans passages just cited, in which, remarks Wedderburn, "Paul's whole argument would be vitiated if any mouth were not stopped by the consciousness of its own guilt before God" ("The Theological Structure of Romans V.12," *New Testament Studies* 19 [1972-73], 351). He further remarks that a reference to individual guilt make the best sense in the light of Jewish parallels (ibid., 352). *Hamartanō* is used of Adam's personal sin in 5:16a, so that the sin of his posterity matches his own.
[83] Dunn, *Romans*, 1.276; U. Wilckens, *Der Brief an die Römer*, Evangelisch-katholischer Kommentar zum Neuen Testament 6. 3 vols. (Zürich/Neukirchen: Benziger/Neukirchener, 1978-82), 1.318, nn. 1053, 1054.
[84] This is what accounts for the otherwise difficult grammatical construction of Rom 3:23-24, where the participle of v. 24 has as its antecedent the main verb of v. 23, "sinned." *Qualitative speaking*, "all," Jew and Gentile, who have sinned and fall short of God's glory are the very same ones who are justified by Christ. Paul then proceeds, in v. 25, to relate that this justification has been procured by none other than Christ's atonement. As Dunn relates, Paul's earliest extant teaching on the death of Christ is to the effect that the cross has broken down the boundary of the law in order to procure the blessing of Abraham for all ("Works of the Law and the Curse of the Law (Galatians 3.10-14)," *New Testament Studies* 31 [1985], 539). See further T. L. Donaldson, "The 'Curse of the Law' and the Inclusion of the Gentiles: Galatians 3.13-14," *New Testament Studies* 32 (1986), 94-112.
[85] In point of fact, the majority of commentators oppose any reference to infants here. See, for example, Moo, Dunn, Cranfield, Schreiner, Calvin, Stuart, Godet, Denny.
[86] See Garlington, *Faith, Obedience, and Perseverance*, 82-84.

[87] Dunn, *Romans*, 1.274.
[88] On the eternity of the law in Jewish literature, see W. D. Davies, *Torah in the Messianic Age and/or the Age to Come*, Society of Biblical Literature Monograph Series 7 (Philadelphia: SBL, 1952); R. Banks, *Jesus and the Law in the Synoptic Tradition*, Society for New Testament Studies Monograph Series 28 (Cambridge: Cambridge University Press, 1975), 49-64, 67-85; id., "The Eschatological Role of Law in Pre- and Post- Christian Jewish Thought," *Reconciliation and Hope: New Testament Essays on Atonement and Eschatology Presented to L. L. Morris on His 60th Birthday*, ed. R. Banks (Grand Rapids: Eerdmans, 1974), 173-85.
[89] In Rom 1:32 and 2:26, *dikaiōma* is the behavior required by the law written on the heart, for which Gentiles are held accountable; in 8:4, it summarizes the obligation of the Sinai covenant as fulfilled in the believer, who, by virtue of the work of Christ and the indwelling Spirit, walks not after the flesh but the Spirit.
[90] In terms of Pauline parenesis, Phil 2:8 and 2:12 in conjunction indicate that this Obedient One is to be obeyed.
[91] Dunn, *Romans*, 1.273. One may agree that "original death" requires a corresponding idea of "original sin." But it is the definition of "original sin" that is the crux of the debate. In Dunn's words: "Paul could be said to hold a doctrine of *original sin*, in the sense that from the beginning everyone has been under the power of sin with death as the consequence, but not a doctrine of *original guilt*, since individuals are only held responsible for deliberate acts of defiance against God and his law" (ibid., 1.291).
[92] Garlington, *Faith, Obedience, and Perseverance*, 98-107.
[93] Ibid., 108-09.
[94] Ibid., 85-88.
[95] Calvin, *The Epistles of Paul to the Romans and to the Thessalonians*, eds. D. W. Torrance and T. F. Torrance (Grand Rapids: Eerdmans, 1973), 111-12; id., *Institutes*, 2.1.8.
[96] Cranfield, *Romans*, 1.278; id., "Problems," 335-40. The Calvin/Cranfield line is taken up by H. Blocher, *Original Sin: Illuminating the Riddle*, New Studies in Biblical Theology (Grand Rapids: Eerdmans, 1997).
[97] Smeaton, *The Doctrine of the Holy Spirit* (Edinburgh: Banner of Truth, 1958), 10-17. See further M. G. Kline, *Images of the Spirit* (Grand Rapids: Baker, 1980), 13-34.
[98] Murray, *Romans*, 1.203-4.
[99] Cranfield, *Romans*, 1.291, n. 1; cf. Dunn, *Romans*, 1.284; Wilckens, *Römer*, 1.328.
[100] Note especially Romans 5:1-11. In the parallelism of vv. 9 and 10, there is a direct equation of justification with reconciliation. The same equation is evident in the "ABA" style of 5:1-11 as a whole. 5:1 commences the section with justification, and v. 11 concludes with

reconciliation. See my *Faith, Obedience, and Perseverance*, 74-79.
[101] Needless to say, perhaps, I cannot endorse R. C. Sproul's assertion that if imputation is passé, then so is the gospel (from the back cover), as though the gospel consisted in imputation.
[102] See my *Faith, Obedience, and Perseverance*, 44-71; K. R. Snodgrass, "Justification by Grace—to the Doers: an Analysis of the Place of Romans 2 in the Theology of Paul," *New Testament Studies* 32 (1986), 72-93; K. L. Yinger, *Paul, Judaism, and Judgment According to Deeds*, Society for New Testament Studies Monograph Series 105 (Cambridge: Cambridge University Press, 1999). It is a little known fact, but Luther also embraced a notion of eschatological justification, at least in seed form. See P. Althaus, *The Theology of Martin Luther* (Philadelphia: Fortress Press, 1966), 237, n. 63.
[103] Hoekema, *Saved By Grace* (Grand Rapids: Eerdmans, 1989), 11-27; Gaffin, *Resurrection and Redemption: A Study in Paul's Soteriology*. 2nd ed. (Phillipsburg, NJ: Presbyterian & Reformed, 1987), 137-42; Garlington, *Faith, Obedience, and Perseverance*, 158-61.
[104] Garlington, *Faith, Obedience, and Perseverance*, 151-61.
[105] O. O'Donovan is correct that to obscure the organic connection of justification and sanctification can lead Protestantism back into "the very uneschatological moralism" from which it sought to deliver us: "The correlate of a 'justification' which has nothing to do with 'righteousness' is a righteousness which has nothing to do with justification, and this soon presented itself to Protestant thought under the heading of 'sanctification'" (*Resurrection and Moral Order: An Outline for Evangelical Ethics* [Leicester/Grand Rapids: Inter-Varsity/Eerdmans, 1986], 254).
[106] See B. Byrne, "Living Out the Righteousness of God: The Contribution of Rom 6:1-8:13 to an Understanding of Paul's Ethical Presuppositions," *Catholic Biblical Quarterly* 43 (1981), 557-81.
[107] J. D. Crossan and J. L. Reed, *In Search of Paul: How Jesus's Apostle Opposed Rome's Empire with God's Kingdom. A New Vision of Paul's Words and World* (San Francisco: HarperSanFrancisco, 2004), 382-83.
[108] Motyer, "Righteousness," 48.
[109] Martyn, *Galatians*, 250.
[110] McGrath, "Justification," *Dictionary of Paul and His Letters*, 518. See also McGrath, *Studies in Doctrine* (Grand Rapids: Zondervan, 1997), 355-453; Dunn, *Theology of Paul*, 334-89 Garlington, *Faith, Obedience, and Perseverance*, chapters four and six; J. Armstrong, "The Obedience of Faith," *Trust and Obey: Obedience and the Christian*, ed. D. Kistler (Morgan, PA: Soli Deo Gloria Publications, 1996), 79-117; J. M. G. Barclay, *Obeying the Truth: A Study of Paul's Ethics in Galatians*, Studies of the New Testament and Its World (Edinburgh: T. & T. Clark, 1988), 236; cf. S. McKnight, *Galatians*, NIV Application Commentary (Grand Rapids: Zondervan, 1995), 119.
[111] Piper illustrates his convictions about imputation on pp. 63-64. On the

promise that his son would clean up his room, he is allowed to go the game that evening. However, the promise is not kept, and so the father cleans up the room for him and then "credits" the clean room to the son's account. To be sure, such may be "grace" or kindness, but to credit a clean room to one who did not in fact do the work is simply a legal fiction. It is no wonder that Protestantism has always been vulnerable to this charge. Contra Piper, if we are exonerated before the bar of God's justice, it is because *in Christ* we have *truly* become righteous people, not because of anything intrinsic in ourselves, but because Christ has *actually* clothed us with the robe of *his righteousness*.

[112] This comes as something of a surprise considering the advantage to which Piper was able to use *Heilsgeschichte* in his study of *The Justification of God: An Exegetical and Theological Study of Romans 9:1-23*. 2nd ed. (Grand Rapids: Baker, 1993).

[113] See G. Hasel, *New Testament Theology: Basic Issues in the Current Debate* (Grand Rapids: Eerdmans, 1978), 13-28.

[114] As evidenced by the insights of a fresh volume of essays, *Biblical Theology: Retrospect and Prospect*, ed. S. J. Hafemann (Downers Grove: InterVarsity, 2002).

[115] Vos, *Biblical Theology* (Edinburgh: Banner of Truth, 1975), 17.

IMPUTATION OR UNION WITH CHRIST?
A REJOINDER TO JOHN PIPER

1. Introduction

The ensuing pages are a rejoinder to John Piper's response to my "Imputation or Union with Christ: A Response to John Piper," *Reformation and Revival Journal* 12 (2003), 45-113.[1] That extended review article was a reaction to Piper's book, *Counted Righteous in Christ: Should We Abandon the Imputation of Christ's Righteousness?* (Wheaton: Crossway, 2002). Dr. Piper's response to my critique appears in same issue of *Reformation and Revival Journal* (121-27). Since the publication of Piper's book, there has appeared *Justification: What's at Stake in the Current Debates?* eds. Mark Husbands and Daniel J. Treier (Downers Grove InterVarsity, 2004). Within this symposium, two papers are especially pertinent to the present exchange: R. H. Gundry, "The Nonimputation of Christ's Righteousness" (17-45), and D. A. Carson, "The Vindication of Imputation: On Fields of Discourse and Semantic Discourse" (46-78).

Because the prime purpose of this essay is to respond to Piper, the interaction with Gundry and Carson has been confined to the endnotes, some of which are rather discursive, particularly in regard to Carson. Because Carson quotes from an "unpublished letter" of Mark Seifrid containing criticisms of my views of sin and perfection, I have replied to Seifrid in the final segment of this paper. In numerous regards, Gundry's assessment of Piper's book runs parallel to my own, and no attempt has been made to reference all the areas of overlap. These are readily discernible to any reader of our respective treatments of imputation.[2] The disagreements with Carson are similarly numerous, but many of these have been addressed in the original response to Piper and in this rejoinder to him. Mainly, my answer to Carson pertains to his critique of my earlier reply to Piper.

2. Rejoinder to John Piper

I will follow Piper's lead by getting straight to Paul's use of Gen 15:6 in Rom 4:3-5. In so doing, I would place a premium on the setting of Abraham's pilgrimage of faith that reaches a climactic point in the declaration that the patriarch was a righteous man, particularly as the Abraham narrative has a decided bearing on

Paul's use of the Greek verb *logizomai* in Romans 4. In a nutshell, it is *the story of Abraham* that determines the meaning of Gen 15:6, which in turn determines Paul's meaning in Romans 4.[3]

The story of Abraham in Genesis extends from 11:27 to 25:11. As a whole, this portion of Genesis may be fairly regarded as the recitation of a new creation. It is on this note that the stories commence, with the call of the patriarch. As depicted by Walter Brueggemann:

> The one who calls the worlds into being now makes a second call. This call is specific. Its object is identifiable in history. The call is addressed to aged Abraham and barren Sarah. The purpose of the call is to fashion an alternative community in creation gone awry, to embody in human history the power of the blessing. It is the hope of God that in this new family all human history can be brought to the unity and harmony intended by the one who calls.[4]

The basic plot moves from tension to unexpected resolution, from the promise of Gen 12:1-3 to its reiteration in Gen 22:15-18. To make a long story very short, the tension/resolution motif surfaces at four strategic junctures in this implementation of the Abraham tradition.

(1) The story line commences with the breakaway of the new community from the old, thereby signaling the radical newness of what has happened with the call of Abraham. Abraham's trust in Yahweh is challenged as he is compelled to leave behind all that is familiar, and especially to forsake the most intimate and cherished of human relationships (12:1-9). At this point, the ideas of land, heir, and new beginning are introduced and made mutually interdependent. Abraham's faith-response is sealed by his willingness to leave his home and family and go wherever Yahweh commands. Joshua 24:2 embodies the tradition that the family of Terah "served other gods," before Yahweh took Abraham from beyond the Euphrates and led him into Canaan. *Jub.* 12:1-5 picks up on this reference and places in Abraham's mouth a protestation against idolatry, which, however, his father and brothers choose to disregard. Shortly thereafter, Abraham burns "the house of idols" (vv. 12-14), prays that his seed may be established forever (vv. 16-21), and is then called into the land of promise (vv. 22-24). Joshua and *Jubilees* thus place Gen 12:1-9 within proximity of Abraham's decision to turn from idols and serve the God of Israel.

(2) Chap. 15 reprises the centrality of Abraham's faith, this time as he is confronted with the reality of his continued childlessness. In order to assure the patriarch that he will not let his promise fail, the Lord swears a self-maledictory oath.

(3) Chap. 17 records the circumcision of the Abrahamic community, which henceforth serves as the sign of Yahweh's covenant. The irony of the situation is intensified by God's renaming of the barren Sarai, who from now on is to be known as Sarah (v. 15). After the promise of a seed is restated with reference to her (v. 16), Abraham laughs in temporary unbelief at his age and that of his wife and pleads that Ishmael might live in Yahweh's sight (vv. 17-18). God refuses, however, and confirms his intention to bring to pass his covenant promises through Isaac (vv. 19-21).

(4) Abraham is put to the ultimate test when he is commanded by Yahweh to sacrifice Isaac (chap. 22). The tension of promise and fulfillment is finally resolved when the angel of Yahweh declares that Abraham fears God, as evidenced by his refusal to withhold his only son (v. 12). The climax of "the generations of Terah" (Gen 11:27) is thus achieved: Yahweh reiterates his promise to bless Abraham and make him the father of a multitude of descendants (vv. 15-18).

These episodes represent, so to speak, the four "mountain peaks" of the testing of Abraham's faith. The center of gravity of each is Abraham's family relations. In the first, the patriarch is compelled to leave home and kindred and strike out on his own. Given the importance of family solidarity in the ancient East, this was a move of no inconsiderable moment: it entailed nothing less than a repudiation of his own relations and their manner of life. From this time onward, Abraham is totally dependent on Yahweh for sustenance, protection, and the establishment of a new family unit. The second portrays the growing, though understandable, frustration of Abraham's continued childlessness. Gen 15:3 gives voice to this frustration and intimates for the first time that Abraham would be happy to have an heir by other means than waiting patient on the promise. Even after the renewal of the promise, as accompanied by an oath, Abraham refuses to wait, choosing rather to produce offspring by Hagar the Egyptian (chap. 16). By the third episode, the frustration has mounted to the point of incredulity: How can an aged couple possibly parent a child? Abraham feels no choice but to cry, "O that Ishmael might live in thy sight!" Finally, there is the threat that the long-awaited seed will be taken away—by Yahweh himself—and with him the hope for the future. It might appear, at least at first sight, that God intended to thwart his own purposes.

In sum, it is within the multilayered development of the promise/fulfillment tension of the Abraham story that Gen 15:6 takes its place. The verse, falling within the second episode of the patriarch's trial of testing, is a thread of the fabric of Gen 11:27-25:11. Consequently, its interpretation cannot be abstracted from the book's overall presentation of "Abraham our forefather" (Rom 4:1).

It is just this complex OT background that Piper overlooked in his original treatment of Gen 15:6 and continues to do so in his response. By approaching the text with a hermeneutical and (systematic-) theological agenda in tow, Piper assumes a meaning for the verb *logizomai*. The problem is compounded by his failure to appreciate the significance of the Hebrew idiom underlying Paul's Greek of Rom 4:3-5. In context, both literary and linguistic, the words "it was reckoned to him as righteousness" (*elogisthē autō eis dikaiosunēn*) embody a declaration that Abraham, in Gen 15:1-6, proves to be a faithful person, trusting Yahweh's promise after all, in spite of temporary doubts.

Piper's reiteration of the familiar view that Gen 15:6, as employed by Paul, marked Abraham's "conversion" is necessary for him to sustain his exegesis of Romans 4. However, even a causal reading of Genesis precludes any such assumption. Abraham was already a believer by the time of Gen 15:6. If further proof is need, it is provided by the explicit statement of Heb 11:8. Referring to Genesis 12, the author reminds his readers that: *"By faith Abraham obeyed* when he was called to set out for a place that he was to receive as an inheritance; and he set out, not knowing where he was going." To postulate, as some must, that the faith in question was something short of "saving faith" is a rather desperate expedient to evade the plain sense of the text. That Abraham was a believer before Gen 15:6 is simply confirmed by the fact that he is marked out as a worshipper of Yahweh by virtue of his erection of an altar to the Lord and calling on his name (Gen 12:8). Indeed, the entirety of the patriarch's deportment from Genesis 12-15 is befitting that of a faithful and obedient servant.

In the OT, by far the most striking parallel to Gen 15:6 is Ps 106:31, the only other occurrence in the Hebrew Bible of the formula, "it was reckoned to him as righteousness." Psalm 106 as a whole is a reproach of Israel's idolatry in the wilderness. However, in the midst of this lengthy indictment there is one glaring exception to the rule:

Then Phinehas stood up and interposed,
and the plague was stayed.
And that has been reckoned to him as righteousness
from generation to generation.

The reference is to Num 25:13. The story of Numbers 25 opens on the note of Israel's fornication with the daughters of Moab, who "invited the people to the sacrifice of their gods, and the people ate, and bowed down to their gods" (v. 2). The episode reaches its dramatic height when Phinehas slays an Israelite man and a Midianite woman engaged in illicit sex. He, according to the historian, was zealous for his God and made atonement for the people of Israel. The wrath of Yahweh was thus averted by the removal of its cause. Because of his heroism, Phinehas became the prototype of those who in subsequent Israelite history were to be "zealous for the law." The author of 1 Maccabees in particular conceives of Mattathias, the father of Judas Maccabeus and his brothers, as a latter-day Phinehas, turning away God's jealous anger by the execution of the unfaithful (1 Macc 2:26, 54; cf. Sir 45:23-24; 4 Macc 18:12).[5]

The mention of Phinehas in Psalm 106 is especially pertinent to our look into Gen 15:6, not only because of v. 31's verbally similar "it was reckoned to him as righteousness," but mainly because Phinehas is placed in conspicuous juxtaposition to the disobedient (idolatrous) of the wilderness generation. More precisely, v. 31 concludes that because of Phinehas' zeal for God righteousness has been reckoned to him from "generation to generation." Ziesler is right in classifying righteousness here as "covenant behaviour."[6] When, therefore, Phinehas burned with zeal for the Lord and slew the adulterous couple, he was regarded by Yahweh as a covenant-keeper by virtue of his abhorrence of the idolatry of the Moabites and his vengeance on the transgressors.

Apart from the factor of violence, which is irrelevant to Gen 15:6, Abraham and Phinehas are a matched pair: both are *considered to be* "righteous" in that they are faithful to Yahweh and his revealed will; both, consequently, are said to be covenant-keepers, because, in point of fact, they are. To be sure, it was Phinehas' *zeal* for Yahweh which was looked upon as covenant faithfulness, whereas it was Abraham's *faith* which was reckoned to be righteousness. However, both zeal and faith have the same referent—the covenant of Yahweh. In point of fact, both are the two sides of the same coin: zeal is the product of faith. Nevertheless, it is precisely Abraham's positioning before the law that enables Paul to make him the paradigm for Gentiles who come to faith in Christ.

Moving to the Dead Sea Scrolls, the document know as 4QMMT, "Some of the Works of Torah," simply confirms the above data drawn from the OT. This "Halakic Letter" was apparently written by a leader of the Qumran community explaining why the sect was splitting from the establishment in Jerusalem and withdrawing into the desert. Its author encourages his readers that he has written "what we determined would be beneficial for you and your people, because we have seen [that] you possess insight and knowledge of the Law" (C27-28). At the end of his letter, the writer challenges his readers with a pair of exhortations. First, "understand all these things and beseech Him to set your counsel straight" (C28-29). Second, "keep yourself away from evil thoughts and the counsel of Belial" (C29). In other words, separate yourself from those who have infected you with their evil thoughts and teaching. The addressees and their associates were perceived to have expressed a willingness to "consort with the enemy."

The purpose of the document can be paraphrased in these terms: "You and I know that the enemy are deadly wrong. Let us, who know and observe the Mosaic Torah, separate ourselves from these abominable sinners." This separation from the unclean sinners and an adherence to the law will have two results. First, "you shall rejoice at the end of time when you find the essence [literally, "some"] of our words true" (col. 30). The messianic era, it is implied elsewhere (col. 21), was soon to arrive. Second, "*it will be reckoned to you as righteousness, in that you have done what is right and good before Him.*" Such is "to your own benefit and to that of Israel" (cols. 31-32). Here, the recipients of the letter will be considered righteous people if they conform themselves to the sect's conception of godly behavior.

This provocative final statement has a familiar ring to readers of the NT: Gen 15:6 and the paradigm of righteous Abraham as advanced by Paul in Romans and Galatians (Rom 4:3; Gal 3:6).[7] However, the Qumran author does not offer righteousness on the basis of "faith alone," but rather "in that you have done what is right and good before Him" (col. 31). According to context, it is the "works of the Law" that fuel such a reckoning. In agreement with the above observations on Phinehas, Abegg maintains that it was not Abraham but Phinehas who provided the model for 4QMMT's employment of the language of "reckoning righteousness."[8] No doubt, he is exactly right, simply because

Phinehas and the entire zealot tradition (as spearheaded by Mattathias) was predicated on the premise of "zeal for the law."[9] By contrast, Abraham can be the father of all who believe because he had no connection with the law. In any event, the reckoning of righteousness, as confirmed by 4QMMT, pertains to an actual quality on the part of the readers which is looked upon as righteousness. The same is true of the numerous rabbinic references to Gen 15:6 and Ps 106:31.[10]

All in all, it is the OT/Jewish materials that form the context and define the semantic significance of the reckoning of righteousness. In virtually every instance where the Hebrew and Greek forms of reckoning occur, a value judgment is made, a judgment based on the actual performance or non-performance of individuals.[11] But as I endeavored to stress in the original response to Piper, it is *in Christ* that one becomes the righteousness of God (2 Cor 5:21) and thereby is reckoned as righteousness. This is the furthest thing from "self-achievement" or synergism, because righteousness is reckoned by faith alone in Christ, apart from "the works of the law."

Returning to Romans 4, Piper complains that my reading of *logizomai* will not do because of the "business analogy" of vv. 4-5. If I may repeat my previous observation, "Piper picks up on the common understanding that Rom 4:4-5 is cast in terms of a commercial transaction. Verse 4, anyway, is capable of such an interpretation, since *logizomai* can use used in the sense of 'calculating' a wage. It may well be that Paul here pauses to draw on an analogy from the business world, because, in terms of contractual relationships, *logizomai* can mean a reckoning of payment for work done."[12] Note that I conceded the possibility that Paul *may* be drawing on the imagery of a commercial transaction. The difference is that Piper is quite sure that such is the case, whereas I merely conceded the possibility. In point of fact, Paul's main focus is covenant relationships, not business. The Hebrew Bible is certainly not oblivious to the reality of wages paid in return for work; but even that, among fellow Israelites, transpires within the parameters of the covenant. It is very telling that Piper and others are much more inclined to invoke secular commercial categories than the Hebrew covenant as the framework of Paul's thought. But at least it brings to the fore the main methodological difference between us: a dogmatic/confessional reading of the text versus a historical or biblical-theological reading.

The control-factor over Paul's choice of words is Gen 15:6. While Rom 4:4 *may* be a reflection on a well-known principle of business practice, 4:5 returns to the idiom of *logizomai eis*: the believer's faith is considered to be his righteousness, just because of faith's object.[13] Piper consistently suppresses this datum. Paul's thought is grounded in the sphere of the Hebrew covenant, according to which individuals are thought to be faithful when they place their confidence in the God of Israel and give concrete expression to their faith by obedience to his commands. The radical thing in Paul, however, is that peoples of all kinds can be looked upon as faithfully obediently quite apart from Torah observance and Jewish ethnic identity. It is those who simply place their trust in Jesus who truly walk in Abraham's footsteps, making the patriarch the father of circumcised and uncircumcised alike (Rom 4:12).

In keeping with the "business analogy" interpretation, Piper consistently renders *logizomai* as "credit."[14] However, both the RSV and the NRSV translate as "reckon."[15] The difference might appear at first glance to be hair-splitting—but it isn't. To "reckon a wage" means that the wage is *calculated in certain terms*. The question is a qualitative one, as underscored by the preposition *kata*, "according to." That is to say, On what basis is the wage to be paid? And the answer is: for "the one who works" the reckoning takes place "according to debt," not "according to grace." On the other hand, for "the one who does not work but trusts him who justifies the ungodly" his faith is "reckoned as" or "considered to be" righteousness.

If it was not clear before, it must be clarified now that in principle Paul certainly does preclude any kind of "works," Jewish covenantal ("covenantal nomism") or otherwise, as the basis of present justification. The gift character of God's righteousness was never called into question.[16] But for the sake of historical exegesis, it must be added that in pursuing his objective in Romans 4, Paul predicates "ungodly" (*asebēs*) of Abraham in the same sense that Jews of this period would have used the term, i.e., *uncircumcised and non-Torah observant*. By way of preaching Paul's text, we may certainly say that "ungodly" depicts all those outside of Christ, in their idolatry and rebellion against God the creator. However, Piper and Carson have missed the irony of the historical situation: the same Abraham who was confirmed as a righteous person in Gen 15:6 would have been deemed "ungodly" by many of his first-century descendants![17] But by a simple "back to the Bible" tack, Paul is able to bypass a considerable layer of tradition and assert that Abraham and the nations are in the same boat. Consequently, analogously to former, the latter need only put their faith in Christ. In blunt terms, Gentiles can forget about the Torah! This is the lead-item on Paul's agenda in Romans 4.

It comes as no surprise that Piper reprises his illustration of imputation from *Counted Righteous* (63-64). On the promise that his son would clean up his room, he is allowed to go the game that evening. However, the promise is not kept, and so the father cleans up the room and then "credits" the clean room to the son's account. My reaction is the same as before: such "imputation" may be a form of "grace" or kindness, but to credit a clean room to one who did not in fact do the work is simply a legal fiction. Contra Piper, if we are exonerated before the bar of God's justice, it is because *in Christ* we have *truly* become righteous people, not because of anything intrinsic in ourselves, but because Christ has *actually* clothed us with the robe of *his righteousness* (Isa 61:10; Jer 23:6; 33:16). What saves justification from "justifiction" is none other than union with Christ.[18] We are declared righteous because we really are righteous, rather than being declared righteous when we really are not.

It is precisely at this juncture that I would press again for union with Christ, in distinction to imputation, as the actual mode of our becoming the righteousness of God. Piper wonders why I insist on making union with Christ an alternative to imputation. In response, it certainly did not go unnoticed that Piper affirms that union with Christ connects us with the divine righteousness (*Counted Righteous*, 51, 84). Rather than an alternative to imputation, he contends, union with Christ is the way it comes about (although it is equally noticeable that the latter received remarkably short shrift as compared to the former). Fair enough, but the premise stands only on the foundational supposition that imputation is demonstrable from Pauline texts. And that, of course, is exactly the issue under debate. I pose union with Christ as an alternative to imputation because there is abundant exegetical evidence for the former but none for the latter. Of course, Piper thinks otherwise; but readers will have to judge for themselves the merits of his case and mine respectively.[19]

Perhaps one point does require further clarification. Piper challenges my employment of the phrase "alien righteousness," which, he says, is misleading because "alien righteousness" bespeaks imputation. This criticism may be legitimate, but with one notable qualification. I used "alien" in the strict sense of the term, i.e., "of another." The righteousness in question is not intrinsically ours; it is Christ's. He is the "other" who clothes us with his righteousness. If, however, readers were confused on this point, I am grateful for the opportunity to correct a possible misimpression. In any event, Piper's allegation that I do not agree with the "historic Protestant view" is at best an oversimplification, because there is no ironclad uniformity among Protestants as regards the relation of faith and righteousness,[20] a consideration that should at least temper claims that the gospel consists in imputation.[21]

Speaking of clarifications, I did not use the word "impartation" in contrast to "imputation," as attributed to me by Piper. He does correctly quote me as saying: "Paul...does not contemplate the obedience of Christ as an end in itself, because it is *through* the one man that obedience has been disseminated *to* all." "Disseminate" means only that Christ's obedience or perseverance is replicated in all those who are in union with him. In distinction to Piper, it is true that my reading of Romans 5 is very much couched in non-imputational terms. But the intention was certainly not to evoke any notion of "infused righteousness" or "self-righteousness:" it was merely to say, as I did say, that Paul does not contemplate the obedience of Christ as an end in itself. *We also have become obedient by virtue of the obedient one—Christ.*[22]

As represented by Piper, my understanding of the relation of justification to sanctification requires even further clarification. True, I did state that "no support can be found for distinguishing between the righteousness of the beginning and the righteousness of the end, between the 'righteousness of faith' and the 'righteousness of life'." It is also true that I think that air-tight distinctions between justification and sanctification, *à la* an *ordo salutis*, have been formulated in the interests of the conflict with Rome. However, it is inaccurate to assert, as Piper does, that, on the biblical-theological model, "justification includes sanctification." It is more proper to say that justification opens the door to the covenant, within which sanctification occurs. With the various refinements scholars might want to make to N. T. Wright's stance on justification and the covenant, the justification of the people of God cannot be abstracted from their identity as members of the covenant. And membership in the covenant entails *ipso facto* the holiness of the covenant and its God.

It is in assessing the relation of justification and sanctification that, once more, methodological issues arise. I normally tell students that if one embraces an *ordo salutis*, then one is obliged to distinguish sharply between justification and sanctification, simply because separate entities are in view. If, however, one follows an *historia salutis*, such a bifurcation is illegitimate because justification and *definitive sanctification* coincide at the point of conversion to Christ or entry into the (new) covenant. It still amazes me that students in the Reformed tradition are mostly unaware of John Murray's essay, "Definitive Sanctification," in which Murray demonstrates that the verbal forms of sanctification-language refer specifically to the passage from death to life.[23] Definitive sanctification means that we can never relapse into our former idolatry "in Adam." In my response to Piper's book, I also cited a passage from Murray's Romans commentary in which he comes remarkably close to the understanding of Rom 6:7 advocated by the proponents of the "new paradigm" (Piper's phrase), i.e., that justification entails liberation from sin.[24] It is disappointing that Piper does not even acknowledge this datum.

In his denial that justification comprehends liberation from the power of sin, Piper is right that there is more than one way "to construe the fact that justified people are obedient people." And given his set of assumptions, the justification/sanctification model is a viable one. Yet his further allegation that I champion the Roman Catholic understanding of Rom 2:13, "because it has been vindicated by the newer biblical-theological approach to justification," is very wide of the mark indeed. My exposition of that passage never promoted a Catholic understanding of justification or that of any other tradition. The purpose was exegesis and the drawing of appropriate conclusions, quite apart from the Catholic/Protestant debate.[25] The case presented was neither Catholic nor Protestant as such. It is certainly worthy of notice that two recent Protestant scholars, Kent Yinger and Simon Gathercole, have both interpreted Romans 2 in terms of an actual end-time justification.[26] But I hasten to add that I certainly do not embrace the classic Tridentine doctrine of justification, especially in view of A. A. Hoekema's exposé of its shortcomings.[27] In this regard, Piper's remarks decidedly convey the wrong impression.

I accept Piper's caveat that biblical theology is as much a system as systematic theology and that is just as complex and controlling. This is a timely warning, because all exegetes bring preunderstanding to the text. Rudolf Bultmann, no devotee of systematic theology, was right that exegesis without presuppositions is impossible.[28] Nevertheless, we all work with a paradigm, and it is a question of the most appropriate paradigm for the materials in question. As in my reply to Piper's book, I would reiterate here that the historical reading of Scripture is in keeping with *the Bible's own story line*.[29] At the end of the day, Old and New Testaments are not dogmatic handbooks, but a story reaching its climax in Christ.[30] Therefore, doctrines such as justification, sanctification, and perseverance must be read against the backdrop of the prophetic Scriptures, particularly in light of such motifs as return from exile and the vindication of the faithful people of God.

In fairness, Piper acknowledges that biblical theology serves as a kind of watchdog over what I would call a "runaway systematic theology." However, his contention that a biblical-theological paradigm comes from only one part of the Bible strikes me as curious. To be sure, some documents are composed in a mainly non-historical style, such as Proverbs and Ecclesiastes. But even these books, in which history recedes into the background, assume a place within the continuum of salvation history. There is nothing purely "topical" as abstracted from the mighty works of Yahweh in history. In a nutshell, the Bible *is* the book of the acts of God: it is story by definition. In practical terms, contra Piper, this means that a salvation-historical methodology, *rightly and consistently implemented*, will not produce incorrect interpretations of any portions of Scripture.

Our differing paradigms surface again in Piper's criticism of my understanding of "redemption" in Rom 3:24. As expected, he is disinclined to view redemption against the backdrop of return from exile and the liberation of Israel from bondage. By way of rejoinder to me, Piper refers to Eph 1:7: "In him we have redemption through his blood, *the forgiveness of our trespasses*" (italics his). Then it is rather baldly stated that "forgiveness is not liberation," along with Piper's skepticism that the new exodus motif governs what Paul has in mind here. Yet while it is impossible in this forum to defend in detail the prophetic framework of Paul's language, I would simply call to mind that the return from exile, according to Jer 31:34, is envisaged precisely as the time when the definitive forgiveness of sins would take place: "I will forgive their iniquity, and remember their sin no more." This promise of forgiveness is contextualized in none other than Jeremiah's majestic vision of the glorious future of the exiles returned from Babylon (Jeremiah 31-33).

This underlying salvation-historical hermeneutic pays very rich dividends, when the prophets of Israel are allowed their place as the most natural matrix of Pauline theology. Familiar doctrines like justification, sanctification, and redemption take on hues and colors, richness and complexities, and particularly *applications* lacking in the flat, one dimensional *loci* approach to Scripture. Since it is just Paul who explicitly roots his gospel in the "prophetic Scriptures" (Rom 1:2; 16:26; Eph 3:1-7), it is hardly arbitrary or artificial to read "redemption" against the background of return from exile. Forgiveness is no mere pronouncement, but the blessed condition of liberation from sin and its devastating power. Would that more preachers would dilate on forgiveness in all its *practical* salvation-historical ramifications!

In winding down, several other matters are in need of some response. For one, Piper thinks my treatment of "the righteousness of God" is too broad and neglects aspects of divine righteousness in both Testaments. He makes a certain point, given that it would require a volume in itself—and a rather large volume at that—to canvass righteousness in all its many occurrences and nuances.[31] In my response to *Counted Righteous*, the immediate object was simply to press that righteousness is God's "saving activity" *in certain texts*. What I said was this:

> To cut to the chase, "righteousness" *in these passages* [from the Prophets and Psalms], and, consequently, in Romans 1:17; 3:21, 22, 25 (26) is not what Piper calls "external righteousness" (= the active obedience of Christ), but rather God's saving activity on behalf of Israel, when he releases Israel from bondage and plants her again in the land never to be moved. This is not to rule out righteousness as an attribute of God. Indeed, it is just the "righteous," covenant keeping, God who springs into action to redeem his people from slavery and graciously renew the covenant with them. Therefore, as the bridge into Romans 4, Romans 3:21-31...argues against "the imputation of external righteousness" and in favor of a salvation-historical reading of Paul, whereby the apostle's intention is seen to be that of announcing the availability of God's saving activity to *all who believe* (1:16; 3:22), because *there is no distinction* (3:22; 10:12).[32]

Perhaps I could add that elsewhere I have sought to address righteousness as "retributive justice," especially as Mark Seifrid has endeavored to make this dimension of righteousness paradigmatic in opposition to righteousness as "covenant faithfulness."[33]

Second, Piper is dissatisfied with my take on the verb "justify" (*dikaioō*) because it is "too broad and puts a construction on the word that goes against its basic meaning and is not demanded by any of the New Testament texts." This is hardly the place to reproduce the data already presented in my prior response to him.

Suffice it to say that the presence of the verb in Acts 13:39 and Rom 6:7, especially as paralleled by "liberate" (*eleutheroō*) in 6:18, argues in the direction of a broader semantic range of *dikaioō* than merely "declare righteous."[34] Several commentators were cited as favoring the translation of *dikaioō* as "freed from sin" in these passages. Again, it is disappointing that Piper does not acknowledge this or even attempt to provide anything like an exegetical rejoinder.

Third, I do appreciate Dr. Piper's agreement that the person of Christ is paramount. And he is right that imputation *ipso facto* does not distance one from Christ. If any readers have received that impression, I am happy to take this occasion to provide further elucidation. Moreover, he is altogether correct that *we ourselves* perform no "transactions"—that is entirely Christ's doing. But even with this concession, it remains that the grace of God does empower us to do his will. There is what Gordon Fee calls "God's empowering presence."[35] The only danger is when "performance" is wrenched from its setting in the covenant and made the basis of an autosoterism, as is the case with the various cults. But when kept within the context of covenant, union with Christ, and the eschatological gift of the Spirit, the "works" of the believer are but the fruit of the Spirit that accompany perseverance (Luke 8:15; Gal 5:22-24).

I would reiterate from my original response that my chief concern is not imputation as such. In the conclusion of that essay, I remarked that it must be placed beyond all doubt that imputation as a concept is hardly objectionable: what evangelical could, at least with any degree of consistency, protest the notion that Christ has become our righteousness in the gospel?[36] Rather, my problems are in those areas that lie adjacent to imputation: the preeminence of the person of Christ with whom we are in union, a salvation-historical hermeneutic as a control over exegesis, and justification as liberation from the power of sin. And once more, I would plead that the actual showcase of the apostle's thought is *not* justification. It is, rather, union with Christ or the "in Christ" experience.[37]

3. Reply to Mark Seifrid

Toward the end of his paper, Carson quite correctly observes that Paul does not think of sin and evil *primarily* in legal terms: the origin of evil is bound up with rebellion, idolatry, and the "de-godding" of God. "What draws down God's wrath, above all things, is the obscenity of competition—for there is no God but God." This is followed up with the comment: "Sin is more than the breaking of rules (though the 'rules' clarify and help to quantify the horrendous breach of idolatry)."[38]

It is in this connection that Carson quotes a paragraph from an "unpublished letter" of Mark Seifrid:

> I shall not here pursue his [my] dilution of the demands of the mosaic covenant by appeal to a certain understanding of "perfection" except to note that he stands at odds with Paul, James, the author of Hebrews, Jesus, the prophets of Israel and Moses himself. Other than that, he is in perfect agreement with Scripture. He doesn't understand that our acts of sin are expressions of unbelief and the desire to annihilate God. This desire resides in all our hearts. If it were not there, we would sin no more. The Law merely exposes us for what we are. He should let it do its work, because apart from it Christ's work means nothing.[39]

For Carson, this not too strong in light of my supposed "insistence that the Old Testament does not demand 'utter righteousness, utter holiness'."[40]

If I may say, not only is Seifrid's evaluation too strong, it is completely wide of the mark, so much so that it calls forth the following response. If there has ever been instance of not recognizing oneself in the portraiture of another, this is it. What impresses me straight-off is that Seifrid and Carson provide no documentation for such a reading of my materials. I can only surmise that the prime reference is to portions of my monograph on Romans, the essay on Gal 3:10-13, and possibly the review of Seifrid's contribution to *Justification and Variegated Nomism*.[41] Assuming that such is the case, I would like very much to set the record straight.

(1) Had Seifrid and Carson given *Faith, Obedience, and Perseverance* a evenhanded reading, they would have taken on board chapter four: "The Obedience of Christ and the Obedience of the Christian" (72-109). Integral to this chapter is the proposition that man's quintessential problem is idolatry, an idolatry committed by the first Adam that has bequeathed to all his posterity a condition of apostasy, as everyone "in Adam" is born into this creation devoid of the Spirit of God. Although I did not use the phrase, this is "total inability," the doleful and hopeless plight of man outside of Christ. Consequently, individual sins are

but symptomatic of the underlying problem of idolatry. Furthermore, chapter two of the book (32-43) applies the idolatry motif to Israel. One may agree or disagree with the precise thesis of that chapter, but the fact remains that I endeavored to trace Israel's failure back to her repetition of Adam's primal rebellion against God. In the case of Adam and Israel respectively, self-idolatry is the root of evil. I would add to the mix that the article on Gal 3:10-13 labors to show that each of the OT passages quoted by Paul has idolatry lurking in the background. All acts of sin stem from the worship of other deities than Yahweh.[42] Therefore, on the basis of what I have actually written, I would beg to differ with Seifrid's allegation that I don't understand that our acts of sin are expressions of unbelief and the desire to annihilate God.

Seifrid does a similar thing in his *Christ, Our Righteousness*.[43] In responding to my treatment of Romans 7 in *Faith, Obedience, and Perseverance* (110-43), Seifrid complains that the weakness of my work resides it its "failure to come to grips with the judgment of God upon fallen humanity in Paul's thought." For him, I embrace the "anthropological optimism of early Judaism," so that, in my reading of Paul, Adam bequeaths to his descendants merely "a disadvantage," namely, the absence of the Spirit, but not guilt. He continues: "Our 'wretchedness' is no longer our just condemnation, but our temporary lack of power to do what we otherwise would. The human being is basically free and good, but weak. What need is there then for the cross?" Romans 7, consequently, is for me "a narrative of struggle, rather than the recognition of the power of sin." By the time Seifrid is through, my theology has been recreated in the image of Pelagius!

Seifrid's misreading of my comments on sin, etc., revolves around one fundamental mistake, namely, the failure to discern my argument respecting Rom 7:14-25. In line with historic Reformed exegesis of the passage, I understand Paul to be writing of the Christian who struggles against indwelling sin, not generic humanity placed at a mere "disadvantage" by Adam ("disadvantage" is Seifrid's word; I never used it). True, I don't think that Adam's guilt is imputed to his descendants, but Seifrid merges and confuses separate chapters of *Faith, Obedience, and Perseverance*. In the exegesis of Rom 7:14-25 (chapter five), "weakness" pertains to *the believer*, who is flesh and Spirit at the same time.[44] Seifrid has extrapolated these remarks directed toward man in Christ and has applied them illegitimately to man in Adam. But in light of chapter four of the book, pertaining to Adam and Christ, to *impute* to me the position that "the human being is basically free and good, but weak" is to engage in hermeneutical jujitsu, no less! If I may be forthright, to transmute remarks about those who possess the Spirit into a declaration concerning those who don't is an irresponsible handling of these materials. As for the "anthropological optimism of early Judaism," this is a construction placed on the materials by Seifrid. Jewish writers were anything but optimistic about the nations;[45] and their assessment of themselves assumed the framework of the covenant; they were hardly Pelagians before Pelagius.[46]

(2) There is the matter of my alleged insistence that the OT does not demand "utter righteousness, utter holiness." In part, this misreading of my intentions stems from Seifrid's take on portions of *Faith, Obedience, and Perseverance*, as addressed above. But since no documentation is provided, I can only assume that the other reference is to "Role Reversal and Paul's Use of Scripture in Galatians 3:10-13." In the essay, it is true enough that I maintain that the law of Moses never required perfect obedience. Yet it is a proposition that forms part and parcel of a larger field of discourse. The thesis of the article is that Paul brings passages from the Torah (Deut 27:26; Hab 2:4; Lev 18:5; Deut 21:23 respectively) to bear on his opponents in Galatia. In brief, these texts, which speak of idolatry and apostasy from the covenant, apply to the Judaizers because they are latter-day apostates from God's purposes in Christ. In their very observance of the law the opponents have not kept it, because they have not "upheld" it in its eschatological design, i.e., to point Israel to Jesus of Nazareth as the one who has done away with the barriers of separation between nations.

In the pursuit of this thesis, it was necessary to deal with the common interpretation that, in Gal 3:10, there is a suppressed premise, namely, the law demands perfect obedience, but no one can actually render that obedience. This tradition of exegesis supposes that if one would be justified by the law, one must lead a sinless existence. As such, the law of Moses is perceived to be a kind of "covenant of works." By contrast, I maintain:

> The "reach of the law" [Peter Craigie's phrase] is not perfect compliance with its demands, or anything approaching it, but fidelity to the God who graciously gave it to Israel.... Obedience to the Torah in the Hebrew Scriptures themselves (as distinct from later theologies) is never portrayed as an unobtainable goal. Rather, according to Deut 30:11-20, it is a thing within Israel's grasp ("this commandment...is not too hard for you, neither is it far off," v. 11). One is able to say this

because..."keeping the law," "obedience," and such expressions, speak of perseverance, not sinless perfection.[47]

Further on, I assert that the key issue, in the Torah and in Galatians, is perseverance versus apostasy, not sinless perfection. As stated, "the Judaizers are not under the curse because they have failed to keep the law 'perfectly,' but because they have proven defective in the central matter: fidelity to the God of Israel."[48]

Apparently, from such sentiments Seifrid and Carson have deduced that my intention was to lower the standards of the covenant, so that "utter righteousness, utter holiness" are made optional. Just two points of clarification. One, it is repeatedly stated in the exegesis of the Torah passages cited by Paul that doing the will of the covenant Lord is paramount and indispensable: the faithful Israelite must flee idolatry and keep Yahweh's statutes and commandments with all his heart. No one can give this portion of the essay a fair reading and not come away with this impression. Two, an unbiased approach to these materials would have grasped the point: although the standard of the law was always complete conformity to the revealed will of God, perfection was never required *to remain in covenant standing*. The sacrificial system existed for the very purpose of covering the sin and failure of the believer; and the only sin that could separate a person from the covenant was apostasy. In his excellent study of OT ethics, Gordon Wenham conveys the root of the matter:

> Obviously the behaviour of the chief actors [of the Old Testament narratives] in many instances falls miserably short of the ideal, and they often suffer in some way for their mistakes. Yet it is clear too that they are not deserted by God despite their sinfulness. So there is a paradox in Old Testament narrative ethics: on the one hand God is terribly demanding, he looks for nothing less than godlike perfect behaviour, yet on the other, despite human failings, he does not forget his covenant loyalty to his people, and ultimately brings them through the suffering that their sin has brought about. Old Testament ethics are therefore as much about grace as about law: they declare that God, the all-holy, is also God, the all-merciful.[49]

The same is true of the new covenant: the Christian strives for complete conformity to the image of Christ. Nevertheless, if we sin, we have an advocate with the Father; if we sin, he is faithful and just to forgive our sins and cleanse us from all unrighteousness. Seifrid may find it "paltry comfort," but I, for one, find it enormously comforting that "notwithstanding our many failures, there is no condemnation as long we as desire to remain within the covenant bond, true to Christ the Lord."[50]

As much as anything else, it is pastorally important to lay to rest the myth that the Torah of Moses functioned as a "covenant of works," for whatever reason such a formulation has been imposed on it. While one certainly agrees that there is an "utter righteousness, utter holiness," for which every believer strives, is it likewise true that "we all stumble in many points" (Jas 3:2).[51] A pietism that burdens the conscience unnecessarily by majoring on the observance of commandments and minoring on persevering faith is to be resisted at all costs. The problem with the various Jewish enclaves was not that they were "legalistic" but *pietistic*. The strenuous law-keeping of these groups, that often went beyond what is written, was grounded in a pietism that too often has been replicated in the history of the Christian church. In principle, I would hope that Seifrid and Carson agree, especially as it is Carson who writes that "sin is more than the breaking of rules (though the 'rules' clarify and help to quantify the horrendous breach of idolatry)."[52] If the essence of sin is idolatry, it follows that the essence of righteousness is fidelity. God forgives our weaknesses; it is only apostasy that makes it impossible to be restored to repentance (Heb 6:4).[53]

(3) There is, to be sure, a biblical doctrine of "perfection," as per "Paul, James, the author of Hebrews, Jesus, the prophets of Israel and Moses himself." The problem is that Seifrid and Carson function with a conception of perfection that is not really the biblical conception. I will leave it with a portion of my review of Seifrid's essay in *Justification and Variegated Nomism*:

> It is regrettable that Seifrid does not define "perfection" in biblical terms, leaving the impression with the general reader that the term is to be understood more or less as it is in English. But the fact of the matter is that in the Jewish milieu, as P. J. Du Plessis has shown, "perfection" is principally a "cultic" and "quantitative" term, indicating "wholeness, entirety and intactness." "Perfection," according to Du Plessis, is wholeness in one's relationship to God.[54] D. Peterson adds that the concept is not formal or abstract. While conceding that perfection in the Old Testament is not essentially a

moral concept, it does involve "*loving obedience to God* as the one who, in his mercy, has initiated the relationship with man."[55] Therefore, to walk in perfection in all God's ways is hardly "sinless perfection," but rather a wholehearted commitment to honor the entirety of the Lord's revealed will. Otherwise put, perfection is simply a David-like desire to seek God and follow his commandments with all one's heart (Psalm 119:2, 10, 34, 69, 145).[56]

As a final word, if I may speak frankly, the cause of Christ is not advanced by Christian teachers fixating on imaginary enemies and constructing straw men out of the honest endeavors of fellow believers to know his mind. In the end, to *impute* to other students of the Word unsound ideas, perhaps with whisperings of heresy, is a failure to "maintain the unity of the Spirit in the bond of peace" (Eph 4:3). I should think that "utter righteousness, utter holiness" demand, at the very minimum, *speaking the truth* and speaking it *in love* (Eph 4:15).[57] As we all endeavor rightly to divide the Word of truth, the bottom line is that theological tradition, even very fine tradition, is not Lord—only Christ is. *Sola Scriptura.*

---

[1] References below are to the original essay.

[2] There are actually two areas of *disagreement* with Gundry. One is that I side with Piper and Carson in believing that it is specifically Christ's righteousness that becomes ours by virtue of union with him (see n. 36 below). The other is that Gundry maintains that 2 Cor 5:21 affirms the imputation of our sins to Christ ("Nonimputation," 18). My own understanding of that verse is stated in "Imputation or Union," 58-59, and will not be repeated here. Suffice it to say that an exchange has taken place: Christ became what we are, in order that we might become what he is (M. D. Hooker, "Interchange in Christ," *Journal of Theological Studies* 22 [1971], 352). Paul does not specify by what modality Christ was "made sin," though he is explicit that we have "become" the righteousness of God because of union with Christ. But perhaps unwittingly Gundry has provided a clue. He informs us that the verb *kathistēmi*, in Rom 5:19, means to "establish" by way of appointment, ordination, or making ("Nonimputation," 26). Thus, it is through Adam's disobedience that human beings "were counted" sinful, whereas through Christ's obedience they are "counted as righteous" (see n. 22 below). It may be, then, that there is an implicit Adam christology lurking behind 2 Cor 5:21. That is to say, on the cross Christ was looked upon and treated as the first Adam in his apostasy. That he endured death in a representative capacity is the least we can say (M. E. Thrall, *A Critical and Exegetical Commentary on the Second Epistle to the Corinthians*,

International Critical Commentary [Edinburgh: T. & T. Clark, 1994], 1.441-42). But his representation and substitution take on a specifically Adamic character as he assumes the role of his predecessor and bears the curse placed on the first man when he fell away from the living God. Having made this association, I recalled (happily) that J. D. G. Dunn had already said the same thing decades ago (*Christology in the Making: An Inquiry into the Origins of the Doctrine of the Incarnation* [London: SCM, 1980], 112-13).

[3] The new book of F. Watson, *Paul and the Hermeneutics of Faith* (London/New York: T & T Clark International, 2004), has demonstrated amply that Paul, in his letters, is retelling the story of the Pentateuch.

[4] Brueggemann, *Genesis*, Interpretation (Atlanta: John Knox), 105.

[5] See M. Hengel, *The Zealots: Investigations into the Jewish Freedom Movement in the Period from Herod I until 70 A. D.* (Edinburgh: T. & T. Clark, 1989), 171-77; D. Garlington, *'The Obedience of Faith': A Pauline Phrase in Historical Context*, Wissenschaftliche Untersuchungen zum Neuen Testament 2/38 (Tübingen: Mohr-Siebeck, 1991), 113-14.

[6] J. A. Ziesler, *The Meaning of Righteousness in Paul: A Linguistic and Theological Enquiry*, Society for New Testament Monograph Series 20 (Cambridge: Cambridge University Press, 1972), 181.

[7] Carson ("Vindication," 56) cites a couple of passage from the *Mekhilta* (a midrash or commentary) on Exodus as evidence that in "Jewish exegesis" Gen 15:6 was connected with Genesis 22, as providing a basis for Abraham's merit. From that, Carson postulates that Paul certainly knew of these traditions and was interpreting Gen 15:6 in quite a different way to his upbringing. He then claims that I cite some Jewish texts to argue that what *Paul means* is precisely what *they mean*, i.e., in his words, "Abraham's faith is imputed to him as righteousness precisely because his faith showed him to be faithful to covenant and thus endowed with covenant righteousness." According to Carson, this reading domesticates Paul by attributing to him the meaning found in the Jewish texts and thus fails to take seriously the profoundly *polemical* context of Romans 3-4 (ibid., n. 26 [italics his]). To Carson, I run the risk of "parallelomania" (the term coined by the Jewish scholar, Samuel Sandmel). Several matters arise here.

(1) Two passages in same document, the *Mekhilta*, hardly establish a trend in "Jewish exegesis." Martin Abegg cites several other rabbinic texts that allude to Gen 15:6—and none them presses a case for Abraham's merit, which, in any case, is not what Carson supposes it to be (Abegg, "4QMMT, Paul, and 'Works of the Law,'" *The Bible at Qumran: Text, Shape, and Interpretation*, Studies in the Dead Sea Scrolls and Related Literature, ed. Peter Flint [Grand Rapids: Eerdmans, 2001], 209-12). Abegg's evidence is to the effect that the most prominent association of Gen 15:6 is not with Genesis 22 but Ps 106:31 and the zeal of Phinehas. For these authors, Abraham and Phinehas are a matched pair.

(2) Carson's texts, with whose traditions Paul was supposedly familiar, are later than Paul. That such traditions could have existed in his day is a distinct possibility. But the fact remains that the two texts cited by Carson postdate Paul, and one simply cannot be so sure that he was *au fait* with them. The texts to which I appealed (Sir 44:20; CD 3:2; *2 Apoc. Bar.* 57:2) are much closer to Paul's actual lifetime and are concerned not to promote merit but the proposition that Abraham kept the law of Moses before Sinai.

(3) Carson ascribes to me just the opposite of what I argued from the Jewish texts. To begin, I certainly did not say that "Abraham's faith is *imputed* to him as righteousness." The whole point of the essay is to maintain that there is no imputation as such. What I said was that Abraham was regarded as (*logizomai eis*) a covenant keeper because of his perseverance in faith: he was looked upon as a righteous person because he was righteous (from the time of Gen 12:1 onward). Most importantly for the argument of Romans 4, the genius of Paul's use of Gen 15:6 is that he predicates righteousness of Abraham before his circumcision and the giving of the law. The Jewish materials, by rather stark contrast, make the patriarch out to be righteous by virtue of his devotion to the Torah. Paul thus uses Gen 15:6 in a manner that radically distances him from the contemporary understanding of the relation of Abraham's righteousness to the law of Moses. Such being the case, I would maintain that I do indeed take seriously the polemic of Romans 3-4, just because that polemic is to the effect that righteousness is now detachable from circumcision and Torah-observance, i.e., "apart from the law" (Rom 3:21). Might I be so bold as to suggest that Carson's employment of the Jewish materials comes closer to "parallelomania" than my own?

(4) Rather than domesticating Paul, the intention is to *contextualize* Paul. Everyone agrees that Paul is to be understood on "his own terms." But the question is, What are Paul's "own terms?" For some of us anyway, Paul's "own terms" are only fully explicable in light of his actual life setting. Certainly, the texts cited by me do not make Paul conform to his inherited tradition(s). Quite the contrary: Paul is 180 degrees away from his contemporaries' assessment of Abraham's righteousness in relation to the Torah.

[8] Abegg, "4QMMT," 208-9.
[9] See Hengel, *Zealots*, 149-228.
[10] Abegg, "4QMMT," 210-12.
[11] Carson maintains that in some instances the Hebrew idiom *hashab l^e* is used in such a way that non-X is reckoned to be X. In Gen 31:15, we read (Rachel and Leah speaking): "Are we not regarded by him as foreigners? For he has sold us, and he has been using up the money given for us?" In another case, Lev 7:18, a sacrifice uneaten by the third day will not be "credited to" the worshipper. According to Num 18:27, 30, the "tithe of the tithe" of the Levites will be reckoned to them as though it were the

grain of the threshing floor and as the fullness of the wine press. By way of reply, a few matters arise.

(1) The several passages cited by Carson are not the most germane to the discussion. While they do contribute to overall semantic range of *logizomai*, O. P. Robertson, as quoted by Carson, certainly makes a quantum leap from Lev 7:18 to Romans 4 by claiming that the text "envisions a situation in which righteousness could be 'reckoned' to a person, even though the individual concerned is admittedly as sinner" (Robertson, "Genesis 15:6 New Covenant Expositions of an Old Covenant Text," *Westminster Theological Journal* 42 [1980], 266). If anything is foreign to Leviticus 7, it is the notion of the imputation of righteousness, and it is highly questionable that the appearance of *logizomai* here provides a base for an imputational understanding of Romans 4. Robertson would have us buy into an "apples and oranges" comparison. Besides, the actual point is to the opposite effect claimed by Robertson: the sacrifice of the peace offering will not be credited to the offerer *because of his own actions*!

(2) Although it is true that, in Gen 31:15, non-X is reckoned to be X in a certain qualified sense, the complaint against Laban falls into line with the dominant meaning of *logizomai*. Rachel and Leah are, in Laban's eyes, regarded and treated as foreigners because of his diminished regard for Jacob (Gen 31:2). In a dream, Jacob is told to return to the land of his birth (v. 13); and because Rachel and Leah are his wives and will leave with their husband, they have become virtual foreigners to their father, now with no inheritance. That this reckoning on the part of Laban is the result of some process of "imputation" is certainly what the text does not say. In his view, his daughters now belong to Jacob's household exclusively and are no longer his. Laban's attitude is based on a value judgment regarding the status of Rachel and Leah. In this case, the distance between non-X and X is not as expansive as Carson seems to think; it fact, it hardly exists.

(3) Previously, I cited the LXX of Lev 7:11-18; 17:1-9; Num 18:25-32; 2 Sam 19:20; Prov 27:14; Ps 106:31 in support of a non-imputational understanding of *logizomai*, generally translated "regard as" ("Imputation or Union," 103, n. 4). To these I now add 4QMMT C31-32 (In Hebrew, not Greek). Carson thinks it strange to bring these texts into play, because, in his words, in them "there is *not* a strict equivalence as supporting a 'non-imputational' reading of *logizomai*" ("Vindication," 58, n. 32 [italics his]). I am not precisely sure what this sentence means, but after a rereading of these texts, I would still retain them, including Lev 7:11-18; 17:1-9; Num 18:25-32. Even these passages do not provide a launching pad for imputation in the traditional theological sense: non-X is regarded as X only in a qualified sense. In the case of Num 18:27, 30, the tithe of the Levites is counted as the entire harvest, a quantitative, not qualitative, reckoning; as it were, an "apples and apples" comparison, not "apples and oranges." In God's eyes, the tithe represents the whole, not

that an "imputation" has taken place, transforming one entity into another. Moreover, when a worshipper is not credited with a sacrifice (Lev 7:18), or a person is credited with bloodguilt (Lev 17:4), or the Levites' tithe is reckoned as the grain of the threshing floor and the fullness of the wine press (Num 18:30), it is because of actions performed or not performed by them. This is just the opposite of imputation. A crediting does take place, but the credit is applied or withheld depending on the conduct of the individual.

(4) Most importantly, Carson's tack does not take into account the panorama of the Genesis story as it bears on Romans 4 and Paul's use of Gen 15:6. The fallacy of the Piper/Carson/Robertson type of approach is that it zeroes in on isolated texts in which *logizomai* can mean "credit" and then disregards the fact that Gen 15:6, with *its employment* of the verb, is but one of the steps along the way of Abraham's pilgrimage of faith. Within the story line of Genesis, Abraham is considered and declared to be righteous because of his continued trust in Yahweh's promise of a seed. The same Abraham who obeyed God's call to leave his home (Gen 12:1-4 = Heb 11:8) renews his faith(fulness) when the expected seed seems to be slow in arriving. Carson seems to have forgotten his own counsel in *Exegetical Fallacies* (Grand Rapids: Baker, 1984), 66. A similar instance of narrowly focusing on linguistic data to the exclusion of a biblical theology is Mark Seifrid's attempt to detach righteousness from covenant fidelity ("Righteousness Language in the Hebrew Scriptures and Early Judaism," *Justification and Variegated Nomism. Volume 1: The Complexities of Second Temple Judaism*, eds. D. A. Carson, P. T. O'Brien and M. A. Seifrid [Grand Rapids: Baker, 2001], 415-42).

It is surely telling that the only other place in the Hebrew Bible where righteousness is said to be reckoned to someone is Ps 106:31, where Phinehas is regarded as righteous because of his zeal on behalf of the purity of the covenant. Instead of forming a contrast to Abraham, the example of Phinehas confirms that the reckoning of righteousness is the recognition that one is already righteous. If there is any difference between the two, it is that Abraham was righteous before the era of the Torah, which is why Paul cites him in the first place. How "sinners" can be reckoned righteous needs no further elaboration at this point in time.

(5) In light of all the above, Carson's allegation that I prejudge the meaning of *logizomai* by labeling it as "non-imputational," and thus "distort the flow of Paul's argument," can be turned on him. By labeling the verb "imputational," or at least as providing a basis for imputation, he too can be accused of prejudgment for the sake of enforcing a conclusion. As much as anything, it is the "flow of Paul's argument" that is in dispute. If one conceives of that "flow" as a polemic against works-righteous legalism, then Carson has a point. But if the intention is to level the playing field for Jew and Gentile alike ("there is no distinction"), then

it is Carson who has distorted the flow of Paul's argument by turning it a dispute over "legalism" versus "grace."
¹² Garlington, "Imputation or Union," 50.
¹³ While commending my acknowledgment that faith's object that is crucial in Paul's argument, Carson thinks that I want to have my cake and eat it too ("Vindication," 68, n. 46). This criticism misspeaks on several counts. (1) My "gratuitous reference to boundary markers, which are scarcely central to Paul's concerns in the opening chapters of Romans," is not so "gratuitous" after all. While the boundary markers hardly exhaust the law of Moses, they are part and parcel of "the works of the law" that do indeed play a central role in the opening chapters of Romans. As Ben Witherington puts it, the law was a "package deal, and one cannot separate out one portion of its commandments from another. All must be obeyed if one is under the Law" (*Grace in Galatia: A Commentary on Paul's Letter to the Galatians* [Grand Rapids: Eerdmans, 1998], 353). Moreover, *the* preeminent boundary marker, circumcision, stands out rather conspicuously in the early going of Romans. Rom 2:25-3:1 makes quite a point of it; and the polemic of Rom 4:9-12 revolves precisely around circumcision: Abraham was considered to be a righteous person before his circumcision and the advent of the law.

(2) Carson maintains that it is far from clear that Paul accepts faith "in place of allegiance to the law of Moses" because "faith shuts out the law, which condemns." Precisely. Righteousness is now revealed apart from the law (Rom 3:21), and it is just Abraham who proves the point, because he exercised faith(fulness) toward Yahweh long before the advent of the Torah. The law that condemns is none other than *Moses'* law. This is why Israel must come to see that Christ is the end of the law and must submit to *God's righteousness* that is now localized in him, not the Torah (Rom 10:3-4). Undergirding the entire discussion of faith, righteousness, and law in Romans is a teleology of the law. It has had its day and must now recede into the background because of the advent of the one to whom it pointed. Now that he has come, our faith is "reckoned as" or "considered to be" righteousness because of faith's object.

(3) According to Carson, I define faith's "quintessential meaning" as "conformity to the will of God." In the process, I surreptitiously make this faith essentially the righteousness which is then rightly imputed to believers as righteousness. Such, language, he says, is "notoriously slippery." He continues: "Like most who take this line, Garlington has not come to terms with Paul's insistence that the faith he has in view is not in any sense properly seen as something intrinsically the believer's and so 'good' that it earns this imputation as righteousness. Rather, it is categorized as a 'gift' (Rom 4:4), which is given to the ungodly."

This assessment creates a whole subset of problems. (a) I did not define *faith's* "quintessential meaning" as "conformity to the will of God." Rather, I said that the "quintessential meaning" of *righteousness* is "conformity to the will of God." This is what I actually wrote: "It is just such an appraisal of the reckoning of righteousness that opens up the intention of Rom 4:6: *because of its object*, faith, and faith alone, is accepted in the place of allegiance to the law of Moses, including, most prominently, the various boundary markers of Jewish identity. In strict terms, faith is *reckoned as* righteousness: our faith in Christ is looked upon as tantamount to righteousness in its quintessential meaning — conformity to the will of God—because *in Christ* we have become God's very righteousness (2 Cor 5:21)" ("Imputation or Union," 51). Rather obviously, Carson did not read carefully enough.

(b) I never wrote of faith as "essentially the righteousness which is then rightly imputed to believers as righteousness." Throughout, my contention is that nothing is *imputed*, as such, to the believer. That my language is "surreptitious" (i.e., "dishonest") and "slippery" is a judgment-call on Carson's part, stemming from polemical ambitions, not the actual import of my words, especially as Carson has substituted "faith" for "righteousness" in my sentence regarding "conformity to the will of God."

(c) To allege that I, and others, have not come to terms "with Paul's insistence that the faith he has in view is not in any sense properly seen as something intrinsically the believer's and so 'good' that it earns this imputation as righteousness" is not fair or accurate in the least. Neither I nor anyone else I know imagine that believers do anything to "earn imputation as righteousness." To couch the issue in such terms is to contort my actual statements beyond recognition. Abraham was certainly not inherently righteous apart from the grace of God; but *as empowered by that grace*, he clung in faith to God's promise of a seed. For that reason, says Paul, "it was reckoned to him as righteousness." Note Rom 4:20-22: "No distrust made him waver concerning the promise of God, but he grew strong in his faith as he gave glory to God, fully convinced that God was able to do what he had promised. *That is why [dio]* his faith was 'reckoned to him as righteousness'."

[14] The same is true of Carson ("Vindication," e.g., 59-63), in disregard of the Semitic underpinning of *logizomai eis*.

[15] See the assemblage of passages by Gundry, "Nonimputation," 18-22. Gundry's consistent rendering of *logizomai eis* as "counted to be" is tantamount to my translation, "regard as." In the previous response, reference was made to G. Von Rad, "Faith Reckoned as Righteousness," *The Problem of the Hexateuch and Other Essays* (London: SCM, 1984), 125-30. However, I neglected to mention Hans-Wolfgang Heiland, *Die Anrechnung des Glaubens zur Gerechtigkeit: Untersuchungen zur Begriffsbestimmung von* hasab *und* logizesthai, Beiträge zur Wissenschaft vom Alten und Neuen Testament 18 (Stuttgart: Kohlhammer, 1936); id., "logizomai, logismos," *Theological Dictionary of the New Testament*, eds. G. Kittel and G. Friedrich. 10 vols. (Grand Rapids: Eerdmans, 1964-76), 4.284-92.

[16] Nobody would disagree with Carson that the object of Abraham's faith is the God who graciously promises ("Vindication," 66). Nevertheless, in the Abraham narrative of Genesis, God's gracious promises are complemented by the patriarch's steadfast "obedience of faith," without which the promises would not have been realized. Carson and Piper fail to remind us that it is Yahweh himself who insists that Abraham walk before him and be blameless (Gen 17:1). It is frequently overlooked that by the time Paul finishes Romans 4 he stresses none other than the persevering quality of Abraham's faith (vv. 20-25). By way of analogy, a neglected text is 1 Kgs 3:6 (2 Chron 1:8) (Solomon speaking): "You have shown great and steadfast love to your servant my father David, *because he walked before you in faithfulness, in righteousness, and in uprightness of heart toward you*; and you have kept for him this great and steadfast love, and have given him a son to sit on his throne today." See also Ps 103:17-18.

[17] Carson's generic reading of *asebēs* ("Vindication," 60-61) disregards the historical significance of the word and is out of touch with the polemic of Romans 1-4. In the two centuries or so before Paul, "ungodly" was applied to those outside the parameters of the covenant with Israel, either pagans or apostate Jews. See my *Obedience of Faith*, 84-86, passim (consult the subject index). The equivalent term "sinners" is unpacked by J. D. G. Dunn, *Jesus, Paul, and the Law: Studies in Mark and Galatians* (Louisville: Westminster/John Knox, 1990), 71-77.

[18] "Justifiction" is an ironically humorous typographical error occurring in E. P. Clowney's essay, "The Biblical Doctrine of Justification by Faith," *Right with God: Justification in the Bible and World*, ed. D. A. Carson (London/Grand Rapids: Paternoster/Baker, 1992), 49.

[19] Carson and P. T. O'Brien similarly contend that I have constructed a false dichotomy (Carson, "Vindication," 56, n. 26). To be sure, if there were a textual basis for imputation, then the alternative of imputation *versus* union with Christ would be illegitimate. But it is just such a textual basis that is lacking.

[20] See my "Imputation or Union," 52-54.

[21] For example, on the part of R. C. Sproul (from the back cover of Piper's book).

[22] Gundry observes that the verb *kathistēmi*, in Rom 5:19, means to "establish" by way of appointment, ordination, or making ("Nonimputation," 26). In line with my own interpretation of the verse, Gundry proposes that through Adam's disobedience human beings "were counted" sinful, whereas through Christ's obedience they are "counted as righteous." This being so, the categories of imputation and infusion are simply irrelevant to Paul's argument. Moreover, Gundry is quite right that "all have sinned" (Rom 3:23; 5:12) has reference to the lack of distinction between Jew and Gentile in the matter of sin, not to the imputation of Adam's guilt to his posterity. On the experiential level, Paul says nary a word about imputation. Rather, "all have sinned" means that "under the

influence of sin all have sinned for themselves, not that they sinned in the original sin of Adam" ("Nonimputation," 28).

[23] Murray, "Definitive Sanctification," *Collected Writings of John Murray*, 4 vols. (Edinburgh: Banner of Truth, 1977), 2.277-84.

[24] Murray, *The Epistle to the Romans*, New International Commentary on the New Testament. 2 vols. (Grand Rapids: Eerdmans, 1959, 1965), 1.222. Even more explicit is T. R. Schreiner, *Romans*, Baker Exegetical Commentary on the New Testament (Grand Rapids: Baker, 1998), 319.

[25] Garlington, *Faith, Obedience, and Perseverance: Aspects of Paul's Letter to the Romans*, Wissenschaftliche Untersuchungen zum Neuen Testament 79 (Tübingen: Mohr-Siebeck, 1994), 44-71, 144-63.

[26] Yinger, *Paul, Judaism, and Judgment According to Deeds*, Society for New Testament Studies Monograph Series 105 (Cambridge: Cambridge University Press, 1999), 146-82; Gathercole, *Where is Boasting? Early Jewish Soteriology and Paul's Response in Romans 1-5* (Grand Rapids: Eerdmans, 2002), 201.

[27] Hoekema, *Saved By Grace* (Grand Rapids: Eerdmans, 1989), 163-69.

[28] Bultmann, "Is Exegesis without Presuppositions Possible?" *Existence and Faith* (New York: World, 1960), 342-51.

[29] I would refer again to my essay on the biblical-theological method, *Exegetical Essays*, 1-15. The article appeared originally in *Acorns to Oaks: The Primacy and Practice of Biblical Theology*, ed. M. G. Haykin (Dundas, ON: Joshua Press, 2003), 25-42.

[30] See notably N. T. Wright, *The Climax of the Covenant: Christ and the Law in Pauline Theology* (Minneapolis: Fortress, 1991); *The New Testament and the People of God*, Christian Origins and the Question of God 1 (Minneapolis: Fortress, 1991); *Jesus and the Victory of God*, Christian Origins and the Question of God 2 (Minneapolis: Fortress, 1996).

[31] To be sure, righteousness in Paul has been understood variously. See the handy compendium provided by N. T. Wright, *What Saint Paul Really Said: Was Paul of Tarsus the Real Founder of Christianity?* (Grand Rapids: Eerdmans, 1997), 101.

[32] Garlington, "Imputation or Union," 57 (italics original). See Gundry, "Nonimputation," 36-38, for numerous texts that place "righteousness" and "salvation" in parallel.

[33] Garlington, *Exegetical Essays*, 340-74.

[34] In the first response to Piper, reference was made to my study of *dikaioō*, in which I endeavored to establish that the semantic range of the verb does indeed transcend "declare righteous" ("A Study of Justification by Faith," *Reformation and Revival Journal* 11 [2002], 55-73 = *Exegetical Essays*, 285-99.

[35] Fee, *God's Empowering Presence: The Holy Spirit in the Letters of Paul* (Peabody: Hendrickson, 1994).

[36] The heart of Gundry's thesis is that it is *God's* righteousness, not Christ's, that has become ours when our faith is counted as righteousness.

On the practical level, imputation is objectionable to Gundry because it can impede holiness ("Nonimputation," 43-44, quoting Mark Seifrid and John Wesley). His concern for sanctification as godly living is certainly valid if imputation is used as a pretext for a lack of growth in grace. My assumption, however, is that this is not necessarily, or normally, the case with those who espouse imputation.

On the other side, in agreement with Piper and Carson ("Vindication," 72-77), I should think that Gundry has artificially distanced God from Christ in the matter of whose righteousness is made ours. In strict terms, Paul does speak of "God's righteousness" or a "righteousness from God" (2 Cor 5:21; Phil 3:8-9). Yet there are counterbalancing factors. For one, Phil 3:9 expresses Paul's desire to be found "in him." The righteousness he longs for comes "from God;" yet it is none other than a righteousness that is *"in him."* How can a righteousness "in Christ" somehow be distanced from Christ himself? For another, Paul is not to be read in isolation from the rest of the NT. Particularly the Gospel temptation narratives and the Letter to the Hebrews make it abundantly clear that Jesus is the man of faith who fulfills the obligations of the covenant (Matt 3:15—"all righteousness").

Gundry is correct to challenge the growing consensus that Paul's own phrase "faith of Jesus Christ" (*pistis Iēsou Christou*) ought to be rendered "the [covenant] faithfulness of Jesus Christ" ("Nonimputation," 19, n. 2). Even so, R. B. Hays has still demonstrated that underlying Galatians is a Jesus-narrative as derived from the Gospels (*The Faith of Jesus Christ: An Investigation of the Narrative Substructure of Galatians 3:1-4:11*, Biblical Resource Series. 2nd ed. [Grand Rapids: Eerdmans, 2002]). If Jesus and the Father are one (John 10:30), then by definition God's righteousness *is* Christ's righteousness, especially given that the Lord whose righteousness clothes the eschatological people of God (Isa 61:10; Jer 23:6; 33:16) is actually the Lord Jesus. In a recent article, "Rethinking the 'Sure Mercies of David' in Isaiah 55:3" (*Westminster Theological Journal* 69 [2007], 279-304), P. Gentry has argued cogently that the "sure mercies of David" (Isa 55:3) are David's own acts of covenant fidelity and righteousness. David is thus the paradigm of Jesus the Christ, whose faithful deeds are granted to Israel (Acts 13:34). I am most grateful to Professor Gentry for a draft of his article.

[37] The phrase "in Christ" has at least a threefold significance for Paul. (1) The *historical*. To be in Christ is to belong to that era of world history inaugurated with his coming. This is the complex of new covenant/new creation as contrasted with what has gone before. Paul thinks of Christ as the new realm God is now establishing in the world. (2) The *personal*. To be "in Christ" is to know him and the power of his resurrection (Phil 3:10), to "live in" him (Gal 2:20), be a member of his body (Rom 12:4-5; 1 Cor 6:15; Eph 1:23; 4:13; 5:30) and to be conformed to his image (Rom 8:29). (3) The *messianic*. Paul's use of "in Christ," "body of Christ," etc., is to be understood in terms of membership within the royal family, the

"Messiah-people." See further my *An Exposition of Galatians: A New Perspective/Reformational Reading*. 2nd ed. (Eugene, OR: Wipf & Stock, 2004), 80-81.

[38] Carson, "Vindication," 71.

[39] Ibid.

[40] Ibid.

[41] Garlington, *Faith, Obedience, and Perseverance*; "Role Reversal and Paul's Use of Scripture in Galatians 3.10-13," *Journal for the Study of the New Testament* 65 (1997), 85-121. The article is reprinted in *Exegetical Essays*, 213-47, which will be cited in the ensuing discussion. The review of Seifrid is likewise in *Exegetical Essays*, 340-74.

[42] Garlington, *Exegetical Essays*, 222-32.

[43] Seifrid, *Christ, Our Righteousness*, New Studies in Biblical Theology 9 (Downers Grove: Inter Varsity, 2000), 136, n. 21.

[44] Still brilliant and relevant is J. D. G. Dunn's "Rom. 7,14-25 in the Theology of Paul," *Theologische Zeitschrift* 31 (1975), 264-73.

[45] As *Jub.* 22:16 not so delicately puts it: "Separate yourself from the Gentiles, and do not eat with them, and do not perform deeds like theirs. And do not become associates of theirs. Because their deeds are defiled, and all of their ways are contaminated and despicable, and abominable."

[46] See my *Obedience of Faith*, e.g., 31-33.

[47] Garlington, *Exegetical Essays*, 224. "Doing the law" is hardly an expression of some program of self-justification. Rather, to do the law is to maintain covenant faithfulness with God. The interplay of covenant faithfulness and such terms as keeping Yahweh's statutes (tantamount to keeping the covenant) or doing the law is evident in Deuteronomy. Crucial is an appreciation of the centrality of the Torah in Israel's self-consciousness of being the chosen people. It is the book of Deuteronomy that gives the classic statement of the role of the Torah in the life of the people. The heart of the book (chaps. 5-28) consists of a restatement of the covenant made at Sinai. Deut 29:1 sums up the whole of that block of material: "These are the words of the covenant which the Lord commanded Moses to make with the sons of Israel in the land of Moab, besides the covenant which He had made with them at Horeb." Throughout the book, the emphasis of covenant life is sustained and reinforced in numerous restatements of the promise (and warnings): "This do and live" (Deut 4:1, 10, 40; 5:29-33; 6:1-2, 18, 24; 7:12-13). This promise does not originate in Deuteronomy, because Lev 18:5 had already said: "So you shall keep My statutes and My judgments, by which a man may live if he does them; I am the Lord."

[48] Garlington, *Exegetical Essays*, 235.

[49] Wenham, *Story as Torah: Reading Old Testament Narratives Ethically* (Grand Rapids: Baker, 2000), 4. Wenham adds that Isaac's deathbed blessing of Genesis 27 is an episode that is most revealing in the way it brings out the viewpoints of the different actors. "It is also one of many in the Old Testament which show the depth of its moral insight and its

avoidance of simple black-and-white judgments. It deals with a world where there are few perfect saints and few unredeemable sinners: most of its heroes and heroines have both virtues and vices, they mix obedience and unbelief" (ibid., 15).

[50] Garlington, *Faith, Obedience, and Perseverance*, 163.

[51] See Dunn's timely counsel, "Rom. 7,14-25 in the Theology of Paul," 272.

[52] Carson, "Vindication," 71.

[53] See the excellent study of Scot McKnight, "The Warning Passages of Hebrews: A Formal Analysis and Theological Conclusions," *Trinity Journal* ns 13 (1992), 21-59.

[54] Du Plessis, *TELEIOS: The Idea of Perfection in the New Testament* (Kampen: Kok, 1959).

[55] Peterson, *Hebrews and Perfection: An Examination of the Concept of Perfection in the Epistle to the Hebrews*, Society for New Testament Studies Monograph Series 47 (Cambridge: Cambridge University Press, 1982), 24 (italics mine). Hence, "perfect" is tantamount to "blameless" (cf. Luke 1:6; Phil 2:15). 4 Macc 7:15 makes the righteous Eleazar's loyalty to the law "perfect" or "complete" by his martyrdom (cf. Peterson, *Hebrews*, 25).

[56] Garlington, *Exegetical Essays*, 361.

[57] As P. T. O'Brien aptly comments, the claims of truth and love should not be held in tension. "The truth as proclaimed should not be dissociated from love or promoted at the expense of love, while a life of love should embody the truth of the gospel" (*The Letter to the Ephesians*, Pillar New Testament Commentary [Grand Rapids: Eerdmans, 1999], 312).

A REVIEW ARTICLE

John Piper, *The Future of Justification:
A Response to N. T. Wright,*
Wheaton: Crossway, 2007

John Piper's new book, as its subtitle indicates, is a rejoinder to N. T. Wright's take on justification in the letters of Paul. The volume consists of eleven chapters and six appendices, all endeavouring to lay bare what Piper considers to be the shortcomings of Wright's understanding of justification and related matters. In his Acknowledgements (11), Piper informs us of his intentions and expectations in a quotation from Solomon Stoddard: "The general tendency of this book is to show that our claim to pardon and sin and acceptance with God is not founded on any thing wrought in us, or acted by us, but only on the righteousness of Christ." By thus framing the issue, Piper's book functions as a broadside against any and all attempts, especially those of Wright, to introduce things "wrought in us" or "acted by us" into the Pauline preaching of justification by faith, thereby detracting from "the righteousness of Christ only." A certain amount of hype has attended the advent of this publication, particularly the "warning" that any other than Piper's outlook on Paul is playing fast-and-loose with the apostle's teaching. According to Piper's web page, "Piper is sounding a crucial warning in this book, reminding all Christians to exercise great caution regarding 'fresh' interpretations of the Bible and to hold fast to the biblical view of justification." In the Conclusion (184), Piper clarifies that the book's title is intended to draw attention to where the doctrine of justification may be going, as well to "the critical importance of God's future act of judgment when our justification will be confirmed."

The Introduction to the book commences on a sombre note. That is to say, eternal life hangs in the balance: "How we live and what we teach will make a difference in whether people obey the gospel or meet Jesus in the fire of judgment.... This is why Paul was provoked at the false teaching in Galatia. It was another gospel and would bring eternal ruin to those who embraced it" (14). Now, Piper's "conviction" is that Wright himself is not under the curse of Gal 1:8-9 (cf. 24, n. 30), and yet the latter's "portrayal of the gospel—and of the doctrine of justification in particular—is so disfigured that it becomes difficult to recognize it as biblically faithful" (15). Piper further maintains that Wright has engaged in no less than a "top-to-bottom rethinking of Paul's theology largely different from the way most people have their New Testament in the last fifteen hundred years." Hence, "When someone engages in such a thorough reconstruction, critics must be extremely careful" (16-17). Wright's reconstruction is "global" in proportions and as such has collided with more traditional outlooks on Paul's theology, especially as regards justification: "his paradigm for justification does not fit well with the ordinary reading of many texts and leaves many ordinary folk not with the rewarding 'ah-ha' experience of illumination, but with a paralyzing sense of perplexity" (24). Consequently, Piper prefers the older guides to the new when it comes to the "deeper issues of how justification really works both in Scripture and in the human soul..." (25, cf. 37-38).

This manner of posing the argument makes for two rather noticeable inconsistencies. For one, if Wright's portrayal of the gospel is what Piper claims, then how could the former *not* be under the curse of Gal 1:8-9, if his portrayal is so *disfigured* that it becomes difficult to recognize it as *biblically faithful*? Is that not, more or less, what Paul thought of the "other gospel" of his opponents in Galatia? Of course, Wright is hardly under the curse, but these are strong terms and, as we will see immediately below, Piper does not carry them through uniformly. Second, it is none other than Wright who thoroughly concurs that "how we live," as well as "what we teach," has an effect on others. Ironically enough, it is Piper who downplays or at least refocuses the all-encompassing demands of the gospel as articulated by Paul's phrase "the obedience of faith" (Rom 1:5; 16:26) as it relates to final justification.

Piper's initial sweeping criticisms are modified, if not mollified, as the book progresses. (a) Wright's definition of justification may not be a devastating mistake, because it may simply conflate denotation and implication when it comes to the matter of covenant membership (44). (b) Wright does indeed use "justification" in more traditional ways (44). (c) Wright is quoted to the effect that in Jesus of Nazareth God had overcome evil and was creating a new world in which justice and peace would reign supreme (45), meaning in principle that Wright does see justification as a creative act. (d) For Wright, justification is both-and: the declaration of God the judge that one is in the right and one's sins are forgiven and that one is a member of the covenant family, the people belonging to Abraham (53). (e) Wright even sounds Protestant (119-20).

At the head of this volume, there is Piper's disavowal of the now standard scholarly procedure of setting New Testament texts within their historical milieu. There are three problems, so says Piper, with such a method: misunderstanding the source, assuming agreement with a source when there is no agreement, and misapplying the meaning of a source. Consequently:

> It will be salutary, therefore, for scholars and pastors and laypeople who do not spend much of their time reading first-century literature to have a modest skepticism when an overarching concept or worldview from the first century is used to give "new" or "fresh" interpretations to biblical texts that in their own context do not naturally give rise to these interpretations (36).

These objections to historical exegesis, I must say, are hardly compelling. Scholars of the stripe of Wright are not unaware of the complexity of historical research and the many occasions on which historians must withhold judgment just because of the uncertainties entailed. The caveats advanced by Piper are well-known, and no scholar of repute would engage in the oversimplified procedure envisioned by him. That said, it *is* possible to trace trajectories of Jewish thought from Ben Sira to the Mishnah; it *is* possible to have a reasonably certain grasp of the theology engaged by Paul and the other New Testament authors. At this point in time, it should not have to be said that the New Testament documents were not, in the first instance, addressed to us; and a common sense recognition of this basic datum must inevitably result in a certain amount of reconstruction of the context of Paul. This is not to make the context more important than the text, nor is it to say that Paul is not to be understood on "his own terms." Rather, it is just Paul's life-situation that serves to illuminate what "his own terms" actually are. When it comes to such central vocabulary items as "law," "covenant," "righteousness," and "justification," there is sufficient intelligibility from the sources that the so-called New Perspective on Paul may fairly claim to have shed considerable light on the actual issues under debate in Paul's day. Certainly, caution must always be exercised in the weighing of historical texts. But even with all the caveats in place, the cause of biblical exegesis is not served by turning back the clock. Once a Copernican revolution has occurred, it will not do to retreat into a pre-Copernican universe.

Piper, rightly in my view, maintains that justification for Paul entails more than a declaration that one is a member of the covenant (*à la* Wright). Instead, quoting Simon Gathercole: "God's act of justification is not one of recognition but is, rather, closer to creation. It is God's determination of our new identity rather than a recognition of it" (42). Even with the various qualifications allotted to Wright, Piper effectively scores some points regarding justification as the experience of salvation by arguing successfully throughout the book that it is a false distinction to bifurcate "justification" and "salvation." In this particular regard, Piper's discussion makes for helpful and even stimulating reading.

From another angle, however, Piper's criticisms fall short of the mark. Restating a thesis from previous publications, that God's righteousness is "his unwavering commitment to act for the sake of his glory," Piper calls into question Wright's conception of righteousness as God's covenant faithfulness, on the basis of Rom 3:1-8, 25-26. The problem is that Piper has failed to appreciate the factors of eschatology and theodicy. In 3:1-8, the issue at stake is God's fidelity in the face of Israel's infidelity (theodicy), a proposition to be unpacked in detail in Romans 9-11. The passage thus confirms, not disproves, Wright's definition. In 3:25-26, eschatology and theodicy combine. The sins committed under the old covenant were not dealt with finally and definitively because God had predetermined (*proetheto*) that Christ would be the "mercy seat" (*hilastērion*): Christ is the ultimate expression of his faithful promise to forgive sins. This is eschatology. The theodicy factor is evident when the participle of 3:26 is read as concessive: "even while justifying the one who has faith in Jesus." Paul's entire statement, then, is to this effect: because of his determination that Christ would be the "mercy seat" for sins, he has remained faithful to his long-term plan to forgive his people's trespasses, and all this *even while justifying* Jew and Gentile alike by the same means—faith in Christ. In so doing, God has not forsaken his people Israel. Rather, as Romans 9-11 is at pains to argue, his (pre)determination to save them was always by means of the gospel of Paul's proclamation.

"The Place of Our Works in Justification" (Chapter 7) is largely a discussion of Rom 2:13. Piper evokes the traditional category of the *basis* or *ground* of justification, in the present and at the end. As familiar as the approach is, methodologically it starts out on the wrong foot. The fact is that Paul hardly ever uses the language of "basis" or "ground." Philippians 3:9, "the righteousness of God based on faith," is the only clear instance, and even here the subject matter is not the "basis of justification," according to the customary jargon. Rather, what characterizes Paul is prepositions of origin and sphere, mainly *ek* and *en*. Thus, contra Piper, "from works of the law" (*ex ergōn nomou*) (Rom 3:20, etc.) and "in the law" (*en nomō*) (e.g., Gal 3:11; 5:4) designates the realm of the Torah, within which one might seek to be justified. By contrast, for Paul, one is justified "in Christ" (e.g., Gal 2:17) and "from faith in Jesus Christ" (e.g., Rom 3:26; Gal 2:16). (I have argued this in some detail in a forthcoming article in *Journal of Biblical Literature*, "Paul's 'Partisan *ek*' and the Question of Justification in Galatians.") Thus, to cast the issue in terms of the "basis" of future justification is to muddy the waters from the outset.

There are two other problems plaguing Piper's treatment of Rom 2:13. One is the disregard of the Jewish backdrop to "the doers of the law." Paul's language is derived from Leviticus 18:5 and the recurring refrain of Deuteronomy, "this do and live" (4:1, 10, 40; 5:29-33; 6:1-2, 18, 24; 7:12-13; cf. 29:9, 29; 30:2, 6, 8, 10, 11, 16, 20; 31:12-13; 33:46). Moreover, in 1 Macc 2:67, the exact phrase "the doers of the law" designates loyalist Jews who would be vindicated by divine justice over against Gentile oppressors. The same combination of words occurs notably in the Qumran *Habakkuk Commentary* (1QpHab) 7:11; 8:1; 12:4. Paul thus lifts the working principle of "covenantal nomism" from the pages of Leviticus and Deuteronomy and transposes it into the eschatological context of faith's obedience as directed toward Christ. For him, it is those who render faithful obedience, the "fruit of the Spirit" (Gal 5:22-24), to Christ who will be vindicated in the last judgment. Wright, then, is correct that Rom 8:3-4 is the explanation of 2:13.

The other exegetical difficulty is that of reducing Rom 2:13 to "public evidence and confirmation of faith at the Last Day for all who will finally be saved" (110). Quoting R. B. Gaffin, Piper is of the conviction that our works are not "(co-) instrumental…for appropriating divine approbation as they supplement faith" (116).

But Rom 2:13 and kindred passages do not read well as simple evidence. Rather, "doing the law" is the precondition of eschatological vindication. Piper has abstracted 2:13 from 2:7: "to those who by patiently doing good seek for glory and honor and immortality, he will give eternal life." On the other side, "for those who are self-seeking and who obey not the truth but wickedness, there will be wrath and fury" (2:8). Rom 2:7, 8 balance each other, and the courses of action depicted by them dictate the outcome of the judgment. Elsewhere in Romans, Paul likewise makes suffering with Christ (8:17) and confession of Christ (10:9-10) preconditions of future eschatological salvation. Reading Paul in this manner does not jeopardize grace, but rather informs us of how the covenant operates, with human response to God's grace as the *sine qua non* of making the covenant "work." It is true that Wright speaks of "evidence" (as quoted on 119-20), but the term is to be coordinated with his contention that obedience is produced in one's life by the Spirit (119, 120). Piper accuses Wright of being unclear how being "in Christ" provides the foundation for final justification (121). However, the former's quotations of the latter on 120 and 129 are as clear as can be. In point of fact, Wright is not at all ambiguous, as Piper alleges.

Not unexpectedly, Piper is concerned to press for the doctrine of the imputation of Christ's active obedience, measured against which Wright falls short. Since I have replied at length to Piper's earlier and kindred work, *Counted Righteous in Christ: Should We Abandon the Imputation of Christ's Righteousness?* (Wheaton: Crossway, 2002, in my *In Defense of the New Perspective on Paul: Essays and Reviews* [Eugene, OR: Wipf & Stock, 2005], 107-97), I will simply cut to the chase here. (a) By Piper's own admission, Wright's remark on Gal 2:19-20 places him in virtual agreement with the sum and substance of imputed righteousness (126). All the benefits of Christ's work are to be had by Wright's understanding of union with Christ without the mechanics of imputation. (b) Piper advances a succession of *non sequiturs*, if one "says no to imputed obedience," as though without imputation there is no foundation for a future justification (128-29). Again, "in Christ" provides the foundation. (c) There is the matter of "faith alone," which, Piper claims, is undermined by Wright's correlation of the verdict of the last day with the entirety of one's life (129). Once again, however, when Wright is allowed to speak for himself, as per the quote on 130-31, precisely the opposite turns out to be the case. Wright's excellent comments on "the obedience of faith" maintain that faith and obedience are not antithetical, and these remarks are not at all ambiguous and unclear, in spite of what Piper claims. Besides offering no comment at all on the important verse Rom 1:5, in his zeal for "faith alone," Piper has failed to distinguish between the Already and the Not Yet. Wright acknowledges that Already-justification is by faith alone, but Not Yet-justification entails faith's obedience consisting in perseverance and covenant service. The brand of *sola fide* forwarded by Piper is simply not in the New Testament (as per, e.g., Rom 4:19-25; 2 Cor 5:10; Jas 2:18-26). Ironically, to be sure, Piper commences his book with the quotation from Solomon Stoddard, but it was just Stoddard's illustrious grandson, Jonathan Edwards, who espoused a clear-cut theology of future justification inclusive of the obedience of the Christian.

Chapter 10 engages Wright's take on Paul in relation to Second Temple Judaism. Piper presses for a "legalistic" understanding of the Judaism of this period, arguing that legalism and ethnocentrism are virtually one and the same, inasmuch as both are rooted in self-righteousness. Regarding 4QMMT in particular, Piper simply asserts that Wright's understanding of justification is not served by this text, without presenting any particular analysis of it. However, a truly responsible treatment of MMT, such as Martin Abegg, "4QMMT, Paul, and 'Works of the Law,'" *The Bible at Qumran: Text, Shape, and Interpretation* (Grand Rapids: Eerdmans, 2001), 203-16, demonstrates ably enough that Wright is more in tune with the intention of the document than Piper. And because of his "pre-Copernican" outlook on first-century Judaism, there is a strained and unconvincing attempt to read "legalism" and "self-righteousness" into the portrait of Pharisaism found in the gospels.

The final chapter takes up again the question of righteousness, which Piper here defines as God's "commitment to do what is right" (164). Later (179) it is categorically denied that righteousness is "the covenant faithfulness of God." One wonders how God's "commitment to do what is right" can be abstracted so arbitrarily from the covenant relationship, but there it is. More serious is Piper's out-of-context quotation of Wright (165-66):

> This is why, when Paul looks ahead to the future and asks, as well one might, what God will say on the last day, he holds up as his joy and crown, not the merits

and death of Jesus, but the churches he has planted who remain faithful to the gospel.

Piper is astonished that Wright would pen such a sentence, especially given the impact he fears that such a statement will have on preaching, which is why this book was written (167, 187-88). Yet all one has to do is read the page from which this quote is lifted. Wright is not denying "the merits and death of Jesus" for Paul's theology as such, but rather they are not the focus of Rom 8:1-11!

The chapter proceeds to defend imputation at further length and is essentially a distillation of Piper's *Counted Righteous in Christ*. Piper does score a point as regards Wright's take on 2 Cor 5:21. Here the traditional reading makes more sense: in Christ God's righteousness has become ours. A parallel text is Phil 3:9: "the righteousness *from* God," itself an echo of Isa 54:17 ("their righteousness from me").

Piper's Conclusion is at heart a plea not to let "works" "add to the perfection and beauty and all-sufficiency of Christ's obedience..." (187). To do so would be a "double tragedy." However, such alarmism is simply unnecessary and misjudges positions taken by Wright and others. Effectively, Piper gives the whole case away when he underscores the necessity of the fruit of the Spirit on the part of the believer (186-87). And his fear that such obedience might add to the work of Christ is, for the most part, not grounded in reality.

In sum, Piper's response to Tom Wright is worth reading for those interested in the seemingly never ending debate over justification. On the couple of issues noted above, I should think that Piper has the better of the argument. But for the most part, he has failed to demonstrate that Wright is wrong. The claim that the latter's paradigm for justification "leaves many ordinary folk not with the rewarding 'ah-ha' experience of illumination, but with a paralyzing sense of perplexity" (24) is simply too subjective to be a useful criterion. In a nutshell, this book is mostly a defense of traditional doctrines, with a minimum of persuasive exegesis and a heavy reliance on confessionalism.

As a pastor, it is understandable that Dr. Piper has a pastoral concern. But is Wright's theology of justification so dire that it is apt to result in Piper's "double tragedy?" I think not, especially given Piper's concessions as indicated above. In my estimation,

Wright is the one who has "delivered the goods" when it comes to penetrating exegesis and, dare one say, *fresh* insight into the letters of Paul. It is also understandable that Piper would want to allay the "confusion" he senses on the part of his church members. However, I must say that such "laypersons" would have to be theologically literate indeed to tackle this volume, not least its microscopic footnotes. Otherwise, the confusion is liable to remain!

As much as anything, this book is flawed by its near phobia of anything that smacks of newness and freshness, which, for Piper, must be suspect by definition. This is why we are exhorted to be suspicious of "our love of novelty" and eager to test biblical interpretations by "the wisdom of the centuries" (38). Agreed, but surely "the wisdom of the centuries" includes our own century. Wright is precisely correct: we are "to think new thoughts *arising of the text* and to dare to try them out in word and deed" (quoted on 37, italics added). Piper would do well to recall Matt 13:52: "And he said to them, 'Therefore every scribe who has been trained for the kingdom of heaven is like a householder who brings out of his treasure *things new and old*.'" I would say the appropriate response to matters "new" and "fresh" is not skepticism but the Beroean spirit of searching the Scriptures to see if these things are so (Acts 17:11).

A REVIEW ARTICLE

D. A. Carson, Peter T. O'Brien, and Mark A. Seifrid (eds.), *Justification and Variegated Nomism. Volume I. The Complexities of Second Temple Judaism.* Grand Rapids: Baker, 2001.

If it is a truism that there is no end to the making of many books (Eccl 12:12), then Qoheleth's famous complaint would appear to be uncommonly appropriate in the face of the unending flow of books, dissertations and articles that have kept the presses rolling ever since the entrée of the "New Perspective" on Paul in his relation to Second Temple Judaism. Appearing in rather close conjunction with certain other responses to the New Perspective,[1] the study under review seeks to shift the paradigm away from the "Sanders/Dunn trajectory," as Moisés Silva calls it,[2] back to a more traditional Reformational reading of Judaism, especially as it impacts on the doctrine of justification by faith.

1. The New Perspective on Paul in His Relation to Second Temple Judaism

In order to clarify the *raison d'être* of this book, it will be helpful to summarize the position to which it takes exception, as encapsulated by E. P. Sanders' now famous phrase "covenantal nomism." Sanders himself explains:

> Covenantal nomism is the view that one's place in God's plan is established on the basis of the covenant and that the covenant requires as the proper response of man his obedience to its commandments, while providing means of atonement for transgression..... Obedience maintains one's position in the covenant, but it does not earn God's grace as such.... Righteousness in Judaism is a term which implies the maintenance of status among the group of the elect.[3]

In one place, he summarizes his position under the following points:

> (1) God has chosen Israel and (2) given the law. The law implies both (3) God's promise to maintain the election and (4) the requirement to obey. (5) God rewards obedience and punishes transgression. (6) The

law provides for means of atonement, and atonement results in (7) maintenance or reestablishment of the covenantal relationship. (8) All those who are maintained in the covenant by obedience, atonement and God's mercy belong to the group which will be saved. An important interpretation of the first and last points is that election and ultimately salvation are considered to be by God's mercy rather than human achievement.[4]

J. D. G. Dunn further clarifies Sanders' outlook:

> This covenant relationship was regulated by the law, not as a way of entering the covenant, or of gaining merit, but as the way of living *within* the covenant; and that included the provision of sacrifice and atonement for those who confessed their sins and thus repented.... This attitude Sanders characterized by the now well known phrase "covenantal nomism"—that is, "the maintenance of status" among the chosen people of God by observing the law given by God as part of that covenant relationship.[5]

Additionally, N. T. Wright epitomizes Sanders' work in these terms:

> His major point, to which all else is subservient, can be quite simply stated. Judaism in Paul's day was not, as has regularly been supposed, a religion of legalistic works-righteousness. If we imagine that it was, and that Paul was attacking it as if it was, we will do great violence to it and to him. Most Protestant exegetes had read Paul and Judaism as if Judaism was a form of the old heresy Pelagianism, according to which humans must pull themselves up by their moral bootstraps and thereby earn justification, righteousness, and salvation. No, said Sanders. *Keeping the law within Judaism always functioned within a covenantal scheme.* God took the initiative, when he made a covenant with Judaism; God's grace thus precedes everything that people (specifically, Jews) do in response. The Jew keeps the law out of gratitude, as the proper response to grace—not, in other words, in order to *get* into the covenant people, but to *stay* in. Being "in" in the first place was God's gift. This scheme Sanders famously labelled as "covenantal nomism" (from the Greek

nomos, law). Keeping the Jewish law was the human response to God's covenantal initiative.[6]

To these explanations, I have attempted to summarize covenantal nomism under three basic propositions:

> (1) Israel became the people of God by his electing grace as manifested in the Exodus. (2) The covenant forms the context of law-keeping. In other words, Israel is bound to keep the law not in order to earn salvation, but in order to maintain her side of the covenant bond. Thus, the stress falls not on legalism but on fidelity to the covenant...and preservation of the community. (3) Sanders, therefore, epitomizes his understanding of Jewish religion with the phrases "getting in" and "staying in." One "gets in" the covenant by being born into the Jewish community, which was formed in the first place by the electing grace of God. One "stays in" the covenant by keeping the law, not perfectly and certainly not for the purpose of establishing a claim on God, but out of a sincere intention to remain loyal to the God of grace. And if one sinned, God has provided the sacrifices to atone for sin and restore one to his standing within the community.[7]

In the midst of all the debate over these issues and the inevitable confusion on the part of some, Dunn calls to mind that the phrase "covenantal nomism" does indeed consists of two parts: covenant and *nomos* (law).

> It is important to note...that Sanders did not characterize Judaism solely as a "covenantal" religion. The key phrase he chose was the double emphasis, "covenantal nomism". And Sanders made clear that the second emphasis was not to be neglected. The Torah/ law was given to Israel to be obeyed, an integral part of the covenant relationship, and that obedience was necessary if Israel's covenant status was to be maintained. Even if obedience did not earn God's grace as such, was not a means to "*get into*" the covenant, obedience *was* necessary to maintain one's position in the covenant, to "*stay in*" the covenant. So defined, Deuteronomy can be seen as the most fundamental statement of Israel's "covenantal nomism". Given the traditional emphasis on Judaism's "nomism" it is hardly surprising that Sanders should have placed

greater emphasis on the "covenantal" element in the twin emphasis. But in his central summary statements he clearly recognized that both emphases were integral to Judaism's self-understanding.[8]

While it is true that Sanders was hardly the first to espouse such an avenue of approach to the sources,[9] it may be safely said that his work represents a watershed in the history of interpretation.[10] Since the publication of his book in 1977, Sanders' assessment of pre-destruction Judaism has become increasingly popular among historians of religion and NT scholars. This not to deny, of course, that there are notable exceptions to the growing consensus, as evidenced conspicuously by the volume herein reviewed.

The actual phrase "New Perspective" was coined by James Dunn, in his Manson Memorial Lecture of 1982, entitled "The New Perspective on Paul."[11] Dunn builds on Sanders' construction of pre-destruction Judaism, but levels the criticism that "Sanders' Paul hardly seems to be addressing Sanders' Judaism."[12] In other words, the Paul of Sanders takes his countrymen to task for precisely the same reason that Luther did! Dunn thus distances himself from Sanders' Paul by defining the apostle's phrase "the works of the law" not as a generalized principle of obedience for the purpose of earning salvation, but as those works done in response to the covenant in order to maintain the bond between God and Israel (the works of "staying in"). Dunn does maintain that "the works of the law" encompasses the whole Torah, but within the period of the Second Temple certain aspects of the law became especially prominent as the boundary and identity markers of the Jewish people: prominently circumcision, food laws, purity laws, and sabbath.

Dunn is frequently misrepresented on this point, as though he restricts "the works of the law" to the "boundary markers," without allowing that the whole Torah is in view when Paul employs the phrase. But just the opposite is the case. He states, in point of fact, that circumcision and the other ordinances were *not* the only distinguishing traits of Jewish self-identity. However, they were the focal point of the Hellenistic attack on the Jews during the Maccabean period. As such, they became *the acid tests of one's loyalty to Judaism.* "In short...the particular regulations of circumcision and food laws [et al.] were important not in themselves, but because they *focused* Israel's distinctiveness and made visible Israel's claims to be a people set apart, were the clearest points which differentiated the Jews from the nations. The law was coterminous with Judaism."[13]

It is just to this appraisal of ancient Judaism and Paul's response that *Justification and Variegated Nomism* takes exception.

2. Summary of Contents and General Evaluation

This book is the first of a two volume project, the primary purpose of which is to re-evaluate Sanders' identification of the "pattern of religion" of pre-destruction Judaism as "covenantal nomism." In point of fact, the end in view is to shift the paradigm back to a "pre-Sanders" reading of the Jewish sources. The editors have chosen to proceed much as Sanders himself did: volume one is entirely devoted to the study of Jewish literature in close chronological proximity to Paul, while volume two will be devoted to reading Paul in light of this freshly evaluated literary context.

The motivation of the project is spelled out clearly in the introduction: Sanders' work has been enormously influential, particularly in the way it constitutes the foundation, or at least the touchstone, for the "New Perspective" on Paul. The editors rightly claim that the work of New Perspective scholars does not represent one monolithic perspective on Paul, but that they generally share an appreciation for the way in which Sanders exposed the biases underlying the study of Paul. Sanders attempted to provide a historically grounded picture of ancient Judaism based directly on the Jewish sources within which Paul is to be situated. The present book thus sets about to test whether Sanders' notion of "covenantal nomism" adequately characterizes the Judaism of Paul's day.

Not including the "Introduction" and "Summary and Conclusions," both of which are written by D. A. Carson, *Justification and Variegated Nomism* contains 14 essays: Daniel Falk, "Prayers and Psalms;" Craig Evans, "Scripture-Based Stories in the Pseudepigrapha;" Peter Enns, "Expansions of Scripture;" Philip Davies, "Didactic Stories;" Richard Bauckham, "Apocalypses;" Robert Kugler, "Testaments;" Donald Gowan, "Wisdom;" Paul Spilsbury, "Josephus;" Philip Alexander, "Torah and Salvation in Tannaitic Literature;" Martin McNamara, "Some Targumic Themes;" David Hay, "Philo of Alexandria;" Markus Bockmuehl, "1QS and Salvation at Qumran;" Mark Seifrid, "Righteousness Language in the Hebrew Scriptures and Early Judaism;" Roland Deines, "The Pharisees Between 'Judaisms' and Common Judaism."

What strikes the reader immediately is that no "party line" is taken in this book; neither is it uniform in the way each author approaches the literature and relates the question of covenantal nomism to the texts under discussion. While the lack of uniformity might be perceived as a problem of methodological consistency, the diversity of approaches is illuminating in its own way. Had the issue of covenantal nomism been treated with precise uniformity in each chapter, this book would have been entirely predictable, not to say needlessly repetitive.

In the main, the essays are well written, handle the subject matter responsibly and evenhandedly, and attempt to update and build on Sanders' work rather than dismiss or defend it simplistically. In many cases, updating or building on Sanders' work has meant evaluating literature that Sanders did not include in *Paul and Palestinian Judaism*. Most of the authors recognize the complexity of bringing a modern agenda to ancient writings that may have had a completely different agenda and, consequently, may not easily yield answers to the questions posed. Also, most recognize the complexity of the literature itself and are appropriately cautious in drawing anything resembling sweeping conclusions.

Nevertheless, the volume as a whole has a few drawbacks. First, in the years since Sanders' seminal work, the amount of material evidence respecting Jewish history, archaeology and theology that has come to light is enormous. And yet a notable amount of this evidence has gone unnoticed. One is left with the impression that at least several of the essays were written in some haste. To be fair, the volume claims to be surveying Jewish literature, not Jewish history generally. Still, because the work aspires to be a comprehensive assessment of whether covenantal nomism is the dominant "pattern of religion" for ancient Judaism broadly speaking, it would have been greatly enhanced by at least some reference to this material.

Second, Carson, as well as a few of the contributors, makes mention of Sanders' failure to analyze certain works in light of the concept of covenantal nomism, and they imply that Sanders' selective use of texts skewed the argument. Carson, for example, is perplexed as to why Sanders did not make use of Josephus (522). But it goes unnoticed that Sanders specifically writes in *Paul and Palestinian Judaism* that his goal (one of six stated on p. xii) is "to argue a case concerning Palestinian Judaism (that is, Judaism as reflected in material of Palestinian provenance) as a whole." Thus, Sanders did not claim to be providing an exhaustive study of all relevant Jewish literature; his exclusion of Diaspora literature was quite intentional. How his clearly stated intentions could have escaped the notice of the editors of this book is puzzling.[14]

Third, Carson's summaries and conclusions are conspicuously at odds with the majority of the essayists enlisted by him.[15] Most of the contributors actually affirm that "covenantal nomism" is an adequate designation of the Jewish understanding of the relationship between Israel and her God. Carson acknowledges that several authors give qualified validation to covenantal nomism, but he concludes that "the fit isn't very good" (547); or that, while "Sanders is not wrong everywhere...he is wrong when he tries to establish that his category is right everywhere" (543). But in view of the fact that Sanders limited his corpus of documents, and since he himself recognized the diversity of expression in this varied literature, Carson's criticisms are too severe and too polemical.

Even more remarkable is that his conclusions do not coincide with those drawn by the majority of the authors, whose critiques of Sanders are considerably more nuanced and far less aggressive than his own. As Eisenbaum comments, the incongruity is most apparent when Carson calls covenantal nomism "reductionistic" and "misleading"—a charge that might well be leveled against him in relation to the body of work he purports to be summarizing! With some justification, then, Dunn can query:

> Was Carson reading a different version of the essays he then published? He complains that the phrase is "too doctrinaire". But it seems to be he himself who so regards it; I am not aware of advocates of "the new perspective" who treat it so. Perhaps by presenting it as something rigid it becomes easier to attack. Whereas the findings of most of the contributors to his volume are in effect that "covenantal nomism" serves well as a summary phrase, so long as one recognizes the variations in emphasis, depending on different styles and circumstances—"variegated *covenantal nomism*".[16]

In spite of my own disagreements with the conclusions drawn by Carson and some of the contributors, the volume comprises a very useful contribution to scholarship. Irrespective of Carson's personal biases, the essays as a whole demonstrate that "covenantal nomism" remains an appropriate category for assessing Second Temple literature. A case in point is Richard Bauckham's appraisal of *4 Ezra* and *2 Baruch*. Sanders conceded that *4 Ezra*, as a conspicuous exception to the "rule" of covenantal nomism, lapses into out-and-out legalism, although *2 Baruch* already undertakes to correct the outlook of its author.[17] Bauckham, by contrast, thinks that these two documents represent a variety of covenantal nomism that places extra stress on law-obedience.[18]

As regards this book's applicability to Paul's theology, we must await volume two. However, we may anticipate that book by posing what would appear to be a piece of presumptive reasoning, as this first installment is meant to lay the groundwork for the second. To judge from what one may piece together from the editors' intentions, it would seem that the argumentation is as follows: Second Temple Judaism was diverse; therefore, there were legalists in Paul's day; therefore, Paul is arguing against the "legalists" (as opposed to the "covenantal nomists"). Time will tell how the editors intend to pursue this apparent agenda. But at this stage of the game, one senses that the entire enterprise may well prove to be reductionistic.

It is fair to say that scholars generally acknowledge that the Judaism of the Second Temple period was diverse. In fact, it is normally taken for granted that one should speak, these days, of *Judaisms* rather than Judaism.[19] Even so, we may legitimately continue to speak of the "four pillars of Second Temple Judaism," which provided an element of unity amidst all the diversity.[20] Thus, it is possible to overwork the diversity angle. But even granting to this volume that pre-destruction Judaism was diverse, its real title, as Dunn proposes, should have been *Justification and Variegated **Covenantal Nomism**!*[21]

In rounding off this segment of the review, just a couple of technical notes. For one, the editors should have exercised a heavier hand in breaking up long and complex paragraphs, of which there are many, for the sake of easier reading. For another, the volume is beautifully printed, but one wonders why the peculiar Hebrew font was chosen, one that certainly does not facilitate the reading process.

3. Specific Response to Mark Seifrid

Mark Seifrid's essay on "Righteousness Language in the Hebrew Scriptures and Early Judaism" is of particular interest because it brings us to the heart of the recent debate respecting justification and related issues. Because volume one is intended to pave the way for volume two of this undertaking on justification, it will be worth the while to examine what promises to be one of the more significant foundational articles for the exegesis of Pauline texts that is to follow.

Summary of Seifrid's Argument

Seifrid's essay commences with a very competent and helpful survey of scholarship pertaining to righteousness. (One only wishes that, for the sake of the general reader, the German quotations had been translated.) In this introductory segment, Seifrid is concerned to resist conceptions of righteousness that limit it to only a relationship and seek to dismiss any notion of a righteous status and a righteous norm. Correspondingly, he also takes scholars to task who fail to grasp the punitive component of righteousness language in its Jewish setting.

The nub of the matter resides in Seifrid's downplay of righteousness as covenant fidelity. According to Seifrid, we have been mislead by scholars who equate the "righteousness" word-group (the Hebrew verb *tsadaq*, the nouns *tsedek* and *tsdeqah* and the adjective *tsadiq*) with "covenant" (*berith*). He is convinced of this because, on his count, there are only seven passages in the OT in which the terms come into "any significant semantic contact" (423). The passages are: Neh 9:32-33; Ps 50:1-6; 111:1-10; Isa 42:6; 61:8-11; Hos 2:16-20; Dan 9:4-7. Seifrid concedes that a full explanation for the infrequency of the convergence of these terms would have to be quite detailed, and that the relation of righteousness to covenant may be approached from historical and theological perspectives rather than of lexical semantics. Such matters, however, lie beyond the scope of his concern.

In pursuing his agenda that "righteousness" = covenant fidelity is misleading, Seifrid proposes that the word "covenant" signifies "a distinct relationship, which often calls forth quasi-forensic and familial language." In biblical terms, he says, one does not "act righteously or unrighteously" with respect to a covenant. Rather, one "keeps," "remembers," "establishes" a covenant, or the like. Conversely, one "breaks," "transgresses," "forsakes," "despises," "forgets" or "profanes" a covenant. He notes that charges of covenantal infidelity appear in the Prophets in the form of familial metaphors (e.g., Isa 1:2; Hos 1:2). Expressed positively, a covenantal relation demands love and loyalty (Hos 6:6). For this reason, "to act in faithfulness and love in a covenant is to act righteously, of course, so that it is not surprising to find righteousness language in occasional connection with *hesed* ("loving kindness" or "covenant love") and *'emunah* ("faith/faithfulness")" (424). Such data lead Seifrid to conclude:

> Just as a covenant is a particular kind of relation, righteousness takes the particular form of love and loyalty in a covenantal relation. All "covenant-keeping" is righteous behavior, but not all righteous behavior is "covenant-keeping." It is misleading, therefore, to speak of "God's righteousness" as his "covenant-faithfulness." It would be closer to the biblical language to speak of "faithfulness" as "covenant-righteousness" (ibid.).

Next in the argument, Seifrid proffers that the biblical understanding of righteousness, in the first instance, has to do with creation rather than covenant. This, for him, accounts for the infrequent collocation (statistically speaking) of righteousness and covenant language. In favor of this conclusion, Seifrid points to the frequency with which "righteousness" is associated with the vocabulary of "ruling and judging," particularly in the case of the king of Israel. At root, however, the biblical conception of kingship bears a universal dimension stemming from creation. The frequent association of "righteousness" language with "ruling and judging," therefore, strongly supports the claim that "righteousness" has to do with creational theology. As Seifrid contends, "For the biblical writers, the demand for social justice derives from God, the divine king, who has determined to secure the good and beneficial order of creation" (426). It is just because of this juridical background of righteousness as the expression of the divine king's function to restore and promote social order that explains, for Seifrid, the frequent association of "salvation" and "deliverance" words with "righteousness."

Seifrid buttresses his argument by noting that frequently in these instances in which "salvation" and "righteousness" stand in parallel "righteousness" is represented by the feminine form of the noun, *tsdeqah*. In so observing, he presses a distinction between the feminine and masculine genders of "righteousness," as both occur in the Hebrew Bible. His claim is that there is a difference of usage between the two: "the feminine tends to refer to a concrete thing such as a righteous act or vindicating judgment. The masculine usually signifies the more abstract concept of 'right order' or 'that which is morally right'" (428). On this basis, Seifrid then maintains that the feminine form of the noun is favored by biblical writers to articulate the vindicating and punitive acts of

God. God is thus said to be "righteous" (*tsadiq*) when he rewards righteous people and punishes the guilty. Therefore—and this is the point at which Seifrid is driving—the relative frequency of the idea of "saving righteousness" (*iustitia salutifera*) is accounted for by God's promises to intervene to "right" the wrongs in a fallen world. Presumably, Seifrid elaborates this proposition in an attempt to root the synonymous parallelism of "righteousness" and "salvation," found in some prominent OT texts,[22] not so much in God's "covenant fidelity" as in his role of king and judge, the one who brings retributive justice to the earth.

Now ensues a survey of righteousness language in extrabiblical Jewish writings stemming from the end of the exile to the production of the Mishnah. Seifrid rightly notes that, for various reasons, the task of analyzing this language is exceedingly complex. His own analysis of the lexical data looks first to the Dead Sea Scrolls and thereafter to rabbinic literature.

With respect to the Qumran materials, Seifrid concedes that "covenant" is often associated with righteousness terminology (see 434, n. 90 for references). However, he questions that Sanders' framework of interpretation holds even here: "The community regarded the covenant into which they had entered as the true will of God, which one was obliged to perform" (434). Then, citing passages from the *Community Rule* (1QS) 1:7-8; 3:9b-12), he fastens on the demand for the sect to walk in perfection in all God's ways. Such expressions as "perfection of way" and "uprightness of heart," he writes, are not general references to piety, but rather represent "the essence of the life and worship of the community" (437). From this he concludes: "Even though the divine saving intervention is still anticipated, the Qumran covenant does not save as a promise prior to and independent of obedience, but precisely *as* the 'perfection of way' in which righteousness is found" (435).

Seifrid's attention is particularly devoted to 1QS 11:2-4, according to which the author praises God for the righteousness that has blotted out his transgressions and vindicated him. Repeating his earlier interpretation of this passage,[23] Seifrid prefers a reconstruction of the Hebrew text that would make the psalmist say: "with *my* righteous deeds he blots out my transgressions," rather than "with *his* [God's] righteousness he blots out my transgressions."[24] Given this rendering, it follows that:

> The thought of 1QS 11:3 remains firmly grounded in the saving action of God. The righteousness of the

psalmist is given to him by God, in the life and worship of the community. It is no contradiction to this thought, that the Qumran writers also speak of human beings as having no righteousness. The righteousness which they have is not theirs, but is found in the community which God founded. Likewise, the various references to hope in or the experience of God's righteousness (singular) in the context of 1QS 11:3 do not make the reading we have offered less likely. The point to be taken from this reading of 1QS 11:3 is simply that for the Qumran community covenantal forgiveness is found in the doing of God-given deeds of righteousness, not apart from them, as Sanders has claimed (437-38).

The final segment of Seifrid's essay is taken up with a consideration of rabbinic literature. His thesis is that the usage of "covenant" (*berith*) in these materials is far more complicated than Sanders was willing to allow. Drawing on the work of Friedrich Avemarie, Seifrid forwards several points. (1) The rabbis associate Israel's election with the Abrahamic covenant and circumcision, not the Sinai covenant and exodus. (2) The rabbis most frequently use "covenant" as an act of obedience in association with the Abrahamic covenant. (3) Therefore, Sanders' use of the phrase "being in the covenant" to convey the notion of "participating in salvation" does not fit the nature of the rabbinic usage, since the idea of obedience is often attached to "covenant," as in the Scriptures. (4) Furthermore, when Sanders speaks of the obligation of the righteous as "faithfulness to the *covenant*," he has deviated from the rabbinic perspective, which placed emphasis on submission to the "yoke of heaven," i.e., love and fear toward the one true God. This faithfulness to God is to be manifested in actual obedience, which, as it was assumed, the human being has the ability to perform, not merely obeying the law to the best of one's ability.

When it comes to righteousness language in rabbinic authors, Seifrid employs the opposite tack of claiming that *tsadiq* is narrower than Sanders would have us believe. He points to the well known fact that *tsadiq* comes to mean "almsgiving" in this literature (this usage finds some precedent in the books of Sirach and Tobit). More to the point, Seifrid contests Sanders' definition of "righteous" as "the general term for one who is properly religious." For him, the word is narrower: "the term sets forth the ideal of obedience for the community, as is evident from its exceedingly rare application to contemporaries, and more frequent association with notable figures from the past" (439). Furthermore, it is clear enough that the rabbis could view God's righteousness in terms of a retributive justice applicable to all creation.

For Seifrid, the bottom line is that these usages of righteousness terminology make it quite clear that Sanders' description of "righteousness" as "(Israel's) covenant status" is inadequate. The rabbinic application of the title of "righteous" to Gentiles indicates that for them, just as in biblical usage, righteousness terminology has to do with creational thought, not merely God's covenant with Israel. "Righteousness," then, can be used with reference to conformity to divine demands, and not merely membership within Israel.

The essay concludes with the concession that the task of plotting the semantic field of righteousness terminology in the Hebrew Scriptures and early Jewish writings lies far beyond the scope of Seifrid's study, and perhaps is not even feasible, owing to its complexity. Nevertheless, he remarks, the works of David Hill, J. A. Ziesler and others are indicative of "the need for greater sensitivity to the distinction between concepts and word meanings in the treatment of righteousness terminology" (441).[25]

More significantly, he believes that his observations call for a reassessment of recent interpretations of Paul's understanding of "the righteousness of God" and "justification" as God's "covenant faithfulness" to Israel. The associations from the Psalms and Isaiah, which Paul evokes by speaking of the "revelation of God's righteousness" (Rom 1:17), belong to creational thought. God appears in such texts as creator, Lord, and king, who "rules and judges" the entire earth. It is conceded that God acts in faithfulness toward his people, contends with their enemies, and executes judgment on their behalf. Yet his acts of "justification" do not represent mere "salvation" for Israel, or even merely "salvation." They constitute the establishment of justice in the world which Yahweh made and governs. Indeed, they may be seen to entail his own justification as the true God over against the idols. The nations are to anticipate that Yahweh will bring about justice for them, even as he has brought it about for Israel. Moreover, in both the Hebrew Scriptures and early Judaism, the usage of righteousness language includes the idea of retributive justice, which is taken up by Paul in his own elaboration of justification.

Response

Without attempting anything like a definitive rejoinder to Seifrid's essay, he has raised a number of issues that deserve some attention.

At the outset, it is to be acknowledged that this study is of positive value in that it (re)establishes that "righteousness" possesses decided components of a righteous status and norm, and that the notion of retributive justice cannot be dismissed, as too many scholars are prepared to do.[26] I would add that it is just this punitive side of righteousness that underlies Rom 1:18-3:20, as it follows upon 1:17: the revelation of the wrath of God from heaven as the "dark side" of the revelation of his righteousness in the gospel.

Having said that, this essay is largely concerned to downplay righteousness as covenant fidelity. Seifrid is quite sure that we have been misled by scholars who equate the "righteousness" word-group with "covenant." In attempting a response, it will be convenient to proceed, as much as possible, point by point.

(1) A mainstay of Seifrid's methodology is a statistical analysis of the conjoined occurrences of "righteousness" and "covenant." As noted before, Seifrid concedes that a full explanation for the infrequency of the convergence of these terms would have to be quite detailed, and that the relation of righteousness to covenant may be approached from historical and theological perspectives as opposed to lexical semantics. Such matters, he avers, lie beyond the scope of his concern. Consequently, instead of looking to covenant as the matrix of righteousness language, Seifrid invokes creation categories, especially as creation provides the basis for the retributive justice of the sovereign king of the universe. The upshot of the whole discussion is that he wants to remove righteousness as much as possible from the relational sphere in order to stress its forensic side. Seifrid leaves the impression that if the equation of righteousness with justice were to be established, then the component of covenant fidelity could be relegated to a subordinate position.

Yet it is just here that the methodological flaws of this study are the most evident. For one, Seifrid's approach is defective in that it is restricted to lexical semantics and does not take into account the historical and theological perspectives needed to form a fully rounded and biblically accurate picture of righteousness. As Dunn observes, Seifrid limited himself to passages in which the actual word "covenant" occurs in conjunction with "righteousness." But surely, as most student of the Bible are aware, concepts may occur even when specific lexical entries are not present.

For another, one of the most telling defects of Seifrid's argumentation is the failure to recognize that creation and covenant are overlapping and complementary to a considerable degree. Studies such as those of W. J. Dumbrell and Robert Murray have demonstrated beyond any reasonable doubt that the various biblical covenants recapitulate creation ideas: each covenant is a kind of new creation.[27] This being so, to root righteousness in creation is, *ipso facto*, to anchor it in covenant as well. The effect of Seifrid's distancing of creation from covenant is a false dichotomy of entities that are, for all theological and practical purposes, indivisible.

(2) By merely listing the passages in which righteousness and covenant coincide (Neh 9:32-33; Ps 50:1-6; 111:1-10; Isa 42:6; 61:8-11; Hos 2:16-20; Dan 9:4-7), Seifrid has failed to convey their central significance. As we take a closer look at these texts, it will be seen that they hardly exist in a vacuum; rather, each is a kind of epitome of a broader spectrum of covenantal thought in which righteousness as fidelity to a relationship plays a principal role.

Nehemiah 9:32-33 is part of Ezra's penitential prayer, confessing the infidelity of Israel and the fidelity of God. Yahweh's faithfulness, in this instance, pertains to his removal of the people from the land because of their idolatry.[28] This prayer, along with similar ones in Ezra 9 and Daniel 9, gave rise to the penitential prayer tradition of Second Temple Judaism.[29] As a whole, the prayer is rooted in numerous biblical traditions.[30] As Werline notes, the prayer, like Deuteronomy 32, Psalm 106 and passages from Isaiah 56-66, is a retelling of Israel's past as a history of sin (I would prefer to say a history of idolatry).[31] Although vv. 32-33 of the prayer fasten on the punitive side of God's righteousness, they do take us to the heart of the "righteousness" word-groups in Hebrew and Greek. That is to say, the covenant stands or falls by virtue of fidelity or infidelity. The land suffers the ravages of chaos (Isa 32:14; Jer 4:23-26) and the nation is taken off into a foreign land when idolatry reaches the point of no return. In the mind of Ezra the scribe, the essence of righteousness is the maintenance of loyalty, from both the divine and human sides.

It is particularly noteworthy that the kindred prayer of Ezra 9 is rooted in the Day of Atonement (Leviticus 16) and the blessings and curses of Leviticus 26 and Deuteronomy 28-30, as Werline has shown.[32] This means that the acknowledgement of Israel's spiritual adultery and God's husbandly faithfulness is far from incidental or peripheral to a biblical definition of righteousness. The very existence of the marriage-covenant is contingent on the righteous/ faithful behavior of its partners.[33]

Daniel 9:4-7 is like Neh 9:32-33.[34] Set in the exile, Daniel's confessional prayer recounts the same problems as Ezra's: Israel has been banished from the land because of idolatry. Whereas God keeps covenant and steadfast love with those who love him and keep his commandments, "we have sinned and done wrong, acted wickedly and rebelled, turning aside from your commandments and ordinances. We have not listened to your servants the prophets, who spoke in your name to our kings, our princes, and our ancestors, and to all the people of the land" (vv. 4-6). For this reason, Daniel is compelled to acknowledge that "righteousness is on your side, O Lord, but open shame, as at this day, falls on us, the people of Judah, the inhabitants of Jerusalem, and all Israel...." (v. 7).

Like the prayer of Ezra, Daniel's confession presupposes the blessings and curses of Leviticus and Deuteronomy. As John Goldingay remarks, the prayer's opening allusion to God's keeping his covenant commitment is not an implicit appeal for mercy, but an acknowledgment that Yahweh has kept his side of the covenant and bears no responsibility for its collapse.[35] But as distinct from Ezra, Daniel prays in positive terms by linking righteousness to God's covenant love toward those who love him and keep his commandments. Goldingay comments that this is the point that Dan 9:23 echoes: "the history of Israel is the story of God's faithfulness to them; his promises, his protection has been constant."[36]

The text is explicit and emphatic in its identification of righteousness with covenant commitment. It is on this basis that Daniel pleads with God: "O Lord, in view of all your righteous acts, let your anger and wrath, we pray, turn away from your city Jerusalem, your holy mountain; because of our sins and the iniquities of our ancestors, Jerusalem and your people have become a disgrace among all our neighbors" (v. 16). The "righteous acts" (*tsdeqoth*) of Yahweh recall Judg 5:11b; 1 Sam 12:7; Ps 103:6; Isa 45:24; Mic 6:5. Again Goldingay speaks to the point. These right acts are his actions on behalf of Israel attacked or afflicted by oppressors in Egypt, in the wilderness, in the period of the Judges and in the exile. At the beginning of Daniel's plea (v.

15), he refers specifically to the exodus, Yahweh's paradigm "righteous acts." According to Goldingay, "God brought Israel out of Egypt by strength of hand and thus established his reputation for doing what is right."[37]

Psalm 50 strikes the theme of the appearance of Yahweh for judgment, cast in terms of theophany, and probably echoing the giving of the law on Sinai (especially in view of v. 5).[38] Its contents, as A. A. Anderson comments, are reminiscent of the classical prophets, with their admonitions and conditional promises.[39] Thus, in keeping with this prophetic atmosphere of the Psalm, vv. 1-6 depict Yahweh as the coming judge. In a manner recalling Deut 4:26; 30:19; 32:1; Isa 1:2, heaven and earth are called upon as witnesses to the judgment (see also Mic 6:1-2; Jer 2:12).[40] In accordance with what scholars have called the "*rib* motif" (*rib* is the Hebrew verb for "contend"), God intrudes theophanically to engage his people in covenant lawsuit.[41]

In commencing the judgment, Yahweh commands: "Gather to me my faithful ones, who made a covenant with me by sacrifice!" (v. 5, probably alluding to Exodus 24). The term translated "faithful ones" is the Hebrew *hasid*. This is the same adjective employed by David in Ps 32:6, where he implores "everyone loyal to Yahweh's covenant" (Anderson's translation) to pray. Craigie states that the term "designates specifically those who were committed to God in the relationship of a covenant."[42] Later in Jewish history, this term would distinguish the Israelite loyalists from apostate Jews during the Maccabean crisis (e.g., 1 Macc 2:24; 7:13).

The occurrence of *hasid* in the present passage might be unexpected, since the Psalm has to do with the judgment of an apparently less than faithful people. Anderson suggests that "faithful ones" may convey a touch of irony, unless we understand the phrase as equivalent to "my covenant people," i.e., "those whose main characteristic is not so much any special virtue or obedience, as their responsibility to God and his laws."[43] A. Weiser concurs: the phrase "my godly ones" (his translation) "addresses the members of the people of God not on account of their special virtues but on the strength of their responsibility, which follows from their relationship with God."[44] If these appraisals of the "faithful ones" are correct, then it is simply underscored that the center of gravity of a covenant is a *relationship*, so much so that even a people ripe for judgment can be depicted in terms of the alliance they are bound to maintain.

In the Psalmist's mind, therefore, it is only natural to invoke the righteousness of God: "The heavens declare his righteousness, for God himself is judge" (v. 6). Anderson thinks that "righteousness" is tantamount to Yahweh's "righteous claim." However, it is more natural to maintain the traditional translation of "righteousness" and refer the term to the Lord's obligation to uphold the curses of the covenant (see above). As in the case of Neh 9:32-33, the "dark side" of righteousness is brought into view, as stressed by the predication of this attribute to God the judge. To be sure, Ps 50:5-6 is a strong text for establishing a retributive element of righteousness (it is somewhat surprising that Seifrid does not make more of it). Nevertheless, the notion of righteousness here does not appear out of the blue, nor does it occur in the abstract, simply because this Psalm is steeped in the covenant theology of Exodus, Deuteronomy and the Prophets. If Yahweh the judge brings retributive justice upon Israel, it is precisely because *the covenant* has been violated.[45] Accordingly, the "faithful ones" are to renew with sacrifice the covenant that was ratified by sacrifice (Exodus 24), in order to see the salvation of God (vv. 14, 23).

Psalm 111 is a hymn of praise. Kraus' summary of its contents is apropos for our purposes:

> (1) This psalm is a hymnic and didactic record of God's gracious attention to his chosen people. It glorifies the reliable, foundational event of the covenant and the continuous salvific faithfulness of Yahweh in history and worship. The foundational traditions of the OT are addressed by means of short references. (2) The singer wants to provide his hearers with a new relation to Yahweh's management and rule. An inner appropriation, joy and fear, is to be determinative.[46]

The two points affirmed by Kraus are typical of all the seven passages under consideration: Psalm 111 presupposes the foundational event of the covenant and God's faithfulness to it, and then seeks to apply "Yahweh's management and rule" to its own day.

In this Psalm, the righteousness of God that endures forever (v. 3) is demonstrated by his "works" (v. 2) and "wonderful deeds" (v. 4). In short, "the Lord is gracious and merciful" (v. 4), proof positive of which is that "He provides food for those who fear him; he is ever mindful of his covenant" (v. 5). It is by virtue of such "works," "wonderful deeds," "grace" and "mercy" that he has given his people the heritage of the nations (v. 6). Apart from these adulations, the faithfulness of Yahweh is particularly stressed in vv. 7-9:

> The works of his hands are faithful and just;
>   all his precepts are trustworthy.
> They are established forever and ever,
>   to be performed with faithfulness and uprightness.
> He sent redemption to his people;
>   he has commanded his covenant forever.
> Holy and awesome is his name.

If anything is conspicuous from this Psalm, it is that the faithfulness of God is assessed in no other terms than that of covenant. The *righteousness* of God that endures forever (v. 3) is just his *fidelity* that has been revealed in the "works" and "wonderful deeds" that have procured a heritage for his people. In performing such works, he is "*mindful of his covenant*" (v. 5).

On the people's part, the corresponding attitude is articulated as the fear of the Lord which is the beginning of wisdom; all those who practice it have a good understanding (v. 10). That the bottom line of the Psalm is the fear of God is of more than passing significance. If the Lord has "commanded [literally, "cut" or "made"] his covenant forever," then the fear of God is the primal response on the part of the human participants in the covenant. In his study of the fear of God in the OT, J. Becker has demonstrated that the phrase "fear of God" is the OT equivalent of "religion," i.e., devotion to the Lord who has redeemed his people by grace.[47] In practical terms, the fear of the Lord is obedience to the divine will. In his study of the theology of the Psalms, Kraus appropriately subsumes "the fear of God" under "The Faith of the Righteous." He notes that in English we do not have terms that could reproduce the loyal, intimate and trusting relationship of life and service, the commitment and devotion of those who are faithful to God. Nevertheless:

> The most frequent expression in the Psalms for this relationship is "those who fear Yahweh" (Ps. 22:23; 25:12, 14; 31:19; 34:7, 9; 61:5; 66:16; 85:9; 103:11, 13; 112: 1; 128:4; 130:4; 147:11). Those who fear Yahweh live in obedience to God's will, in permanent attentiveness and submission. What is involved here is a never-ending commitment to the God of Israel and to his commandments, an always present "knowledge of God".... For those who fear Yahweh, God is a living

> reality. They look for the self-disclosure of God and are always alert to receive him. Undoubtedly, the phrase "fear Yahweh" became less vivid with the passage of time and occasionally it became a mere formal designation. But the basic meaning of real fear never disappeared, fear that knows that God is the judge and is aware of his incomprehensible sovereignty and freedom (Ps. 119:120). Fear does not exclude love.... Yahweh's people turn to him in love (Ps. 5:11; 18: 1; 31:23; 40:16; 69:36; 97: 10; 122:6; 145:20). They are constantly attentive to God and always long to be near him. Therefore they love the temple as the place where they meet God (Ps. 26:8; 27:4; 84:4).[48]

So, even while the actual term "righteousness" is not predicated of the faithful, it comes down to that all the same. Those who fear the Lord are none other than his covenant keeping people. As though the covenant setting of the Psalm needed further confirmation, the provision of food (v. 5) probably harks back to Israel in the wilderness. The Psalmist's thought is thereby anchored to the exodus and the establishment of the law at Sinai. Once more in Kraus' words: our Psalm *"glorifies the reliable, foundational event of the covenant and the continuous salvific faithfulness of Yahweh in history and worship."*[49]

Isaiah 42:6 (7) comes in the midst of one of the great servant songs of the prophet's volume of consolation for Israel:

I am the Lord, I have called you in righteousness,
   I have taken you by the hand and kept you;
I have given you as a covenant to the people,
   a light to the nations,
   to open the eyes that are blind,
to bring out the prisoners from the dungeon,
   from the prison those who sit in darkness.

After the identification of the called one in Isa 42:1-5, vv. 6-7 inform us of the manner and purpose of his calling. Here, Yahweh announces that he has called this personage "in righteousness." E. J. Young interprets "in righteousness" to be "in the sphere of righteousness." Young then defines righteousness as "conformity to a fixed norm or standard." To "act in righteousness," therefore, is to act in accordance with what is right, with absolute justice. However, since there is no abstract standard of justice apart from God, the servant acts in accordance with God's will and purpose.[50]

Young's appraisal of Isaiah's language is correct as far as it goes. Yet he is guilty of abstracting "conformity to a fixed norm or standard" from its moorings in the covenant *relationship*, a relationship that permeates all the servant songs with their atmosphere of mutual intimacy and trust between Yahweh and his servant. Besides, strictly speaking, the servant does not "act in righteousness," but is *"called* in righteousness." The reference is indeed to the sphere of his calling, and, as such, the sphere is just that of covenant commitment.

Given that the arena of the servant's calling is "righteousness," we are not surprised that the design of his commission is to be a "covenant to the people" and "a light to the nations." Exegetically, there is the question of whether "people" has Israel specifically in mind or is synonymously parallel to "nations."[51] For our purposes, it is necessary only to observe that the servant is depicted as though he himself were a covenant. In the abstract, this might seem odd: How can a person be a covenant? However, given the characteristic nature and ethos of a biblical covenant, the point is that the servant has been called to be the very embodiment of God's own faithfulness to all nations.[52]

If Ernst Käsemann was right, then the thought of Isaiah 42:6 is grounded in the creation. God's righteousness, according to Käsemann, is none other than his commitment to the creation; and in the act of justification God is seen to reclaim the creation as his own.[53] The creation reference is confirmed by the "light" that the servant will shed on the nations. "Light" is generally a metaphor for "salvation," but ultimately it stems from Gen 1:3, as brought forward by numerous passages from both Testaments. As the light-bearer, the servant is the bringer of a new creation to the entire globe of sinful humanity—"far as the curse is found." It is he who causes a new order to emerge from the chaos of sin by virtue of the knowledge of himself (cf. Isa 53:11; John 17:3).

In biblical-theological perspective, this servant is Jesus the Christ, who is placed before our view as the man of faith exemplifying covenant steadfastness and fidelity (especially in the Gospel temptation narratives and the Letter to the Hebrews).[54] It is he who shines eschatologically upon the nations (Matt 4:15-16 [= Isa 9:1-2]; John 1:4-5, 9; 3:19; 8:12; 9:5, etc.). If, then, Christ embodies in his own person and work new covenant/new creation realities, it is he who empowers "all the nations" to render to God the creator "the obedience of faith" (Rom 1:5; 16:26). The obedient one has created a race of creatures in his own image (Rom 5:12-19; 1 Cor 15:49).[55]

We see in Isa 42:6, therefore, another instance in which a passage draws together vocabulary, images and conceptions founded much earlier in the biblical record. By virtue of this intertextuality, it is confirmed once more that the intermingling of righteousness and covenant is embedded in the consciousness of a scriptural author.[56] There is, in point of fact, a covenant theology that pervades the Hebrew Scriptures and is regarded as a given and an axiom among its writers.

Isaiah 61:8-11 is likewise part and parcel of a servant song. In these verses, Yahweh declares that he will faithfully recompense his people and make an everlasting covenant with them (v. 8). Their descendants shall be known among the nations and all who see them shall acknowledge that they are a people whom the Lord has blessed (v. 9). In explicit terms, God's faithfulness is directed toward his covenant: it is "in faithfulness" (*emeth*) that the eternal covenant will be established. This covenant is, no doubt, the new covenant to be ratified by the work of the servant. The effect of God's covenant faithfulness is twofold. First, there will be a recognizable Israelite offspring, an echo of Gen 12:2; 15:5; 17:5-8: the ancient promise to Abraham will be kept. Second, not only will Israel survive, the nation will be a witness to the world.

Next, there is a declaration of joy, cast in terms of wedding imagery (vv. 10-11):

I will greatly rejoice in the Lord,
   my whole being shall exult in my God;
for he has clothed me with the garments of salvation,
   he has covered me with the robe of righteousness,
as a bridegroom decks himself with a garland,
   and as a bride adorns herself with her jewels.
For as the earth brings forth its shoots,
   and as a garden causes what is sown in it to spring up,
so the Lord God will cause righteousness and praise
   to spring up before all the nations.

Although the identity of the speaker is a matter of some debate, the majority of commentators opt for Zion. This makes the most sense, because the singer has been made the recipient of "salvation" and "righteousness" (cf. Jer 23:6; 33:16). Here we find the synonymous parallelism of these two familiar terms: the latter is tantamount to the former.

Next, the imagery switches from a wedding to horticulture. Just as the earth yields its produce, "the Lord God will cause righteousness and praise to spring up before all the nations." The picture is consonant with numerous prophetic passages in which the age to come is depicted as a fruitful field. We first encounter fruit in the Genesis creation account and later in the flood narrative (itself a new beginning) (Gen 1:11, 12, 22, 28, 29; 3:2, 3, 6, 12; 8:17; 9:1, 7). Later, one of the central promises of the Abrahamic covenant is fruitfulness in terms of the patriarch's descendants (Gen 17:6; 28:3; 35:11; 47:27; 48:4; Exod 1:7). In the Prophets, the fruitfulness of the land features prominently in the prophecies respecting Israel's return from exile (Isa 4:2; 27:6; 29:17; 32:15-16; 65:21; Jer 23:3; 31:5; Ezek 17:23; 34:27; 36:8, 11, 30; 47:12; Amos 9:14; Joel 2:22; Zech 8:12). In the prophetic vision, Palestine was to be made like the Garden of Eden before Adam's fall, a veritable new creation.[57]

The righteousness which is salvation is to take the form of Israel's renewed commitment to the covenant. In plain language, "those whom he wraps in his robe of righteousness experience not only deliverance from unrighteousness and its effects but also divine enablement to live out his righteousness."[58] Directly parallel is Isaiah 32: a king will reign in righteousness (v. 1); the Spirit will be poured from on high; the wilderness will become a fruitful field (v. 15); and "then justice will dwell in the wilderness, and righteousness abide in the fruitful field. The effect of righteousness will be peace, and the result of righteousness, quietness and trust forever" (vv. 16-17).[59]

In brief, the equation of righteousness and covenant fidelity—on both the divine and human sides—is glaringly obvious in Isa 61:8-11. Yet the passage hardly occurs in isolation and is far from representing a mere incidental or minority outlook on the righteousness language of the OT. Quite the contrary, it takes its place alongside the other six texts that themselves are the heirs of an articulated and developed covenant theology, according to which righteousness is none other than an irreversible commitment to a familial bond established by grace.

Hosea 2:16-20 takes its place within the promise of the restoration of Israel after the judgment due to her adultery = idolatry (2:1-13). Cast in terms of the creation account, as taken up by Noachic covenant, the prophecy looks forward to a new covenant when the curse will be removed: war will come to an end, and even the wild animals will no longer pose a threat to Israel's peace and security. On that day, the broken marriage between Yahweh and his spouse will be restored: "I will take you for my wife forever; I will take you for my wife in righteousness and in justice, in steadfast love, and in mercy. I will take you for my wife in faithfulness; and you shall know the Lord" (v. 19).

Righteousness and covenant are linked in terms of conjugal fidelity: Israel will no longer call Baal her husband, but Yahweh (v. 16). Commenting on this image, A. A. Macintosh can say: "in this situation Hosea seeks to redeem the notion of love between man and woman from the murky confusion into which Baalism had dragged it and to exalt it to a representation of the faithful love of the just and true God for the people that he had chosen of old."[60] Therefore, righteousness is conceived of as loyalty to this familial bond of commitment to be reestablished at the time of the nation's restoration to the land.

God's devotion to the covenant is articulated as the "steadfast love" and "mercy" that have compelled him to end the exile and renew the marriage. From the people's side, although they had been no better than the prophet's own adulterous wife, in the restoration they will become "my people" (v. 23), a phrase that hearkens back to "my peculiar possession," or Israel as a "kingdom of priests" (Exod 19:5-6). "On that day" (v. 16), the ideal relationship of Israel to her God will be realized and consummated. The terms of vv. 19-20, remark F. I. Andersen and D. N. Freedman, "constitute a profound theological statement describing the foundational components of the marriage relationship, which derive from the character of Yahweh himself."[61]

In sum, the seven passages just examined demonstrate that the correspondence of righteousness and covenant is far from casual or incidental. In point of fact, the notion of covenant forms the indispensable context and subtext of the talk of righteousness. Each of the seven presupposes and echoes previous strands of biblical tradition, and each seeks to apply to its own day foundational concepts reaching back into the earliest stages of Israel's nationhood. Statistically speaking, one may argue, as Seifrid does, that seven texts do not a major motif make. But the passages in question are not to be relegated to the status of prooftexts, as Seifrid is in danger of doing. A mere lexical analysis is insufficient to assess the fundamental significance of ideas that form the substrata and axioms of OT biblical theology. If anything, these passages take us to the heart of what covenant theology is all about—righteousness as the fidelity required of both the divine and human partners of the marriage bond that bears the name of *berith*.

(3) Seifrid has proposed that, in biblical terms, one does not "act righteously or unrighteously" with respect to a covenant. Rather, one "keeps," "remembers," "establishes" a covenant, or the like. Conversely, one "breaks," "transgresses," "forsakes,"

"despises," "forgets" or "profanes" a covenant. Just as a covenant is a particular kind of relation, righteousness takes the particular form of love and loyalty in a covenantal relation. All "covenant-keeping" is righteous behavior, but not all righteous behavior is "covenant-keeping." It is misleading, he insists, to speak of "God's righteousness" as his "covenant-faithfulness." It would be closer to the biblical language to speak of his "faithfulness" as "covenant-righteousness."

My impression is that this formulation is rather convoluted and difficult to understand. At best, Seifrid is guilty of hair splitting by maintaining that all "covenant-keeping" is righteous behavior, but not all righteous behavior is "covenant-keeping." Even more conspicuous is the assertion that is misleading to speak of "God's righteousness" as his "covenant-faithfulness." Supposedly, it would be closer to the biblical language to speak of "faithfulness" as "covenant-righteousness." Yet the very passages cited by him, as examined above, link inextricably righteousness and the covenant. That being so, it is really inconceivable that there should be a righteous behavior which is not at the same time covenant-keeping. Seifrid's distinction can only exist in the abstract, not in the concrete and everyday realities of covenant life. Moreover, to insist that it would be better to speak of God's "faithfulness" as "covenant-righteousness" rather than of his "righteousness" as "covenant-faithfulness" is a meaningless distinction, which most certainly would be lost on most readers of the Bible.

Besides, his argument is self-contradictory. Seifrid plays on terms such as "keeping," "remembering," "establishing" a covenant, or, conversely, "breaking," "transgressing," "forsaking," "despising," "forgetting," "profaning" a covenant. In so observing, he wants to maintain that one does not "act righteously or unrighteously" with respect to a covenant. Yet he goes on to state that a covenantal relation is familial and demands love and loyalty (Hos 6:6). For this reason, "to act in faithfulness and love in a covenant is to *act righteously*, of course, so that it is not surprising to find righteousness language in occasional connection with *hesed* ("loving kindness" or "covenant love") and *'emunah* ("faith/ faithfulness")" (424 [italics mine]). By his own admission, then, one *does* "act righteously or unrighteously" with respect to a covenant![62]

(4) Seifrid's attempt to locate righteousness in creation rather than covenant categories has been addressed above. He leans particularly on the frequency with which righteousness language is associated with "ruling and judging." The demand for social

justice derives from God, the divine king, who has determined to secure the good and beneficial order of creation. This, for Seifrid, explains the frequent association of "salvation" and "deliverance" words with "righteousness."

Certainly, he has demonstrated amply that righteousness language, in at least some instances, pertains to "ruling and judging." He is equally correct that God's role as the divine king accounts, partially anyway, for the relation of righteousness and salvation/deliverance. But given the overlapping and interpenetrating character of creation and covenant in biblical theology, rather than disproving the connection of righteousness with covenant, his data only prove it. Seifrid is obviously concerned to keep retributive justice at the fore of righteousness, at the expense of the relational component. But in so doing, he has committed himself to two methodological mistakes. One is the artificial bifurcation of creation and covenant. The other is the failure to recognize that even where righteousness is retributive justice, the retribution is meted out as a result of the violation of a covenant relationship. Even in the case of wrath directed toward pagan peoples (*à la* Rom 1:18-3:20), the *creation covenant* is still operative (see the appendix).

In his endeavor to distance God's righteousness, as retributive justice, from covenant fidelity and root it in his role as king and judge, Seifrid appeals to certain lexical data, namely, the distinction between the feminine and masculine forms of the nouns for "righteousness." "The feminine tends to refer to a concrete thing such as a righteous act or vindicating judgment. The masculine usually signifies the more abstract concept of 'right order' or 'that which is morally right'" (428). On this basis, Seifrid then maintains that the feminine form of the noun is favored by biblical writers to articulate the vindicating and punitive acts of God. God is thus said to be "righteous" when he rewards righteous people and punishes the guilty.

On the surface, this may seem like a compelling argument. But without disputing Seifrid's findings as such, I would add the caution that there is such a thing as overinterpretation of linguistic data, which loads onto individual words more freight than they can bear. As numerous scholars have taught us, in pursuing the task of exegesis, we must read words within words; that is, words do not exist on their own, but form part of an entire segment of discourse.[63] Therefore, while it may be true that the feminine and masculine forms of "righteousness" *tend* (his word) to refer to concrete and abstract conceptions respectively, ultimately the semantic range of terms is determined by actual usage with a broader context. In the case of righteousness in particular, that context is the covenant, though covenant finds its rootage in creation. This means that even in those instances in which *tsdeqah* and cognates designate a vindicating judgment, that judgment falls in response to covenant infidelity.

To this I would add that "righteous acts" (feminine plural) in a passage like Dan 9:16 (cf. Judg 5:11b; 1 Sam 12:7; Ps 103:6; Isa 45:24; Mic 6:5) are retributive with regard to Israel's enemies, but salvific on behalf of his covenant people. If anything, this datum indicates that one may overplay the retributive dimension of this form of the noun. Moreover, if Goldingay is correct, then the "righteous acts" of God in Dan 9:16 serve to establish "his reputation for doing what is right."[64] Here, the feminine falls into Seifrid's more abstract (masculine) category of "that which is morally right."

(5) Seifrid's handling of the postbiblical materials is of necessity limited,[65] and he is right that the task of analyzing these materials is exceedingly complex. First come the Qumran texts. Although he concedes to Sanders that "covenant" in the Scrolls is often associated with righteousness terminology, he questions whether Sanders' framework of interpretation actually holds. He fastens on the demand for the sect to walk in perfection in all God's ways (1QS 1:7-8; 3:9b-12). Such expressions as "perfection of way" and "uprightness of heart" are not general references to piety, but rather represent "the essence of the life and worship of the community." From this he concludes that the Qumran covenant does not save as a promise prior to and independent of obedience, but precisely *as* the "perfection of way" in which righteousness is found.

In response, it is regrettable that Seifrid does not define "perfection" in biblical terms, leaving the impression with the general reader that the term is to be understood more or less as it is in English. But the fact of the matter is that in the Jewish milieu, as P. J. Du Plessis has shown, "perfection" is principally a "cultic" and "quantitative" term, indicating "wholeness, entirety and intactness." "Perfection," according to Du Plessis, is wholeness in one's relationship to God.[66] D. Peterson adds that the concept is not formal or abstract. While conceding that perfection in the OT is not essentially a moral concept, it does involve "*loving obedience to God* as the one who, in his mercy, has initiated the relationship with man."[67] Therefore, to walk in perfection in all God's ways is hardly "sinless perfection," but rather a wholehearted commitment to honor the entirety of the Lord's revealed will. Otherwise put, perfection is simply a David-like desire to seek God and follow his commandments with all one's heart (Ps 119:2, 10, 34, 69, 145).

This being so, the "legalistic" edge is taken off Seifrid's reading of the Scrolls. Granted, the Qumran covenant does not envision salvation as taking place independently of obedience. But "salvation" for a Second Temple Jew was understood eschatologically as the vindication of his fidelity to God in final judgment. Many Christian writers fail to grasp this point and consequently assign a synergism to ancient Judaism that is entirely inappropriate, as though Jews of this period were Pelagians before Pelagius. If, in Seifrid's words, this covenant saves "precisely as the 'perfection of way' in which righteousness is found," then nothing more need be involved than perseverance in God's commandments as the pre-condition of final vindication. With this the canonical Scriptures are entirely in agreement.[68]

Not only so, passages like 1QS 11:1-3, 5, 11-12, 13-15 and 1QH 4:30-33; 7:30-31; 13:17 graphically illustrate that the Qumran sect held to justification by the free grace of God. The point is not that the sectarians embraced a "justification by decency,"[69] but rather *justification was restricted to the community* as a "private reserve."[70] This is the real point and precisely the conclusion of Otto Betz, which is only to be expected since, in his words, "at Qumran *the righteousness of God has absolute priority over human activity*. It leads to obedience to the law, but this does not turn into merit."[71]

Among the Scrolls, Seifrid's attention is particularly turned to 1QS 11:2-4. The gist of his argument is that the Hebrew text of v. 3 should read: "with *my* righteous deeds he blots out my transgressions," rather than "with *his* [God's] righteousness he blots out my transgressions." From this it follows, says Seifrid, that for the Qumran community covenantal forgiveness is found in the doing of God-given deeds of righteousness, not apart from them, as Sanders has claimed.

First, as in the case of Avemarie's book on the rabbinic materials (see below), Seifrid, at best, has oversimplified Sanders. If anything, Sanders clearly acknowledged that forgiveness is linked to God-given deeds of righteousness. To quote him at length:

> God's grace and the requirement of performance on the part of man are both stressed so strongly in the Scrolls

that it is difficult to state the precise relationship between grace and works. This is Burrows's formulation: "The sons of light are saved by the faithful study and observance of the law, but they are able to keep the law only because they have been placed under the dominion of the spirit of light." I should prefer not to say that they are saved by study and observance. It appears more accurate to say that they are saved by the electing grace of God *when it is responded to with repentance and commitment*, and that they keep the commandments, with God's help, as a *consequence* of the election and as a *condition* for remaining in the covenant.[72]

Later, Sanders writes in pointed terms that at Qumran "obedience is the condition *sine qua non* of salvation."[73] And in the conclusions of his survey of the Scrolls, he remarks that the soteriological patterns to be found in them are consistent. There may be differences here and there on points of *halakah* (application of the law), but the general pattern of religion is not affected by such differences.

We find no layer in the Qumran material in which obedience to the law is not required or in which transgression is not punished. Further, the place of obedience in the overall scheme is always the same: it is the *consequence* of being in the covenant and *the requirement for remaining* in the covenant.... Obedience to the commandments was not thought of as earning salvation, which came rather by God's grace, but was nevertheless required as a *condition of remaining in the covenant*; and not obeying the commandments would damn.[74]

If these statements of Sanders' seem to be at variance with his overall thesis of covenantal nomism, the solution resides in the fact that, in the Judaism of this period, grace and works, or grace and law, were not juxtaposed as they are in Western systematic theology.

The heightening of the perception of God's grace and the requirement of obedience is instructive for understanding Judaism generally, for it indicates that "grace" and "works" were not considered as opposed to each other in any way. I believe that it is safe to say that

> the notion that God's grace is in any way contradictory to human endeavour is totally foreign to Palestinian Judaism. The reason for this is that *grace and works were not considered alternative roads to salvation.* Salvation…is always by the grace of God, embodied in the covenant.[75]

The only way that Seifrid's allegation will work is if "forgiveness" is given the narrowest definition possible and is somehow detached from "salvation," especially considering that salvation for Jews of this period was dominantly eschatological in nature, corresponding to the restoration of Israel.[76] Sanders is as clear as anyone could be that forgiveness and salvation hinge precisely on devotion to the Torah, not "legalistically" conceived, but as the appropriate response to God's covenant grace.

Second, perhaps the best answer to Seifrid's treatment of 1QS 11 is the essay of Marcus Bockmuehl, "1QS and Salvation at Qumran," which appears in this very volume and of which Seifrid could have taken advantage. Bockmuehl first surveys the significance of the *Community Rule* as a whole. In the discussion of election and the people of God (the corporate dimension) in the *Rule*, he demonstrates that the notion of covenant holds sway in the sect's conception of itself. True, covenant is restricted to the members of the Dead Sea community. Nevertheless, the Scrolls give no indication that a belief in the basic continuity of the covenant promises has been surrendered (391). This is a very telling consideration in light of Seifrid's downplay of covenant as a framework of interpretation for righteousness.

Next, Bockmuehl analyzes 1QS in terms of voluntarism and predestination (the individual dimension). As ironic as it may seem, one chooses to enter the community and commit oneself heart and soul to the standards of the sect; yet this choice has been predetermined by God. Though on the surface it might seem like 1QS embraces a merit-based system of salvation, this is not the case.

> Salvation, on this view, could never be a matter of human merit. The covenanters do not know themselves elect by their works but, on the contrary, their works bear witness to their election. God has "caused them to inherit the lot of the Holy Ones" (1QS 11:7-8), "caused them to draw near" to the covenant (so 1QS 11:13; cf. 1QH 6[=14]:13). It is his agency that supremely determines a person's standing, and which underwrites

human choice in the first place. Although Josephus suggests that it was the Pharisees who held divine providence and human free will in a fine balance (*J. W.* 2.162f.; *Ant.* 13.172; cf. *m. 'Abot* 3:19), in these texts we do in fact find a comparable co-existence of these two theological topoi in tension. Here lies the paradox of Qumran's view of salvation: although the sons of light freely choose to belong to the covenant and thus to be saved, the very fact that they do so is itself an expression of the overruling grace of God, whose sovereign design disposes over both the saved and the damned. At the same time, even the sect's evident determinism in relation to historical and cosmological events serves fundamentally only to reinforce and confirm this eternal predestination of the elect (397).

Consonant with this outlook is Bockmuehl's conclusion respecting righteousness and justification in the *Rule*:

Thus, the *Serekh*'s [*Rule*'s] view of justification clearly rides on a cosmic order of God's righteousness whose revelation constitutes both the final salvation of his people and the final destruction of the forces of darkness. The revelation of that righteousness, moreover, does not depend on either the predicament or the achievements of believers, but is determined solely by God himself (399).

This reading of the 1QS is simply buttressed by its conceptions of sin and atonement (399-402).

In sum, Bockmuehl is aware that his findings are "not fundamentally incompatible" with those of Sanders. "Qumran manifests an eschatological faith in which salvation and atonement for sins are not humanly earned but divinely granted by predestined election and membership in the life of the observant covenant community" (412).

Given this highly responsible and entirely plausible reading of 1QS, Seifrid's attempt to rewrite 1QS 11:3 is destined for failure. On the strictly paleographical level, and in the abstract, his argument for "*my* righteous deeds" rather than "*his* [God's] righteous deeds" might fly. But in the light of the doctrine of salvation in this Scroll, his translation comes across as a piece of special pleading; and it is doubtful that many objective readers of the Scrolls will be convinced.

After Qumran, there is a perusal of rabbinic texts. Seifrid's thesis is that the usage of "covenant" (*berith*) in these materials is far more complicated than Sanders was willing to allow. His four essential points about "covenant" in this literature are summarized above, and I will simply respond to them here.

(a) Even if the rabbis associate Israel's election and circumcision with the Abrahamic covenant rather than the Sinai covenant, the fact remains that *her identity as a chosen people is bound up with a covenant*. That circumcision in particular should be associated with Abraham instead of Moses follows quite naturally from the fact that circumcision is the sign of the Abrahamic covenant (Gen 17:11; Rom 4:11), not the Mosaic, which was the sabbath (Exod 31:12-17). The only way that Seifrid's observation can carry any weight is to assume that rabbinic authors somehow conceived of the Abrahamic covenant in abstraction from the Mosaic, which most certainly was not the case.

(b) His second point is linked to the first, namely, that rabbinic writers frequently use "covenant" as an act of obedience in association with the Abrahamic covenant. One would readily grant that this is case; but the problem for Seifrid is that this datum does not carry any more conviction than his first observation. He seems to assume that obedience to the Abrahamic covenant is in some way detachable from the covenant under which these authors lived, the Mosaic.

(c) The third point is the contention that Sanders' use of the phrase "being in the covenant" to convey the notion of "participating in salvation" does not fit the nature of the rabbinic usage, since the idea of obedience is often attached to "covenant," as in the Bible. It should be obvious by this time that we have here another of Seifrid's false alternatives. Participation in salvation is not to be distinguished from obedience, since the latter is proof positive of the former. It is only by placing a "legalistic" construction on "obedience" that Seifrid is able draw such a sweeping conclusion.

(d) The fourth point charges that when Sanders speaks of the obligation of the righteous as "faithfulness to the *covenant*," he has deviated from the rabbinic perspective, which placed emphasis on submission to the "yoke of heaven," i.e., love and fear toward the one true God. This faithfulness to God is to be manifested in actual obedience, which, as it was assumed, the human being has the ability to perform, not merely obeying the law to be best of one's ability.

At the risk of repetition, the "yoke of heaven" can be viewed as but another way of speaking of "faithfulness to the covenant." Seifrid, by placing a negative spin on "yoke," has created a presumption against the Sanders-type reading of the Tannaitic sources. It would appear to be characteristic of his work that terms like "obedience" and "works" are consistently placed in such a pejorative light. That faithfulness to God is to be manifested in actual obedience is a given. However, the implication that the human being, in Jewish/rabbinic thought, had the inherent ability to perform the law (apart from grace) is an assumption imposed on the materials in question. Some such reading of these texts is characteristic of a number of scholars who have reacted to the New Perspective.[77] The question is obviously complex, but suffice it to say that I have argued elsewhere that any "anthropological optimism," as it is called, is due to the awareness that one sustains a covenant relationship to God and is enabled by his grace to obey.[78]

As related in the summary of Seifrid's essay, when it comes to righteousness language in rabbinic authors, he employs the tack of claiming that *tsadiq* is narrower than Sanders would have us believe.[79] He argues against Sanders' definition of "righteous" as "the general term for one who is properly religious," because, for him, the word is narrower: "the term sets forth the ideal of obedience for the community, as is evident from its exceedingly rare application to contemporaries, and more frequent association with notable figures from the past" (439). Furthermore, it is clear enough that the rabbis could view God's righteousness in terms of a retributive justice applicable to all creation. For Seifrid, the bottom line is that these usages of righteousness terminology make it quite clear that Sanders' description of "righteousness" as "(Israel's) covenant status" is inadequate. The rabbinic application of the title of "righteous" to Gentiles indicates that for them, just as in biblical usage, righteousness terminology has to do with creational thought, not merely God's covenant with Israel. "Righteousness," then, can be used with reference to conformity to divine demands, and not merely membership within Israel.

Some of these points are well taken in themselves. Several rabbinic authors do conceive of "righteous Gentiles," and very possibly righteousness terminology does have to do with creational thought, not merely God's covenant with Israel. That said, we should remind ourselves that covenant and creation do not exist in hermetically sealed containers. To say that (righteous) Gentiles conform to creational standards is virtually to admit that they comply with various sanctions of the Mosaic law. Once again, Seifrid's attempt to divorce covenant and creation is unsuccessful.

As for Sanders' definition of "righteous" as "the general term for one who is properly religious," it is difficult to think that Seifrid has improved upon it. If, in Seifrid's words, the term sets forth "the ideal of obedience for the community," I, for one, find it rather arbitrary to distinguish between this and "properly religious" deportment. Seifrid's definition may be technically more accurate, but at the end of the day, his and Sanders' definitions come down to pretty much the same thing. That the sources more frequently apply "righteous" to notable characters from the past than to contemporaries proves nothing in itself, simply because Jewish authors were accustomed to placing paradigm figures before their readers for the purpose of emulation in the present.[80] The righteous of days past are called to mind in order to engender righteousness in their descendants. The most famous of such encomiums is Ben Sira's "Praise of Famous Men" (Sirach 44-50).

All in all, Seifrid has hardly refuted Sanders' take on the rabbinic materials. Additionally, Seifrid leaves the impression, from Avemarie's work, that rabbinic religion was heavily "works" oriented in the pejorative sense. In point of fact, Avemarie's book includes lengthy engagements of such matters as obedience to God from the vantage point of knowledge of God and community.[81] The conclusion to that particular discussion is that "the Torah not only comes from God, *it leads to him as well.*"[82] The conclusion to the entire book is: "The Torah is, according to the rabbinic understanding, the means and way to life, the medium of salvation. But it is more than that. Israel keeps it because God has given it and because she loves it."[83] Even more strikingly, Avemarie grants that throughout this literature it is possible to speak of a "covenantal nomism" (*Bundesnomismus*)! The Torah of the rabbis cannot be divorced from this context in which the law was given: in this sense, Sander's coinage of the phrase, says Avemarie, is certainly justified![84]

Therefore, the actual data emerging from rabbinic texts hardly support the expectations of those who go looking for a *quid pro quo* relationship, wherein reward was dished out in proportion to a mechanical obedience. That God's grace, forgiveness and provision for sin loom large in rabbinic literature is amply demonstrated by specialists in the area. Correspondingly, the dominant mentality of the sources is that "works" are but the human response to the covenant grace of God.[85] To be sure, many scholars have established that works feature prominently in the sources and that the destiny of individuals hinges on the performance of such works. But that is only to be expected, given that works are just the other side of the coin to faith—and the NT hardly forms an exception to this rule (e.g., Matt 7:21-27; 12:33-37; 25:31-46; Luke 8:15; Rom 1:5; 2:13; 16:26; Jas 2:14-26; Rev 2:19; 3:2; 22:12).[86]

(6) It remains only to say a word or two about Seifrid's concluding reflections. He believes that the works of Hill, Ziesler and others are indicative of the need for greater sensitivity to the distinction between concepts and word meanings in the treatment of righteousness terminology. But more significantly, he believes that his observations call for a reassessment of recent interpretation of Paul's understanding of "the righteousness of God" and "justification" as God's "covenant-faithfulness" to Israel. In his view, the associations from the Psalms and Isaiah which Paul evokes by speaking of the "revelation of God's righteousness" (Rom 1:17) belong to creational thought. God appears in such texts as creator, Lord, and king, who "rules and judges" the entire earth. God does act in faithfulness toward his people, yet his acts of "justification" do not represent mere salvation for Israel, they constitute the establishment of justice in the world which Yahweh made and governs. Accordingly, Seifrid places a good deal of stress on righteousness as retributive justice, which, he believes, is taken up by Paul in his own elaboration of justification.

Granted, some scholars might possibly want to increase their sensibilities to the distinction between concepts and word meanings in the treatment of righteousness terminology. If so, then we are grateful to Seifrid for the challenge. I would qualify, however, that Hill spends the first twenty-two pages of his book discussing lexical semantics, in order to prepare the ground for his word studies. Perhaps his approach is dated to a degree, but at least there was an effort to address the appropriate concerns.

While biblical scholars must always be prepared to reassess their work, my impression is that Seifrid has presented insufficient data to discredit the current paradigm of the righteousness of God as God's covenant faithfulness to Israel. The claim that righteousness is more properly associated with creation rather than covenant has been addressed above, as has Seifrid's focus on righteousness as retributive justice. Suffice it to say here that the OT picture of God as king and righteous judge in no way lessens his role as the Lord of the covenant, who is ever mindful of the needs of his chosen people. To be sure, the ultimate purpose for God redeeming his people is the establishment of justice throughout the entire earth. Yet to speak of "mere" salvation for Israel is to overlook the obvious: it is through the restoration and justification of the remnant of Israel that the light of salvation was meant to shine to the ends of the earth.[87] Once again, Seifrid has set at odds entities that are meant to coexist in harmony. God's covenant fidelity to Israel and his determination to set right the wrongs of this world are of a piece.

Finally, the claim that retributive justice forms the backbone of Paul's doctrine of justification will, presumably, be addressed in the second volume of this undertaking. For the present, the case remains unproven. However, I can say with little hesitancy that none of the data marshaled by Seifrid encourage us to think that a significant paradigm shift will take place anytime soon away from the consensus reading of righteousness as covenant fidelity.[88] Why Seifrid is particularly concerned to press for retributive justice is not altogether certain at this point. Yet one senses that by playing down covenant fidelity and playing up retributive justice, the intention is to land a broadside against the growing conviction that eschatological justification (vindication) is contingent on fidelity to a covenant commitment. We shall see.

Conclusions

Seifrid's essay has presented a challenge to the New Perspective understanding of righteousness. In so doing, Seifrid has argued for a renewed appreciation of righteousness as retributive justice, in keeping with the OT portrayal of God as a king and judge. To the degree that he has been able to redress the balance in favor of a neglected dimension of righteousness, we are in his debt. Certainly, he has raised a number of issues that deserve to be weighed carefully; and it is always good to have our assumptions subjected to careful scrutiny.

Having said that, the downside of this paper far outstrips its positive benefits. Methodologically, the essay starts off on the wrong foot. By confining himself mainly to lexical matters, excluding for the most part biblical-theological concerns, Seifrid has cut himself, and his readers, off from the single most valuable source of information respecting righteousness. Surely, any resolution to the current debate on righteousness and justification must be pursued on the basis of exegesis, an exegesis informed by the panorama of salvation history. Symptomatic of Seifrid's approach is his mere listing of passages in which righteousness and covenant come into "any significant semantic contact" (his words).

Had these texts been expounded to any degree, it would have been seen that their function is that of a conduit through which broad streams of covenant theology are allowed to flow. As it is, we are presented with a myopic conception of righteousness.

To the degree that theological motifs are pursued, Seifrid is eager to bifurcate creation and covenant. By so doing, he is able, at least to his satisfaction, to shift attention away from righteousness as covenant fidelity and shift it onto the component of retributive justice. As intimated above, his motives remain to be seen. Until these are clarified, it certainly appears that Seifrid is guilty of driving a wedge between categories that overlap, interpenetrate and exhibit reciprocity to a considerable degree, as though we were forced to choose between one or the other. Even where he concedes that righteousness and covenant are found in combination, the relevance of such data tend to be submerged in favor of righteousness as retribution. What Seifrid has failed to realize is that retributive justice itself is relational in terms of covenant relationships, even in the case of peoples outside of Israel, who live in contradiction to the ideals of the creation covenant. The bottom line is that his linking of righteousness with creation to the practical exclusion of covenant is misleading in the extreme.

While one appreciates the necessity of limiting the materials under examination, especially in a symposium such as this, the fact remains that Seifrid's handling of the sources is very one-sided indeed. Scant attention is paid to texts that support the relational component of righteousness, especially as they might bear on justification and kindred issues. The effect is a reductionism, which, ironically enough, is just Carson's complaint against Sanders!

A rather troubling matter is Seifrid's misrepresentation, not to say, at times at least, distortion of Sanders, with whom he disagrees, and Avemarie, with whom he wants to agree. The particulars of these misrepresentations are indicated above; and it is sufficient to say in these conclusions that Seifrid's case and credibility are not enhanced by his inaccuracy in reporting the views of others.

4. Appendix:
The Creation Covenant

Because anything like a full examination of the relation of creation and covenant is impossible within this review, I want simply to convey some indications that Genesis 1 and 2 have a covenant relationship in view.[89] A significant portion of Seifrid's argumentation rests on the assumption that righteousness, in the main, is to be understood within the confines of creation categories rather than covenantal. As I have sought to counter above, the distinction is artificial and represents a false alternative, inasmuch as covenant stems from creation. It might be objected that the actual term "covenant" (*berith*) is not used in the creation account. However, I would argue that all the constituent elements of a covenant, with the exception of ratification by blood, are present.

First, there is a family relationship established by virtue of the creation of a man and a woman, and from them progeny. It is just the family that is made to be the paradigm of covenant relations. In this light, a covenant may appropriately be defined as *a familial bond of commitment*. The well known biblical figures of parent-child and husband-wife as images of God and his people take their point of departure from creation. Adam was the son of God (Luke 3:38), and Adam and Eve together were the recipients of God's fatherly and husbandly care. And in their relationships with their own children, the first human pair were intended to mirror the Lord's care and provision for them.

Second, there are what might be called covenant stipulations, or the "house rules" regulating the relationship. These are: (1) the creation mandates (subduing the earth and procreation); (2) the prohibition against eating the fruit of the tree of knowledge of good and evil, the focal point of Adam's testing. Adam, in other words, was obliged to follow a course of obedience, i.e., to persevere in the life which had been given him. He was to continue listening to the voice of God, accept his interpretation of reality, and bear his likeness in all things, all the while accomplishing the mandate to subdue and protect the earth. In case of disobedience, a penalty is specified (Gen 2:17).

Third, there are covenant privileges. (1) Life, both physical and spiritual. In all the covenants, life is the pinnacle point of blessing. The statement of John 17:3 ultimately derives from the creation: to know God is to have eternal life. In Rev 2:7; 22:2, 14, John the seer depicts the life of the new creation as access once more to the tree of life. The course of salvation history is thus brought full circle; the end represents a return to the beginning, as eschatology corresponds to protology. From the vantage point of life as covenant privilege, Eden is the symbol of Adam's life and the presence of God. (2) Man is given the position of creator and regent. In his original condition of creation, he was only "a little lower than the angels" (Ps 8:5; Heb 2:6-8), with the potential of rising above them (1 Cor 6:3).

Fourth, there is the immediate presence of God, which forms the basis of "the promise" of Eph 2:12, i.e., "I will be their God and they shall be my people" (Jer 31:33). Eden is the aboriginal symbol of God's presence. Later in the biblical record, Eden-like ideas are taken up and applied to the land of Palestine, especially as the temple occupies the central portion of the land and stands on its holiest ground. In the new creation, once again the dwelling of God is with men (Rev 21:3), in the person of the Word who became flesh and dwelt among us (John 1:14).

Fifth, there is a covenant servant, Adam. In Gen 2:15, Adam was to "serve" (*abad*) the ground. As being of the earth and earthy, he had direct responsibility to the earth. Each of the subsequent covenants is likewise organized around a servant who embodies the covenant in his person (Noah, Abraham, Moses, David, Christ).

Sixth, according to the most natural understanding of Hos 6:7, the Adamic relationship is a *berith*.[90] As Adam, according to the prophet, Israel has broken the (Mosaic) covenant. This is buttressed by Deuteronomy, which repeatedly represents Israel as the "son of God" who is enduring testing, only this time in the wilderness.

Seventh, the absence of a formal oath is no argument against the essentially covenantal character of the creation relationship. It is true, as O. P. Robertson says, that the covenants entail a "verbalized declaration of the character of the bond being established."[91] But one of the most impressive features of the creation account is the persuasiveness of the speech of God. In other words, God's creative speech is his commitment to his creatures. This is so from two perspectives. One is that his creative *fiat* entails a commitment to preserve what he has made (see Ps 104:30). The other is that his pronouncement of blessing upon his creatures (Gen 1:22, 28) is his assurance to them that he will be faithful to his commitment to them. Because sin is not yet a reality, a formalized oath is superfluous: trust is fully operative (contrast Heb 6:13-18). It is just in these terms that J. H. Stek rightly argues that the reason why the word covenant does not appear in Genesis 1-2 is that it only applies in a fallen world, where relationships of love, loyalty and trust need to be bolstered by oaths.[92]

Finally, the absence of blood sacrifice to ratify the covenant is likewise no insurmountable obstacle. For one thing, the Davidic covenant makes no mention of sacrifice, but it is a *berith* nonetheless (Ps 89:3). More importantly, in the pre-fall condition, death had not yet entered the picture: there was no necessity for one life to be forfeited in place of another; there was no debt to be paid. Therefore, blood sacrifice would have been totally inappropriate. Perhaps this is why *berith* is not used in Genesis 1 and 2, because Genesis is written for the emerging nation of Israel, for whom covenantal commitment was inseparable from animal sacrifice (e.g., Exod 24:4-8).

All in all, the data supporting an equation, or at least an overlapping, of creation and covenant is impressive enough to resist Seifrid's efforts to banish righteousness, by and large, from the latter and localize it in the former. The distinction is simply unwarranted.

---

[1] P. Stuhlmacher, *Revisiting Paul's Doctrine of Justification: A Challenge to the New Perspective* (Downers Grove: InterVarsity, 2001); A. A. Das, *Paul, the Law, and the Covenant* (Peabody: Hendrickson, 2001); S. Kim, *Paul and the New Perspective: Second Thoughts on the Origins of Paul's Gospel* (Grand Rapids: Eerdmans, 2002); S. J. Gathercole, *Where is Boasting? Early Jewish Soteriology and Paul's Response in Romans 1-5* (Grand Rapids: Eerdmans, 2002); S. Westerholm, *Perspectives Old and New on Paul: The "Lutheran" Paul and His Critics* (Grand Rapids: Eerdmans, 2004).

[2] Silva, "The Law and Christianity: Dunn's New Synthesis," *Westminster Theological Journal* 53 (1991), 341.

[3] Sanders, *Paul and Palestinian Judaism: A Comparison of Patterns of Religion* (Philadelphia: Fortress, 1977), 75, 420, 544.

[4] Ibid., 422.

[5] Dunn, *Romans*, Word Biblical Commentary 38 a, b. 2 vols. (Dallas: Word, 1988), 1.lxv. See additionally Dunn's *The Theology of Paul the Apostle* (Grand Rapids: Eerdmans, 1998), 335-40.

[6] Wright, *What Saint Paul Really Said: Was Paul of Tarsus the Real Founder of Christianity?* (Grand Rapids: Eerdmans, 1997), 18-19 (italics mine).

[7] D. Garlington, "A Review Article: Mark Adam Elliott, *The Survivors of Israel: A Reconsideration of the Theology of Pre-Christian Judaism*," *Reformation and Revival Journal* 10 (2001), 181.

[8] From Dunn's review of *Justification and Variegated Nomism*, *Trinity Journal* ns 25 (2004), 111.

[9] One thinks of such pioneering efforts as G. F. Moore, "Christian Writers on Judaism," *Harvard Theological Review* 14 (1921), 197-254; id., *Judaism in the First Centuries of the Christian Era: The Age of the Tannaim*. 3 vols. (Cambridge, MS: Harvard University Press, 1927); M. Limbeck, *Die Ordnung des Heils: Untersuchungen zum*

Gesetzesverständnis des Frühjudentums (Düsseldorf: Patmos, 1971). R. N. Longenecker was also ahead of his day, though this is frequently overlooked (*Paul: Apostle of Liberty* [New York: Harper & Row, 1964], 65-85). Longenecker characterizes the piety of Hebraic Judaism as "nomism," not "legalism" in the conventional sense.

[10] Of the many summaries of Sanders' work, handy compendia are provided by Wright, *Saint Paul*, 18-20; Westerholm, *Perspectives*, 159-63.

[11] Dunn, "The New Perspective on Paul," *Bulletin of the John Rylands University Library of Manchester* 65 (1983), 95-122. The article is reprinted in Dunn's *Jesus, Paul, and the Law: Studies in Mark and Galatians* (Louisville: Westminster/John Knox Press, 1990), 183-214.

[12] Dunn, "New Perspective," 121.

[13] Dunn, "Works of the Law and the Curse of the Law (Galatians 3.10-14)," *New Testament Studies* 31 (1985), 526 (this essay is likewise reprinted in *Jesus, Paul, and the Law*, 215-41). See further his "Yet once more—'The Works of the Law': A Response," *Journal for the Study of the New Testament* 46 (1992), 99-117. Dunn justifiably issues a note of protest in *Theology of Paul*, 358, n. 97.

[14] The criticism that Sanders limited the scope of his investigation is oft-repeated and well taken. In fairness, though, it would have taken a multi-volume work to canvass *all* the relevant sources. I attempted to fill a gap as far as the Apocrypha is concerned in my *'The Obedience of Faith': A Pauline Phrase in Historical Context*, Wissenschaftliche Untersuchungen zum Neuen Testament 2/38 (Tübingen: Mohr-Siebeck, 1991). That limitations to any study are in order is illustrated by the thesis of Mark Seifrid, one of the editors of this volume, who confined his study of justification mainly to the Dead Sea Scrolls and the *Psalms of Solomon* (*Justification By Faith: The Origin and Development of A Central Pauline Theme*, Novum Testamentum: Supplements 68 [Leiden: Brill, 1992]).

[15] An observation made by a number of reviewers: Dunn; P. Eisenbaum, "Review of Biblical Literature" (accessible to members of the Society of Biblical Literature at the SBL home page); J. Byron, "Review of Biblical Literature;" I. W. Scott, "Review of Biblical Literature;" C. Blomberg, "Denver Journal" (accessible at the home page of Denver Seminary); M. Bockmuehl, in a Cambridge Ph.D. seminar, accessible at http://www.tyndale.cam.ac.uk/Tyndale/staff/Head/J&VN.htm.

[16] Dunn, *Trinity Journal* ns 25 (2004), 113. Dunn relates the sagacious counsel of C. F. D. Moule that statements may vary quite strikingly in emphasis due to the very different circumstances to which they are addressed.

[17] Sanders, *Paul*, 427-28.

[18] With regard to *4 Ezra*, Bauckham makes several points. (1) Salvation is not represented as the result of weighing an individual's deeds, but as the reward for the kind of life the righteous person has led in faithfulness to

God and the Torah. (2) It is a false alternative to posit that there is an inconsistency between God's grace and keeping the law. God gives salvation to those members of his elect people who have kept the terms of the covenant. (3) *4 Ezra* illustrates how the basic and flexible pattern of covenantal nomism could take forms in which the emphasis is overwhelmingly on salvation by obedience to the law. *2 Baruch* endorses essentially the same outlook. My only qualification is that Bauckham applies the term "merit" to the process of keeping the terms of the covenant. I would say, rather, that keeping the terms of the covenant is "righteousness."

[19] See Garlington, *Obedience of Faith*, 263-64.

[20] J. D. G. Dunn, *The Partings of the Ways: Between Christianity and Judaism and Their Significance for the Character of Christianity* (Philadelphia: Trinity Press International, 1991), 18-36. Note as well J. M. G. Barclay, *Jews in the Mediterranean Diaspora: From Alexander to Trajan (323 BCE-117 CE)* (Edinburgh: T. & T. Clark, 1996), 401.

[21] Note again Bauckham's appraisal of covenantal nomism as flexible enough to accommodate even an extra heavy stress on law-keeping (*Variegated Nomism*, 174). In the case of *4 Ezra* and *2 Baruch* in particular, account must be taken of the circumstances of their composition, i.e., in the wake of the destruction of Jerusalem. Bauckham quotes J. J. Collins to the effect that the pessimism of *4 Ezra* "springs not so much from its lofty standards as from historical experience" (ibid.).

[22] Ps 98:2-3, 8-9 (LXX 97:2-3, 8-9); Isa 45:22-25; 51:5-6; 62:1-2. Noteworthy as well are Ps 35:27-28 (LXX 34:27-28); 72:1-4 (LXX 71:1-4, 7); 85:11-13 (LXX 84:12-14); 96:13 (LXX 95:13); Isa 9:7 (LXX 9:6); 11:1-2, 5; 45:8, 22-25; 51:5-6; 53:10-11; 61:11; Jer 23:5-6; Mal 4:2 (LXX 3:20).

[23] Seifrid, *Justification by Faith*, 100-03.

[24] The argument is based on the contention that the Hebrew letters *waw* and *yodh*, which form the pronominal suffixes of the noun "righteousness," are indistinguishable from one another in 1QS. This allows Seifrid to opt for "*my* righteous deeds" rather than "*his* righteous deeds."

[25] The reference is to Hill, *Greek Words and Hebrew Meanings: Studies in the Semantics of Soteriological Terms*, Society for New Testament Studies Monograph Series 5 (Cambridge: Cambridge University Press, 1967); Ziesler, *The Meaning of Righteousness in Paul: A Linguistic and Theological Enquiry*, Society for New Testament Studies Monograph Series 20 (Cambridge: Cambridge University Press, 1972).

[26] Seifrid's case would have been strengthened by a reference to *The Prayer of Azariah*. The *Prayer* contains an acknowledgment of the justice of God's judgment against a covenant-breaking people (vv. 4-5, 8-9). God, according to Azariah, is "righteous" (*dikaios*) because he has upheld his covenant threats to punish a disloyal nation (cf. Neh 9:33; Tob 3:2; Add Esth 14:6-7; 1QS 1:26).

[27] Dumbrell, *Covenant and Creation: An Old Testament Covenantal Theology* (Exeter: Paternoster, 1984); Murray, *The Cosmic Covenant: Biblical Themes of Justice, Peace and the Integrity of Creation*, Heythrop Monographs 7 (London: Sheed and Ward, 1992). See also B. W. Anderson, *From Creation to New Creation: Old Testament Perspectives*, Overtures to Biblical Theology (Minneapolis: Fortress, 1994), esp. 146-64.
[28] As taken up and applied by later literature: Pr Azar 4-5, 8-9; Tob 3:2; Add Esth 14:6-7; 1QS 1:26.
[29] See R. A. Werline, *Penitential Prayer in Second Temple Judaism: The Development of a Religious Institution*, Society of Biblical Literature: Early Judaism and Its Literature 13 (Atlanta: Scholars Press, 1998).
[30] See the tabulation of passages by J. M. Myers, *Ezra-Nehemiah*, Anchor Bible 14 (Garden City: Doubleday, 1965), 167-69.
[31] Werline, *Prayer*, 57. On the motif of Israel's unfaithfulness, see R. C. Ortlund, *Whoredom: God's Unfaithful Wife in Biblical Theology*, New Studies in Biblical Theology (Grand Rapids: Eerdmans, 1996).
[32] Werline, *Prayer*, 46-53.
[33] That the covenant is a marriage-like relationship is well known. But see the detailed study of G. P. Hugenberger, *Marriage as a Covenant: Biblical Law and Ethics as Developed from Malachi*, Biblical Studies Library (Grand Rapids: Baker, 1994).
[34] See Werline, *Prayer*, 67-86.
[35] Goldingay, *Daniel*, Word Biblical Commentary 30 (Dallas: Word, 1989), 242.
[36] Ibid.
[37] Ibid., 243.
[38] On the theophany motif of the Psalm, see H. J. Kraus, *Psalms 1-59*, Continental Commentary (Minneapolis: Fortress, 1993), 491-92.
[39] Anderson, *The Book of Psalms*, New Century Bible. 2 vols. (Grand Rapids/London: Eerdmans/Paternoster, 1972), 1.381.
[40] P. Craigie notes that in the original covenant the people accepted Moses' invocation of heaven and earth (*Psalms 1-50*, Word Biblical Commentary 19 [Waco: Word, 1983], 365; id., *The Book of Deuteronomy*, New International Commentary on the Old Testament [Grand Rapids: Eerdmans, 1976], 376). But now, the same heaven and earth testify as "hostile witnesses" against them.
[41] With regard to Isa 1:2, J. Oswalt rightly notes that Isaiah's references to covenant are not as explicit as those of Jeremiah. In fact, Isaiah does not use *berith* at all. Nevertheless, it cannot be denied that Isaiah knows of the covenant. Covenant would appear to be the ground of all the prophet's thinking; it is a pattern for living, without which life cannot be sustained (*The Book of Isaiah*, New International Commentary on the Old Testament. 2 vols. [Grand Rapids: Eerdmans], 1.85). A consideration such as this should have been weighed more carefully by Seifrid.
[42] Craigie, *Psalms, 1-50*, 365.

43 Anderson, *Psalms*, 1.384.
44 Weiser, *The Psalms: A Commentary*, Old Testament Library (Philadelphia: Westminster, 1962), 395.
45 One of Seifrid's objections to *berith* as the matrix of righteousness is that it has received "the same abstract treatment" as *tsdeqah*. He complains that scholars are not clear in their delineation of "God's covenant faithfulness." Is the reference to the Sinaitic, Abrahamic, Davidic or Noachic covenant, or something else? He questions whether it is historically and theologically legitimate "to collapse all of the biblical covenants into one" (425, n. 47). However, this particular problem is imaginary, not real. No one is suggesting that the various covenants be collapsed into one. God's faithfulness to his people pertains historically and theologically to whatever covenant they find themselves under at any given period of salvation history, with its own peculiar demands and privileges. Far from being abstract, God's righteousness as covenant faithfulness is a principle that transcends the various epochs of *Heilsgeschichte* and yet is localized in each.
46 Kraus, *Psalms 60-150*, Continental Commentary (Minneapolis: Fortress, 1993), 359.
47 Becker, *Gottesfurcht im Alten Testament*, Analecta Biblica 25 (Rome: Biblical Institute Press, 1965).
48 Kraus, *Theology of the Psalms* (Minneapolis: Augsburg, 1986), 157-58. So fundamental is the fear of God that the scribe Jesus Ben Sira made it one of the outstanding themes of his wisdom book. See J. Haspecker, *Gottesfurcht bei Jesus Sirach: Ihre religiöse Struktur und ihre literarische und doktrinäre Bedeutung*, Analecta Biblica 30 (Rome: Biblical Institute Press, 1967). According to Ben Sira, the fear of God is tantamount to trust in God (Sir 1:14), an equation surely derived from the Hebrew Scriptures themselves. J. Snaith comments that "the fear of the Lord implies neither childish terror nor merely formal respect for authority." Rather, "It is to be understood...as a warm, personal trust and reverence" (*Ecclesiasticus or the Wisdom of Jesus the Son of Sirach*, Cambridge Bible Commentary [Cambridge: Cambridge University Press, 1974], 11).
49 Kraus, *Psalms 60-150*, 359 (italics mine).
50 Young, *The Book of Isaiah*, New International Commentary on the Old Testament. 3 vols. (Grand Rapids: Eerdmans, 1965-72), 3.118.
51 See the discussions of Oswalt, *Isaiah*, 2.117-18; Young, *Isaiah*, 3.119-20.
52 Cf. Young, *Isaiah*, 3.120-21.
53 Käsemann, "'The Righteousness of God' in Paul," *New Testament Questions of Today* (Philadelphia: Fortress, 1969), 168-82.
54 Many scholars are convinced that Paul articulates this conception of Christ the covenant-keeper by means of the Greek phrase literally translated as "faith of Jesus Christ" (*pistis Iēsou Christou*) (e.g., Rom 3:22, 26; Gal 2:16). For discussions of the phrase, with other literature,

see my *Galatians*, 127-28, 142; I. G. Wallis, *The Faith of Jesus Christ in Early Christian Traditions*, Society for New Testament Studies Monograph Series 84 (Cambridge: Cambridge University Press, 1995); essays by R. B. Hays, J. D. G. Dunn and P. J. Achtemeier in *Pauline Theology. Volume IV: Looking Back, Pressing On*, eds. E. E. Johnson and D. M. Hay. Society of Biblical Literature Symposium Series 4 (Atlanta: Scholars Press, 1997), 35-92.

[55] See D. Garlington, *Faith, Obedience, and Perseverance: Aspects of Paul's Letter to the Romans*, Wissenschaftliche Untersuchungen zum Neuen Testament 79 (Tübingen: Mohr-Siebeck, 1994), 72-109.

[56] Intertextuality is not so easy to define formally, but the gist of it is that later passages of Scripture echo earlier ones. This field of study is one of the hot buttons of hermeneutics at present. Amongst the massive amounts of literature, see R. B. Hays, *Echoes of Scripture in the Letters of Paul* (New Haven: Yale University Press, 1989); D. C. Allison, *The Intertextual Jesus: Scripture in Q* (Harrisburg: Trinity Press International, 2000).

[57] This considerable "fruit tradition" lies behind the "fruit of the Spirit" in Gal 5:22-23 (Garlington, *Galatians*, 253-54).

[58] Oswalt, *Isaiah*, 2.575.

[59] It is frequently overlooked that Isa 32:16-17 is the backdrop to Rom 5:1. See Garlington, *Faith, Obedience, and Perseverance*, 75-76.

[60] Macintosh, *Hosea*, International Critical Commentary (Edinburgh: T. & T. Clark, 1997), 79. On the confusion of the names Baal and Yahweh, see ibid., 80.

[61] Andersen and Freedman, *Hosea*, Anchor Bible 24 (Garden City: Doubleday, 1980), 283. On the marriage imagery of this passage, see G. I. Emmerson, *Hosea: An Israelite Prophet in Judean Perspective*, Journal for the Study of the Old Testament: Supplement Series 28 (Sheffield: JSOT Press, 1984), 21-26.

[62] The interplay of covenant faithfulness and such terms as keeping Yahweh's statutes (tantamount to keeping the covenant) or "doing the law" is evident in Deuteronomy. Crucial is an appreciation of the centrality of the Torah in Israel's self-consciousness of being the chosen people. It is the book of Deuteronomy that gives the classic statement of the role of the Torah in the life of the people. The heart of the book (chaps. 5-28) consists of a restatement of the covenant made at Sinai. Deut 29:1 sums up the whole of that block of material: "These are the words of the covenant which the Lord commanded Moses to make with the sons of Israel in the land of Moab, besides the covenant which He had made with them at Horeb." Throughout the book, the emphasis of covenant life is sustained and reinforced in numerous restatements of the promise (and warnings): "This do and live" (Deut 4:1, 10, 40; 5:29-33; 6:1-2, 18, 24; 7:12-13). This promise does not originate in Deuteronomy, because Lev 18:5 had already said: "So you shall keep My statutes and My judgments, by which a man may live if he does them; I am the Lord."

I have sought to demonstrate the equation of law-obedience or covenant-keeping with fidelity to the God of the covenant in my essay, "Role Reversal and Paul's Use of Scripture in Galatians 3.10-13," *Journal for the Study of the New Testament* 65 (1997), 95-106 (now reprinted in *Exegetical Essays*. 2nd ed. [Eugene, OR: Wipf & Stock, 2003], 197-231).
[63] See, among many, J. Barr, *The Semantics of Biblical Language* (Oxford: Oxford University Press, 1961); D. A. Carson, *Exegetical Fallacies* (Grand Rapids: Baker, 1984); M. Silva, *Biblical Words and Their Meaning: An Introduction to Lexical Semantics* (Grand Rapids: Zondervan, 1983); P. Cotterell and M. Turner, *Linguistics and Biblical Interpretation* (Downers Grove: InterVarsity, 1989).
[64] Goldingay, *Daniel*, 243.
[65] See his treatment of the Qumran materials and the *Psalms of Solomon* in *Justification by Faith*, 78-135. That these texts by themselves require a full-length study is evident from B. Przybylski, *Righteousness in Matthew and His World of Thought*, Society for New Testament Studies Monograph Series 41 (Cambridge: Cambridge University Press, 1980); M. Winninge, *Sinners and the Righteous: A Comparative Study of the Psalms of Solomon and Paul's Letters*, Coniectanea biblica, New Testament 26 (Stockholm: Almqvist & Wiksell, 1995).
[66] Du Plessis, *TELEIOS: The Idea of Perfection in the New Testament* (Kampen: Kok, 1959).
[67] Peterson, *Hebrews and Perfection: An Examination of the Concept of Perfection in the Epistle to the Hebrews*, Society for New Testament Studies Monograph Series 47 (Cambridge: Cambridge University Press, 1982), 24 (italics mine). Hence, "perfect" is tantamount to "blameless" (cf. Luke 1:6; Phil 2:15). 4 Macc 7:15 makes the righteous Eleazar's loyalty to the law "perfect," i.e., "complete," by his martyrdom (cf. Peterson, *Hebrews*, 25).
[68] See the splendid study of K. L. Yinger, *Paul, Judaism, and Judgment According to Deeds*, Society for New Testament Studies Monograph Series 105 (Cambridge: Cambridge University Press, 1999).
[69] F. F. Bruce, *The Spreading Flame: The Rise and Progress of Christianity from its First Beginnings to the Conversion of the English* (Exeter: Paternoster, 1958), 336, writing of the soteriology of Pelagius.
[70] E. Käsemann, "The Faith of Abraham in Romans 4," *Perspectives on Paul* (Philadelphia: Fortress, 1971), 88.
[71] Betz, "Rechtfertigung in Qumran," *Rechtfertigung: Festschrift für Ernst Käsemann zum 70. Geburtstag*, eds. J. Friedrich, et al. (Tübingen/Göttingen: Mohr-Siebeck/Vandenhoeck & Ruprecht, 1976), 34 (italics his).
[72] Sanders, *Paul*, 295 (first italics mine, second his).
[73] Ibid., 304.
[74] Ibid., 320.
[75] Ibid., 297 (italics his). It is noted that M. Bockmuehl, in the essay "1QS and Salvation at Qumran," appearing in this book, reminds us that

Sanders had access to only four main documents among the Scrolls. He is right that "no serious student would today attempt to describe 'the Qumran pattern of religion' without reference to the large number of additional texts that have become accessible since 1977" (*Variegated Nomism*, 383).

[76] The salvation = restoration motif is taken up by E. P. Sanders, *Jesus and Judaism* (Philadelphia: Fortress, 1985), 61-119; N. T. Wright, *Jesus and the Victory of God*, Christian Origins and the Question of God 2 (Minneapolis: Fortress, 1996); S. McKnight, *A New Vision for Israel: The Teachings of Jesus in National Context* (Grand Rapids: Eerdmans, 1999); S. M. Bryan, *Jesus and Israel's Traditions of Judgement and Restoration*, Society for New Testament Studies Monograph Series 117 (Cambridge: Cambridge University Press, 2002).

[77] For example, D. A. Carson, *Divine Sovereignty and Human Responsibility: Biblical Perspectives in Tension*, New Foundations Theological Library (Atlanta: John Knox, 1981); T. Laato, *Paul and Judaism: An Anthropological Approach*, South Florida Studies in the History of Judaism 115 (Atlanta: Scholars Press, 1995).

[78] See my *Obedience of Faith*, 19-20, 31-33 (note n. 99).

[79] The appearance of "righteousness" as "almsgiving" is a subsidiary point, but still one worth addressing. Carson finds the presence of almsgiving in the book of Tobit to be evidence for an incipient merit theology (*Sovereignty*, 51). In Tobit, the Greek term is not "righteousness" but *eleēmosunē* (related to the word for "mercy," *eleos*). However, rather than merit, *eleēmosunē* is simply righteousness as directed manward in love for neighbor. See my *Obedience of Faith*, 165-66. The point may not be so significant in itself, but it does illustrate how scholars can read texts tendentiously.

[80] See G. W. E. Nickelsburg and J. J. Collins (eds.), *Ideal Figures in Ancient Judaism: Profiles and Paradigms*, Society of Biblical Literature Septuagint and Cognate Studies 12 (Chico: Scholars Press, 1980). Cf. my own treatment of various paradigm figures, *Obedience of Faith*, 35-48, 163-91, 216-27.

[81] Avemarie, *Tora und Leben: Untersuchungen zur Heilsbedeutung der Tora in der frühen rabbinischen Literatur*, Texte und Studien zum Antiken Judentum 55 (Tübingen: Mohr-Siebeck, 1996), 244-61.

[82] Ibid., 261 (italics mine).

[83] Ibid., 584.

[84] Ibid., n. 40.

[85] References are easily located throughout Moore, *Judaism*; Avemarie, *Tora und Leben*; S. Schechter, *Aspects of Rabbinic Theology: Major Conceptions of the Talmud* (New York: Schocken, rep. 1961); E. Urbach, *The Sages: Their Concepts and Beliefs* (Cambridge MS: Harvard University Press, rep. 1987); C. G. Montefiore and J. Loewe, *A Rabbinic Anthology* (New York: Schocken, rep. 1974).

[86] The unity of faith and works is disrupted, for example, by Das, who argues for "Deserving Obedience in Early Judaism" (*Paul, the Law*, 12-44).

[87] Prophetic passages such as Isa 42:1 ("he will bring forth justice to the nations") and Hab 2:14 ("But the earth will be filled with the knowledge of the glory of the Lord, as the waters cover the sea") are set precisely in the context of return from exile.

[88] Seifrid claims that the associations from the Psalms and Isaiah, which Paul evokes by speaking of the "revelation of God's righteousness" (Rom 1:17), belong to creational thought (exclusively). But he disregards the fact that lying behind Rom 1:17 is Ps 98:2, 9: "The Lord has made known his salvation; before the nations he has revealed his righteousness.... For he comes to judge the earth; he will judge the world in righteousness and the peoples with uprightness." In Paul's mind also must have been such Psalm texts as 9:8; 96:13. The Psalmist's mention of the "nations" may very well echo creation. But the fact remains that Psalm 98 is cast primarily in exodus terms, with the call for Israel to sing to the Lord a "new song," recalling the "old song" of Moses in Exodus 15. That Paul proceeds to quote Hab 2:4 simply nails down the point, as this prominent text embodies the vision of return from exile—a new Exodus. This means that Rom 1:17 adapts an *Israel* text and applies it to a new people. God's covenant faithfulness in reversing the exile is now extended to the Gentiles.

[89] See further S. Hafemann, "The Covenant Relationship," *Central Themes in Biblical Theology: Mapping Unity in Diversity.* eds. Scott J. Hafemann and Paul R. House. (Grand Rapids: Baker Academic, 2007), 40-42.

[90] See B. B. Warfield, *The Selected Shorter Writings of Benjamin B. Warfield*, ed. J. E. Meter. 2 vols. (Nutley, NJ: Presbyterian & Reformed, 1970), 2.116-29; S. J. Hafemann, "The Covenant Relationship," *Central Themes in Biblical Theology: Mapping Unity in Diversity* (eds. S. J. Hafemann and P. R. House (Grand Rapids: Baker Academic, 2007), 40-42.

[91] Robertson, *The Christ of the Covenants* (Grand Rapids: Baker, 1980), 6.

[92] Stek, "'Covenant' Overload in Reformed Theology," *Calvin Theological Journal* 29 (1994), 12-41. I am grateful to my friend, Professor Peter Gentry, for this reference.

A REVIEW ARTICLE

Simon J. Gathercole, *Where is Boasting? Early Jewish Soteriology and Paul's Response in Romans 1-5*. Grand Rapids: Eerdmans, 2002.

This publication is the incarnation a Ph.D. thesis presented to the University of Durham, under the supervision of J. D. G. Dunn. The book is of particular interest because the stance assumed by the student is conspicuously at odds with that of the teacher. In the preface, Gathercole compliments his mentor as "a tireless, gracious, and tolerant sparring partner in debate;" but, I would add, a *sparring partner* all the same. In personal conversation, Professor Dunn confirmed that, in fact, his interaction with Gathercole was comprised of several years of very intensive exchange.

Gathercole tackles the question of "early Jewish soteriology" from the vantage point of Israel's boasting as it pertains to her confidence before God and her distinctiveness from the nations. Structurally, the book follows the more or less traditional pattern of a research project, in this instance: (1) an introductory survey of boasting and related matters in recent scholarship; (3) a study of pertinent Jewish texts that bear on the issue of obedience and final vindication in early Judaism; (3) an exegesis of Romans 1-5.

1. Overview of Gathercole's Argument

Much of the "Introduction" is occupied with a review of the New Perspective on Paul (NPP), as represented prominently by the work of E. P. Sanders, J. D. G. Dunn and N. T. Wright. In this survey, Gathercole singles out statements of Dunn and Wright, in agreement with Sanders, to the effect that (supposedly) in Jewish thinking final acceptance by God at the judgment does not rest on obedience to the Torah. Clearly, says Gathercole, *if* this picture of Jewish soteriology is right, then boasting in obedience, or basing one's confidence of final salvation in one's observance of Torah, is very unlikely to be in evidence. Accordingly, the model of boasting articulated by Dunn and Wright, of confidence based on national election and vocation, would more likely be the correct one.

However, Gathercole is adamant that this model is *not* correct. Indeed, it is "dangerously one-sided," because obedience as a condition of and basis for final vindication and salvation at the eschaton is fundamental to Jewish thought. He qualifies that the reconstruction of NPP scholars is not always wrong in what it asserts, but "it is extremely one-sided and leads to serious distortions when we come to examine the relation between early Judaism and Paul" (13).

Since the purpose of this book is to assess the role of boasting in Paul's response to Jewish soteriology, Gathercole summarizes the issue in these terms: "The debate hinges on whether these works are identity markers, defining one as belonging to the true people of God, or whether these works also have a functional role as a criterion for final salvation. Broadly, adherents of the New Perspective on Paul hold the first position, while critics of the New Perspective emphasize the second position" (13). Gathercole thus presents us with an either/or option; and ultimately he will come down on the side of boasting as a species of human "achievement."

Integral to this either/or schema is the "grace-works axis" (K. L. Yinger). On the one side are scholars who emphasize the continuity between Judaism and Paul as pertains to the relation of grace and works. Yinger, for example, maintains that Paul and Judaism alike are no more "monergistic" or "synergistic" than each other. Indeed, Paul's stance toward works in relation to the final judgment is entirely consistent with Jewish precedents.[1] On the other side, interpreters such as T. Laato and T. Eskola adopt an "anthropological" approach, according to which Paul's appraisal of human nature is much more pessimistic than that of Judaism. For these scholars, Paul stresses predestination and grace, whereas his Jewish contemporaries, with their "higher view" of human nature, are "synergistic" in their sympathies.

The introduction is rounded off by various methodological considerations. Here, Gathercole is concerned to underscore a number of factors. (1) Sanders downplayed the eschatological dimension of Second Temple Judaism. (2) Judaism is to be understood not only on "its own terms," but as well on "Paul's terms." (3) Hellenistic Jewish texts have not been given the weight they deserve in the reconstruction of Jewish soteriology. (4) Nomenclature such as "legalism" and "works-righteousness," as traditionally conceived, is not appropriate for the literature of this period. The real point is that not enough of a distinction has been made by the NPP between salvation as *getting in* and final vindication at the last judgment.

Gathercole then epitomizes his book as being concerned with the impact of two key questions on the exegesis of Paul. (1) What were the criteria for God's saving vindication at the eschaton, according to Jewish thought? (2) Did Jewish groups believe they would be vindicated on the basis of God's election, or on the basis of their own obedience? His thesis argues that Jewish soteriology was based both on divine election and on final salvation by works. Paul, by contrast, opposes the view that justification is by obedience to the Torah (as contra the NPP).

After the introduction commences "Part I: Obedience and Final Vindication in Early Judaism." This survey of materials subdivides into five segments that canvass a variety of literature, including selected NT passages.

Gathercole's conclusion from Apocrypha, Pseudepigrapha and Qumran is just what was stated in the Introduction: "God is portrayed as saving his people at the *eschaton* on the basis of their obedience, as well as on the basis of his election of them" (90). As far as the Dead Sea Scrolls in particular are concerned, he is bothered that the Sanders-type reading of the sources upsets the balance between realized and future eschatology. For him, "final judgment on the basis of works permeates Jewish theology" (111). This, in turn, sets the stage for the argument that Paul was reacting against a Judaism which believed that one earned final salvation as a result of works.

The treatment of Jewish soteriology in the NT yields the same conclusion: works are a precondition to a favorable verdict in the last judgment. In this, the NT itself is in line with Jewish precedents. Particularly as regards Paul, the theology of final judgment according to obedience exhibits both continuity and discontinuity in relation to Jewish texts: continuity as to obedience being a criterion for final judgment, discontinuity as to the character of the obedience. Therefore, Paul's theology does not fit comfortably into either a Lutheran or Reformed framework. But neither can covenantal nomism suffice as a description of either Judaism or Christianity because of the function of works at final judgment. If it seems like Jewish and Pauline soteriological patterns are more or less the same, Gathercole assures us that such a comparison runs aground on the rocks of Paul's pneumatology. In his conception, unless the apostle's contemporaries were synergistic, "then the Holy Spirit came at Pentecost for nothing" (134)! Nevertheless, there has not been sufficient recognition of the common ground between the traditions of early Christianity and early Judaism. "It is not that both consist in initial grace that fully accomplishes salvation, followed by works which are evidence of that; rather, *both share an elective grace and also assign a determinative role to works at final judgment"* (135 [italics mine]).

The chapter on obedience and final vindication in the aftermath of 70 CE surveys *4 Ezra, 2 Baruch,* Josephus and rabbinic literature, including the targums. The findings are the same as in the case of the previous materials: works count in the final judgment, thus rendering the covenantal nomism model inadequate. Of particular note is that in summarizing and embracing F. Avemarie's work on the Tannaitic materials,[2] Gathercole chides Sanders for a systemizing approach that, on the one hand, under-interprets texts that are problematic for him and, on the other, stretches supporting texts beyond their limits.

The treatment of boasting in Second Temple Judaism endeavors to steer a course somewhere between traditional views of Israel's boasting and the outlook of the NPP. According to the former, Paul sees lack of assurance as one of the most significant problems within Judaism. The problem is solved by the gospel of justification by faith. For the latter, the people of God based their confidence in final vindication purely on God's election and not on their works. Their assurance of vindication came from God's faithfulness to his promises and was not earned by their own obedience. In contrast to both, this chapter "aims to demonstrate that the element of obedience was indeed believed by a number of Jewish writers to be not only possible but also accomplished, both by the nation as a whole as well as by individuals. As a result, it can be said that works too, not just divine election, are a basis for confidence in final vindication" (163).

Gathercole's consideration of the Jewish materials is rounded off by the chapter on boasting in Second Temple Judaism. He discovers that Israel's boasting was not only in election and national distinctiveness, but in actual obedience to the law. In brief, the Israelite had to perform the Torah in order to be considered faithful to it. Gathercole believes that this latter strand of boasting has been excluded by the NPP, because, in his words, "obedience, as well as election, is the basis of Israel's confidence before God" (194). Predictably, Sanders continues to be the whipping boy. In the face of so much evidence that boasting is grounded in real performance, Gathercole feels compelled to take Sanders to task for a "minimalistic" understanding of covenant faithfulness that reduces righteousness to "mere intention."

The remainder of the book is comprised of "Part 2: Exegesis of Romans 1-5." The first segment of this division pertains to "Paul's Assessment of Jewish Boasting in Romans 1:18-3:20." The discussion here is organized around Paul's problem with his interlocutor in Rom 2:1-16: what was he guilty of? For Gathercole, Paul's dialogue partner is unrepentant and apostate. This Jew, who represents Israel as a whole, believes he is far better than he actually is. Therefore, all of Paul's energies in this portion of Romans are directed toward convincing this person of the extent of his guilt, because "...*this was precisely what was missing in the self-assessment of the Jewish nation*" (211 [italics his]). It is to this end that Gathercole adduces passages from Romans 2 and 3, which indict the Jew of his failure to keep the law.

Given his conclusions from the previous survey of the Jewish materials, in Romans 2, Gathercole maintains: "Paul is countering the Jewish view that obedience to Torah is the way to final justification, not that salvation is restricted to a certain sphere" (214). He is of the opinion that numerous Jewish texts speak of "a sense of innocence as far as sin was concerned" (214). This means that Paul is opposing "a Jewish confidence at the final judgment that is based on election in conjunction with obedient fulfillment of Torah. Paul is trying to persuade his interlocutor that his sin runs much deeper than he thought, and so the interlocutor's obedience to Torah is by no means comprehensive enough for his justification" (214).

All this is set in contrast to the NPP, which, supposedly, mainly views boasting as possession of the Torah only, not performance of its requirements. Such "antinomian ethnocentrism" is objectionable because "God's election and Israel's obedience are consistently held together, and neither is emphasized at the expense of the other" (203).

The exegesis of Romans 1-5 carries on with "Paul's Reevaluation of Torah, Abraham, and David in Romans 3:27-4:8." In this chapter, Gathercole revisits the views of Sanders, Dunn and Wright, with more criticisms offered, mainly relating to the perceived imbalance on the part of the NPP that restricts Jewish "works" to the boundary markers and does not extend to include comprehensive obedience to the law. Gathercole offers comments on Paul's use of Abraham and David in Romans 4 and presses the point that both were justified as "ungodly" sinners, thus providing the paradigm for Israel which is disobedient and ungodly. The issue is not boundary markers, but Israel's failure to keep the law.

The final chapter bears the title of "The Resurrection of Boasting in Romans 5:1-11." Here, Gathercole takes up the relationship between boasting in Rom 2:17 and 5:2, 3, 11. The first passage condemns a certain kind of boasting, while the latter ones resurrect a form of boasting that Paul not only approves of but actually commends. In agreement with the consensus among commentators, Gathercole defines boasting as the confidence or assurance of eschatological salvation. He offers the pertinent exegetical observation that Paul's use of the preposition "in" as construed with the verb "boast" specifies the ground of Christian boasting: the hope of the glory of God, our sufferings and God himself. The final segment of the chapter, and of the book, considers the difference between Jewish and Pauline boasting. The difference is twofold. (1) The Christian's boast in God *through Christ*. (2) The boasting of Paul's Jewish interlocutor in Romans 2 is illegitimate and unfounded because he is unrepentant and unable actually to fulfill the law because of his sinfulness; thus, the ground of the Jew's confidence is undercut.

2. Response

Dr. Gathercole is to be congratulated on a fine piece of scholarship. His book is exemplary as a well-researched, well-argued and attractively presented thesis. The writing style as a whole is easy enough to follow. In places, a more deliberate phrasing would have facilitated the reading process, but only infrequently does he get bogged down by excessive subordinate clauses and parenthetical explanations, a rare achievement in this kind of literature.

The argument itself is comprised of two intertwining themes: judgment according to works and the consequent boasting of those who have performed such works as to be approved in the final judgment. As to the first, it is not, he says, a matter of initial grace that fully accomplishes salvation, followed by works that are (mere) evidence of that grace; rather, *elective grace assigns a determinative role to works at the final judgment* (135). Given such a premise, the second point follows naturally enough, that boasting entails more than pride in election and national privileges; actual performance lies at the root of the boast. I should think that Gathercole has established both prongs of his thesis beyond any reasonable doubt, and to the extent that these findings provide a necessary counterbalance to some approaches to the Jewish sources, we are in his debt.

By way of critical response, a number of observations are in order. It will be possible only to respond in principle to those aspects of the book that are liable to criticism, and not to offer a detailed appraisal of much of the exegesis of Romans 1-5.

(1) As pertains to the relation of works to judgment, Gathercole's thesis is not unique: that (covenantal) works loom large in the literature of this period has hardly escaped the notice of scholars. One acknowledges that he is attempting to insert the thin end of the wedge into the door of the NPP; and anyone who has engaged in a similar research project can well appreciate that a Ph.D. thesis hinges on a creative use of materials that have been explored countless times. Nevertheless, Gathercole has not really advanced us beyond Yinger's work. He has devoted more detailed attention to some of the sources than Yinger, for which we are thankful; but, in principle, he has not told us anything that Yinger and others before him have not already said. I might add that a number of other secondary sources were only glanced at or ignored altogether.

(2) Gathercole's representation of the NPP is misleading and prejudicial in some particulars. For one thing, he paints a rather reductionistic picture. The main target in his crosshairs is the Sanders-Dunn-Wright axis, with occasional references to other scholars such as Yinger. One is not surprised by this, and his occupation with the "big three" is not out of line. In fairness, Gathercole acknowledges that there are discrepancies between these three particular scholars (221). Nevertheless, the phrase "New Perspective" is normally used in such a manner as to convey impression that the movement that bears this title is, more or less, a monolithic entity. In point of fact, such is not the case. It is surely telling that D. A. Carson acknowledges that the NPP cannot be reduced to a single perspective. "Rather, it is a bundle of interpretive approaches to Paul, some of which are mere differences in emphasis, and others of which compete rather antagonistically."[3] Some of us who embrace a modified form of the NPP are entirely in agreement with Gathercole that works count in the last judgment and that Israelite boasting pertains not merely to possession of the Torah and national privileges, but as well to an actual and factual performance of the law. Given that such is the case, the edge of his argument is blunted to a certain degree, at least in the case of those of us who believe that the NPP is not a "package deal" that has to be bought into lock, stock and barrel.

Second, the book starts off on the wrong foot by pressing a rather rigid either/or distinction between works as identity markers and works as serving as a criterion for final salvation.[4] In fairness, he does state that "broadly" adherents of the NPP hold the first position, while its critics emphasize the second position (13). Yet as the thesis unfolds, the former is almost exclusively attributed to a highly selective number of proponents of the NPP. As intimated above, I, for one, do indeed think that works as tokens of election and works as the precondition of final acceptance go hand in hand. Dunn offers this very observation: if Sanders has been criticized for polarizing in favor of election at the expense of obedience, Gathercole is in danger of polarizing in the opposite direction. Those who come in on the next phase of the debate will have the responsibility to ensure that the pendulum settles in a truer position.[5] I would add that Gathercole tends to chide Sanders for his systematic methodology. Yet his own determination to have works as the basis of final salvation is as systematic as Sanders' approach ever was. Only this is a systemization in reverse: whereas Sanders is open to the charge that his approach resulted in a downplay of works, Gathercole's systemization gives rather short shrift to election and the covenant.[6]

As Dunn further points out, for all that Sanders is open to criticism, his key phrase, "covenantal nomism," does attempt to provide a balance—covenant *and* law. This is nowhere more evident than in Sanders' treatment of the Dead Sea Scrolls. According to Sanders, there is no layer in the Qumran materials in which obedience to the law is not required or in which transgression is not punished. Obedience to the commandments was not thought of as earning salvation, which came by God's grace; but obedience was nevertheless required as a condition of remaining in the covenant, and not obeying the commandments would damn.[7] Sanders writes in pointed terms that at Qumran "obedience is the condition *sine qua non* of salvation."[8] If nothing else, such statements give the lie to Gathercole's allegation that Sanders reduces obedience to "mere intention" and operates with a "minimalistic" conception of the works required by the covenant (182-84, 187-88). To attribute to Sanders the attitude that "it doesn't matter what you do as long as you are sincere" (183) is an injustice to him.

Third, Gathercole's portraiture of the work of Dunn is at least in need of qualification. As quoted by him (12), Dunn would appear to distance himself from the proposition that, in Jewish theology, final acceptance by God is conditioned on obedience.[9] However, in his monumental work on Paul's theology, Dunn agrees that judgment according to the law was taken for granted: "...the need actually to *do* the law was characteristic of historic Judaism."[10] Moreover, the citation of Dunn's comment on Rom 4:2 needs to be set in context. Dunn does say: "Paul is not speaking about 'good works' done by Abraham, but about faithful obedience to what God requires."[11] But the fact that "good works" is placed in inverted commas is a giveaway that he means "works" *in the pejorative sense of earning salvation*. This is evident from the introduction of his commentary, where he explains that the traditional approach to Judaism has assumed that Paul, in Romans, addresses "the *merit* of *good works*."[12]

Gathercole also perpetuates the common misconception that Dunn reduces the entirety of "the works of the law" to the boundary markers. The truth, however, is that Dunn recognizes very clearly that these "works" encompass the whole Torah. But within the period of the Second Temple, certain aspects of the law became especially prominent as the badges of Jewish identity: prominently circumcision, food laws, purity laws and sabbath. He states, in point of fact, that circumcision and the other ordinances were *not* the only distinguishing traits of Jewish self-identity. However, they were the focal point of the Hellenistic attack on the Jews during the Maccabean period. As such, they became *the acid tests of one's loyalty to Judaism*. "In short...the particular regulations of circumcision and food laws were important not in themselves, but because they *focused* Israel's distinctiveness and made visible Israel's claims to be a people set apart, were the clearest points which differentiated the Jews from the nations. The law was coterminous with Judaism."[13] No wonder, Dunn justifiably issues a note of protest.[14]

In the fourth place, Gathercole joins a growing list of scholars who have enlisted the labors of Avemarie as a counterbalance to Sanders' reading of rabbinic literature. Admittedly, Avemarie has provided an exacting and invaluable study of these materials, and his results are to be weighed carefully. If nothing else, his findings remind us that neither Sanders nor anyone else is to be accepted uncritically. However, like Mark Seifrid before him,[15] Gathercole leaves the impression from Avemarie's book that rabbinic religion was heavily works-oriented in the "legalistic" sense. In point of fact, Avemarie includes lengthy engagements of such matters as obedience to God from the vantage point of "knowledge of God and community."[16] The conclusion to that particular discussion is that "the Torah not only comes from God, *it leads to him as well*."[17] The conclusion to the entire book is: "The Torah is, according to the rabbinic understanding, the means and way to life, the medium of salvation. But it is more than that. Israel keeps it because God has given it and because she loves it."[18] Even more strikingly, Avemarie grants that throughout this literature it *is* possible to speak of a "covenantal nomism" (*Bundesnomismus*)! The Torah of the rabbis cannot be divorced from the context in which the law was given. In this sense, Sander's coinage of his phrase, says Avemarie, is certainly justified![19]

(3) A fundamental flaw of this thesis is that Gathercole, like other scholars of his persuasion, tends to abstract Jewish "works" or "obedience" from the covenant. To be sure, he is not unaware of the factor of covenant and often enough speaks of obedience in covenantal terms. Nevertheless, practically speaking, a notable distancing of obedience from covenant is in evidence. As Dunn reminds us, Sanders did not characterize Judaism solely as a "covenantal" religion, because the key phrase he chose conveyed a double emphasis—"covenantal nomism." And Sanders made it clear that the second emphasis was not to be neglected. But given the traditional emphasis on Judaism's "nomism," it is hardly surprising that Sanders should have placed greater emphasis on the "covenantal" element in the twin emphasis, though in his central summary statements he clearly recognized that both emphases were integral to Judaism's self-understanding.[20] It is just this balance of "covenant" and "nomism" that is lacking in Gathercole's presentation of the materials. Consequently, he persists with the old notion that the Judaism contemporary with Paul was self-reliant and exhibited no real sense of dependence on the grace and mercy of God. Many examples could be cited to the contrary, but here I would refer only to a couple of the Dead Sea Scrolls (1QS 11:1-3, 5, 11-12, 13-15; 1QH 4:30-33; 7:30-31; 13:17) and the considerable penitential prayer tradition of Second Temple Judaism.[21]

Apart from effectively disjointing law from covenant, Gathercole has not appreciated *the implications of covenant as the matrix of obedience.* Particularly given the setting of Deuteronomy, the Sinai covenant was established by grace and maintained by grace. The declaration of Deut 5:6, "I am the LORD your God, who brought you out of the land of Egypt, out of the house of slavery," roots the covenant in none other than "redemptive grace." Throughout the Hebrew Scriptures generally, the pervasive metaphors of father/son and husband/wife, to depict Israel's relationship to Yahweh, carry connotations of love, intimacy and *enablement*. If Gathercole and others are prepared to charge Jews of this period with a kind of autosoterism, then Deut 30:11-14 is liable to the same accusation. Says Moses: *"You can do it"* (v. 14)! But, of course, the underlying assumption is that one can do the law as enabled by the Lord of the covenant himself. To suppose that Second Temple Jews were unaware of the way the covenant operates makes for presuppositionalism, not historical objectivity. It is only an effective bifurcation of covenant and obedience that sparks the quantum leap from works as the precondition of final salvation to "earning salvation" and "synergism."

An even more glaring omission is Gathercole's failure to connect works with faith in the Jewish materials. One gains the impression that faith was practically a nonentity in the life of the Jewish communities and the peculiar possession of the Christian church. At the risk of tooting my own horn, Gathercole might have had a look at my own thesis (*Obedience of Faith*), also written under Dunn's supervision, in which I endeavored to demonstrate that the Second Temple texts are replete with the language of faith, especially in connection with obedience. Indeed, it was my conclusion that Paul actually coins the phrase "the obedience of faith" (Rom 1:5; 16:26) with Jewish precedents in mind. I would call attention to a passage such as Sir 1:14, where the scribe Jesus Ben Sira equates trust in God with the "fear of God," the nearest OT circumlocution for "religion."[22]

In light of the realities of covenant grace and faith, Gathercole's depiction of obedience in Judaism and Paul respectively as an "apples and oranges" kind of comparison (my phrase) falls by the wayside. With a wave of the hand, he disavows any close parallels to Paul's theology of divine empowerment by the Spirit in Second Temple literature, except at Qumran, and even that, he thinks, is questionable. However, this claim founders on the evidence presented by C. S. Keener that the Spirit does appear as the Spirit of purity (and prophecy) in numerous texts.[23] It is evident enough, from Keener's data, that the Spirit cleanses and creates a new heart; one is not left to one's own devices.[24] Especially lame is Gathercole's contention that references to the Spirit in the Dead Sea Scrolls pertain to illumination rather than empowerment. It is highly doubtful that the community would have distinguished the two.

Provocative, to say the least, is the contention that unless Judaism was synergistic, the Spirit came for nothing on Pentecost! To be sure, the doctrine of the Spirit does not emerge with conspicuous clarity until the advent of the Lord who is the Spirit (2 Cor 3:17); and it is just the Pentecostal outpouring of the Spirit that marks out the community of Jesus as the latter-day Israel endued with power from on high. Nevertheless, his characterization of predestruction Judaism as a religion practically devoid of the enablement of the Spirit pushes the envelope too far. To say, as he does, that Paul has an understanding of obedience that is "*radically different* from that of his Jewish contemporaries," because "for him [as opposed to Judaism] divine action is both the source and the continuous cause of obedience for the Christian" (264), simply begs the question.

(4) In line with scholars such as Eskola and Laato, Gathercole plays the "anthropological card" in support of his thesis. In reviving a very old position indeed, he reiterates the notion that ancient Jews thought they were much better than they actually were, with some supposed innate ability to perform the will of God apart from divine aid. Such, however, is supposition not fact. A glance at the Qumran Hymns and the penitential prayer tradition, as referenced above, is a sufficient argument to the contrary, along with Keener's (and Levison's) survey of the Spirit in the relevant materials. Gathercole's claim that Paul and his contemporaries "clearly disagree" about whether human obedience without transformation by Christ and the Spirit can ever be the basis for justification (249) is only partially correct. As we shall see momentarily, the real difference between the two revolves around christology.

I would submit that Paul's actual critique of his interlocutor in Romans 2 has to do with *idolatry*, a significant substratum of Rom 1:18-3:20 that goes unnoticed by Gathercole. Without attempting to reproduce my previous study of this motif,[25] suffice it to say that Israel's idolatry, according to Paul's allegation, consists in her tenacious clinging to the law to the exclusion of Christ. His debate partner, who engages in sacrilege or idolatry (the verb *hierosuleō*, 2:22), is the none other than the one who boasts in the law. The implication is that Paul's polemic is directed not toward such moral shortcomings that would render the Jew "sinful" or "unworthy" in the most general terms. Rather, he is addressing Israel's age old problem: idolatry. Only now the face of the idol has changed—it is the nation's own Torah!

(5) Closely related to the charge of idolatry is the central issue between Paul and his contemporaries, namely, *christology*. If the Jew is idolatrous, for Paul, it is because he has refused to have Jesus of Nazareth as his Messiah and Lord; he has refused to submit to God's righteousness which has now been localized in Christ (Rom 10:3-4). Given the premise that Christ is the "end" (*telos*) of the law (Rom 10:4), both as the law's goal and its termination, not to believe in him is to prove unfaithful to God's eschatological purposes. Gathercole insists that the interlocutor is

unrepentant. True enough, but he is unrepentant with regard to Christ, not with regard to his covenantal duty under the Torah. The Jew is not the "bad" person, morally speaking, Gathercole portrays him to be;[26] rather, he is the one who has effectively renounced Yahweh's plan for the end of the ages in his Son. It is in this sense that the interlocutor may be regarded as apostate.[27] For all that Protestantism has insisted that justification is the "article of standing and falling of the church" (*articulus stantis et cadentis ecclesiae*), christology really is. *The church stands or falls with Christ*.

(6) Naturally, the phenomenon of boasting itself calls for some comment. Germane to Gathercole's argument is that Jewish boasting is bad because it entails "performance," as taken in the disapproved sense of "earning salvation." I would submit that boasting in performance is not necessarily a bad thing and that Gathercole has placed too negative a spin on the activity in question. His tack overlooks a noteworthy text such as Psalm 119, in which the Psalmist "boasts" over and over again. He makes no bones about it: he has loved the law of God and has keep its statues. Other Psalmists rejoice in the fact that Yahweh has rewarded them according to their righteousness and integrity (Ps 7:8; 18:20, 24). Just as striking, Paul, in Gal 6:4, commends boasting in one's own work, as opposed to denigrating the character of others. Ultimately, the believer's boast is in Christ and his cross (Gal 6:14); but stemming from this boast is the ability to perform such "work" (*ergon*) as one may glory in.[28] In Romans 2, Paul's problem with the interlocutor is not that he boasts as such, but that the object of his boasting is wrong: instead of the Torah, his boast should be in Christ. This becomes evident as one keeps reading further in the letter. In representing Jewish boasting in the manner he does, Gathercole treads the same path as D. A. Carson's study of divine sovereignty.[29] That is to say, Jewish attitudes are made to exist in a kind of time-warp between the two Testaments, in which people lapsed into a retrograde legalism. For such scholars, the "intertestamental period" serves as a convenient foil for various theses pertaining to NT theology.

(7) In the company of numerous scholars, Gathercole believes that in both Jewish and Pauline eschatology there is a tension between election and grace, on the one hand, and final vindication according to works, on the other (226, 265). Yet this is where Gathercole could have profited from Yinger's work. Yinger's thesis is precisely that, in the Jewish milieu, there is no actual tension between the two categories; the tension exists only in the

minds of Western (systematic) theologians. Ps 62:12, normally considered to be the source of Rom 2:6, actually says: "to you, O Lord, belongs *steadfast love*, for you requite a person *according to his work*." Apparently, the Psalmist is unaware of any "tension." Gathercole's own formulation is that "elective grace assigns a determinative role to works at the final judgment." Such is not a tension, but the logical outworking of grace; and Paul is not "radically different" after all from his Jewish contemporaries. Nor are Paul's criteria for past and future justification "slightly different" (266). Both are due to the believer being "in Christ." If for the sake of a theological formulation we wish to categorize Paul's thought, then the "basis" of justification, now and in the judgment, is *union with Christ*.[30]

(8) In view of the above, Gathercole's portrayal of Jewish justification requires some examination. The case is made that Abraham's justification, in various texts, was not eschatological, nor was it justification at the beginning of his covenant relationship. Rather, it was an event that took place at some point subsequent to the promise and Abraham's belief, as well as subsequent to his obedience to the commandments. What we find in all these texts, he says, is that faith/faithfulness becomes evident subsequent to Abraham's trials, in contrast with the biblical portrayal of faith being clearly present before the trials. So, justification, in the Jewish mindset, is subsequent to trials and to being found faithful.

This formulation is right and wrong at the same time. Right because the vindication (justification) of Abraham does take place subsequent to his entrance into the covenant relationship; but wrong because the biblical portrayal of Abraham does in fact depict the patriarch as faithful/believing in the midst of trials. Abraham's vindication, according to Genesis, is subsequent to trials and to being found faithful. In support of this alternative interpretation, I would call attention to the fact that Gathercole and other commentators understand Gen 15:6 as Abraham's "conversion;" before this point in the Genesis narrative, Abraham is only an "ungodly idolater" (250). However, this supposition founders on the progression of the Genesis story itself. Abraham's pilgrimage of faith begins in Genesis 12, as confirmed by Heb 11:8: "*By faith Abraham obeyed* when he was called to set out for a place that he was to receive as an inheritance; and he set out, not knowing where he was going."

By the time the narrative reaches chapter 15, Abraham's faith is beginning to wane. But once God assures him again of the promise, Abraham continues to believe and is declared to be a righteous, covenant-keeping person. This is his "justification" in Genesis: the Lord's vindication of him as a faithfully obedient person. All this plays into Paul's hands in Romans 4. One of the "exegetical traditions" of Judaism was that Abraham kept specifically the law of Moses (Sir 44:20; CD 3:2; *2 Apoc. Bar.* 57:2).[31] In a rather glaring omission, Gathercole does not even call attention to this datum, apart from simply quoting CD 3:2. Here we have the actual background to Romans 4 and the point of dispute. Based on the chronology of the biblical record, it is Paul's contention that Abraham was considered to be a righteous person before circumcision and the law. Not surprisingly, Rom 4:9-15 takes up none other than these two "pillars" of Jewish faith and life: circumcision and the Torah. The polemical value for Paul is that Gentiles can be received as the faithful ones of God apart from the assumption of Jewish identity. All they need do is "walk in the footsteps of Abraham" *who had faith before his circumcision*. In order to be the children of Abraham, it is not first necessary for them to become "honorary Jews."

In pursuing this objective, Paul predicates "ungodly" (*asebēs*) of Abraham in the same sense that Jews of this period would have used the term, that is, *uncircumcised and non-Torah observant*. Herein resides the irony of the situation. The same Abraham who was confirmed as a righteous person in Gen 15:6 would have been deemed "ungodly" by many of his first-century descendants! But by a simple "back to the Bible" tack, Paul is able to bypass a considerable layer of tradition and assert that Abraham and the nations are in the same boat. Consequently, analogously to former, the latter need only put their faith in Christ. In blunt terms, Gentiles can forget about the Torah! Therefore, Gathercole's contention that Paul's doctrine of the justification of the ungodly by faith without works is not integrally related to the inclusion of the Gentiles (251) is simply wrong. From the outset of the Roman letter, Paul has maintained this very thing: God's righteousness is for *all who believe, Jew and Greek* (1:16-17).

All this being so, the schema constructed by Gathercole is at least in need of modification. On his reading, Jewish obedience results in justification, and justification results in boasting (250). Given that "justification," or "vindication," in the Jewish outlook, normally pertains to the last judgment, this sequence is correct. The problem is that Gathercole attempts to set this formulation over against Pauline justification and boasting. By this time, it is necessary only to reiterate that in Paul's mind too a favorable eschatological judgment rests on covenant obedience, to which Gathercole himself assents. The difficulty is that he tries to equate Jewish justification, which is eschatological, with "phase one" of Pauline justification, an "apples and oranges" comparison. In so doing, Gathercole confuses the works of "getting in" with the works of "staying in." The reality is that ancient Jews were born into the covenant and could expect their ultimate vindication as a result of covenant faithfulness. Over against this expectation, Paul retorts that justification/vindication is to be found in Christ, and Torah works have nothing to do with it. For him, justification from beginning to end is christological: it is *in Christ* that one becomes the righteousness of God (2 Cor 5:21), now and in the last day. It is for this reason that the Christian boasts not in the law, but *in the Lord* (1 Cor 1:31).

Gathercole certainly does acknowledge that the christological dimension of the Christian's boast is a "crucial new component" (261). But having said that, he lapses into the anthropological mode by insisting that the Jew is sinful and unrepentant, with the result that his boast is "something very different from the boast of the Christian" (261). He is right, but not for the reasons given. Rather, the two boasts emerge from two separate spheres: Torah and Christ. One cannot dwell in both at the same time. Again, Gathercole plays up anthropology at the expense of christology.

(9) Gathercole's argument from Paul's use of David in Romans 4 does present a legitimate challenge to at least some proponents of the NPP. He is quite sure that David is the "smoking gun" that proves that Paul's focus is on anthropological matters, not the badges of Jewish identity. His point is that both Abraham and David were "ungodly" in the same sense of moral failure. By way of citing some Jewish sources as a foil, he refers to the "exegetical tradition" that David was accepted by God and justified on the basis of his works (CD 5:5 and 4QMMT, C24-25). The problem is that neither text speaks of *justification*! David is simply viewed as a righteous man whose deeds ascended to God and who was delivered from his enemies. Gathercole is here in danger of "parallelomania."

Even so, an honest reading of Rom 4:6-8 requires that we come to terms with the role of David in Paul's argument, as derived from Psalm 32. Gathercole is so confident that David is the "smoking gun" that he can write: "*It is crucial to recognize that the New Perspective interpretation of 4:1-8 falls to the ground on this point: that David although circumcised, sabbatarian, and kosher, is described as without works because of his disobedience*"

(247 [italics his]). His case is compelling in that David's behavior is called to the fore and challenges the assumption that Paul's polemic in Romans 4 is concerned *only* with boundary markers. Nevertheless, there is a failure to recognize that "ungodly" carries strong overtones of covenant infidelity. It is this very term, along with "lawless" and "sinners," that the writer of 1 Maccabees employs in his denunciation of Jews who apostatized to Hellenism.[32]

One may quite legitimately speak of David's ethical failure, but it is the very nature of that failure that rendered him as one outside the covenant. By his twofold sin of adultery and murder, David lowered himself to the level of the pagan world and ceased to be the representative of Yahweh on earth—*he became as one uncircumcised*. Particularly in Pauline perspective, when David broke the tenth commandment by coveting his neighbor's wife, he was turned into an idolater (Col 3:5). Such a reading makes perfect sense of Paul's argument, because Gentiles may be assured that they are acceptable to God in a sense qualitatively similar to David, who, at the time of his sin, was no better *covenantally speaking* than they. No wonder, Paul can say that David pronounces a blessing on those who are forgiven apart from "works," i.e., Torah-works. Out-and-out pagans can take assurance that they can be forgiven and accepted apart from the "nomistic service" required by the law.

Gathercole recognizes a certain validity to this reply, but he avers that in this case Paul would be conceiving of the entirety of Israel as under sin and outside the covenant since they are without works of Torah (247). But this rejoinder is simply unmindful of the idolatry motif of Rom 1:18-3:20, with its attendant irony. Paul fully concedes that his contemporaries have performed Torah-works. But that is precisely the problem! It is their zeal for the works of the law that have obscured their vision of the Messiah, Jesus of Nazareth, and a recognition that God's righteousness has now been embodied in him (Rom 9:16; 10:2-3).[33] As argued above, it is Israel's rejection of God's eschatological plan in Christ that has rendered her unfaithful, especially considering that perfect obedience was never required of Israel as God's covenant partner. The issue was never moral imperfection, but idolatry.

Whether one accepts this explanation or not, the fact remains that Gathercole's argument respecting David is valid only in the case of those who maintain that Paul's concern is restricted to boundary markers. His critique does indeed apply to some NPP scholars, but there is a notable company who would wish to dissent.

3. Summary

Gathercole's book serves as a useful and welcomed corrective to an imbalance on the part of some practitioners of the NPP. It is true, as he notes many times, that there has been a tendency to play up sociological matters (Jewish distinctiveness and self-identity) and to play down the Torah's own requirement that one really and truly "do the law." As stated above, the divide between the two on the part of certain notable scholars is not as stark as Gathercole would have us believe. Nevertheless, to the degree that he has redressed the balance in favor of a reading of Judaism and Paul that more accurately reflects the actual data, we are in his debt.

Perhaps the book's most valuable contribution is actually a byproduct of its main intention. Gathercole joins the growing consensus of NT scholars who believe that the eschatological vindication (justification) of "the doers of the law" (Rom 2:13) is to be understood in actual, not hypothetical, terms. *Even in Paul, works do count in the judgment.* Gathercole does think that this portion of the Roman creates a tension within Paul's overall theology, which, in my view, falls short of his otherwise insightful exposition. Nevertheless, he has honestly come to terms with the language and implications of the text, which many in the Reformed and Evangelical tradition are reluctant to do.

On the problematic side, Gathercole continues to perpetuate some of the same wrongheaded ideas about the character of Second Temple Judaism as his many of his predecessors. His approach to the sources is certainly an improvement over the imposition of terms like "legalism" and "works-righteousness" onto the Jewish materials by the likes of Schürer, Weber, Billerbeck, Bultmann, etc. But even so, his conclusions, in the end, are close enough to the "old school" approach to call for the criticisms proffered above. What he presents is a more enlightened and sensitive approach to the materials; but, at the end of the day, Judaism remains a religion devoid of the Spirit and dependence on the grace of God. While avoiding some of the extremes of traditional Christian assessments of predestruction Judaism, essentially Gathercole's book is but another reassertion of the Reformation understanding of the character of Paul's controversy with his Jewish contemporaries.

As much as anything else, this book wrongly endorses the "majority report" that soteriology as such is the lead-item on

Paul's agenda in Romans (and elsewhere). To be sure, the gospel is God's power to save everyone who believes (Rom 1:16). Yet prior even to salvation is the datum that Paul's gospel concerns *God's Son* (Rom 1:3). It is on this note that Paul begins the letter, making it the embodiment of his *christological gospel*.[34] In a very real sense, Rom 10:4 is the fulcrum of the epistle: Israel's striving to perform her covenantal duty is vain (9:16; 10:2-3) because the law is now passé; Christ is the *telos* of the law. The actual showcase of the apostle's thought is *not* justification, as time-honored as that notion is in traditional theology. It is, rather, union with Christ or the "in Christ" experience. From this vantage point, Col 1:18 exhibits the very life blood of Paul's preaching—that *in all things he may have the preeminence.*

In context, it is none other than christology that occasions Paul's very question, "Where is Boasting?" Of course, the answer is that "it is excluded" by virtue of "the law of faith" as opposed to "the law of works" (Rom 3:27). But given that faith, for Paul, is always specifically trust in Christ ("Christic faith"), the juxtaposition of "faith" and "works" is but his familiar contrast of Christ and the Torah. That Paul was not opposed to boasting as such is evident from Gal 6:4, as observed above. The Christian has not ceased to boast, but now his boasting is in Christ, in his cross, and in the hope of the glory of God (Rom 5:2; Gal 6:14; Phil 3:3). Phil 3:3 is especially telling inasmuch as it relocates boasting from the law to Christ: believers are those who "boast in Christ Jesus and place no confidence in the flesh." "Flesh," as the ensuing discussion clarifies, is Paul's former pedigree as a "Hebrew of Hebrews." In a nutshell, Paul replaces Torah-boasting with Christ-boasting.[35] It is Torah-boasting that is excluded, because Torah-boasting prevents one from boasting *in Christ*.

This review perhaps represents a "mediating position" between Gathercole and some exponents of the NPP. But it simply underscores that the movement known generically as the "New Perspective" is flexible enough to allow for individual thought and refinement of convictions.

---

[1] Yinger, *Paul, Judaism, and Judgment According to Deeds*, Society for New Testament Studies Monograph Series 105 (Cambridge: Cambridge University Press, 1999).

[2] Avemarie, *Tora und Leben: Untersuchungen zur Heilsbedeutung der Tora in der frühen rabbinischen Literatur*, Texte und Studien zum Antiken Judentum 55 (Tübingen: Mohr-Siebeck, 1996).

[3] D. A. Carson, Peter T. O'Brien, and Mark A. Seifrid (eds.), *Justification and Variegated Nomism. Volume I. The Complexities of Second Temple Judaism* (Grand Rapids: Baker, 2001), 1.

[4] A similar false distinction crops up when Gathercole alleges that the NPP stresses sociological categories to the exclusion of soteriological issues (225), as though the two were mutually exclusive. But, in point of fact, the works required for covenant obedience are just the works that distinguished Israel from the nations. See my discussion in *'The Obedience of Faith': A Pauline Phrase in Historical Context*, Wissenschaftliche Untersuchungen zum Neuen Testament 2/38 (Tübingen: Mohr-Siebeck, 1991), 265-66.

[5] In a personal communication from Professor Dunn.

[6] It is here that a concession is due to Dr. Gathercole. In his response to my review (forthcoming in *Reformation and Revival Journal*), he is quite right that his endeavors to balance election and works in Judaism are more pronounced than I gave him credit for. It should be underscored, however, that the point about polarization was actually Dunn's, as I passed it on from him. The phrase "short shrift" was chosen to say that in comparison with works, election/grace are more in the background than the foreground of Gathercole's book, not that the latter are bypassed altogether. I take his point that *election and works* are the twofold basis of final salvation. I also take the point that Sanders had already substantiated the factor of election and that there was no need to reproduce his discussions. Yet by that very standard, if Gathercole's treatment of texts is acknowledged to be balanced, then so must Sanders' be. However, such a balance Gathercole is apparently unwilling to grant to Sanders when the former ascribes to the latter a "minimalistic" understanding of covenant faithfulness that reduces righteousness to "mere intention." Sanders' handling of the Dead Sea Scrolls proves otherwise.

[7] Sanders, *Paul and Palestinian Judaism: A Comparison of Patterns of Religion* (Philadelphia: Fortress, 1977), 320.

[8] Ibid., 304.

[9] Dunn, "In Search of Common Ground," *Paul and the Mosaic Law*, ed. J. D. G. Dunn (Grand Rapids: Eerdmans), 312.

[10] Dunn, *The Theology of Paul the Apostle* (Grand Rapids: Eerdmans, 1998), 135-36. This consciousness of judgment by works stems from the Torah itself, in particular Lev 18:5 and Deut 4:1, 10, 40; 5:29-33; 6:1-2, 18, 24; 7:12-13, with the familiar refrain, "this do and live."

[11] Dunn, *Romans*. Word Biblical Commentary 38 a, b. 2 vols. (Dallas: Word, 1988), 1.200.

[12] Ibid., lxv (italics his).

[13] Dunn, "Works of the Law and the Curse of the Law (Galatians 3.10-14)," *New Testament Studies* 31 (1985), 526. See further his "Yet once more—'The Works of the Law': A Response," *Journal for the Study of the New Testament* 46 (1992), 99-117.

[14] Dunn, *Theology of Paul*, 358, n. 97.

[15] Seifrid, "Righteousness Language in the Hebrew Scriptures and Early Judaism," *Justification and Variegated Nomism. Volume I. The Complexities of Second Temple Judaism*, eds. D. A. Carson, P. T. O'Brien and M. A. Seifrid (Grand Rapids: Baker, 2001), 415-42.
[16] Avemarie, *Tora und Leben*, 244-61.
[17] Ibid., 261 (italics mine).
[18] Ibid., 584.
[19] Ibid., 584, n. 40.
[20] From Dunn's review of *Justification and Variegated Nomism*, Trinity Journal ns 25 (2004), 111.
[21] See R. A. Werline, *Penitential Prayer in Second Temple Judaism: The Development of a Religious Institution*, Society of Biblical Literature: Early Judaism and Its Literature 13 (Atlanta: Scholars Press, 1998). Werline's work is completely overlooked by Gathercole. That these and other prayers were rooted in biblical texts has been shown by M. J. Boda, *Praying the Tradition: The Origin and Use of Tradition in Nehemiah 9*, Beihefte zur Zeitschrift für die alttestamentliche Wissenschaft 277 (Berlin: de Gruyter, 1999); J. H. Newman, *Praying by the Book: The Scripturalization of Prayer in Second Temple Judaism*, Society of Biblical Literature: Early Judaism and Its Literature 14 (Atlanta: Scholars Press, 1999). A penitential prayer consultation has now been established at the annual meeting of Society of Biblical Literature. Papers and bibliographies can accessed online at: http://macdiv.ca/prayer.
[22] Garlington, *Obedience of Faith*, 19-20.
[23] Keener, *The Spirit in the Gospels and Acts: Divine Purity and Power* (Peabody: Hendrickson, 1997), 6-48. One may agree with Keener that in early Christian literature the Spirit distinguishes Jesus and his community as the true servants of God, who have begun to experience the radically new power of the kingdom era (ibid., 27).
[24] See also J. R. Levison, *The Spirit in First-Century Judaism* (Leiden: Brill, 2002), 73-76.
[25] D. Garlington, *Faith, Obedience, and Perseverance: Aspects of Paul's Letter to the Romans*, Wissenschaftliche Untersuchungen zum Neuen Testament 79 (Tübingen: Mohr-Siebeck, 1994), 32-43, as seconded by J. A. Fitzmyer, *Romans*, Anchor Bible 33 (New York: Doubleday, 1993), 318.
[26] Gathercole points to the charge of Rom 2:21-22 that the interlocutor has engaged in theft, adultery and sacrilege. Commentators such as C. K. Barrett and D. J. Moo note that these three often appear side by side in lists of vices (e.g., Philo, *Conf.* 163; *Spec. Laws* 2.13; 4.87). C. E. B. Cranfield senses the problem occasioned by Paul's application of these three sins to contemporary Israel and opts for the view that Paul is radicalizing the law in much the same manner as Matt 5:21-30 (*A Critical and Exegetical Commentary on the Epistle to the Romans*. International Critical Commentary. 2 vols. [Edinburgh: T. & T. Clark, 1975, 1979], 1.168-69). This makes more sense than the supposition that the typical

Jew overtly engaged in such activities. In any event, given the whole sweep of Rom 1:18-3:20, the debate partner's main problem is his idolatrous boast in the Torah, not in Christ, as God's definitive provision for sin. It is certainly noteworthy that in the OT and later literature, adultery stands as a symbol of idolatry (Garlington, *Obedience of Faith*, 190; R. C. Ortlund, *Whoredom: God's Unfaithful Wife in Biblical Theology*, New Studies in Biblical Theology [Grand Rapids: Eerdmans, 1996]). It should be added that engagement in such sins as Paul enumerates hardly renders the Jew an apostate from the Mosaic standards, as per Gathercole's claim. If that were so, then many Christians could be considered apostates from the new covenant!

[27] I have argued that in Gal 3:10-13 the Judaizers fall under the same condemnation because, for all intents and purposes, they too assume a stance on the wrong side of the eschatological divide and effectively subvert God's plan for the ages. See my "Role Reversal and Paul's Use of Scripture in Galatians 3.10-13," *Journal for the Study of the New Testament* 65 (1997), 85-121, as reprinted in *Exegetical Essays*, 3rd. ed. (Eugene, OR: Wipf & Stock, 2003), 213-47.

[28] See my treatment of the passage in "Burden Bearing and the Recovery of Offending Christians (Galatians 6:1-5)," *Trinity Journal* ns 12 (1991), 178-82; and *An Exposition of Galatians: A New Perspective/ Reformational Reading*, 2nd ed. (Eugene, OR: Wipf & Stock, 2004), 295-96.

[29] Carson, *Divine Sovereignty and Human Responsibility: Biblical Perspectives in Tension*, New Foundations Theological Library (London: Marshall, Morgan & Scott, 1981). Gathercole seconds Carson's claim that, in the Jewish sources, God responds to the "merit" of Israel (15). The problem is that what Carson calls "merit" is actually the people's required response to the covenant. If God responds to "merit" in the postbiblical materials, then the same must be true of Deut 28:1-14. But, we may presume, neither Carson nor Gathercole wants to go there.

[30] Cf. my *Faith, Obedience, and Perseverance*, 70-71.

[31] See further Garlington, *Obedience of Faith*, 37-40; T. R. Schreiner, *Romans*, Baker Exegetical Commentary on the New Testament (Grand Rapids: Baker, 1998), 215-17.

[32] See Garlington, *Obedience of Faith*, 91-102.

[33] Gathercole, as many commentators, takes Rom 10:3 as a statement of Israel's attempt to "establish" its own righteousness (228), an interpretation that carries definite "works-righteousness" overtones. Yet his overview of the Septuagint usage of the verb *histēmi* does not include significant passages in which it means not "establish," but "maintain" the covenant. To be sure, in some cases, it does refer to God's establishment and/or maintenance of covenant relationships (Gen 6:18; 9:11; 17:7, 19, 21; 26:3; Exod 6:4; Lev 26:9; Deut 8:18; 9:5; 29:13; Jer 11:5; Sir 17:12; 45:7, 24). But most relevantly, in other instances, the verb speaks of Israel's responsibility to "maintain" the covenant (Jer 34[LXX 41]:18; Sir

11:20; 44:20; 45:23; 1 Macc 2:27). Particularly relevant in view of Paul's acknowledgment of Israel's zeal are Sir 45:23: Phinehas "stood firm" [*stēnai*] when the people turned away; and 1 Macc 2:27: "everyone who is zealous for the law and who maintains (*histōn*) the covenant, let him come after me." This is Paul's real point: Israel is zealous to *maintain* "her own" (*tēn idian*) covenant righteousness and refuses to submit to God's latter-day embodiment of righteousness in Christ.

[34] N. T. Wright, "The Messiah and the People of God: A Study in Pauline Theology with Particular Reference to the Argument of the Epistle to the Romans," D.Phil. thesis, Oxford University, 1980. Much of this material is included in Wright's *The Climax of the Covenant: Christ and the Law in Pauline Theology* (Minneapolis: Fortress, 1991).

[35] In principle, Gathercole acknowledges this, but his analysis is marred by his insistence that the Jew who boasts is unrepentant (261).

THE NEW PERSPECTIVE, MEDIATION AND JUSTIFICATION: A REPLY TO S. M. BAUGH[1]

1. Introduction

From the outset of this response to Professor S. M. Baugh's essay, "The New Perspective, Mediation, and Justification," necessity compels an accurate perception of what "The New Perspective on Paul" (NPP) actually is. Although J. D. G. Dunn, who coined the phrase, has reiterated his position many times and in many places, perhaps the best entrée into his thought is the recent volume of essays that rather comprehensively engages the debate that has ensued since the publication of his ground breaking essay, "The New Perspective on Paul."[2] Dunn assesses his aims and endeavors in these terms:

> This is what I meant and still mean when I speak of "the new perspective on Paul", as I attempted to work it out in fuller detail some years later in my *Theology of Paul*. In summary: (a) It builds on Sanders' new perspective on Second Temple Judaism, and Sanders' reassertion of the basic graciousness expressed in Judaism's understanding and practice of covenantal nomism. (b) It observes that a social function of the law was an integral aspect of Israel's covenantal nomism, where separateness to God (holiness) was understood to require separateness from the (other) nations as two sides of the one coin, and that the law was understood as the means to maintaining both. (c) It notes that Paul's own teaching on justification focuses largely if not principally on the need to overcome the barrier which the law was seen to interpose between Jew and Gentile, so that the "all" of "to all who believe" (Rom. 1.17) signifies in the first place, Gentile as well as Jew. (d) It suggests that "works of law" became a key slogan in Paul's exposition of his justification gospel because so many of Paul's fellow Jewish believers were insisting on certain works as indispensable to their own (and others?) standing within the covenant, and therefore as indispensable to salvation. (e) It protests that failure to recognize this major dimension of Paul's doctrine of justification by faith may have ignored or excluded a vital factor in

combating the nationalism and racism which has so distorted and diminished Christianity past and present.[3]

Assuming this self-portrait of Dunn's, in my analysis of and reply to Baugh's essay I will simply follow his organization, first by summarizing the arguments and afterward responding to them. In each instance, I would emphasize that the views expressed herein are distinctively my own. If I may recall from a previous publication, there is no such thing as *the* NPP:

> There simply is no monolithic entity that can be designated as the "New Perspective" as such. It is surely telling that D. A. Carson, a noted critic of the NPP, acknowledges that it cannot be reduced to a single perspective. "Rather, it is a bundle of interpretive approaches to Paul, some of which are mere differences in emphasis, and others of which compete rather antagonistically." What goes by the moniker of the "New Perspective" is actually more like variations on a theme; and, in point of fact, this generic title is flexible enough to allow for individual thought and refinement of convictions....[4]

Therefore, though I am much indebted to E. P. Sanders, J. D. G. Dunn, N. T. Wright and numerous others for invaluable insights, the following representation of the NPP does not correspond precisely to any of these scholars.

2. "The Fundamentals of the New Perspective"

After asserting in his Introduction that the NPP consists of "a relatively small but vocal group," and that "the various positions of this group have been subject to considerable critique and rebuttal in scholarly literature, for its underlying analysis of both ancient Judaism and Paul's theology," Baugh proceeds to outline what he perceives to be the fundamentals of the NPP, of which there are three "nonnegotiable ideas" (though Dunn numbers five).

(1) According to Baugh, the NPP has rejected the traditional Protestant vision of Judaism and Paul's Jewish-Christian opponents as "rank legalists." In place of this, ancient Judaism is now understood in terms of E. P. Sanders' now famous "covenantal nomism:" one "gets in" the covenant by God's grace, but "stays in" by works of obedience to God's law.

As a rudimental depiction of Sanders, this is fair enough, though it does suffer from oversimplication, as we will see. To be sure, Baugh is right that NPP scholars have rejected the caricature of Second Temple Jews as "rank legalists," simply because it is a caricature and for that reason *ought* to be rejected and replaced by an appraisal that does actual justice to the sources. That is to say, the main issue before Jewish writers of this time-frame was perseverance in the face of widespread apostasy, not the amassing of merits for the sake of some "self-salvation."[5] However, such a conclusion did not descend "straight down from above" in 1977 with the publication of E. P. Sanders' *Paul and Palestinian Judaism*. Conspicuously absent in Baugh's presentation is a sense of historical perspective, which leaves the impression (from silence) that virtually no one before the advent of the "Sanders/Dunn trajectory" had taken issue with the Reformation understanding of the character of this Judaism.[6] Certainly such is not the case. Around the turn of the twentieth-century, a group of Jewish scholars rightly protested against the Christian mishandling, not to say distortion, of the literature they knew so well. As a result, non-Jewish interpreters of Judaism and Paul, such as G. F. Moore, James Parkes and W. D. Davies, began to reassess.[7] Davies in particular concluded that at point after point in Paul's letters there is agreement between him and the rabbinic teachers, the real difference being the question of whether Jesus of Nazareth is the Messiah.[8] Davies rightly, then, focused the issue on christology.

Strangely overlooked in the NPP debate, especially by evangelicals, has been R. N. Longenecker's *Paul: Apostle of Liberty*.[9] Longenecker's treatment of the piety of Hebraic Judaism is a model of balanced scholarship.[10] He demonstrates, in the words of Israel Abrahams, that there are both "weeds" and "flowers" in the garden of Judaism and that the elements of nomism and spirituality must be kept in proper proportion to one another. Certainly ahead of his time, Longenecker had already distinguished between "acting legalism" and "reacting nomism," with the latter characterizing "the religion of a *nomist*."[11] It is true that Longenecker takes the "weeds" of Judaism to be its tendency toward "externalism." Yet even here he does not absolutize the external factor, because the "essential tension" of predestruction Judaism was not externalism versus inwardness, but "fundamentally that of promise and fulfillment."[12]

In light of the actual development of Jewish and Pauline studies, Sanders' work is but the outcome of a process of rethinking. To be sure, his *Paul and Palestinian Judaism* managed to grab the attention of the scholarly world in a way none had done before. Nevertheless, his was not a unique epiphany straight out of the blue. As was so of Einstein's revolutionary accomplishments, Sanders also has stood on the shoulders of others ("giants") who came before him.[13]

(2) For Baugh, what began as a "new perspective" on Second Temple Judaism has, without further ado, turned into a complete recasting of Paul's theology. In particular, Wright is chided for indicting the Christian church for its supposed misunderstanding of justification for nearly two thousand years.

He is right that Sanders did little exegesis of Paul and that his sketch of Paul's theology has gained few followers. In fact, I have heard it whimsically said, and agree, that Sanders' book should have been entitled *Palestinian Judaism and Paul*! Nevertheless, Baugh's allegation, as it stands, falls short of accuracy. One of the most accessible windows onto the NPP is a segment of Dunn's Introduction to his Romans commentary.[14] In his own reflections on the movement whose name was coined by him, Dunn does indeed maintain that Protestant exegesis has for too long allowed a typically Lutheran emphasis on justification by faith to impose a hermeneutical grid on the text of Romans. The problem lay in what that emphasis was set in opposition to. The antithesis to "justification by faith"—what Paul speaks of as "justification by works"—was understood in terms of a system whereby salvation is *earned* through the *merit* of *good works*. This was based partly on the comparison suggested in Rom 4:4-5 and partly on the Reformation's rejection of a system whereby indulgences could be bought and merits accumulated. But Dunn's qualification is often neglected, i.e., the Reformation's repudiation of indulgences and merits *is* an important emphasis: God is the one who justifies the ungodly (Rom 4:5); and understandably, he says, this insight has become an integrating focus in Lutheran theology with tremendous power.

A careful reading of Dunn reveals clearly enough that his agenda is stated in hermeneutical terms. The protest against merits, etc., was necessary, justified and of lasting importance. But the hermeneutical mistake was to read *this* antithesis back into the NT period and to assume that Paul was protesting in Pharisaic

Judaism precisely what Luther protested in the pre-Reformation church.[15] It is true that this "new perspective" is pursued programmatically throughout Dunn's commentary, but Paul's theology is hardly given an overhaul *in toto*. In many places, Dunn's comments on the text of Romans are as traditional as any other commentator.[16] It would be much more fair and accurate to say that Dunn and others have sought to make appropriate adjustments to our understanding of Paul in the light of his place in history and the issues actually under debate during his lifetime.[17] It is telling that the only aspect of Paul's theology singled out by Baugh is justification. Even if one believes that justification is the "article of standing and falling of the church" (*articulus stantis et cadentis ecclesiae*), it is a *non sequitur* that an adjusted definition of the term is tantamount to a wholesale revision of Paul's preaching, and Baugh has not demonstrated that such a sweeping alteration has in fact occurred.

As for justification, a nuanced approach is indispensable in coming to terms with the apostle's teaching as perceived by the NPP. In so doing, it is necessary to distinguish between Dunn and Wright. Dunn is *not* of the opinion that the church has been "wrong" (as Baugh puts it) for the past two thousand years as regards justification by faith. According to his own statement, he has no particular problem in affirming that the doctrine of justification, in its fully orbed expression, is "the article of standing or falling of the church."[18] Some may question the phrase "fully orbed expression." But even allowing that this choice of words may not sit comfortably with some traditional views of justification, Dunn is basically onside with the Reformation in its recognition of the manner in which God justifies (vindicates) sinners.[19]

> This I say once again is what the "new perspective" is all about for me. It does *not* set this understanding of justification by faith in antithesis to the justification of the individual by faith. It is *not* opposed to the classic Reformed doctrine of justification. It simply observes that a social and ethnic dimension was part of the doctrine from its first formulation, was indeed integral to the first recorded exposition and defense of the doctrine—"Jew first but also Greek".... This is the lost theological dimension of the doctrine which needs to be brought afresh into the light, *not* to diminish the

traditional doctrine, but to enrich the doctrine from its biblical roots and to recover the wholeness of Paul's teaching on the subject.[20]

Wright, by contrast, maintains that justification does not tell us how one can be saved; it is, rather, a way of saying how one can know that one belongs to the covenant community, or, in other words, how are the people of God to be defined?[21] To be sure, such issues are to be judged in light of the covenant context of "the righteousness of God" and similar ideas. On this score, Wright is undoubtedly correct. Paul does indeed address the question, "Who is a member of the people of God." Likewise, it is true that "justification...is the doctrine which insists that all who share faith in Christ belong at the same table, no matter what their racial differences, as together they wait for the final new creation."[22] This much said, it is to be acknowledged that Wright has distinguished too sharply between the identity of the people of God and salvation. In my view, it is closer to the mark to say that (among other things) Romans and Galatians do address the issue of entrance into the body of the saved, meaning that to belong to the new covenant *is* to belong to the saved community. Therefore, justification does indeed tell us how "to be saved," in that it depicts a method of redeeming sinners—*by faith* in Christ—and placing them in covenant standing with the God of Israel. If justification is *by faith*, then, in point of fact, a modality of salvation is prescribed.[23]

Moreover, I should have thought that with all of Wright's admirable and "justifiable" stress on the return from exile motif he would have been more inclined to play up justification as *salvation from bondage*. As he himself has labored to demonstrate, the very term "gospel" originates in Isa 40:9; 41:27; 52:7; 61:1-2; Joel 3:5 (LXX), where the announcement is made that Israel's captivity is at an end and that the people will embark on an exodus from Babylon, just as the wilderness generation had originally come out from Egypt, the "house of bondage." In the broader context of Isaiah 40-66, the "gospel" expands to entail Yahweh's return to Zion, his enthronement there and the commencement of the new creation. But if it is the "righteousness of God" that underlies and impels Israel's release from a new house of bondage, then why is justification not tantamount to a salvation, which, in biblical-theological terms, is played out with Jesus as the binder of the strong man who plunders the latter's goods and releases those bound by him (Matt 12:22-30; Luke 11:14-23; 10-17)?

But all the foregoing notwithstanding, it remains that Baugh has not represented Wright entirely accurately. According to Baugh: "Wright...indicts the church—principally because it has misunderstood ancient Judaism and has 'ransacked' Paul for mere proof-texts; therefore the Christian church has misunderstood Paul on justification 'for nearly two thousand years' and 'has systematically done violence to that text [Romans] for hundreds of years'." But let's examine Wright a bit more closely. In the pages referenced by Baugh,[24] Wright maintains that "the discussions of justification in much of the history of the church, certainly *since Augustine*, got off on the wrong foot—at least in terms of understanding Paul—and they have stayed there ever since."[25] Thereafter, he cites Alister McGrath to the effect that the doctrine of justification as has come to develop a meaning quite independent of its biblical (Pauline) origins. We cannot pursue McGrath at all, but Wright is in essential agreement with him that the origins of justification in Paul lie in his polemics *vis-à-vis* the Judaism of his day. He continues: "Whatever Paul means by a word, if the church has used that word or its equivalents in other languages to mean something else for nearly two thousand years, *that is neither here nor there*." Still, he writes, there remains a problem. In all the church's discussion of "justification," Paul's letters "are ransacked for statements, dare we even say proof-texts, on a subject which he may or may not himself have conceived of in those terms."[26] This leads to the proposal that if Paul meant by "justification" something which is "significantly different from what the subsequent debate has meant," then the appeal to him is "consistently flawed, maybe invalidated altogether."[27] And indeed, Wright does claim that the traditional way of reading Romans has "systemically done violence to that text for hundreds of years, and that it is time for the text itself to be heard again."[28]

In presenting his peculiar approach to justification, Wright leaves no doubt that he is not satisfied with the terms in which the issue has been posed and with the Reformation's reading of Roman in particular. Yet the situation is not dire. For one thing, Baugh gives us a truncated version of Wright's complaint that Paul's letters "are ransacked for statements, dare we even say proof-texts, on a subject which he may or may not himself have conceived of *in those terms.*" Wright's own syntax, it would seem, has been subjected to a proof-texting method, leaving an overly negative impression of his actual claims. Moreover, Wright does not say categorically that the church has misunderstood justification from the get-go. His discussion, unlike Baugh's, is more nuanced than that. Augustine, he writes, is the effective *terminus a quo* of discussions of justification that have "got off on the wrong foot and have stayed there ever since." This is a statement of procedure, not a blanket denunciation of the entire pre-NPP understanding of Paul, especially if it is *neither here nor there* if the church has used "justification" or its equivalents to mean something else for nearly two thousand years.

Baugh has failed to notice Wright's acknowledgment that Paul does discuss the subject-matter that the church has referred to as "justification," though he does not use "justification language" for it. When it comes to a personal knowledge of God in Christ, Paul does not employ the language of justification, but rather he speaks of the proclamation of the gospel of Jesus, the work of the Spirit and the entry into the common life of the people of God.[29] Again, I should think if justification speaks to the issue of the deliverance of the believer from the bondage of sin, it is a false alternative to place this facet of soteriology over against the personal knowledge of God in Christ, as assured by the work of the Spirit and accompanied by our reckoning among the covenant people. Even so, Wright is considerably more balanced than as represented by Baugh, particularly as Wright proceeds to specify that his "threefold grid" for understanding "God's righteousness" is provided by covenant language, law-court language and eschatology.[30] Whether one agrees or disagrees, it is evident that Wright is seeking to shift the terms in which justification has been discussed, from the dogmatic/confession to the exegetical/ historical, in keeping, I would say, with Paul's own world of thought.

(3) Consequently, for Baugh, any reading of Paul that "looks suspiciously like the Protestant view is ipso facto mistaken and excluded from consideration in the new perspective." Correlative with this point of view, writes Baugh, is the "curious fact that the new perspective Paul looks remarkably like his 'covenantal nomist' opponents described in Sanders's portrait of ancient Judaism."

The first element of this allegation is an overstatement and actually attributes to proponents of the NPP an attitude that is not characteristically exhibited by them. I simply defer again to Dunn's introductory essay to *The New Perspective on Paul*, "The New Perspective on Paul: Whence, What, Wither?" I might add my own piece, "The New Perspective on Paul" (especially pp. 26-29).[31]

As for the "curious fact that the new perspective on Paul looks remarkably like his 'covenantal nomist' opponents described in Sanders's portrait of ancient Judaism," it is to be conceded that there is a similarity. According to Baugh's reading of Sanders, one gets into covenant fellowship and salvation through a gracious, corporate election and retains title to these blessings only through "a sort of nonmeritorious obedience through works of law keeping." Yet this is not precisely Sanders' own articulation of his position. To be sure, Sanders does indeed speak of "good deeds" as the condition of remaining in covenant relationship.[32] Likewise, he can state that the "proper response of man" is his "obedience to the commandments." Yet such obedience is but doing the will of the covenant Lord, who has provided atonement for transgressions.[33] In short, the faithful Israelite stayed in the covenant by perseverance, in keeping with Lev 18:5.[34] As Sanders is careful to state, the question is whether one or not one Israelite in good standing. However, simple heredity did not ensure salvation: "That came to all those individual Israelites who were faithful."[35]

Such being the case, I would submit that both Paul and his Jewish counterparts were convinced that one must "get in" and then "stay in." While it is true that he and they differed as to requirements for getting in and staying in, and while it is also true that one is disinclined to speak of Paul's theology in terms of a "nomism" (because Christ takes the place of the law), the basic pattern is the same. The difference is *christology*: for Paul, *Christ* is the "article of standing and falling of the church."[36] One gets in Christ by electing grace and stays in Christ by perseverance or "the obedience of faith" (Rom 1:5; 16:26), which itself is God's gift by virtue of the eschatological Spirit.[37]

3. "Methodological Difficulties in the New Perspective"

(1) The first "methodological difficulty" is "a pervasive tendency" on the part of NPP scholars to use a word, word group or phrase in Paul "as levers to shift our understanding of Paul's doctrines from what has been painstakingly established to their own eccentric

interpretations." While this is obviously an *ad hominem* shot, as though advocates of the NPP are merely "eccentric" and have shirked from painstaking analysis of the data,[38] I can reply in brief to the words and phrases elicited by Baugh.

The first is the hotly debate phrase "faith of Jesus Christ" (*pistis Iēsou Christou*). The meaning of the phrase is not germane to the present purposes. But Baugh's citation of it in (limited) NPP literature is sufficient to illustrate that his analysis is beset with its own methodological problems. By citing only such scholars as Douglas Campbell and Richard Hays, the impression is left that the subjective genitive interpretation of *pistis Iēsou Christou* (Christ's own covenant fidelity) is characteristic of the NPP as such. Yet there is one glaringly obvious omission—J. D. G. Dunn. The scholar who actually coined the title "The New Perspective on Paul" has consistently resisted this reading of "faith of Jesus Christ!"[39] Dunn can thus hardly be accused of an "eccentric interpretation" when he supports fully the traditional reading of Paul's phrase.

Second, according to Baugh, the methodological problems of the NPP are further compounded by the phrase "the righteousness of God." Supposedly, this combination of words, along with the "righteousness" (*dik-*) word-group generally, warrants "the recasting of Paul's whole theology and especially the doctrine of justification in the way in which new perspective adherents desire." His charge is that the NPP has focused too narrowly on a few words and phrases and has not appreciated that justification in Paul is a complex construction which must be established by *statements* and larger units of discourse.

Here once more is a baffling allegation, as though we on "the other side of the fence" have forgotten our basic James Barr.[40] That the NPP has fixated atomisticly or myopically on mere words and phrases apart from an entire field of discourse simply does not comport with the facts. Quite the contrary, justification, as it takes its place within the broader parameters of "the righteousness of God," is rooted in the panorama of the prophetic teaching respecting Israel's return from exile. Paul virtually brackets Romans with the declaration that his gospel is rooted in the prophetic Scriptures of Israel (Rom 1:2; 16:26); and, as we saw above, the very notion of gospel is rooted in the latter chapters of Isaiah.[41] Therefore, since the sum and substance of Isaiah and the other prophets is exile and return, some of us certainly cannot be fairly accused of disregarding Paul's entire universe of discourse in favor of simple words and phrases. Consequently, far from recasting Paul's whole theology, especially the doctrine of justification, I would maintain that we in the NPP "camp" have understood Paul in the manner in which he wished to be understood, i.e., as a theologian of salvation history who took the story of Israel and redrew it around Christ and the church.[42]

Singling out Wright in particular, Baugh cites as an "extreme example" of ignoring context the former's attempt to fix the content of Paul's gospel in two verses in Isaiah.[43] In point of fact, Wright does not limit his reference to the two verses, Isa 40:9 and 52:7. He writes that the Jewish usage of the relevant root "gospel," in its noun (*euangelion*) and verbal (*euangelizesthai*) forms, *includes* these verses. Yet Baugh bypasses the fact that Wright thereafter proceeds to point out that these passages take their place in the company of others like Isa 60:6; 61:1, as they form the climactic statements of the great double theme of *the entire section of Isaiah 40-66*. Moreover, the return from exile was predicted by Isaiah, Jeremiah, Ezekiel and others, as reflected by several of the Qumran texts.[44] It would appear that Baugh is the one who has seized on certain words and has disregarded Wright's *statements* and larger units of discourse.[45]

To add to the problem, Baugh reasons that if Wright's identification of "gospel" with return from exile is correct, then we could just as likely trace Paul's gospel to Jer 20:15, where the prophet curses the man who brought the "gospel" of his birth to his father; "hence, the gospel would be viewed as a curse." The obvious reply is that this particular announcement of "good news" (*ho euangelisamenos*) is not of the same variety as the prophets' heralding of the end of the exile and the subsequent enthronement of Yahweh on Mount Zion.[46] Again, Baugh has neglected the actual *statement* of Jeremiah within his larger unit of discourse. It is he who is guilty of "illegitimate totality transfer" (Barr), not Wright who, if anyone, is sensitive to the breadth of the prophetic setting of Paul's employment of "gospel."[47]

(2) The second problem, for Baugh, pertains to the character of justification. Rather than a declaration by God that the sinner is accounted righteous in Christ by faith alone, the NPP, so says Baugh, envisages "some sort of ongoing relationship in covenant involving both God's obligation to save his covenant people and the individual's own obedience to maintain covenant with God."

Dunn then is cited that such a conception for the NPP is rooted in Hebrew thought, in which righteousness entails "a concept of relation." "Justification," consequently, means "to be acquitted, recognized as righteous...to be counted as one of God's own people who had proven faithful to the covenant."[48] So, as Baugh would have it, Paul turns out for the NPP to be a "covenantal nomist" like his opponents. Central to Baugh's complaint is the supposed opposition, in NPP thinking, between Jewish and Greek conceptions of justice and justification, as though the former allowed no place for a norm (the law) whereby sin was accounted as transgression, and the latter recognized no element of societal relationships. This is why we then are told that a more accurate evaluation of Paul's historical backdrop would be "inconvenient for the rhetorical appeal of the new perspective," as though the rationale and argumentation were rhetorical and rhetorical alone.

At this late date, it is difficult to conceive that anyone *au fait* with biblical studies would dismiss the relational nature of the Hebrew covenant, even if other factors enter in.[49] Even Mark Seifrid, who wants to downplay the definition of righteousness as covenant fidelity, has to concede that there are seven OT texts that make the connection explicit.[50] Given that righteousness is *at least* covenant fidelity, Dunn's appraisal of justification is apropos: Paul's doctrine entails being counted "as one of God's own people who had proven faithful to the covenant."[51] The issue, at the end of the day, is not achievement, merit or anything remotely resembling a method of self-salvation. It is, rather, the eschatological vindication of the servants of Christ who have remained loyal to him. And no, Paul was not a "covenantal nomist" like his opponents, because the "nomists" were devotees of the law, whereas Paul was a devotee of Christ. That such a take on justification is not antagonistic to the traditional understanding of Paul is underscored by the conviction of many of us that the declaration of the last day retains its character of forensic acquittal. By definition, judgment *is* forensic, though we should remind ourselves that all of the judgment texts (Old and New Testaments) base final forensic acquittal on "works," not the works of "saving ourselves" or "contributing to salvation," but the believer's "fruit" (John 15:2, 8, 16; Gal 5:22-23) which is the inevitable product of faith. At the end of the day, what counts is faith(fulness), or, in Hebrew, *'emunah*.[52]

As for the putative antithesis of Jewish and Greek conceptions of justice and justification, Baugh typically paints with a very broad brush, and, apart from an allusion to Dunn, no "new perspective advocates" are named. But if I also may take up Dunn again, two of his most relevant writings in this regard are studies in which he has posed the old issue of righteousness as justice.[53] It is true that Dunn contrasts the Hebrew relational (covenantal) ideal of righteousness with the Greco-Roman, which measured righteousness in terms of absolute ethical norms against which particular claims and duties could be measured. Failure to measure up to this standard involved ethical or criminal liability. By comparison, in Hebrew thought righteousness is something one has precisely in one's relationships as a social being. Individuals are righteous when they meet the claims which others have on them by virtue of their relationship.[54]

Baugh makes a valid point that we should not oversimplify and thus exaggerate the differences between the Hebrew and Greco-Roman notions of righteousness, as though there were no overlap at all. Yet, in his recent volume on Paul, it has not escaped the notice of Udo Schnelle, a decided "NPP sympathizer," that there was a degree of interpenetration between the two worlds.[55] But even with this qualification, the fact remains that Paul moved within the biblical/Jewish world of the covenant of Yahweh with Israel. Whatever relational aspects adhered to pagan notions of behavioral norms are of secondary importance in understanding Paul. It is just in terms of the OT understanding of righteousness that justification find its application within the society of the people of God. The judges of Israel were responsible for recognizing what these various obligations were as imposed on the people and for judging them accordingly, clearing the innocent and not deferring to the great (Exod 23:7-8; Lev 19:15; Deut 25:1; Isa 5:23). This basic datum is a sufficient comeback to any claims that the NPP is concerned solely with relationships and not with the divine demand as expressed in the law. Dunn further comments that the more fully we recognize that Paul's teaching on divine righteousness is the OT doctrine through and through, the more we must also recognize the social dimension of that righteousness (as demanded by none other than the law). By way of application, he writes, "this discovery of the horizontal and social dimension of justification by faith indicates that such social concerns lie at the heart of this so characteristic and fundamental Christian and *Protestant* doctrine."[56]

(3) The third methodological problem "haunting" the NPP is "the consistent tendency to limit the meaning of Paul's own teaching to what his supposed Jewish contemporaries either taught or what they would have understood." Baugh illustrates with Gal 5:3. This verse, in association with Gal 3:10, has been taken to indicate that Paul interpreted the law to require perfect and entire obedience. Consequently, the problem (for Baugh) is that such an interpretation does not fit Sanders' assessment, in Baugh's words, that "both Paul and contemporary Judaism taught a more relaxed view of the law in the form of covenant nomism." If Paul viewed the law as imposing an exacting and exhaustive requirement for personal obedience, then, according to Baugh, Sanders' analysis of Paul's opponents would end in failure.

The problematics of this misrepresentation are evident at a glance. At the very least, it is an oversimplification, and really a caricature, that NPP scholars reduce Paul's understanding to that of his contemporaries. True, Paul shared common values and outlooks with his Jewish kinsmen, particularly such familiar *theologoumena* as covenant, righteousness, faith and judgment. But at the same time, his perception of the role of the law and the Jewish people was radically altered by his encounter with the risen Christ on the Damascus Road.[57] To reiterate form above, Paul cannot be domesticated to Jewish standards simply because his vision of Jesus the Christ breaks the mold of Judaism. For him, the crucified Messiah is all in all; he is the goal and termination (*telos*) of Israel's law (Rom 10:4); he is the reason the Torah was imposed as a disciplinarian on the covenant people (Gal 3:23-25); he is the "body" to whom the shadows pointed (Col 2:17). Consequently, faith for Paul is Christic in orientation: from now on, trust is to be placed specifically in Jesus of Nazareth, the crucified Messiah.[58]

The argument from the conjunction of Gal 5:3 with Gal 3:10 involves a good deal of assumption. As for the former, Paul's reasoning is obvious enough from the standpoint of the Torah itself: "For Paul the Law is a package deal, and one cannot separate out one portion of its commandments from another. All must be obeyed if one is under the law."[59] One was not, in other words, free to pick and choose in cafeteria style from among the commandments. What is in view is the typical Jewish mindset which understood "doing the [whole] law" (Lev 18:5; Deut 4:1,

10, 40; 5:29-33; 6:1-2, 18, 24; 7:12-13) as the obligation and privilege of those within the covenant.[60] The Torah's own demand is a far cry from that which has been imposed on it. In commenting on Deut 27:26, Peter Craigie, for example, maintains that "the reach of the law is so all-pervasive that man cannot claim justification before God on the basis of 'works of the law'."[61] But the "reach of the law," I would respond, is not perfect compliance with its demands, or anything approaching it, but fidelity to the God who graciously gave it to Israel. Craigie's other mistake is a failure to realize that the law is in fact performable. Obedience to the Torah in the Hebrew Scriptures themselves is never portrayed as an unobtainable goal. Rather, according to Deut 30:11-20, it is a thing within Israel's grasp ("this commandment...is not too hard for you, neither is it far off," v. 11). One is able to say this because "keeping the law," "obedience" and such expressions speak of perseverance, not sinless perfection.

In Protestant exegesis, Gal 3:10 too has been understood in the terms suggested by Baugh, i.e., the law demanded perfect, perpetual obedience. If this reading is correct, then Baugh has a case that Sander's analysis of Paul's opponents would end in failure. Yet it has been pointed out more than once that such an analysis is flawed in that it requires the "suppressed premise" that no one can actually keep the law perfectly. Of course, it is a truism that perfect obedience is an impossibility for fallen human beings; but the problem is that one must assume that *this* suppressed premise was actually in Paul's mind as he penned Gal 3:10.[62] This approach, to my mind, has been successfully rebuffed by several scholars.[63] I would suggest, as I have before, that Paul is playing on the preceding portion of Galatians, according to which the Judaizers have become "ministers of sin" and "transgressors" (2:17-18) because of their preaching of "another gospel." Therefore, the apostasy/perseverance texts of Deut 27:26; Hab 2:4; Lev 18:5; Deut 21:23 are directly applicable to them by virtue of the phenomenon of role reversal.[64] The issue in Gal 3:10, as in the Torah itself, is covenant fidelity or perseverance, not a "covenant of works" mentality whereby the law demanded perfection for the Israelite to remain in covenant standing. Baugh and others have forgotten about the sacrificial system.[65]

Since, therefore, these two texts from Galatians can be explained in other terms than those forwarded by various exegetes, we are not compelled to concede that Sanders' analysis of Paul's opponents has ended in failure. In fact, my proposed interpretation is entirely consistent with "the new perspective on Judaism" as advanced by Sanders.

In elaborating his third methodological problem, Sanders remains in Baugh's crosshairs. To cut to the chase, it is simply irrelevant if Sanders changed his mind about Paul's conception of the law in relation to obedience, because Sanders is *not* a supporter of the NPP. As Dunn puts it, Sanders gave NT scholarship a "new perspective" *on Second Temple Judaism*.[66] The very reason why, in his Manson Memorial Lecture of 1982, Dunn coined the phrase "The New Perspective on Paul" was because Sanders, while providing legitimate insight into Judaism, still worked with an "old perspective" outlook on Paul himself. Consequently, to say, as Baugh does, that "the new perspective Paul can never break out of the box of his supposed pre-Christian convictions about the nature of the law and its righteousness" entails a twofold mistake. (a) It dismisses Sanders' accurate portrait of the *pre-Christian* Paul, who understood that what the law required was fidelity, not sinless perfection, and who believed in the efficacy of the sacrificial system. (b) It fails to understand the eschatological situation: for the *Christian* Paul, the law and *its* righteousness has now given way to Christ and *his* righteousness (e.g., Rom 3:21; 10:3-4). To say it one more time, the question pertained to christology in relation to the Torah, and to the degree that Sanders has illuminated the Jewish position, we are in his debt.[67]

(4) The fourth "methodological problem" takes up again the issue of justification, which forms a bridge into a lengthier section on Romans 5. In principle, I have already replied to Baugh's objections. Suffice it to say here that justification as a "definitive, judicial act" is falsely set in opposition to "continuance in the covenant relationship." It is not either/or but both/and. The believer's present justification as God's "definitive, judicial act" sets him upon the path of covenant fidelity—"continuance in the covenant relationship"—that eventuates in future eschatological vindication. Rather than evoke Sanders to the effect that one "gets in" by grace but "stays in" by works of obedience, it would have been more relevant to cite Dunn's affirmation that Paul expected his converts to "lead a life worthy of God" (1 Thess 1:2), which is but their "harvest or fruit of righteousness in their lives" (2 Cor 9:9-10; Gal 5:22-24; Phil 1:11).[68]

In a mere footnote (n. 33), Baugh gives exceedingly short shrift to Paul's pivotal phrase "the obedience of faith" (Rom 1:5; 16:26). We are told that this combination of words is "often misunderstood." We are not apprised of the "correct" understanding, but Baugh is quite sure that faith's obedience cannot be tantamount to "faithfulness" or "works of obedience" (I would add "perseverance"). It is easily countered that Paul's Greek phrase *hypakoē pisteōs* has undergone a great deal of study in contemporary research, and some very competent scholars disagree with Baugh.[69] The lameness of Baugh's resistance of data that has been so "painstakingly established" is underlined by his contention that certain NPP scholars have committed the "etymological fallacy" or "root fallacy,"[70] with regard to the Greek noun *hypakoē* ("obedience") as connected with the Hebrew verb *shama'* ("hear"). According to Baugh, this is an "extreme example" of this particular exegetical failing. Yet once more, an answer is readily at hand: the appeal to *hypakoē* is simply *not* an example of the root fallacy. Carson explains that the etymological approach to word study entails word history and the drawing out "hidden meanings" based on a "meaning" inherent in the root of a word or a particular combination of letters. There are many examples, but Carson illustrates the fallaciousness of the method with the English word "nice," as derived from the Latin *nescius*, "ignorant." In terms of etymologizing, the "nice" person would be "ignorant" by definition![71]

However, NPP (and other) scholars invoke *hypakoē* not because of etymology but because of its usage in context. The LXX translators actually chose three variants of the Greek verb "hear" to render the Hebrew *shama'*, *akouō*, *eisakouō* and *hypakouō*. All three are more or less synonymous. But still the questions arise, why are there variations, and do the variants convey at least different shades of meaning? As far as the verb *hypakouō* and the noun *hypakoē* are concerned, the prefix *hyp* ("under") cannot be dismissed as cavalierly as Baugh has done. While noting Carson's documentation of scholars who have pressed this prefix too far,[72] I would call to mind that as able a linguist as J. A. Fitzmyer—certainly no apologist for the NPP— discerns that: "Though that faith begins for Paul as a 'hearing'...it does not stop there. It involves the entire personal commitment of a man/woman to Christ Jesus as 'Lord'.... The word *hypakoē* implies the '*sub*mission' or total personal response of the believer to the risen Lord."⁷³ Granted, Paul and the LXX translators could have articulated the notions of submission and total personal response with the other forms of the Greek "hear." But, in their minds, there was apparently something about *hypakoē* that was especially suitable to their purposes.

"Hearing" in relation to obedience is significant enough that it is well to recall that in the Hebrew Scriptures the activity entails much more than audio-sensory processes. In point of fact, in Hebrew there are no distinctive words for "obey" and "obedience." Rather, the idea of obedience is consistently expressed by the vocabulary of hearing: to hear rightly is to obey.⁷⁴ As Wilckens affirms, the *Shema* of Deut 6:4—"Hear, O Israel"—has doing in view.⁷⁵ Dunn, then, can add that the respective appellations "hearers of the law" and "righteous" are complementary and overlap in large measure: hearing/believing and works are two ways of saying the same thing.⁷⁶ D. J. Moo is thus quite right that "obedience" (*hypakoē*) and "faith" are mutually interpreting: "Obedience always involves faith, and faith always involves obedience."⁷⁷

As straightforward (and Pauline) as this is, there remains, as Wright observes, an anxiety on the part of generations of theologians that any stress on obedience creates the impression that "good moral works" take priority over "pure faith." Wright, however, appropriately dismisses any such anxiety as missing the point:

> When Paul thinks of Jesus as Lord, he thinks of himself as a slave and of the world as being called to obedience to Jesus' lordship. His apostolic commission is not to offer people a new religious option, but to summon them to allegiance to Jesus, which will mean abandoning their other loyalties. The gospel issues a command, an imperial summons; the appropriate response is obedience.⁷⁸

4. "Covenant Mediation in Romans"

Subsumed under this heading are discussions of "Having Been Justified," "Justification and Mediation" and "The Development of Paul's Thought." As for the first, many of Professor Baugh's observations are well taken and are welcomed contributions to the study of Romans 5. I would simply second Dunn's contention that the aorist tense "having been justified" (*dikaiōthentes*) of Rom 5:1 marks the beginning of the salvation process: justification is not a once-for-all act; it is the initial acceptance by God into restored fellowship.[79] But because "process" can be and has been construed in a synergistic or Pelagian sense, I would just call to mind that the "process" corresponds to the basic architecture of NT eschatology: the familiar "Already" and "Not Yet," or perhaps better, the "inauguration" and "consummation" of salvation. Since the present concern is with Romans 5, I would invoke the same verses as Dunn, Rom 5:9-10:

> If we have been justified by Christ's blood, then (how much more) shall we be saved from (eschatological) wrath.
>
> If we have been reconciled by Christ's death, then (how much more) shall we be saved by his (resurrection) life.

I have treated the passage elsewhere.[80] Suffice it to say here that the past redemptive event in Christ has given rise to hope in the believer, a hope which has as its primary focus the future eschatological consummation of the new creation. Or, as Neil Elliott puts it, vv. 9-10 "relocate the soteriological fulcrum in the apocalyptic future: the gracious justification and reconciliation of the impious is made the basis for sure hope in the salvation to come."[81] Paul thus polarizes past and future as the epochal stages of the salvation experience, with the assurance that although the consummation of redemption is still outstanding, the believer can take comfort that God's purposes cannot fail. In this light, the aorist "having been justified" of Rom 5:1 is to be given its due, but within the spectrum of the "three tenses" of salvation history: "I have been saved, I am being saved, and I will be saved." It is the future tense of salvation that features prominently in Gal 5:5 as well: "For through the Spirit, by faith, we await the hope of righteousness." The verb "await" (*apekdechomai*) is always used by Paul of future eschatological expectation (Rom 8:19, 23, 25; 1 Cor 1:7; Phil 3:20). Paul, then, anticipates a time when the believer's present possession of righteousness will be brought to its crowning conclusion at the end of this age with the full realization of the new character that has already commenced in

Christ.[82] We should not forget that the very first instance of the verb "justify" (*diakaioō*) in Rom is 2:13, where it occurs in the future tense: it is the doers of the law who will be justified (*dikaiōthēsontai*) in eschatological judgment. As I have argued elsewhere, the "doers of the law" are not "legalists," but those who have maintained faith with Christ.[83] Consequently, for Paul *sola fide* includes the obedience of faith.[84]

Under the subheading of "Justification and Mediation," again there is much with which to agree. However, it must be reiterated that synergism is not a characteristic of the NPP reading of Paul; it is, rather, covenant fidelity. Baugh thus mistakenly subsumes "covenantal nomism" under the label of "synergism" and thereby confuses the issue. If anything, covenantal nomism is an expression of perseverance, not "synergism" or "contributing to salvation." Those of us who espouse one variety or other of the NPP have no hesitation in concurring with Baugh: "We have no claim on God derived from anything in ourselves as worthy of redemption."[85] We heartily affirm that our redemption hinges from beginning to end on the mediatorial work of Christ. Likewise, I agree that the Already is the guarantee of the Not Yet. In Baugh's own words, the last-day verdict has already been rendered at the resurrection of Jesus for our justification (Rom 4:25).

Yet the other side of the coin is that Rom 5:9-10 sets up a movement (process) from present to future salvation. It is normally observed that Paul's assertion is akin to the rabbinic *qal wahomer* ("light and heavy") pattern: "from the lesser to the greater." On the surface, it might appear strange that Paul could place the past work of Christ in the "lesser" category. But without minimizing the significance of Christ's death, his sacrifice must eventuate in the final salvation of his people in order to accomplish its goal. The salvific process is commenced with present justification, but it will not be consummated until we are finally "saved." Judith Gundry Volf appropriately comments: "The process of consummating the work of salvation is more like an obstacle course than a downhill ride to the finishline. For the destiny of Christians does not go unchallenged in a world opposed to God's purposes. The powers of evil in the form of afflictions and trials threaten continuity in their salvation."[86] Thus, Cranfield's remark that deliverance from eschatological wrath in relation to (past) justification is "very easy" fails to appreciate the formidable nature of the "obstacle course."[87] Given the "tribulations" (Rom 5:3) that attend the life of faith this side of the resurrection, the great thing, from the perspective of the present passage, is yet to be accomplished. None of this calls into question the efficacy of the work of Jesus the mediator, but it is to affirm that his work is not complete until the day on which the good work he began in us will be completed and perfected (Philippians 1:6).[88] We should recall as well that Reformed theology has always been sensitive to the interplay of the *perseverance* of the saints and the *preservation* of the saints. It is not either/or but both/and.

The final subsection, "The Development of Paul's Thought," contains relevant and useful exegetical observations on Rom 5:12-21. The main point is to reiterate that our justification can in no way hinge on our personal performance of the law, which is backed up by the doctrine of imputation. Since I have already addressed this issue above, there is little to say but that Baugh refuses to recognize that justification, like most things in soteriology, occurs in stages, corresponding to unfolding of salvation history. No one I know in the NPP camp maintains that our present justification is contingent on any kind of "autosoteriosm." Dunn, for one, has expressed himself clearly enough (as quoted above).[89] And as to the justification of the last day, it has also been stated in the plainest terms possible that our ultimate vindication has nothing to do with "performance," "merit," "works-righteousness," "synergism" or any other pejorative terms that might be enlisted. To say it one last time, it is the "obedience of faith" or *the perseverance of the saints* that counts in the judgment. As for imputation, I have addressed the issue elsewhere.[90] It is true that a number of us see no particular exegetical evidence for the doctrine of imputation as espoused, say, in the Westminster Confession. But even so, a stance one way or the other toward imputation is not of the essence of the NPP. And even some who do embrace imputation are still in tune with an eschatological phrase of justification as the outgrowth of faith's obedience.[91]

5. Summary

Professor Baugh's essay has endeavored to expose what he perceives to be the methodological and exegetical weaknesses of the NPP. He is to be commended for his attempt to come to terms with some of the Pauline texts that have been revisited many times since the "Sanders/Dunn trajectory" made its way onto the stage of NT Studies, over a quarter of a century ago now. A number of his exegetical observations on Roman 5 and his reaffirmation of the efficacy of the work of Christ are entirely apropos and are most welcomed. However, the downside of his paper largely outweighs its positive benefits. Throughout, there is the persistent misrepresentation that has plagued the Reformed response to the NPP since the outset of the debate. This includes painting with a very broad brush and, in several instances, "imputing" to proponents of the NPP positions that they do not necessarily advocate. Among other things, Baugh has not appreciated the variegated nature of the movement that generically bears the moniker of "The New Perspective on Paul." For instance, in the matter of justification he fails to take notice of the differences between Dunn and Wright (and others of us who have written on the subject). Especially egregious, moreover, is the allegation that the NPP has engaged in a recasting of Paul's entire theology. But as much as anything else, his essay is tarnished by the various *ad hominem* remarks with which it is punctuated. According to Baugh, the NPP has made the gains it has by the efforts of a small, eccentric, noisy but energetic band of rhetoricians who function as a censorship board to suppress any and all "offending" materials! I would hope that future discussions can be conducted in the spirit of "iron sharpening iron" on the part of those who, after the pattern of the Beroeans, search the Scriptures daily to see if these things are so.

---

[1] Baugh, "The New Perspective, Mediation, and Justification," *Covenant, Justification, and Pastoral Ministry: Essays by the Faculty of Westminster Seminary California*, ed. R. S. Clark (Phillipsburg: Presbyterian & Reformed, 2007, 137-63.
[2] Dunn, "The New Perspective on Paul," *Bulletin of the John Rylands University Library of Manchester* 65 (1983): 95-122.
[3] Dunn, *The New Perspective on Paul: Collected Essays*. Wissenschaftliche Untersuchungen zum Neuen Testament 185 (Tübingen: Mohr Siebeck, 2005), 15.
[4] D. Garlington, "The New Perspective on Paul: An Appraisal Two Decades Later," *Criswell Theological Review* ns 2, no. 2 (2005), 18. See Dunn's own admission in *New Perspective on Paul*, vii-viii. It is of more than passing interest that Dunn acknowledges that N. T. Wright was the first to recognize the significance of the work of E. P. Sanders ("The Paul of History and the Apostle of Faith," *Tyndale Bulletin* 29 [1978], 61-88).

It was Wright who proposed that there should be "a new way of looking at Paul...(and) a *new perspective* on...Pauline problems" (cited by Dunn, *New Perspective on Paul*, 6, n. 24, italics added).

[5] If I may refer to my discussion in *'The Obedience of Faith': A Pauline Phrase in Historical Context*. Wissenschaftliche Untersuchungen zum Neuen Testament 2/38 (Tübingen: Mohr Siebeck, 1991), 120, 265-67.

[6] The "Sanders/Dunn trajectory" is the phrase of Moisés Silva, "The Law and Christianity: Dunn's New Synthesis," *Westminster Theological Journal* 53 (1991), 341.

[7] See the historical overview of E. P. Sanders, *Paul and Palestinian Judaism: A Comparison of Patterns of Religion* (Philadelphia: Fortress, 1977), 1-12.

[8] W. D. Davies, *Paul and Rabbinic Judaism: Some Rabbinic Elements in Pauline Theology*. 4th ed. (Mifflintown, PA: Sigler Press, 1998), 323-24.

[9] Longenecker, *Paul: Apostle of Liberty* (New York: Harper & Row, 1964).

[10] Longenecker, *Paul*, 65-85.

[11] Longenecker, *Paul*, 78, 79-83. Longenecker was later to (re)define "works of the law" as "a catch phrase to signal the whole legalistic complex of ideas having to do with winning God's favor by a merit-amassing observance of the Torah" (*Galatians*. Word Biblical Commentary 41 [Dallas: Word, 1990], 86). This is in apparent conflict with his endorsement of Sanders and the acknowledgement that "First-Century Judaism was *not* fundamentally legalistic" (ibid.). In any event, my point is that in his earlier work Longenecker formed an integral part of a developmental process culminating in Sanders.

[12] Longenecker, *Paul*, 84.

[13] This is especially evident from S. Westerholm's survey of scholarship in *Perspectives Old and New on Paul: The "Lutheran" Paul and His Critics* (Grand Rapids: Eerdmans, 2004), 3-258. It is also well to remember that before Dunn's Romans commentary there was U. Wilckens, *Der Brief an die Römer*. Evangelisch-Katholischer Kommentar zum Neuen Testament 6. 3 vols. (Zürich/Neukirchen: Benziger/Neukirchener, 1978-82). Wilcken's work may fairly be termed the first "NPP" commentary on Romans.

[14] Dunn, *Romans*. 2 vols. Word Biblical Commentary 38 a, b (Dallas: Word, 1988), 1.lxiii-lxxii.

[15] Dunn, *Romans*, 1.lxv. See the similar discussion in Dunn's *The Theology of Paul the Apostle* (Grand Rapids: Eerdmans, 1998), 335-40, and at length *New Perspective on Paul*, 1-88.

[16] The same is true of his appreciation of justification by faith alone. See his *Theology of Paul*, 371-79; *New Perspective on Paul*, 21-22.

[17] In a personal communication, Professor Dunn has confirmed the correctness of this characterization of his work.

[18] Dunn, *New Perspective on Paul*, 21.
[19] Dunn maintains that Luther's translation of Rom 3:28, "by faith alone," may be regarded as faithful to the thrust of Paul's argument so long as the scope of Paul's contrast of faith and works of the law is borne in mind (*Romans*, 1.187). In commenting on Gal 2:16, Dunn doubts that the traditional reading of the verse has quite caught Paul's meaning. Nevertheless, he is entirely sympathetic with the proposition that humans cannot earn their salvation by their own efforts. In theological terms, this is an insight of "tremendous importance" (*The Epistle to the Galatians*. Black's New Testament Commentaries 9 [Peabody: Hendrickson, 1993], 135).
[20] Dunn, *New Perspective on Paul*, 33 (italics original).
[21] Wright, *What Saint Paul Really Said: Was Paul of Tarsus the Real Founder of Christianity?* (Grand Rapids: Eerdmans, 1997), 119, 120-22, 131; id., *Paul: In Fresh Perspective* (Minneapolis: Fortress, 2005), 122.
[22] Wright, *Saint Paul*, 122.
[23] As regards Galatians particularly, better are E. P. Sanders, *Paul, The Law, and the Jewish People* (Philadelphia: Fortress, 1983), 18-19, and C. Cousar, *Galatians*. Interpretation (Louisville: John Knox, 1982), 61, both of whom acknowledge that soteriology lies at the heart of Paul's concerns in the letter.
[24] Wright, *Saint Paul*, 115-17.
[25] Wright, *Saint Paul*, 115.
[26] Wright, *Saint Paul*, 115-16.
[27] Wright, *Saint Paul*, 116.
[28] Wright, *Saint Paul*, 117.
[29] Wright, *Saint Paul*, 117.
[30] Wright, *Saint Paul*, 117-18.
[31] Other attempts to bridge the gap between the NPP and "the Protestant view" (admirably, in an irenic spirit) are M. F. Bird, *The Saving Righteousness of God: Studies on Paul, Justification, and the New Perspective* (Eugene, OR: Wipf and Stock, 2007); M. B. Thompson, *The New Perspective on Paul. Grove Biblical Series* (Cambridge: Grove Books, 2002). Baugh's quotation of Francis Watson (p. 140, n. 11) seems uncommonly like a suspicion that the NPP is ipso facto mistaken and consequently excluded from consideration.
[32] Sanders, *Paul*, 517, as quoted by Baugh.
[33] Sanders, *Paul*, 236, 420.
[34] See further my *Obedience of Faith*, 263-65, and "Role Reversal and Paul's Use of Scripture in Galatians 3.10-13," *Journal for the Study of the New Testament* 65 (1997), 101-4.
[35] Sanders, *Paul*, 237-38.
[36] See further my "New Perspective' Reading of Central Texts in Romans 1-4," in this collection.

[37] As affirmed explicitly by Dunn, *New Perspective on Paul*, 77-80. If no one can call Jesus Lord but by the Spirit (1 Cor 12:3), and if faith itself is the gift of God (Ephesians 2:8), then everything is of grace, from beginning to end.

[38] Such a bewildering contention can hardly be sustained in the face of the massive efforts of various NPP scholars. A fair reading of these materials is sufficient to establish that their labors are neither eccentric nor lacking in painstaking analysis. Besides Dunn and Wright, there are such "NPP sympathizers" as Udo Schnelle, Scott Hafemann, Scot McKnight, James Scott, David deSilva, Marcus Bockmuehl and Gordon Fee. Various non-NPP scholars champion the analysis of the rabbinic materials by F. Avemarie, *Tora und Leben: Untersuchungen zur Heilsbedeutung der Tora in der frühen rabbinischen Literatur*. Texte und Studien zum Antiken Judentum 55 (Tübingen: Mohr-Siebeck, 1996). Yet it is to be noted that Avemarie acknowledges the grace-element in these sources, although he believes that there is a tension between grace/election, on the one hand, and works, on the other. Most strikingly, Avemarie grants that throughout this literature it is possible to speak of a "covenantal nomism." The Torah of the rabbis cannot be divorced from this context in which the law was given. In this sense, Sanders' coinage of the phrase, says Avemarie, is certainly justified (ibid., 584, n. 40).

[39] As illustrated easily enough from Dunn's *Romans*, 1.166-67, and *Galatians*, 138-39. In more detail, see Dunn's "Once More, *PISTIS CHRISTOU*," *Pauline Theology. Volume IV: Looking Back, Pressing On*. eds. E. E. Johnson and D. M. Hay. Society of Biblical Literature Symposium Series 4 (Atlanta: Scholars Press, 1997), 61-81.

[40] Barr, *The Semantics of Biblical Language* (Oxford: Oxford University Press, 1961).

[41] According to Mark 1:1-3, "the beginning of the gospel of Jesus Christ" *is* Isa 40:3 (and Mal 3:1).

[42] *A la* Wright, especially in *Jesus and the Victory of God*. Christian Origins and the Question of God 2 (Minneapolis: Fortress, 1996).

[43] Citing Wright, *Saint Paul*, 42-43.

[44] Wright, *Saint Paul*, 42-43.

[45] Likewise, the citation of Sanders (*Paul*, 544) fails to appreciate Sanders' actual point, which is that the difference between Paul and Judaism resides in a different usage respectively of the "righteous" word-group.

[46] J. A. Thompson points out that the underlying Hebrew is neutral and means merely "bring news," whether good or bad (*The Book of Jeremiah*. New International Commentary on the Old Testament [Grand Rapids: Eerdmans, 1980], 464, n. 4).

[47] See further Wright, "Gospel and Theology in Galatians," *Gospel in Paul: Studies on Corinthians, Galatians and Romans for Richard N.*

Longenecker. eds. L. A. Jervis and P. Richardson. Journal for the Study of the New Testament Supplement Series 108 (Sheffield: Sheffield Academic Press, 1994), 222-39.

[48] Dunn, *Galatians*, 134-35.

[49] The literature is massive, but as good a starting point as any is Dunn, *Theology of Paul*, 334-89; id., *New Perspective on Paul*, 1-15 (both with other literature).

[50] Seifrid, "Righteousness Language in the Hebrew Scriptures and Early Judaism," *Justification and Variegated Nomism. Volume 1: The Complexities of Second Temple Judaism*. eds. D. A. Carson, P. T. O'Brien and M. A. Seifrid (Grand Rapids: Baker, 2001), 415-42.

[51] See Dunn, *New Perspective on Paul*, 63-86; K. Yinger, *Paul, Judaism, and Judgment According to Deeds*. Society for New Testament Studies Monograph Series 105 (Cambridge: Cambridge University Press, 1999), esp. 146-82; Garlington, "New Perspective Reading," 18-24; id., *Faith, Obedience, and Perseverance: Aspects of Paul's Letter to the Romans*. Wissenschaftliche Untersuchungen zum Neuen Testament 79 (Tübingen: Mohr Siebeck, 1994), 44-71.

[52] See further my *Obedience of Faith*, 10-11.

[53] Dunn, "The Justice of God: A Renewed Perspective on Justification by Faith," *Journal of Theological Studies* ns 43 (1992), 1-22; id. (with Alan Suggate), *The Justice of God: A Fresh Look at the Old Doctrine of Justification by Faith* (Grand Rapids: Eerdmans, 1993).

[54] Dunn, "Justice of God," 16.

[55] Schnelle, *Paul: His Life and Theology* (Grand Rapids: Baker, 2005), 460-63 (note Schnelle's comparison of Paul and Dio Chrysostom in particular, p. 463).

[56] Dunn, "Justice of God," 20-21 (italics added).

[57] See my *Obedience of Faith*, 255-58.

[58] C. H. Cosgrove confirms that the believer's faith is not in God per se, but in him as the vindicator of the crucified Messiah ("Justification in Paul: A Linguistic and Theological Reflection," *Journal of Biblical Literature* 106 [1987], 666). Wilckens speaks to the same effect: it is not faith as such that concerns Paul, but faith as directed to the crucified Christ as the basis of all righteousness before God (*Römer*, 1.89).

[59] B. Witherington, *Grace in Galatia: A Commentary on Paul's Letter to the Galatians* (Grand Rapids: Eerdmans, 1998), 353. Cf. Longenecker, *Galatians*, 227; Dunn, *Galatians*, 267.

[60] *If* there is any emphasis on "all" in Deut 27:26, which appears only in the LXX, it is qualitative, not quantitative. Again, Israel was not free to pick and choose from the variety of the commandments: each one had its peculiar importance. It is in this vein that Paul writes in Gal 5:3 that everyone who receives circumcision is bound to keep *the whole law*. Ironically enough, the Judaizers do not keep "the whole law" because of

the absence of love on their part (5:14). Note how in Deut 30:16 loving God is correlated with walking in his ways and keeping his commandments.

[61] Craigie, *The Book of Deuteronomy*. New International Commentary on the Old Testament (Grand Rapids: Eerdmans, 1976), 334.

[62] As championed by B. Estelle in *Covenant, Justification, and Pastoral Ministry*, 124-33.

[63] Dunn, *Galatians*, 171; id., *Jesus, Paul*, 226; Wright, *The Climax of the Covenant: Christ and the Law in Pauline Theology* (Minneapolis: Fortress, 1991), 144-45; S. McKnight, *Galatians*. NIV Application Commentary (Grand Rapids: Eerdmans, 1995), 154-55; G. Howard, *Paul: Crisis in Galatia*. Society for New Testament Studies Monograph Series 35. 2nd ed. (Cambridge: Cambridge University Press, 1990), 51-54.

[64] Garlington, "Role Reversal." My take on Gal 3:10 is supported by J. R. Wisdom, *Blessing for the Nations and the Curse of the Law: Paul's Citation of Genesis and Deuteronomy in Galatians 3.8-10*. Wissenschaftliche Untersuchungen zum Neuen Testament 2/133 (Tübingen: Mohr Siebeck, 2001), 43-62, 154-82, and N. Calvert-Koyzis, *Paul, Monotheism and the People of God: The Significance of Abraham Traditions for Early Judaism and Christianity*. Journal for the Study of the New Testament Supplement Series 273 (London: T & T Clark International, 2005), 96-97.

[65] See further my reply to D. A. Carson and Mark Seifrid in this volume.

[66] Dunn, *New Perspective on Paul*, 5.

[67] In another *ad hominem* barb, Baugh complains: "Anything he [Paul] says that does not conform to the views of this censorship board must be scrubbed of all offending material." Such a snide remark is not worthy of a reply.

[68] Dunn, *New Perspective on Paul*, 63-72, esp. 67-68. Along these lines, an essay that really should have received more play is C. Loewe, "'There is No Condemnation' (Romans 8:1): But Why Not?" *Journal of the Evangelical Theological Society* 42 (1999), 231-50.

[69] In addition to Dunn's and Wright's numerous and various publications, Yinger's monograph and my own efforts to come to terms with "the obedience of faith," similar conclusions have been reached by G. N. Davies, *Faith and Obedience in Romans: A Study in Romans 1-4*. Journal for the Study of the New Testament Supplement Series (Sheffield: Sheffield Academic Press, 1990); J. Miller, *The Obedience of Faith, the Eschatological People of God, and the Purpose of Romans*. Society of Biblical Literature Dissertation Series 177 (Atlanta: Scholars Press, 2000); T. Berkeley, *From a Broken Covenant to Circumcision of the Heart: Pauline Intertextual Exegesis in Romans 2:17-29*. Society of Biblical Literature Dissertation Series 175 (Atlanta: Society of Biblical Literature, 2000). Outside of Paul, there is the excellent study of A. P.

Stanley, *Did Jesus Teach Salvation by Works? The Role of Works in the Synoptic Gospels*. The Evangelical Theological Society Monograph Series 4 (Eugene, OR: Wipf & Stock), 2006.

[70] Referring to D. A. Carson's *Exegetical Fallacies*. 2nd ed. (Grand Rapids: Baker, 1996).

[71] Carson, *Exegetical Fallacies*, 27 (from my first edition of the book).

[72] Carson, *Exegetical Fallacies*, 27-28.

[73] Fitzmyer, "The Semitic Background of the New Testament *Kyrios*-Title," *A Wandering Aramean: Collected Aramaic Essays*. Society of Biblical Literature Monograph Series 25 (Chico: Scholars Press, 1979), 132.

[74] See further Garlington, *Obedience of Faith*, 11-13.

[75] Wilckens, *Römer*, 1.132.

[76] Dunn, *Romans*, 1.97, citing Deut 4:1, 5-6, 13-14; 30:11-14; 1 Maccabees 2:67; 13:48; *Sibylline Oracles* 3:70; Philo, *On the Preliminary Studies* 70; *On Rewards and Punishments* 79; Josephus, *Antiquities* 5.107, 132; 20.44.

[77] Moo, *The Epistle to the Romans*. New International Commentary on the New Testament (Grand Rapids: Eerdmans, 1996), 52-53. Kindred statements can be found in T. N. Schreiner, *Romans*. Baker Exegetical Commentary on the New Testament (Grand Rapids: Baker, 1998), 35; C. E. B. Cranfield, *A Critical and Exegetical Commentary on the Epistle to the Romans*. International Critical Commentary. 2 vols. (Edinburgh: T & T Clark, 1979), 1.66-67; J. Murray, *The Epistle to the Romans*. New International Commentary on the New Testament. 2 vols. (Grand Rapids: Eerdmans, 1959, 1965), 1.13-14; E. Lohse, *Der Brief an die Römer*. Kritisch-exegetischer Kommentar über das Neue Testament. 15th ed. (Göttingen: Vandenhoeck & Ruprecht, 2003), 68.

[78] Wright, "Romans," *The New Interpreter's Bible*. 12 vols. (Nashville: Abingdon, 2002), 10.420.

[79] Dunn, *Theology of Paul*, 386. It should be added that on the same page Dunn clearly acknowledges the reality of continuing sin in the life of the believer, even quoting Luther's famous *simul justus et peccator*. Writes Dunn: "Throughout this life the human partner will ever be dependent on God justifying the ungodly."

[80] Garlington, *Faith, Obedience, and Perseverance*, 74-79.

[81] Elliott, *The Rhetoric of Romans: Argumentative Constraint and Strategy and Paul's Dialogue with Judaism*. Journal for the Study of the New Testament Supplement Series 45 (Sheffield: Sheffield Academic Press, 1990), 229.

[82] See my *An Exposition Of Galatians: A Reading From the New Perspective*. 3rd ed. (Eugene, OR: Wipf & Stock, 2007), 301-3.

[83] Garlington, *Faith, Obedience, and Perseverance*, 56-71.

[84] See further my "New Perspective Reading," 59-63.

[85] See Wright's emphatic affirmation of this in *Saint Paul*, 116.
[86] Gundry Volf, *Paul and Perseverance: Staying In and Falling Away* (Louisville: Westminster/John Knox Press, 1990), 81. G. C. Berkouwer also identifies "continuity in salvation" as the central problem of perseverance (*Faith and Perseverance*. Studies in Dogmatics [Grand Rapids: Eerdmans, 1958], 12).
[87] Cranfield, *Romans*, 1.266.
[88] We should recall that Hebrews focuses so much of its attention on the mediatorial aspect of Christ's priesthood as indispensable "in bringing many sons to glory" (5:10). The entire letter can be looked upon as an elaborate commentary on Rom 5:9-10.
[89] Wright is also clear: "There is simply no way that human beings can make themselves fit for the presence or salvation of God. What is more, I know of no serious theologian, Protestant, Catholic or Orthodox, who thinks otherwise" (*Saint Paul*, 116).
[90] Garlington, *Defence of the New Perspective*, 107-97. See also the telling criticisms of R. H. Gundry, "The Nonimputation of Christ's Righteousness," *Justification: What's at Stake in the Current Debates?* eds. M. Husbands and D. J. Treier (Downers Grove Leicester: InterVarsity/Apollos, 2004), 17-45. I differ with Gundry in my conviction that it is *Christ's* righteousness that becomes ours by virtue of union with him.
[91] For example, at least several of the (Reformed) contributors to the volume, *The Federal Vision*. eds. S. Wilkins and D. Garner (Monroe, LA: Athanasius Press, 2004).

COVENANTAL NOMISM AND THE EXILE:
A REPLY TO I. M. DUGUID[1]

1. Introduction

Professor I. M. Duguid's essay commences with a rudimentary analysis of E. P. Sanders' now famous phrase "covenantal nomism."[2] His concern, however, is not to address Sanders as such but rather "the rise of similar formulations within the modern church." The discussion is intended to focus on "the accuracy of covenantal nomism as a description of the OT relations between God and his people and in particular on the pastoral crisis that faced God's people during and after the exile." The question is: "Can covenantal nomism account for the persistence of God's relationship with his people after the exile." Or, stated otherwise: "After Israel's unfaithfulness had led to the ultimate sanction of exile, did the prophets promise covenant blessing dependent on human faithfulness, or did they look for something new in which God himself would fulfill the covenant conditions?" As in my reply to S. M. Baugh in this volume, this response to Professor Duguid will follow his organization, first summarizing the arguments and then responding to them.

2. "Maintenance of Marriage"

Duguid acknowledges that "at first sight" covenantal nomism may seem to be supported by the analogy of the marriage relationship in the OT. Thus, he remarks, it could be well argued that a wife's faithfulness is necessarily a key element in the marital relationship. By analogy, then, our faithfulness would be a key element in maintaining our relationship with God. But the question is, How is this analogy worked out in Scripture? In answering the question, Duguid appeals to several passages in the prophets. The first is Ezekiel 16. After a vivid depiction of Israel's adoption, nurturing by the Lord and yet adulterous response to his grace, the bottom line is that after Yahweh's wrath is poured out on Jerusalem he will have mercy on her. Judgment is thus not the end of Israel's relationship with her God. According to Duguid, "The Israelites will experience the curses that the covenant threatened, but the covenant relationship itself will not be annulled by their unfaithfulness."

Next, Hosea 2, Isaiah 50 and Jeremiah 3 are considered in tandem. As for Hosea 2, the prophet's unfaithful wife was chosen for no merit in her. When she runs after other lovers, she is punished, but divorce could not be the end of the story, because ultimately the Lord would restore her to himself. Isaiah 50 is stated in similar terms: Yahweh's divorce of Israel was because of her transgressions. Nevertheless, even such iniquities cannot ultimately destroy the marriage. The Lord has remained faithful to his bride and for that reason speaks comfort to Zion. The Lord will raise up a faithful servant who will bring deliverance to his unfaithful bride. Jeremiah 3 pictures the breach between the Lord and his people in the strongest possible terms. But even so, the relationship, writes Duguid, cannot ultimately be severed by their unfaithfulness: "The marriage relationship between God and his people cannot ultimately be destroyed by the unfaithfulness of the bride."

The response to these data can be brief. On the one hand, Duguid is quite right that it is the mercy of God toward Israel that will ultimately restore her to the marriage covenant. This is beyond dispute and is simply not a bone of contention between a "covenantal nomism" reading of God's relation to Israel and any other. On the other side, a rather obvious fact has been downplayed: it is for no other reason than *infidelity* that a divorce has occurred and the nation is sent packing into exile. Hosea 2, Isaiah 50 and Jeremiah 3 all draw on the divorce metaphor and cite as the cause of the dissolution of the marriage Israel's adultery. One may say, as Duguid does, that the marriage relationship between God and his people cannot ultimately be destroyed by the unfaithfulness of the bride. But the fact remains that God's restorative action (return from exile) is intended to repair a relationship that was broken by none other than an unfaithful bride. The old marriage is dissolved, and the Lord "marries" a new "wife" who enters into a "new covenant" with him.

3. "Renovation of the Covenant"

The thesis of this rubric is stated as follows:

> ...the future prospect after the exile is not merely a return to the status ante quo. It would be no comfort to tell a generation who had experienced the full weight of the covenant curses for their disobedience and that of their forefathers that future blessing depended on their future faithfulness. Rather, the prophets repeatedly pointed their hearers to a new intervention of God that would radically alter the constitution of the people.

In pursuing this proposition, appeal is made to the well known passages of Jeremiah 31, Ezekiel 34 and Ezekiel 36. As for Jeremiah 31, the "new covenant" (31:31-34) is radically unlike the Sinai covenant in some significant regards, most notably in terms of internal transformation, the writing of the law on the heart, the universal knowledge of God and the definitive forgiveness of sins. At the same time, Duguid notes, the new covenant represents the fulfillment of the Mosaic covenant, when the blessings of that conditional covenant will be received unconditionally, through a sovereign act of God's mercy and grace. The same, he writes, pertains to the Davidic covenant. Even though the persistent unfaithfulness of David's heirs had now led to comprehensive judgment, Jeremiah promised a renewal of the Davidic covenant in the days to come. To wit: "Neither God's covenant with David nor his covenant with the descendants of Jacob could ultimately be broken, in spite of all of the unfaithfulness of the human parties, for these covenants were as unbreakable as God's covenant with night and day (33:19-26)."

Identical themes emerge from Ezekiel 34. The "covenant of peace" will bring about a new future for Israel. No longer will the exiles undergo the curses of the Sinai covenant, but rather they will now enjoy the blessings of that covenant. Duguid specifies that the "covenant of peace" is "a new covenant in the sense that they will in the future experience the blessings promised in the original (Mosaic) covenant rather than the curses merited by their breaches in the covenant." The same is true of the blessings of the Davidic covenant. In place of the monarchy divided by sin, the returned exiles will be united under one shepherd. They will now know blessing instead of curse. Adam's original act of unfaithfulness will be undone through an act of salvation on the Lord's part.

Such ideas are further developed in Ezek 36:16-38. God's wrath is called forth by Israel's unfaithfulness, as evidenced by her many and various misdeeds. But, says Duguid, this action creates a new problem for God: it now appears that he is unable to bring about what he had promised, i.e., to maintain his people in the land within the special relationship of the Mosaic covenant, as symbolized by the tabernacle, the visible dwelling of God in their midst. The Lord might have blotted out Israel from the pages of history, except for his concern for his own name, which he had inextricably linked to Israel by entering covenant with them. "Because of that sovereign, irrevocable act at Sinai," comments Duguid, "mercy not only may be but must be shown to Israel." Consequently, not only is there a mere physical return to the land, but the people must be redeemed inwardly and effectively. The old heart of stone will be replaced by one of flesh, and as a result: "Israel will experience the blessings of the Mosaic covenant, the fruitfulness of the land, rather than experiencing the covenant curse of famine that had made them such a reproach among the nations." Duguid then rightly maintains that the Lord's favor toward his people does not flow from this inner transformation but is the cause of it. All this corresponds, in Ezekiel, to the new creation that will restore the land to a "better-than-original" condition. The various data from these selected passages are summarized by Duguid:

> The central point being made by the prophet is clear: the blessings promised in all of God's covenants—conditional and unconditional—will ultimately be experienced by God's people. This will take place not through their faithfulness but through a sovereign act of God's grace in providing for them a new and faithful shepherd.

By way of positive reaction, Professor Duguid has presented us with an exceedingly lucid and useful overview of these prophetic texts. His treatment makes for a very handy biblical theology of exile and return. A great many of his points are clearly rooted in the Scriptures, and I know of no one who would take issue with the bulk of his analysis, certainly not respecting the sovereign power and grace of God exercised to restore Israel to the land and to establish a new covenant, wherein the exiles are purged of their old sins, sanctified and renewed in their service of the Lord.

In terms of critical response, several observations are in order. For one, Duguid drives a wedge between the "new intervention of God that would radically alter the constitution of the people" and the necessity of a renewed fidelity on their part. Students of biblical theology are well aware that every covenant is established sovereignly and unilaterally, but always with a view to bilateral relations.[3] Even the Mosaic covenant (modeled on the Hittite Suzerain treaties), with all its declarations of naked sovereignty, has in view the faithful obedience of Israel, the people of a marriage-like bond with Yahweh. The operational principle of this covenant is stated in Lev 18:4-5: "You shall do my ordinances and keep my statutes and walk in them. I am the Lord your God. You shall therefore keep my statutes and my ordinances, by doing which a man shall live: I am the Lord." This is, as it were, covenantal nomism. In context, this demand for obedience stands over against idolatry, in particular: "You shall not do as they do in the land of Egypt, where you dwelt, and you shall not do as they do in the land of Canaan, to which I am bringing you. You shall not walk in their statutes" (Lev 18:3). In short, the faithful Israelite stayed in the covenant by doing the will of the covenant Lord, or perseverance.[4] The same perspective is evident in the recurring refrain of Deuteronomy: "This do and live" (Deut 4:1, 10, 40; 5:29-33; 6:1-2, 18, 24; 7:12-13; cf. 29:9, 29; 30:2, 6, 8, 10, 11, 16, 20; 31:12-13; 33:46). Given that the context of this doing of the law is the covenant graciously established at the time of the Exodus, the point of Lev 18:5 is hardly that of Israel having to earn God's favor or obtain life by performance. Rather, the people would continue to live in the land and enjoy the abundant blessing of the Lord if they remained within the parameters of the law and turned away from idolatry—this is to "do the law."

Second, for Duguid, "It would be no comfort to tell a generation who had experienced the full weight of the covenant curses for their disobedience and that of their forefathers that future blessing depended on their future faithfulness." Moreover, return from exile and the establishment of the new covenant "will take place not through their faithfulness but through a sovereign act of God's grace in providing for them a new and faithful shepherd." Of course, this is undeniably true, but there seems to be some confusion regarding the establishment of the covenant and its continuance—"getting in" and "staying in" (as per immediately above). Israel could never have been the prime mover in the redemptive actions that took place in connection with her deliverance from the bondage of exile. But let's not forget that faithfulness is the intended product of this "sovereign act of God's grace." Everything is of grace, from beginning to end, but it is grace that empowers and enables human fidelity. This is what Gordon Fee calls "God's empowering presence" by the Spirit.[5] Consequently, it is a false dichotomy to set God's power and grace over against the necessity of human fidelity. It is both/and not either/or: the one is the means to the other.

It is true that Duguid singles out the Spirit and his work in the prophetic passages selected. But we need to take matters to another level and consider the relation of Spirit to "fruit" in the prophets. The imagery of fruit is first encountered in the Genesis creation account and later in the flood narrative (itself a new beginning) (Gen 1:11, 12, 22, 28, 29; 3:2, 3, 6, 12; 8:17; 9:1, 7). Later, the fruitfulness of the land features prominently in the prophecies respecting Israel's return from exile (Isa 4:2; 11:1-5; 27:5b-6; 29:17; 32:15-18; 44:2-4; 51:3; 57:18; 60:21; 61:1; 65:21; Jer 23:3; 31:5; Ezek 17:23; 34:27; 36:8, 11, 30; 47:12; Amos 9:14; Joel 2:22; Zech 8:12). In the prophetic vision, Palestine was to be made like the Garden of Eden before Adam's fall, a veritable new creation.[6]

G. K. Beale's study of the prophetic backdrop of these verses has demonstrated that Isaiah 32 and 57, particularly in the Septuagint, are distinguished in their depiction of the restoration of Israel as a time of fruitfulness.[7] But the prosperity goes beyond material abundance to embrace ethical and spiritual qualities. According Isa 32:16-18:

Then justice will dwell in the wilderness,
  and righteousness abide in the fruitful field.

And the effect of righteousness will be peace,
  and the result of righteousness, quietness and trust for ever.
My people will abide in a peaceful habitation,
  in secure dwellings, and in quiet resting places.

Such is the result of the outpouring of the Spirit from on high (v. 15). Likewise, Isa 57:18 contains the assurance:

I have seen his ways, but I will heal him;
  I will lead him and requite him with comfort,
  creating for his mourners the fruit of the lips.

All this carries over into Paul's letter to the Galatians. In commending to his readers "the fruit of the Spirit" (Gal 5:22-23), Paul confirms that the new creation has arrived in Galatia. His converts have entered that new creation not by virtue of Torah observance, but because of the descent of the Spirit upon them in Pentecostal blessing. It is they, uncircumcised as they are, who fulfill the imagery of the productive land; they are the new Israel which has returned from exile; they are the fruitful vine the old Israel failed to be (John 15:2-8, in contrast to Isa 5:1-7; Jer 8:13; Hosea 9:10; 14:6-7; Hab 3:17); they are the nation producing the fruit of the kingdom (Matt 21:43).[8]

Beale further roots the Christian life of 5:22-25 in the resurrection of the end-time Israel. Phrases such as "the fruit of the Spirit," "living by the Spirit" and "walking by the Spirit" are best understood as "resurrection living." It is Ezek 37:3-14 that links resurrection directly with Spirit, and the Septuagint of Isa 57:15-19 assigns to the Spirit the giving of resurrection life. Therefore, Gal 5:22-25 is like Isa 57:15-19 in not only combining "Spirit" and "fruit," along with the mention of "joy," "peace" and "patience," but also in making the Spirit the source of resurrection life. Such resurrection existence finds a precedent in Gal 2:19-20, which sets the pattern of crucifixion-resurrection, whereby the believer's experience is identified with Christ's own death and resurrection.[9] It should be added that these pictures of resurrection and fruitful living stand in the sharpest contrast to the chaos so disturbingly exhibited by "the works of the flesh" in Gal 5:19-21. If the bulk of those works is hatred and its attendant phenomena, mainly discord and strife, then the fruit of the Spirit, commencing with love, finds its unifying factor in a community at rest and enjoying the benefits of mutual understanding, support and encouragement.

All of the above suggests very plainly that the outpouring of the Spirit at the time of restoration from exile and the establishment of the new covenant is to the end that Israel be a fruitful vine (in contrast to what she was in Isaiah's day [e.g., Isa 5:1-7 = Matt 21:33-43]). The writing of the law on the heart (Jer 31:33) has no other purpose than bringing Israel full-circle back to the very terms of the Sinai covenant (Lev 18:5; Deut 4:1, 10, 40; 5:29-33; 6:1-2, 18, 24; 7:12-13; cf. 29:9, 29; 30:2, 6, 8, 10, 11, 16, 20; 31:12-13; 33:46), of being God's people and he being their God.[10] The new covenant thus realizes the purpose for which the old covenant was instituted.[11] If faith, perseverance and fruitfulness were non-negotiables under Moses, the same is true of the eschatological covenant. Not to bear the fruit of the Spirit is by definition to engage in the "works of the flesh" (Gal 5:19-21), the effect of which is that one will not inherit the kingdom of God, but rather reap a harvest of "corruption" (Gal 6:8). Bear in mind that Paul writes Galatians for the purpose of averting the apostasy from Christ that was already under way.[12]

We can now return to Duguid's original proposition: "It would be no comfort to tell a generation who had experienced the full weight of the covenant curses for their disobedience and that of their forefathers that future blessing depended on their future faithfulness." The straightforward reply is that the returned exiles would take comfort from the promise that, at the time of the restoration, the Spirit would be outpoured in copious measure to ensure the inscription of the law on their hearts, i.e., to grant them a heart compliant with the will of the covenant Lord, and to transform them from a fruitless vine into a field that bears abundant fruit. Their renewed and continued fidelity to the new covenant *is* required, but the wherewithal to comply is the gift of the sovereign Spirit. In that they could take supreme comfort and derive ultimate encouragement.

In the third place, there is the issue of conditionality in the covenants. I would submit that each biblical covenant is conditional, in the sense that the human partner is obliged to maintain faith with the God of the covenant.[13] Since it is always best to begin at the beginning, I would first call attention to the *creation covenant* of Genesis 1-3. While there are no "ifs" on the surface of the text, it is obvious enough that Adam was obliged to fulfill the mandates set before him (procreation and subduing the earth), while obeying the command not to eat of the tree of the knowledge of good and evil.[14] If he failed to comply, then on the day he sinned he would die (Gen 2:15-17); and, of course, that is what happened. That Adam died on the very day he sinned makes sense in light of Israel's exile.[15] That is to say, death by definition is banishment from the presence of God, which is precisely what transpired when Adam and Eve were expelled from the garden (Gen 3:22-24). In brief, Adam was the first to suffer the pain of exile = death. The creation does carry on, with two of Adam's sons (Able and afterward Seth) to take the lead of the godly line. But as for Adam himself, Paul can view him as the head of the old creation tainted by sin and death, whose place has been taken by Christ, the life-giving Spirit (Rom 5:12-19; 1 Cor 15:21-22; 45-50). G. C. Berkouwer, then, justifiably writes that although the word "fall" does not occur in Genesis 3, "sin is pictured as *apostasy from God.*"[16] Adam, in short, was the first to break faith and fall away.

As for the *Noahic covenant*, again there are no "ifs" observable. Yet in the narrative of Genesis, the events of the flood and its aftermath are represented as a new creation: the earth is initially covered with water (Gen 1:2) and then the dry land emerges (Gen 1:6-8). In fact, there are numerous parallels, but the essential point is that once the chaos of the flood waters subside, Noah and his family emerge from the ark as the new humanity, a people of a new beginning. Such being the case, one would expect that the Noahic covenant would follow suit with the state of affairs in the garden. One very telling indication that conditionality is involved in this renewed creation covenant is the presence of curse. Ham looked upon the nakedness of his father (euphemistic for a sexual act), and when Noah woke up, he placed the curse on Ham's son Canaan (Gen 9:24). The curse was fulfilled when Israel invaded and conquered the land of Canaan. The very factor of curse argues rather compellingly that one could (and in Ham's case did) forsake the ideals and practices of the creation covenant and thus incur the judgment of the Creator.

As regards the *covenant with Abraham*, the text of Genesis is replete with assurances that the Lord will fulfill his promise of a seed that would become the source of blessing for the nations (Gen 12:1-3, etc.). However, by the time of Genesis 15, his faith begins to wane as he complains that he is still childless (v. 3). In response, the Lord does two things. First, he reassures Abraham that his progeny will be as numerous as the stars of heaven (vv. 4-6), to which Abraham responds in faith. Second, there is Yahweh's self-maledictory oath (vv. 7-16). As is well known by now, the symbolism inherent in the cutting of the animals is that the one who undertakes an oath swears that he will suffer the same fate as the animals if he does not fulfill his covenant commitment. Or, as M. G. Kline explains, "Passing between the slain and divided beasts beneath the threatening birds of prey...God invoked the curse of the oath upon himself should he prove false to it."[17] Later, when the Lord's oath seems to be very much in doubt, Abraham is called upon to sacrifice the son miraculously born in his old age (Genesis 22). But, as we know so well, the Angel of the Lord called from heaven: "By myself I have sworn, says the Lord, because you have done this, and have not withheld your son, your only son, I will indeed bless you, and I will multiply your descendants as the stars of heaven and as the sand which is on the seashore" (vv. 16-17). Here the voice refers back to Genesis 15 and reiterates the familiar promise that Abraham's children would one day be innumerable. We recall that Heb 6:13-18 picks up on both the oath and the word of promise in order to encourage the readers that the same oath and promise are for their benefit as well.

We will revisit the Abrahamic covenant below, but for the moment we note simply that the story of Abraham contains another dimension. According to Gen 17:1-2, a requirement was placed on the patriarch: "When Abram was ninety-nine years old the Lord appeared to Abram, and said to him, 'I am God Almighty; walk before me, and be blameless. And I will make my covenant between me and you, and will multiply you exceedingly'." Gordon Wenham very helpfully observes that the Lord bids Abraham to walk "in his presence," recalling the way in which Enoch and Noah walked with God (Gen 5:22, 24; 6:9). Wenham then defers to Claus Westermann for the meaning of this command: "God directs Abraham (who here represents Israel) to live life before him, a life in which every step is taken looking to God and every day of which is accompanied by him." However, Wenham rightly takes issue with Westermann's denial that this was a high demand, for certainly it was.[18]

Of particular interest is the syntax of 17:2. The requirement that Abraham live a certain kind of life is followed here by the conjunction *waw* as expressing result: "*so that* I may make (literally "give") my covenant with you. As Wenham further explains, this verse goes straight to the heart of the topic: "Whereas inaugurating the covenant was entirely the result of divine initiative, confirming it involves a human response, summed up in v 1 by 'walk in my presence and be blameless' and spelled out in the demand to circumcise every male."[19] It should be added that "blameless" is not sinless perfection but a wholehearted compliance with every aspect of God's revealed will. Noah was the first to be called "blameless" and "righteous" (Gen 6:9; 7:1). Much later, these very terms are applied by Luke to Elizabeth and Zechariah: "they were both righteous before God, walking in all the commandments and ordinances of the Lord blameless" (Luke 1:6; cf. Phil 3:6).[20] Notice the correlation of "righteous," "walking" and "blameless." In both Genesis and Luke, the three are tantamount to one another: all denote perseverance as a godly way of life. A significant confirmation is provided by Heb 6:15. After invoking the oath and the word of God as assuring Abraham, the writer adds: "And thus Abraham, *having patiently endured*, obtained the promise." For this author, there are two side to the same coin: God's assurance and Abraham's perseverance (walking blameless before God).

Conditionality is obvious in the case of the *Sinai covenant*. Deuteronomy 28-30, for example, is all about the blessings of the covenant for obedience and the curses of the same covenant for disobedience. On the one hand, "All these blessings shall come upon you and overtake you, *if* you obey the voice of the Lord your God (28:2);" and "The Lord will establish you as a people holy to himself, as he has sworn to you, *if* you keep the commandments of the Lord your God, and walk in his ways" (28:9). On the other, "But *if* you will not obey the voice of the Lord your God or be careful to do all his commandments and his statutes which I command you this day, then all these curses shall come upon you and overtake you" (28:15). Such is a constant refrain throughout this section of the book, having to do with exile and return. The whole is distilled in 30:15-20. Even a glance at the text is sufficient to establish that the issue placed before the nation is not the mere loss of rewards but life itself, if she chooses to disregard the Lord's commandments, statutes and ordinances in favor of idols.[21] For this reason, Moses pleads with the people to choose life instead of death.[22]

The promise to *David* constitutes a covenant within the covenant, with a specific view to a future Israelite ruler who would take charge of the kingdom. It is true that, according to 2 Sam 7:15, God's steadfast love would never be removed from David's progeny. But in virtually the same breath, the Lord requires obedience on his part, and when such obedience is not rendered, then he will be chastised "with the stripes of the sons of men" (2 Sam 7:14). Additionally, Ps 89:29-33, as it echoes 2 Sam 7:14-15, speaks precisely in the same terms:

I will establish his line for ever
   and his throne as the days of the heavens.
If his children forsake my law
   and do not walk according to my ordinances,
if they violate my statutes
   and do not keep my commandments,
then I will punish their transgression with the rod
   and their iniquity with scourges;
but I will not remove from him my steadfast love,
   or be false to my faithfulness.

Here too, the Lord promises continued fidelity to David, but to the end that his descendents will fulfill the terms of the covenant. And *if* they do not do what is required, certain consequences will result, which is precisely what happened when Israel was banished into Babylonian exile (as preceded by the dispersion of the two northern tribes into Assyrian captivity).

As for the *new covenant*, foreseen by Israel's prophets, the one who established it in his blood (Luke 22:20) speaks in this manner (John 15:1-11):

I am the true vine, and my Father is the vinedresser.

> Every branch of mine that bears no fruit, he takes away, and every branch that does bear fruit he prunes, that it may bear more fruit. You are already made clean by the word which I have spoken to you. *Abide* in me, and I in you. As the branch cannot bear fruit by itself, unless it *abides* in the vine, neither can you, unless you *abide* in me. I am the vine, you are the branches. He who *abides* in me, and I in him, he it is that bears much fruit, for apart from me you can do nothing. *If* a man does *not abide* in me, he is cast forth as a branch and withers; and the branches are gathered, thrown into the fire and burned. *If* you *abide* in me, and my words *abide* in you, ask whatever you will, and it shall be done for you. By this my Father is glorified, that you bear much fruit, and so prove to be my disciples. As the Father has loved me, so have I loved you; *abide* in my love. *If* you keep my commandments, you will *abide* in my love, just as I have kept my Father's commandments and *abide* in his love. These things I have spoken to you, that my joy may be in you, and that your joy may be full.

The imagery of the passage is derived from Ps 80:8-19; Isa 5:1-7; 27:2-11; Jer 2:21-28; Ezek 15:1-8; 19:10-14, where Israel is depicted as an unfruitful vine. In each instance, the consequence is exile. As Andreas Köstenberger observes, in contrast to Israel's failure, Jesus claims to be the "true vine," who brings forth the fruit that the nation failed to produce. "Thus Jesus, the Messiah and Son of God, fulfills Israel's destiny as the true vine of God" (Ps 80:14-17).[23] And as an advance on the vine imagery of the OT, Jesus is not only the vine, the disciples are the "branches" that adhere to him: they derive their life and identity by virtue of union with him; without him, they can do nothing.

Of the many factors that stand out in the passage, Jesus' relationship to the disciples is characterized by conditionality, by "ifs." If one does not abide in Christ the vine, judgment is the sure outcome. But if one abides in him and keep his commandments, the result is fruit-bearing and continuance in his love. Note especially the latter: Christ's love for individuals is contingent on keeping his commandments. No doubt, there are systems of theology that would gladly explain away the *prima facie* meaning of the text, but it will always resist every effort.[24] Below we will take up the question of the divine and the human in the process of perseverance and fruitfulness. Suffice it to say here that both dimensions of the evidence must be marshaled in support of an overall understanding of the perseverance of the saints as balanced by the preservation of the saints.

Apart from "if," of particular interest is the phrase "abide in" or "remain in," which occurs no less than ten times in John 15:1-11. The English renders the Greek *menō en*. In fact, Jesus' language is rooted in the Septuagint of Deut 27:26: "Cursed be he who does not confirm the words of this law by doing them." The Septuagint translates the verse as "cursed is every man who does not *remain in* all the words of this law to do them." The underlying Hebrew of the Greek "remain" (*emmenō*) is a verb which literally means "to uphold" (*yakim*) the words of the Torah. The force of *yakim* is not to be overlooked: the Israelite was to "uphold" or "support" "the words of this law," which were given to regulate the relationship between Yahweh and Israel. In so doing, one would honor one's prior faith-commitment to the Lord.[25] At heart, then, the point of Deut 27:26 is: "Cursed be anyone who is fundamentally disloyal to the law—anyone who does not, by his actions, show that he is on the side of the law and anxious to 'make the law stand'."[26]

That the Septuagint chose *emmenō* for *yakim* is understandable, given that the verb has the meaning of "remaining within a specified territory."[27] Its selection may reflect the climate in which portions of the translation took place, i.e., the necessity of persevering in "the holy covenant" (1 Macc 1:15) in the face of the Hellenistic onslaught. Elsewhere, *emmenō* likewise means "persevere in" (Sir 2:10; 6:20; 11:21 [in parallel to "believe" = *pisteuō*]; 1 Macc 10:26, 27; Philo, *Preliminary Studies* 125; Josephus, *Against Apion* 2.257; cf. Num 23:19). Furthermore, in other crucial passages in Deuteronomy, the kindred *menō en* (as it reproduces *dabaq b^e*) denotes dedication to Yahweh and continuance in his ways (e.g., 11:22; 13:4; 30:20; cf. Josh 22:5; 23:8-11). In these verses, the phrase stands in parallel with the synonymous expressions "keeping the commandments" and "loving Yahweh." It is just this usage that carries over into John 15:1-11, according to which the disciples must "abide in" (*menō en*) him, the vine.[28] That such "abiding" is tantamount to continuing faith is evident from John 14:1: "Keep on believing in God, and keep on believing in me."[29]

By way of qualification, there are differences between John and Deuteronomy. (1) Christ takes the place of the Torah: the believer remains in him, not the law. (2) Consequently, Jesus provides the model for us: it is he who has kept the Father's commandments and has remained in his love. (3) There is the factor of mutual indwelling, a characteristic of the Fourth Gospel. Not only do the disciples abide in Christ, his words abide in them, as he himself does (17:23). And not only so, there is the advent of "the Spirit of truth" who dwells with them and is in them (14:17). Here is the factor of divine enablement: by virtue of Christ and the Spirit (as sent by the Father, 14:26), the disciples will go forth and fulfill the mandate of the service of their Lord (cf. 16:1-4). Perhaps the best summary of the farewell discourses of John 14-17 is 14:23-24. In answer to a question by Judas, Jesus replies: "*If* a man loves me, he will keep my word, *then* [*kai*] my Father will love him,[30] and we will come to him and make our home with him. He who does not love me does not keep my words; and the word which you hear is not mine but the Father's who sent me." It is surely striking that divine sovereignty and enablement are not set over against the conditionality of loving Christ and keeping his word. Rather, entirely in keeping with the character of a biblical covenant, it is both at the same time.

In light of such considerations, one may say with Duguid that the blessings of the covenant are *received* unconditionally when the exile comes to an end. But as the return from exile motif carries over into the NT, we find the same outlook as in the Torah and the prophets, namely, that blessings unconditionally received *must result* in the bearing of much fruit and the keeping of Christ's commandments. Conditionality characterizes life not only under Moses but under Christ as well: "*If* you love me, you will keep my commandments. *Then* [*kai*] I will pray the Father, and he will give you another Counselor, to be with you forever" (John 14:15-16, as elaborated by 14:21-24). Certainly without meaning to do so, I should think, Duguid leaves the impression that faithful obedience (perseverance) is unnecessary for members of the new covenant community. But if that were so, documents such as Hebrews and 1 John (and several others) were written for no purpose.

4. "Transformation of the People"

Under this heading are subsumed several passages, Ezekiel 37, Haggai 2 and Zechariah 3, all making the same essential point: resurrection and cleansing from defilement are the products of a divine transformation, with the result that the people experience blessing. These observations are well-taken, apropos and could hardly be called into question. But once more, such data do not preclude a "covenantal nomism" understanding God's relations with Israel. Indeed, Duguid's assessment falls directly into line with my own: "The order of these two acts of God [resurrection and change of status before God] is irreversible: first the people must be made clean and acceptable in God's sight; only after that could the process of being transformed into a new obedience be begun." I would only underscore what I have written above: such divine deeds are to the end that Israel be a faithful and fruitful people, not merely as desirable commodities, but as constituting the *sine qua non* of covenant responsibilities and privileges.

Duguid makes a particular issue of the enjoinder of the Angel of the Lord to the high priest Joshua: "Thus says the Lord of hosts: If you will walk in my ways and keep my charge, then you shall rule my house and have charge of my courts, and I will give you the right of access among those who are standing here" (Zech 3:7). This follows upon the injunction for Joshua to exchange his filthy garments for clean ones. Duguid concedes that the "right of *access*" is not certain, but the important point (for him) is that what is dependent on Joshua's faithfulness is "not his standing in the covenant community but the experience of extraordinary blessing." Duguid perceives Joshua's "standing in the Lord's presence" as more akin to prophetic privilege than that of a "normal Israelite," "a blessing beyond mere salvation." In any event, the passage is sufficiently singular that little, if anything, of it can be placed in service of Duguid's desire to play down the factor of conditionality in the covenant, especially as Duguid himself is not certain of the meaning of "right of access."

5. "Rewards for Faithfulness"

In this segment, Duguid takes up his thesis derived from Zechariah 3, as now buttressed by Haggai 2 and Ezekiel 40-48. That is to say, the theme of faithfulness *is* important, not as the means of staying within the covenant but rather as the source of receiving rewards. In taking up Haggai 2, Duguid maintains that because of Zerubbabel's faithfulness in obeying the Lord during the day of small things (Zech 4:10), he is promised "special status" on the day of cosmic shaking (Hag 2:6-7). The presence of Zerubbabel, the chosen "signet ring," is evidence that the stump is not dead; he is a green shoot emerging from the stump of the old line. The question is: "What has Zerubbabel done to deserve this mark of approval?" The answer is: "He has simply done what the kings of Judah ought to have done, but often failed to do, namely listen to God's word through the prophet and obey it." Consequently, Zerubbabel would effectively hear: "Well done, good and faithful servant! You have been faithful over a little; I will set you over much. Enter into the joy of your master" (Mathew 25:21).

Up to a point, these observations are fair enough. Duguid is certainly right that the issue is that of Zerubbabel's faithfulness over against the failure of the kings of Judah to obey. But there is a flaw in his line of argumentation. Rather than disproving that continued covenant blessings are contingent on faithfulness, the case is *proven* just by the obedience of Zerubbabel. Had he fared like his predecessors, Jerusalem and the temple would not have been rebuilt. When the eschatological shaking of the heavens and the earth would occur, there would be no place to serve as a repository of the wealth of the nations that was to flow into the new temple (Hag 2:6-9). The city and the temple must be rebuilt, and the rebuilding is contingent on the fidelity of the workers, and especially that of Zerubbabel, the governor. To be sure, "desert" is not even an issue, because the Lord was with Zerubbabel (Hag 1:13; 2:4). But if anything, it is nothing other than the fidelity factor that is placed in "boldface print" by the books of Ezra and Nehemiah. According to those accounts, the workers were required to be loyal and true to the task, with defectors and opponents singled out for particular scorn. In order to take his meaning, the prophecy of Haggai has to be read in the historical context of his ministry to the returned exiles.

One may grant that Zerubbabel enjoyed a "special status" in salvation history. Yet the issue was not merely reward for himself as an individual; rather, his privilege was that of being a vital link in the chain that would eventuate in the coming of the new creation, as symbolized apocalyptically by the shaking of the heavens and the earth. It is surely impressive that Heb 12:25-29 takes up this passage in Haggai and applies it to the necessity of perseverance in view of the coming last day. The writer's bottom line is: "Therefore let us be grateful for receiving a kingdom that cannot be shaken, and thus let us offer to God acceptable worship, with reverence and awe; for our God is a consuming fire" (v. 29). For this author, the events that transpired in Zerubbabel's day find their definitive fulfillment in the *parousia* of Christ and the necessity of our faithfulness against that day. Notice in this text the presence of the two elements that form a constant in the biblical outlook for the future: (1) the kingdom cannot be shaken because of God's sovereignty and determined purpose; (2) it is possible to refuse him who is speaking (v. 25) and thus be devoured by the "consuming fire" that is the eschatological wrath of God.

It is well to add that Duguid's reference to Mathew 25:21 is appropriate enough, but with one important proviso. According to the parables of Mathew 25 and parallels, there are *unfaithful servants*. In the very parable of the "Talents," there is the condemnation of the "wicked and slothful servant" who is consigned to "outer darkness," where there will be weeping and grinding of teeth—the unmistakable language of judgment as reflective of ancient Oriental funerals (cf. Luke 7:32; 8:52). See further Matt 24:48-51; Luke 12:45-46; 19:19-27. According to Jesus, the good and faithful servants will indeed enter into the joy of their Lord, but the others will be put with the unfaithful (Luke 12:46). The issue, then, is much larger than individual rewards: *nothing less than life and death are at stake.*

Duguid's argument is thereafter extended into Ezekiel 40-48, which, he believes, supports the principle of reward for faithful service. In particular, it is the faithful Zadokite priests who are rewarded with the central role in the new temple. They are not perfect, but because they have been the most faithful, they may expect a reward in the heavenly realm. By contrast, the Levites had been unfaithful in their spiritual adultery. Yet even they are not excluded from the visionary promised land because of their unfaithfulness; they are restored to their God-given place as ministers of the sanctuary. The covenant between the Lord and the tribe of Levi cannot be broken by their faithlessness. For Duguid, "All of God's chosen people enter and remain in the covenant relationship through the Lord's faithfulness, yet there are greater rewards for those who have been more faithful in that service. Faithfulness in the Lord's service finds its reward in enhanced access to the presence of the Lord."

To judge by the comments of another commentator on Ezekiel, Daniel Block, Duguid's observations on the text of Ezekiel 44 are entirely accurate. Block shows how vv. 10-11 and 12-14 respectively of chapter 44 stand in parallel.[31] The upshot is that the Levites are held accountable for their idolatry, but even so, they are reinstated and reassigned to different duties. They may not function as priests, but theirs is still a privileged role.[32] The covenant with Levi, therefore, remains unbroken (Jer 33:20-22).

The problem, however, is one of methodology in the application of these observations. Without expressly invoking the category of "typology," the only way to make real sense of Duguid's proposal is to assume that he sees the Levites telegraphing ahead of time glimpses of the actual new temple, with a constituency of faithful and not so faithful priestly servants. Otherwise, an appeal to Ezekiel 44 is simply irrelevant, if there is no parallel to be encountered in the new covenant community. But as in the case of Joshua in Zechariah 3, there is a failure to appreciate that something as singular and context-specific (not to say obscure) as the service of the Levites in Ezekiel's temple can hardly be paradigmatic for the relationship that believers sustain to Christ in the new covenant. Reasoning in terms of a biblical typology, this projected temple serves to foreshadow in a grandiose manner the eschatological sanctuary, which ultimately will expand to encompass the new heavens and the new earth.[33] Nevertheless, typology does not normally, if ever, conform to a one-for-one correspondence between the respective elements of prediction and fulfillment; it is normally "looser" than some are willing to allow. What is important in typology is the conviction that there is an overall consistency of divine activity in salvation history: God's acts in the OT set in motion a rhythmic pattern which is brought to a climax in the NT. R. T. France expresses it well: "New Testament typology is…essentially the tracing of the constant principles of God's working in history, revealing a 'recurring rhythm in past history which is taken up more fully and perfectly in the Gospel events'."[34] Scripture thus largely consists of parallel persons and events that culminate in the Christ-event.[35]

Such being the nature of typology, one must be very careful in bringing elements of the type over into the finished antitype. The points of correspondence between the two were never meant to be precisely exact. If the type were perfect, there would be no need for an antitype, and we must ever resist the temptation to confuse typology with allegory. In the present case, it will not do to import idolatrous Levites into the body of Christ, destined to inherit the universe.[36] Duguid's argument is that even though the Levites were faithless and idolatrous, they are still occupy a place in the new temple, though with a reassignment of responsibilities and diminished access into the presence of God. But the suggestion that "Levites" can be translated into "carnal Christians" who still get "in" the "heavenly realm" (if that is the point) simply does not wash with the NT (or the Old). Myriads of texts could be cited, but some rather obvious ones are Rom 1:18-32 (all about idolatry); 8:5-8; 13:11-14; 1 Cor 6:9-10 (including idolaters); Gal 6:19-21; Heb 12:14; Rev 21:8 (again idolaters). Perhaps Duguid understands the Levites to be "penitent sinners." But apart from the fact that the text of Ezekiel does not actually say so, the fundamental problem is still that of extrapolating from a very specific setting and making the application far too broadly.[37] It is the whole flow of salvation history that must inform not only our conception of typology but the constituency of the people of God; and in light of the "big picture" of the redemptive narrative, Duguid's proposal fails to measure up to the ideal and the reality of covenant relationships.

6. "Theological Reflections"

Professor Duguid's essay moves into its final phase with this series of theological reflections. In introducing this segment, Duguid recapitulates what has gone before: "All of the OT covenants, both conditional and unconditional, would have ended in failure if left to the faithfulness of sinful human beings." To this is added the comment that although the covenants with Abraham, Israel (Sinai) and David were endangered on several occasions, human faithlessness could not annul God's covenant commitment.

At the risk of belaboring the point, the foundational problem with this formulation is that there are no unconditional covenants in Scripture. At the very least, the data presented in the previous part of this undertaking are sufficient to call into question Duguid's claim that such covenants are in evidence. At bottom, it is an oversimplification to push the divine determination to maintain the covenant at the expense of the bilateral character of the arrangement. As intimated more than once, Duguid is not wrong that the final deciding factor is God's covenant commitment. At the end of the day: "so shall my word be that goes forth from my mouth; it shall not return to me empty, but it shall accomplish that which I purpose, and prosper in the thing for which I sent it" (Isa 55:11). Yet it is Isaiah 55 as a whole which is so very instructive. On the one side, there is the proclamation of v. 11 that nothing can thwart the Lord's purposes in regathering Israel from her dispersion among the nations. But on the other, if anything characterizes this specimen of "gospel preaching," it is the repeated and impassioned pleas for the people to return to the Lord and thus enter into the blessings of the new creation; and unless they return, the covenant will not be established.

Texts can be multiplied many times over, but simply sticking with the instances cited by Duguid—the patriarchs, Israel and David (Levi)—we can briefly review the data. As for Abraham and his progeny, it was pointed out above that Abraham was required to walk before God and be blameless (Gen 17:1); and there is no reason why the same operative principle should not apply to Isaac and Jacob. In fact, the entire narrative of Jacob can be viewed as the process of turning the "rascal" Jacob into the man he should have been, all culminating in his wrestling with the Angel of the Lord and his consequent transformation (Gen 32:22-32).[38] Additionally, we should not forget about Esau, the one who despised his birthright by bartering it away (Gen 25:29-34). Equally a member of the Abrahamic community, it is Esau who is set forth as a prototype of the Christian apostate by the Letter to the Hebrews (12:15). Of course, the covenant continued and found its fulfillment in the Mosaic and Davidic covenants and finally in the new covenant. Even an Esau could not frustrate the Lord's designs. Nevertheless, Esau and those like him function as warning posts to the reality of apostasy.

Regarding the Sinai covenant, comment has been offered previously. Duguid correctly points to Moses' impassioned appeal that the people choose life rather than death (Deut 30:19). It is likewise obvious that the repeated unfaithfulness of the people did not demolish the bond established on the mountain—nor could it. Yet something rather conspicuous has been omitted, namely, on those occasions when there was an egregious display of rebellion against the Lord, reprisal was taken against those who chose to denounce Yahweh as their God: they were cut off from the covenant. One is the worship of the golden calf (Exodus 32). Moses' intercession for Israel staves off the total destruction of the congregation, but even so, about three thousand of them are put to the sword by the Levites because of their breach of faith (vv. 25-29). It is just in this setting that the question rings out, Who is on the Lord's side (v. 26)? One had to decide and come to Moses, or not. Another occasion is that related in Num 21:4-9. When the Israelites began to "murmur" against God and Moses—the noise of rebellion and apostasy—the fiery serpents killed many of them.[39] Yet the community is not entirely obliterated because of the brazen serpent placed on a standard to be their salvation. Here again we see both sides of the coin. A third instance is refusal to trust God in view of the report of the spies, Joshua and Caleb (Numbers 13-14). Again, there is murmuring which provokes the anger of the Lord and calls forth his judgment. Only Joshua and Caleb are allowed to enter the promised land, while the entire generation of those who left Egypt were consigned to wander in the wilderness for forty years. We may say that the two men who remained faithful represent a "remnant" of the larger community. The Lord rewards their fidelity, and their entry into the land ensures that the covenant will continue. Yet a terrible price is paid by those who chose rebellion and unbelief.

The covenant with David is of the same species as the others. We may acknowledge with Duguid that the narrator of 2 Samuel demonstrates that human unfaithfulness cannot annul God's covenant commitment. But again, a vital datum has been overlooked. Even a year after David's twofold sin of adultery and murder, there was no repentance on his part. And because there was no admission of guilt, Nathan the prophet was sent to denounce David as one who had stolen the ewe lamb of another (2 Sam 12:1-15). It is only when Nathan exclaims "you are the man" that David realizes the depth of his sin and repents of it (as echoed in Psalms 32 and 51). As in all the examples examined in this study, a bilateral arrangement is in place here. Yes, God is resolved that the covenant not be annulled, yet his determination is not played out in the abstract, because apart from David's repentance and renewal of the covenant, no son of his would sit on the throne of Israel. (I think it is quite on purpose that the birth of Solomon follows immediately upon David's confession and the death of the child conceived out of wedlock with Bathsheba.) God's determination to sustain the covenant is enacted in no other way than in bringing David to repentance and confession. We may say that the Lord's dealings with David were the means to the end of ensuring the perpetuity of the covenant with him.

Before descending to the particulars of this final portion of Duguid's essay, I should say that all the above observations are commonplace to any reader of the OT, and I have sought only to remind us of what we know already. Yet these familiar stories are to be read in the scope and breadth intended by their authors in order to determine their overall aims and objectives. It is thus the full weight of the narratives that are to be brought to bear on "covenantal nomism" debate, simply because one of the worst enemies of biblical interpretation is imbalance and oversimplification in one direction or the other.

Marshaled under this concluding rubric of "Theological Reflections" are two subheadings. The first is "Jesus Christ, the Fulfiller of the Covenants." The question is, "If Israel is a nation of promise breakers, how then will these covenants be fulfilled and bring about the blessing that God has irrevocably committed himself to give his people?" The answer of the OT is twofold: "there must be a substitute who suffers in the place of his people and a covenant keeper who takes Israel's place (and, even more profoundly, Adam's place) in fulfilling the righteousness that God demands as the condition of the blessing." The answer of the NT is that Jesus Christ is the suffering substitute and obedient servant. This premise is then unpacked with reference to various biblical texts.

The great bulk of what Duguid has written is indisputable. I know of no evangelical who endorses covenantal nomism as an accurate evaluation of Judaism or who embraces the new perspective on Paul who would call into question the substitutionary work of Christ, the one who endured the curse for us, with a view to the fulfillment of the blessings that all the covenants promised to covenant keepers.[40] It is in this regard that Christ's death and resurrection are "the climax of the covenant." "He *is* Israel, going down to death under the curse of the law, and going through that curse to the new covenant life beyond."[41] Nor is it a matter of debate that Christ has clothed us with the garments of his own righteousness (Isa 61:10; Jer 23:6; 33:16). This section of Duguid's essay is excellent gospel preaching, but, I must say, it is preaching to the converted!

My only critical comeback concerns the stance that "covenantal nomists" take toward the OT sacrificial system. According to Duguid, too much weight is placed by them on the efficacy of the sacrifices. But the answer is easy. First of all, a recognition of the place and function of the sacrifices is not peculiar to covenantal nomism. It is only a matter of coming to terms with the typological significance of this portion of the cultus. Certainly, the offering of animals, including the day of atonement, was provisional for old covenant Israel and had no inherent efficacy; its only purpose was to point forward to Christ and his sacrifice of himself. Such things are simply not in dispute. Second, those of us who embrace a covenantal nomism understanding of Judaism are *not* "covenantal nomists." Covenantal nomism is an assessment of Judaism, not Christianity. Christ has taken the place of the law. We are devotees not of the law but of Christ![42]

Finally, we come to "The Place of Human Faithfulness." Duguid's recapitulated thesis is that our faithfulness is to be rewarded, but it is not the condition by which we remain in the covenant. Then follows a brief discussion of reward, with the bottom line being: "There is only one way to enter this reward of eternal life in the close presence of God: through faith in that looks to his righteousness imputed to us and depends on his faithfulness—not our own—to bring to completion our salvation."

In light of the entire above discussion and analyses of texts, there is little to say but that this is a decided oversimplification, even to the point of distortion. Of course, the finished work of Christ, including not least his faithfulness, is the reason for our salvation. But to say that our fidelity is not the condition for remaining in the covenant does violence to every Old and New Testament passage we have considered. Duguid would have us decide between the faithfulness of Christ and our own. Yet if there was ever a false alternative, this is it, just because Christ's work is not complete until the day on which he perfects the "good work" that he has begun in us (Phil 1:6). According to Rom 5:9-10, there is a salvation yet to be. For Paul, the past redemptive event in Christ has given rise to hope in the believer, a hope which has as its primary focus the future eschatological consummation of the new creation.[43] It is not either Christ's faithfulness or ours: it is both at the same time. But since the fidelity of the believer is an obvious bone of contention for Duguid, let me affirm once more that Christ, the Servant of the Lord, has fulfilled the conditions of the covenant, but in so doing he has imparted the gift of his Spirit to ensure our own covenant fidelity and thus to bear his image.[44] If no one can call Jesus Lord but by the Spirit (1 Cor 12:3), and if faith itself is the gift of God (Eph 2:8), then everything is of grace, from beginning to end. A recognition of our faithfulness is hardly a denial of divine mercy and grace.

Quite the contrary, it is none other than God's empowering presence that enables us to run the race set before us, looking to Jesus, the author and perfecter of *our faith* (Heb 12:2).

7. Summary and Reflections

In his essay, Professor Duguid has endeavored to challenge the ideology lying behind the coinage of E. P. Sanders' phrase "covenantal nomism." The gist of the argument is that this moniker cannot be an accurate portrayal of covenant relationships, because it is the faithfulness of the Lord, not human beings, that ensures the continuance of the covenant. According to Duguid, there are both conditional and unconditional covenants in Scripture. Among the most prominent of the conditional covenants is the Mosaic. But even the blessings of that covenant are to be received unconditionally, through a sovereign act of God's mercy and grace, at the time of Israel's return from exile, when the new covenant is established. In the final analysis, it is Christ the covenant servant who has fulfilled the conditions of the covenant. As I read him, however, these findings are placed in service of a rather startling conclusion: for all practical purposes, *perseverance is unnecessary and unrequired*. I doubt that Duguid would want to express it in these terms, but such is the consistent outcome of his thesis.

In my response, I have concurred that God's grace is always primary, indispensable and the source of every blessing that flows from the covenant(s). Each biblical covenant is initiated sovereignly and graciously in fulfillment of the Lord's eternal design to have a people for himself, and we are kept by the power of God for a salvation to be revealed in the last day (1 Peter 1:5). And yes, the Lord Jesus Christ is the faithful and obedient servant (Phil 2:5-11) who has fulfilled the conditions of the covenant. None of these data are in dispute, and it is inconceivable that any believer would call them into question. *Without him, we can do nothing*.

Where I differ is in my assertion that every covenant is conditional, in the sense that the human partner is obliged to maintain faith with the God of the covenant. Therefore, if

Christ has fulfilled the conditions of the covenant, it is to the end that we do the same. In the very context where Paul declares Jesus to be the servant obedient unto death, he calls on the Philippians to imitate his example: the obedient one is to be obeyed, and the readers are to work out their own salvation with fear and trembling (Phil 2:12-13; cf. Heb 5:9). As Gordon Fee so aptly comments, the connection of "work out your own salvation" with "obedience" is verified by both the grammar and the context. As he remarks, the outworking of the Philippians' common salvation consists in their continued obedience to Christ. In their concrete situation, the immediate demand is for them to stop their internal squabbling (4:2-3) and get on with being God's blameless children in pagan Philippi. As regards the qualification that God is at work in them, Fee adds that Paul writes this not to protect himself theologically, but to encourage the readers that God is really on the side of his people actively working on their behalf.[45] Fee's introductory remark to this passage is telling. He notes that the text has long been difficult for evangelical Protestants, who cannot imagine that Paul is suggesting that salvation is something that must be "worked out," even with God's help.[46] Yet Fee's exposition demonstrates clearly that Paul is making such a demand.[47] I would add that Phil 2:12-13 furnishes an outstanding instance of how theology must adapt itself to the text of Paul and not force the text into its mold.

Therefore, given that Christ is the man of faith, who made his own trek through the wilderness of this world, and given that we can do nothing apart from him, it follows that our feet are to tread where his have trod. If we are being conformed to his image (Rom 8:29; Eph 4:24; Col 3:10), then we are to learn obedience in precisely the same manner as he, i.e., through testing, trial and temptation. According to the author of Hebrews: "Although he was a Son, he learned obedience through what he suffered; and being made perfect he became the source of eternal salvation *to all who obey him*" (Heb 5:8-9). Faithful obedience to Christ, or perseverance, is so much of the essence of new covenant life that Paul had to exercise self-control in all things, lest, having preached to others, he himself would be rejected (1 Cor 9:24-27). As Fee explains, the image in view is that of being "disqualified" (*adokimos*) to receive the eschatological prize of the Christian race. "This has been the point of the [athletic] metaphors from the beginning, that the Corinthians exercise self-control lest they fail to obtain the eschatological prize."[48]

In Phil 3:12-14, Paul again invokes the figure of the race: because he has not yet attained to the resurrection of the dead, he presses on toward the goal of the upward calling of God in Christ. In the immediately preceding statements of 3:10-11, Paul wants to know Christ and the power of his resurrection, as well as participate in his sufferings and death (v. 10), "that, if somehow, I may attain the resurrection from the dead." The phrase "if somehow" (*ei pōs*) appears curious, if not troubling. Peter O'Brien points to recent interpretations of 3:11 that seize on the route by which Paul will experience the resurrection, either through martyrdom or some other kind of death, or he might be alive at Christ's coming.[49] In this case, Paul writes, "if by whatever means...." Such makes for a plausible reading and avoids a potential clash with Paul's stated confidence elsewhere that he will certainly be with the Lord (e.g., Phil1:23; 2 Cor 5:1-9). Be that as it may, we should not miss the obvious: Paul has not yet been raised eschatologically with Christ, and for that reason he must forget what lies behind and press on to lay hold of the future prize. Even he must persevere to that end.

All this serves to underscore what I have attempted to say in the body of this response: because of sovereign grace, the covenant itself can never be broken, but there are individuals who may and do forsake it. The pronounced weakness of Duguid's approach to the materials is one of imbalance: only one part of the evidence is presented and the other is virtually ignored. But when both sides of the coin are kept in sight, it should be self-evident that it is not either/or but both/and. In Christ, God has reconciled the world to himself (2 Cor 5:19) by establishing an everlasting covenant with a new humanity, the "Israel of God" (Gal 6:16). Yet the Lord of this new covenant not only requests but requires that his "branches" abide in himself, the "vine." If they do, they will bear abundant fruit; if they do not, they will be cut off and cast into the fire (John 15:1-11). And once more, the author of Hebrews understood very well that Christ has offered to the Father the sacrifice that ends all sacrifice (9:11-14). Yet the cross does not render endurance unnecessary, but rather mandates it: "let us run with perseverance the race that is set before us" (12:1), of course, "looking to Jesus the pioneer and perfecter of our faith," the very one who apprised his disciples that "he who endures to the end will be saved" (Matt 10:22).

The perseverance debate is hardly new, as per the encounters of Calvinism and Arminianism over the centuries. But I fear that these interchanges may have actually muddied the waters. The problem is that the "five points" of both systems are schematized and tend to be artificial, as both are based on a systematic rather than a biblical theology. Without reproducing my observations on the Already and the Not Yet in the reply to Professor Baugh, God's grace *and* "the obedience of faith" on our part (Rom 1:5; 16:26) are simply what one would expect, given that the salvation inaugurated here and now must be consummated hereafter (Rom 5:9-10). Our trek through the wildness has commenced, but we have not yet entered into God's eschatological rest, and the possibility remains that some may fail to enter because of "the disobedience of unbelief" (Hebrews 3).[50] Note especially the parallel of Heb 3:18-19: "And to whom did he swear that they should never enter his rest, but to those who were *disobedient*? So we see that they were unable to enter because of *unbelief*." The Already is the guarantee of the Not Yet, but not in such a manner as to preclude the necessity of perseverance.

For some, what I am proposing may seem like a contradiction of terms, or, at the very least, a theological tension. It is in the study of Paul in particular that recent debate has centered around whether there is such a "tension" in his thought respecting election and grace, on the one hand, and final vindication according to faith's obedience, on the other. Even someone as conservative as Simon Gathercole believes that such is the case, and the massive volume of Gathercole's Aberdeen colleague, Francis Watson, has this putative tension as its central thesis.[51] In my view, however, such an assessment of Paul's theology fails to "get into his head," as he assumes his place in the context of Second Temple Judaism, with the OT as common to both. Altogether on target, I would say, is Kent Yinger's study of *Paul, Judaism, and Judgment According to Deeds*.[52] According to Yinger's findings, there simply is no tension in Jewish thinking between God's grace and God's demand; the two simply coexist in complete harmony.⁵³ For a final time, we do not have to choose between either/or, because it is always both/and at the same time. As a notable instance, Ps 62:12 (normally considered to be the source of Rom 2:6), actually says: "to you, O Lord, belongs *steadfast love*, for you requite a person *according to his work*."⁵⁴ It is for this reason that the great "assurance chapter" of Scripture, Romans 8, promises "no condemnation for those who are in Christ Jesus" (v. 1); and yet the recipients of this guarantee are those who walk according to the Spirit and put to death the deeds of the body (vv. 4-8). To set the mind on the Spirit is life, but the mindset of the flesh must result in death (v. 6).⁵⁵

On a final note, I would ask why Professor Duguid did not engage more of the recent literature devoted to the return from exile motif. He does touch base briefly with a couple of Wright's books.⁵⁶ But Wright's pursuance of the matter hardly ends there, and others have taken up the cause as well. To be sure, the literature on the motif is voluminous, but in addressing the theme in relation to "covenantal nomism," some interaction with these scholars would have been appreciated.⁵⁷

---

[1] Duguid, "Covenant Nomism and the Exile," *Covenant, Justification, and Pastoral Ministry: Essays by the Faculty of Westminster Seminary California*, ed. R. S. Clark (Phillipsburg: Presbyterian & Reformed, 2007, 61-87.

[2] Throughout Sanders' *Paul and Palestinian Judaism: A Comparison of Patterns of Religion* (Philadelphia: Fortress, 1977).

[3] For example, O. P. Robertson, *The Christ of the Covenants* (Grand Rapids: Baker, 1980), 3-15.

[4] See further my *'The Obedience of Faith': A Pauline Phrase in Historical Context*. Wissenschaftliche Untersuchungen zum Neuen Testament 2/38 (Tübingen: Mohr Siebeck, 1991), 263-65, and "Role Reversal and Paul's Use of Scripture in Galatians 3.10-13," *Journal for the Study of the New Testament* 65 (1997), 101-4.

[5] Fee, *God's Empowering Presence: The Holy Spirit in the Letters of Paul* (Peabody: Hendrickson, 1994).

[6] One of the central promises of the Abrahamic covenant is fruitfulness in terms of the patriarch's descendants (Gen 17:6; 28:3; 35:11; 47:27; 48:4; Exod 1:7). This carries over into Galatians: Paul's Gentile converts are the actualization of Abraham's seed.

⁷ Beale, "The OT Background of Paul's Reference to 'the Fruit of the Spirit' in Galatians 5:22," *Bulletin for Biblical Research* 15 (2005), 1-38.
⁸ Beale shows that in certain strains of Jewish literature eschatological Israel was expected to be spiritually fruitful ("Background," 16-20).
⁹ Beale, "Background," 20-22.
¹⁰ See the excellent treatment of Jer 31:33-34 by C. F. Keil, *The Prophecies of Jeremiah*. Commentary on the OT. 10 vols. (Peabody: Hendrickson, rep. 2006), 8.282-85. Among other insights, Keil relates that the writing of the law on the heart is tantamount to an animating life-principle (2 Cor 3:3).
¹¹ Duguid thinks that Isaiah's "covenant of peace" (Isa 54:10) is a *new* covenant in the sense that the returned exiles will experience the blessings promised in the original (Mosaic) covenant rather than the curses merited by their breaches of that covenant. Without denying the validity of this insight, I would stress that the new covenant is *eschatologically* new. It is rooted in the old covenant and brings its essential ideals to realization. Yet, in terms of Jesus' own teaching, the new covenant brings a new wine that cannot be contained by the old wine skins (Mark 2:21-22, as accompanied by 2 Corinthians 3 and Hebrews 8). By definition, newness is an eschatological concept. See C. B. Hoch, *All Things New: The Significance of Newness for Biblical Theology* (Grand Rapids: Baker, 1995). The new covenant is not simply the old covenant *redivivus*. Despite the continuity observable between old and new, the discontinuity of the two is underscored by the datum that, according to Ezekiel 37 and numerous other passages, the exile is reckoned as Israel's death, to be followed by her resurrection. See D. E. Gowan, *Theology of the Prophetic Books: The Death and Resurrection of Israel* (Louisville: Westminster/John Knox, 1998); J. D. Levenson, *Resurrection and the Restoration of Israel: The Ultimate Victory of the God of Life* (New Haven: Yale University Press, 2006). The difference between the two Israels is thus like the disparity of life and death. By contrast, the new covenant for Second Temple Judaism was, as S. Lehne writes, "a return to the *old* relationship with God and a *renewal* of the old covenantal promises by God in response." As she further notes, the Qumran sectarians' ideal of the new covenant "consists in a return to the original intentions of the Mosaic Torah as they have come to understand its true import under the guidance of the Teacher of Righteousness" (*The New Covenant in Hebrews*. Journal for the Study of the New Testament Supplement Series 44 [Sheffield: Sheffield Academic Press, 1990], 58).
¹² On the apostasy factor, see T. A. Wilson, "Wilderness Apostasy and Paul's Portrayal of the Crisis in Galatia," *New Testament Studies* 50 (2004), 550-71.
¹³ Duguid cites a comment from my review of D. A. Carson, P. T. O'Brien and M. A. Seifrid, eds., *Justification and Variegated Nomism*.

Volume 1: The Complexities of Second Temple Judaism (Grand Rapids: Baker, 2001): "The very existence of the marriage-covenant is contingent on the righteous/faithful behavior of its partners." This was written in response to Mark Seifrid's downplay of righteousness as covenant fidelity. And the point still stands: our righteousness and God's are required to maintain the marital bond known as a covenant. On the identification of marriage and covenant, see G. P. Hugenberger, *Marriage as a Covenant: Biblical Law and Ethics as Developed from Malachi*. Biblical Studies Library (Grand Rapids: Baker, 1994). It is in terms of the marriage-covenant that "grace" and related words make sense as God's "covenant love" and "and covenant fidelity." See N. Glueck, *Hesed in the Bible* (New York: KTAV, 1975); G. R. Clark, *The Word Hesed in the Hebrew Bible*. Journal for the Study of the OT Supplement Series 157 (Sheffield: Sheffield Academic Press, 1993); N. H. Snaith, *The Distinctive Ideas of the OT* (London: Epworth, 1944), 94-130; T. F. Torrance, *The Doctrine of Grace in the Apostolic Fathers* (Grand Rapids: Eerdmans, 1959), 10-20. As Torrance in particular puts it, "grace" is God's self-giving to Israel (*Grace*, 15). If God gives himself to Israel in a marriage-like relationship, then he commits himself to the maintenance of his bond with her. The classic passage is Exod 33:19-34:9, especially against the backdrop of the golden calf incident (Exodus 32).

[14] Bryan Estelle's excellent account of the creation covenant (*CJPM*, 99-116) is rich and rewarding and, if anything, serves to confirm the conditional character of that covenant. I would just submit that rather than a "covenant of works," the relationship depicted in the opening chapters of Genesis is simply a conditional covenant, like any other. As for Estelle's treatment of Rom 5:12-21 and Gal 3:10, which, for him, support the traditional doctrine of the covenant of works, I have proposed alternative understandings respectively in *Faith, Obedience, and Perseverance: Aspects of Paul's Letter to the Romans*. Wissenschaftliche Untersuchungen zum Neuen Testament 79 (Tübingen: Mohr Siebeck, 1994), 79-108; "Role Reversal and Paul's Use of Scripture in Galatians 3.10-13," *Journal for the Study of the New Testament* 65 (1997), 85-121.

[15] Again, Gowan, *Theology of The Prophetic Books*; Levenson, *Resurrection and the Restoration of Israel*.

[16] Berkouwer, *Sin*. Studies in Dogmatics (Grand Rapids: Eerdmans, 1971), 268 (italics added). Likewise, Calvin, *Institutes*, 2.1.4. See at more length my *Faith, Obedience, and Perseverance: Aspects of Paul's Letter to the Romans*. Wissenschaftliche Untersuchungen zum Neuen Testament 79 (Tübingen: Mohr Siebeck, 1994), 79-109.

[17] Kline, *By Oath Consigned: A Reinterpretation of the Covenant Signs of Circumcision and Baptism* (Grand Rapids: Eerdmans, 1968), 16-17.

[18] Wenham, *Genesis 16-50*. Word Biblical Commentary 2 (Dallas: Word, 1994), 20.

[19] Wenham, *Genesis 16-50*, 20. Confirmation is provided by V. P. Hamilton, *The Book of Genesis*. New International Commentary on the OT. 2 vols. (Grand Rapids: Eerdmans, 1990, 1995), 1.461-63.

[20] See further J. Nolland, *Luke 1-9:20*. Word Biblical Commentary 35a (Dallas: Word, 1989), 26-27; J. Green, *The Gospel of Luke*. New International Commentary on the New Testament (Grand Rapids: Eerdmans, 1997), 65. Green notes that the image of living lives that conform to God's will as a journey is an important one for Luke, as developed the central "journey" section of the Gospel.

[21] Robertson stresses this very factor: "A covenant is a bond-in-blood. It involves commitments with life-and-death consequences. At the point of covenantal inauguration, the parties of the covenant are committed to one another by a formalizing process of blood-shedding. This blood-shedding represents the intensity of the commitment of the covenant. By the covenant they are bound for life and death" (*Christ of the Covenants*, 14-15).

[22] The "covenant lawsuit" of Isaiah 1 echoes Deuteronomy: "If you are willing and obedient, you shall eat the good of the land; But if you refuse and rebel, you shall be devoured by the sword; for the mouth of the Lord has spoken" (vv. 19-20).

[23] Köstenberger, *John*. Baker Exegetical Commentary on the New Testament 4 (Grand Rapids: Baker, 2004), 450. The Septuagint of Jer 2:21 names Israel a "true vine," but the succeeding context makes it plain that this "true vine" was deeply flawed.

[24] The same pertains to the conditionality inherent in Matt 6:14-15: "For *if you forgive* men their trespasses, your heavenly Father also will forgive you; but *if you do not forgive* men their trespasses, neither will your Father forgive your trespasses." Plainly, the precondition of eschatological forgiveness is our forgiveness of others here and now.

[25] The same note of allegiance to (or renewal of) the covenant is sounded by the hiphil stem of the verb *qum* in, e.g., 2 Kgs 23:3, 24. By way of further illustration, 1 Sam 15:11, 13; Jer 35:15, 16 present us with a study in contrast: as over against those who have broken faith with the Lord, there are individuals who have "upheld" the Torah.

[26] J. Bligh, *Galatians: A Discussion of St. Paul's Epistle*. Householder Commentaries 1 (London: St. Paul, 1970), 257.

[27] H. Schlier, *Der Brief an die Galater*. Kritisch-exegetischer Kommentar über das Neue Testament. 5th ed. (Göttingen: Vandenhoeck & Ruprecht, 1971), 132.

[28] Not surprisingly, the idea of "remaining"/"abiding"/"cleaving" is taken up by later Jewish literature. Ben Sira, for example, more than once correlates cleaving to God with obedience (e.g., Sirach 11:22; 13:4; 30:20). To cleave to God entails dispositions such as love, fear and faith, virtues commended by the scribe throughout his book.

[29] Because in the present tense the Greek indicative and imperative assume the same form, John 14:1 can actually be translated in four different ways. But the rendering that makes the most consistent sense is to take *pisteuō* as imperative in both instances.

[30] That *kai* can function to introduce an apodosis ("then") is well documented. See, for example, *BDAG*, 494-95. *Kai* here is much like the *waw* of Gen 17:2.

[31] Block, *The Book of Ezekiel: Chapters 25-44*. New International Commentary on the OT (Grand Rapids: Eerdmans, 1998), 627.

[32] Block, *Ezekiel*, 632. Block denies that the Levites are demoted in privilege. It would appear to me that they are, but Duguid's essential point remains intact.

[33] See G. K. Beale, *The Temple and the Church's Mission: A Biblical Theology of the Dwelling Place of God*. New Studies in Biblical Theology 17 (Downers Grove: InterVarsity, 2004), 335-64.

[34] France, *Jesus and the OT: His Application of OT Passages to Himself and His Mission* (Downers Grove: InterVarsity, 1971), 39, quoting G. W. H. Lampe, *Essays on Typology*. Studies in Biblical Theology 1/22 (London: SCM, 1957), 27.

[35] See, for example, D. C. Allison, *The New Moses: A Matthean Typology* (Minneapolis: Fortress, 1993), 11-95.

[36] Especially in light of Rev 21:1-22:5, according to which the coming universe is depicted as a city, a temple and a garden all-in-one. It is into this realm that no unclean thing can enter. See Beale, *Temple*, 23-25, 365-73.

[37] Even granting that the Levites might be viewed as "penitent sinners," the fact remains that restoration always follows upon genuine *repentance*, i.e., turning from idols to serve the true and the living God (1 Thessalonians 1:9). In this case, renewed fidelity as embodied in repentance is hardly optional. And the picture of a temple served by the "more faithful" and the "less faithful" is incongruous in terms of obedience as the worship and service of the Creator rather than the creature. Some believers may be more fruitful and productive than others, but faithfulness by definition is commitment to the person of the Lord and the standards of his covenant. Idolatry is *ipso facto* precluded.

[38] Geerhardus Vos describes the Jacob narrative in these terms: "The main principle embodied in the history of Jacob-Israel is that of subjective transformation of life, with a renewed stress of the productive activity of the divine factor." Vos acknowledges, as everyone must, that Jacob is represented as the least ideal of the patriarchs. But, "This is done in order to show that divine grace is not the reward for, but the source of noble traits. Grace overcoming human sin and transforming human nature is the keynote of the revelation here" (*Biblical Theology: Old and New Testaments* [Edinburgh: Banner of Truth, rep. 1975], 93).

[39] In Phil 2:14-16, Paul is concerned that his readers not repeat the murmuring and questioning of Israel in the wilderness. Rather, they should be the blameless children of God who shine as lights in the midst of a perverse and crooked generation, so that his labors among them would not have been in vain.

[40] Among other considerations, Duguid's appeal to Jesus' wilderness experience, succeeding where Israel failed, is certainly to the point. Both the Gospel temptation narratives and Hebrews set forth Jesus as the man of faith who persevered through the wilderness. Perhaps I could pass on my own study, "Jesus, the Unique Son of God, Tested and Faithful," *Exegetical Essays*. 3rd ed. (Eugene, OR: Wipf & Stock, 2003), 79-132. An abbreviated version appears in *Bibliotheca Sacra* 151 (1994), 284-308.

[41] N. T. Wright, *The Climax of the Covenant: Christ and the Law in Pauline Theology* (Minneapolis: Fortress, 1991), 152 (italics original). See as well J. M. Scott, "Paul's Use of the Deuteronomic Tradition," *Journal of Biblical Literature* 112 (1993), 217-221.

[42] I have addressed this in my reply to S. M. Baugh in this book.

[43] See my discussion of Rom 5:9-10 in the reply to S. M. Baugh.

[44] See J. D. G. Dunn, *The New Perspective on Paul: Collected Essays*. Wissenschaftliche Untersuchungen zum Neuen Testament 185 (Tübingen: Mohr Siebeck, 2005), 77-80, along with the relevant portion of my reply to S. M. Baugh.

[45] Fee, *Paul's Letter to the Philippians*. New International Commentary on the New Testament (Grand Rapids: Eerdmans, 1995), 235-36, 237-38.

[46] Fee, *Philippians*, 231.

[47] Fee's recent volume on Paul's christology makes the same point. In responding to those commentators on Phil 2:6-8 who have an aversion to the idea of imitating Christ, as though ethics were based finally on self-effort rather than on grace, Fee writes: "But these objections are based on a fundamental misunderstanding of *imitatio* in Paul's thought, which does not mean 'repeat after me' but rather (in the present context) 'have a frame of mind which lives on behalf of others the way Christ did in his becoming incarnate and dying by crucifixion.' One can appreciate the desire not to let this profound passage lose its power by making it simply an exemplary paradigm, but Paul himself seems to have done that very thing. He then follows up with his own story in 3:5-14 as one who lives out the Christ paradigm and urges the Philippians to follow his example of following the primary example (3:15-17) and thus to live in the present in a cruciform way" (*Pauline Christology: An Exegetical-Theological Study* [Peabody: Hendrickson, 2007], 372, n. 6).

[48] Fee, *The First Epistle to the Corinthians*. New International Commentary on the New Testament (Grand Rapids: Eerdmans, 1987),

440. Fee adds: "...we have been called to a higher life of service that includes self-control and the willingness to endure hardship as concomitants. Perhaps too many contemporary Christians have lost sight of their eschatological goal and are running aimlessly, if they are in the 'contest' at all" (ibid., 441).

[49] O'Brien, *The Epistle to the Philippians*. New International Greek Testament Commentary (Grand Rapids: Eerdmans, 1991), 412-13.

[50] See the excellent studies respectively of S. McKnight, "The Warning Passages of Hebrews: A Formal Analysis and Theological Conclusions," *Trinity Journal* ns 13 (1992), 21-59; D. deSilva, "Entering God's Rest: Eschatology and the Socio-Rhetorical Strategy of Hebrews," *Trinity Journal* ns 21 (2000), 25-43.

[51] Gathercole, *Where is Boasting? Early Jewish Soteriology and Paul's Response in Romans 1-5* (Grand Rapids: Eerdmans, 2002), 226, 265; Watson, *Paul and the Hermeneutics of Faith* (London: T & T Clark International, 2004).

[52] Yinger, *Paul, Judaism, and Judgment According to Deeds*. Society for New Testament Studies Monograph Series 105 (Cambridge: Cambridge University Press, 1999).

[53] Brad Young very helpfully confirms that Paul's thinking is Jewish in character, a telling point when it comes to comprehending and unpacking his universe of discourse. Those who scruple about hard-and-fast distinctions between "justification" and "sanctification" should consider that what appears to the Western mind to be a "blurring" of ideas is, in the Jewish mindset, what Young calls "a cycle of interactive concepts." According to Young, "The apostle understands God and his great love for all humanity as a vibrant whole. One concept belongs to a complex of interactive ideas. Each term he uses to communicate his thought is clustered with other interactive concepts concerning God's relationship to people.... When the contours of Pauline thought are considered in a cycle of interactive concepts rather than in a straight line where each new idea supersedes and eliminates the previous one, the apostle's conceptual approach to God is given fresh vigor. It is a Jewish way of thinking" (*Paul the Jewish Theologian: A Pharisee among Christians, Jews, and Gentiles* [Peabody: Hendrickson, 1997], 40-41, 42). The hermeneutical impact of this observation should be apparent enough: modern interpreters must be prepared to undergo a paradigm shift to this Jewish way of thinking in order to enter the thought processes of Paul and the other biblical writers.

[54] On the theology of Romans 2, see further my *Faith, Obedience, and Perseverance*, chapter 3; K. R. Snodgrass, "Justification by Grace—to the Doers: an Analysis of the Place of Romans 2 in the Theology of Paul," *New Testament Studies* 32 (1986), 72-93.

⁵⁵ See further C. Loewe, "'There is No Condemnation' (Romans 8:1): But Why Not?" *Journal of the Evangelical Theological Society* 42 (1999), 231-50. At the risk of throwing out an inflammatory term, we should remember that classic antinomianism was devoted to the proposition that grace does not entail obligation.

⁵⁶ Wright, *Climax of the Covenant*, and *What Saint Paul Really Said: Was Paul of Tarsus the Real Founder of Christianity?* (Grand Rapids: Eerdmans, 1997).

⁵⁷ I think particularly of Levenson, *Resurrection and Restoration*; N. T. Wright, *The New Testament and the People of God.* Christian Origins and the Question of God 1 (Minneapolis: Fortress, 1991); id., *Jesus and the Victory of God.* Christian Origins and the Question of God 2 (Minneapolis: Fortress, 1996); id., *The Challenge of Jesus: Rediscovering Who Jesus Was and Is* (Downers Grove: InterVarsity, 1999); id., *Paul: In Fresh Perspective* (Minneapolis: Fortress, 2005); J. M. Scott, ed., *Exile: OT, Jewish, and Christian Conceptions.* Supplements to the Journal for the Study of Judaism 56 (Leiden: Brill, 1997); C. A. Evans, "Jesus and the Continuing Exile of Israel," *Jesus and the Restoration of Israel: A Critical Assessment of N. T. Wright's Jesus and the Victory of God.* ed. C. C. Newman (Downers Grove: InterVarsity, 1999), 77-100; B. Pitre, *Jesus, the Tribulation, and the End of the Exile: Restoration Eschatology and the Origin of the Atonement* (Grand Rapids: Baker, 2005); M. Fuller, *The Restoration of Israel: Israel's Re-gathering and the Fate of the Nations in Early Jewish Literature and Luke-Acts.* Beihefte zur Zeitschrift für die neutestamentliche Wissenschaft und die Kunde der älteren Kirche 138 (Berlin: de Gruyter, 2006). There are also the older contributions of M. Knibb, "The Exile in the Literature of the Intertestamental Period," *Heythrop Journal* 17 (1976), 253-72; id., "Exile in the Damascus Document," *Journal for the Study of the OT* 25 (1983), 99-117.

A REVIEW ARTICLE

Gordon J. Wenham, *Story as Torah: Reading Old Testament Narratives Ethically*. Grand Rapids: Baker, 2000.

This *is* a book to read and study. Gordon Wenham has provided a study of OT ethics that strikes the balance, as well as any book could, between "law and grace," or the demands of the covenant, as equalized by God's fatherly compassion toward his children.

1. Summary of Wenham's Argument

Wenham epitomizes his thesis at the outset:

> Obviously the behaviour of the chief actors [of the Old Testament narratives] in many instances falls miserably short of the ideal, and they often suffer in some way for their mistakes. Yet it is clear too that they are not deserted by God despite their sinfulness. So there is a paradox in Old Testament narrative ethics: on the one hand God is terribly demanding, he looks for nothing less than godlike perfect behaviour, yet on the other, despite human failings, he does not forget his covenant loyalty to his people, and ultimately brings them through the suffering that their sin has brought about. Old Testament ethics are therefore as much about grace as about law: they declare that God, the all-holy, is also God, the all-merciful (4).

Later on, Wenham adds that Isaac's deathbed blessing of Genesis 27 is an episode that is most revealing in the way it brings out the viewpoints of the different actors. Moreover, "it is also one of many in the Old Testament which show the depth of its moral insight and its avoidance of simple black-and-white judgments. It deals with a world where there are few perfect saints and few unredeemable sinners: most of its heroes and heroines have both virtues and vices, they mix obedience and unbelief" (15). Complementary to this real life assessment of the OT saints is Wenham's equation of "perfect" with "blameless," as per the example of Noah (30).

The opening chapter establishes the categories of "implied author" and "implied reader," which serve as fundamental categories for Wenham's approach to the OT narratives. To be illustrated by two particular books, Genesis and Judges, Wenham seeks to argue that ethical readers should aim to discover the views of the implied author, and this requires them to engage with his ideas and to share his stance on many issues. To become a sensitive reader involves understanding the implied author's outlook and adapting oneself to the implied reader. Accordingly, the reader is not concerned with the process of composition, but with what the implied author is communicating by telling the narrative. This involves careful study of the final form of the different books to determine the message that they were attempting to communicate to their implied readers.

Wenham then turns to the rhetorical function of Genesis. This is a chapter chock-a-block with insights into the first book of the Bible, including its relation to other OT narratives. The "ethics of Genesis" revolve around monotheism (which functions as a persistent critique of Near Eastern theology) and the human being as the image of God. Over against the Babylonian creation and flood myths, Genesis envisions God as the provider for human needs, not the other way around, with mankind providing "care and feeding for the gods." Thus, in Genesis a far more positive view is taken of man in the order of creation, with Adam an Eve represented as his image. In the context of the ancient Near East, the king was regularly called the "image" of the gods; but Genesis democratizes the idea—"every human being is a king and responsible for managing the world on God's behalf" (25).[1] The patriarchal narratives confirm that the task of subduing the earth is fully operative even in the aftermath of Adam's fall. Genesis thus presents *a mixture of realism and idealism* in discussing the creation mandates, including marriage and procreation, both of which have their happy and not so happy sides.

After Genesis comes the rhetorical function of Judges. Again, the commentary on the structure and theology of the book is richly insightful and rewards careful reading. As to the atmosphere of Judges, it is quite different from Genesis. The latter begins with the triumphant account of God creating the world in six days and ends with Joseph confidently looking forward to his burial in the promised land. By contrast, Judges opens with the ineffective efforts of the Israelite tribes to conquer the land and concludes, after a dreadful civil war, with the gloomy reflection: "every man did what was right in his own eyes." Moreover, whereas Genesis has a fairly positive attitude towards the past, Judges has a much darker one. For Wenham, most of the stories in the book seem to be told to shock the reader or at least make the reader ask himself what the characters in the stories ought to have done. In other words, the narrative embodies a set of values and ethical norms that the reader must somehow tune into if he is not to read the stories "against the grain," i.e., in ways that are contrary to the message that the author intended to convey. According to Wenham, in Judges "we have fewer clues than usual in the Old Testament to give away the author's assumptions, and this coupled with its portrayal of non-normative behaviour makes it one of the most difficult books in the canon to interpret from an ethical perspective" (45).

With some qualification, Wenham is sympathetic with classifying Judges as part of the "Deuteronomistic History," i.e., the books from Deuteronomy to 2 Kings, which recount the history of Israel from the conquest to the exile. His reservation is that a recognition of Deuteronomistic elements in the book does not make it simply one volume within that history, because Deuteronomistic ideas pervade the OT as a whole. Even so, read in this way, Judges is seen to exemplify the ideals of the book of Deuteronomy, particularly its message that disobedience to the law leads to divine displeasure and suffering for the nation.

The "ethics of Judges" consist in fidelity to Yahweh. The two prologues of the book, 1:1-2:5 and 2:6-3:6, predict what the rest of the book will describe: Israel has broken the covenant by not expelling the Canaanites and will go further by worshipping their gods; in turn, the Canaanites will become Israel's adversaries. But this gloomy scenario is prefaced by a ray of hope: "I will never break my covenant with you." "Despite the repeated tales of Israel's faithlessness that are about to begin, God's loyalty to Israel is not in doubt. So although the book's horizon becomes ever darker as the story progresses and it ends with the blackest of episodes, God's promise gives hope of new and better days" (50). "As in Genesis human sinfulness does not nullify God's graciousness. Israel may break the covenant, and suffer for it, but God will still hear their prayer when they repent. God's readiness to answer prayer runs through the book of Judges and relieves its otherwise gloomy message" (58).

This fidelity versus idolatry theme has particular application in the case of the judges and the would-be king Abimelech. In all but one instance, Othniel, the various savior-judges fall short of wholehearted allegiance to the Lord and foreshadow the time when a king "after God's own heart" would ascend the throne of Israel. Judges portrays Israel becoming progressively more lax in its Torah-observance and ever more prone to disunity between the tribes. In the epilogue, both trends reach a climax with outright idolatry among the Danites and a civil war that could have destroyed the nation. "The reader is driven to conclude: this must not continue, if the nation is to enjoy harmony at home and peace abroad. A new way of life under new leadership is required, if Israel is to survive in Canaan" (69).

In sum, "as in the book of Genesis the heroes of Judges are by no means sinless: yet despite the book's portrayal of their many faults it still affirms that God in his grace may use them to fulfil his purpose" (69).

Wenham next turns to "Ethical Ideals and Legal Requirements." In this chapter, he proceeds to argue that obedience to the rules is not a sufficient definition of OT ethics, but that much more is looked for from members of the covenant people. Ethics is more than keeping the law, or, to put it in biblical terms, righteousness involves more than living by the Decalogue and the other laws in the Pentateuch. Thereafter follows a sketch of the importance of virtue, community values, and the imitation of God for an understanding of the values of the biblical narrators.

The ensuing discussion is based on the premise that while laws generally set a floor for behavior within society, they do not prescribe an ethical ceiling. Therefore, the study of legal codes within the Bible reveal only the limits of the tolerance of the law-givers and may not be an index to what they approve of as ideal conduct (80). In the OT, what takes us to the heart of the ethical ideal is the avoidance of idolatry and the love and worship of the only God. In his words, the Bible goes beyond legal sanctions and negative commands, because its ethico-religious ideal is wholly positive:

> Israel is enjoined to love the Lord with all her heart, soul and strength. To walk after, cleave to, and to love him. Though it has been correctly pointed out that these are the actions required of loyal treaty partners, and that love and fear of God is expressed chiefly through keeping his commandments, it is wrong to reduce love to obedience. It is obedience, but more than obedience. This covenantal loyalty is also the attitude looked for within a family, between children and parents, and between spouses. Israel's loyalty to and affection for her God should mirror his love for her. In the Psalms there are glimpses of the human spirit reaching out towards this goal (81).

Wenham maintains that the first commandment illustrates what he calls the "gap between law and ethics" (82). The law merely punished extreme forms of disloyalty to God, i.e., apostasy and idolatry, and prohibited actions such as intermarriage that might lead to the ultimate religious disloyalty. But fearing, loving, cleaving to the Lord was not fulfilled just by avoiding the worship of other gods. The ethico-religious goal was far deeper and more embracing: it involved both loyalty to God and an enjoyment of his presence.

Wenham's gap between law and ethics is illustrated by sexual ethics. The law itself discriminated against women and created an environment in which marriages were easily terminated on the part of the male. However, just looking at the law gives a misleading view of what actually went on in ancient Israel and does no show how the biblical writers in fact hoped for a much higher standard of sexual ethics than the law insisted on. After a brief survey of materials, Wenham surmises that in the realm of marriage there was a gap between the ideals or hopes of the implied writers and the lesser demands of the law.

As this chapter continues to unfold, Wenham discusses the issue of "character and virtue," both of which consist in obedience to the declared will of God as the cardinal religious and ethical ideal. Such is illustrated by Noah and Abraham. As regards the latter, Wenham insightfully observes that the patriarch's career begins and ends with "two dramatic and costly examples of his absolute obedience to God's commands, his leaving home and his sacrifice of his only son" (87-88). He then suggests three main criteria for determining that a character's behavior is regarded by the implied author as virtuous: (1) The behavior pattern is repeated in a number of different contexts; (2) The character trait is exhibited in a positive context; (3) outside the narrative material of the OT, the legal codes, Psalms, and wisdom books often shed light on the various attitudes toward virtue and vice. However, even when the focus of the stories is on individual examples of piety, the communal dimension of biblical ethics, especially family solidarity, remains foundational.

In sum this chapter argues two propositions. One, the ethical expectations of the OT are higher than the legal rules. Simply keeping the laws is insufficient. It is not enough to avoid worshipping other gods—the Lord wants Israel to love him with her whole heart, mind, and strength. Likewise, it is not good enough not to commit adultery—the OT expects husbands and wives to love, care for and protect each other. Two, By portraying the biblical repeatedly acting in certain ways, the narratives are implicitly defining certain virtues and vices, encouraging its readers to imitate the former and avoid the latter. These virtues cannot be defined by law alone: rather the stories offer paradigms of behavior that apply in various situations.

Yet foundational to these two prongs of OT ethics is the imitation of God. The vertical dimension of man imitating God has its effects in man's treatment of his fellow man. The historical narratives, especially Genesis, thus set out a very lofty ideal of human behavior. It does not show its heroes simply keeping the law in their individual actions or illustrating typical human virtues. Rather, it sets out a vision of human beings made in the image of God and thus obligated to imitate God in their dealings with one another and with other creatures. Sometimes the stories show, for example, the patriarchs acting in exemplary fashion: they not only keep the law and model virtue, but exhibit truly godly characteristics as those made in the image of God should. Sometimes they fall very far short. But most often their deportment is mixed, neither outstandingly virtuous nor catastrophic. Nevertheless, their mixed ethical achievement does not generate a sense of complacency in the reader. On the contrary, it serves as a reminder that God still keeps his promises and is loyal to his people despite their shortcomings.

Before turning to the NT, Wenham concentrates on the "Problematic Tales" of the rape of Dinah (Genesis 34) and the story of Gideon (Judges 6-8). After a thorough recitation of the various solutions to the problems, Wenham himself concludes that in the case of Dinah no one comes out of the episode very credibly on the Israelite side, let along the Shechemite side. Even so, Jacob and his sons escape scot-free. "Here as in many other Old Testament stories God treats his people much more kindly than they deserve in order to demonstrate his faithfulness to his promises" (119). As for the Gideon-episode, there are many aspects of Gideon's character and actions that raise questions: like the other judges he is not meant to be imitated in every detail.

> But he is a great example of how God can act through less than perfect people. The story of Gideon, like the rest of Judges, demonstrates God's power over Israel's enemies and their gods. It demonstrates the Lord's faithfulness to his covenant despite Israel's infidelity and his patience towards those whom he calls to lead

his people despite their own wavering faith and obedience (127)

The concluding chapter on "New Testament Perspectives" is based on the proposition that the NT, like the OT, is telling a story. Wenham ties into the work of Ben Witherington, *Paul's Narrative World of Thought*.[2] According to Witherington, in Paul's vision of human history there are four major stories: (1) the story of a world gone wrong, i.e., the fall of Adam and the consequences described in Genesis 1-11; (2) the story of Israel in that world; (3) the story of Christ; (4) the story of Christians, including Paul himself, which arises out of all three of these previous stories and is the first full installment of the story of a world set right again. Paul's theology is set within the framework of this grand narrative which begins with creation and ends with Christ's second advent and the resurrection of the dead. For both Paul and his Jewish contemporaries, the story of salvation began with the call of Abraham. With him began the process of the retrieval of fallen mankind and the restoration of Eden. "When Paul thinks of the human beginnings of paradise regained, he thinks of that first great example of faith. Paul does not believe that there are several stories of God's redeeming work; there is essentially only one that leads from Abraham to Christ and beyond" (130, quoting Witherington). Over against the Jewish appeal to the stories of Moses and David, says Witherington, Paul chose to concentrate on Adam and Abraham because of their more universal appeal to Gentiles.

Given this narrative character of Pauline theology, and that of the NT as a whole, it follows from the unity of God's historical purpose that there is a unity of ethic before and after Christ. Thus, it is likely that Paul, among others, expected the same principles to govern behavior of the people of God before and after Christ. This is buttressed by the way various parts of the NT appeal to the OT as models for Christian behavior. Using Hebrews as an example, Wenham notes that the author presupposes not just a familiarity with the stories of the OT, but that there is a continuity between those people and his readers. "They are part of the one people of God sharing in one story of salvation. That is why the achievements of the Israelites of the past should inspire the Christians of the first century" (134).

The question is, How can this theological continuity be maintained in the realm of ethics? Does not the NT advocate a quite different stance in such matters as the food laws, marriage and divorce, and violence? In order to resolve the question, Wenham surveys the OT laws pertaining to purity, holiness, and food. As for *purity*, in and through the multitude of regulations, the key principle is that God is the supremely holy being, and anyone who wishes to come into his presence must be holy too. *Holiness*, in the ritual system, stands opposite uncleanness. Since God is perfectly holy, the unclean are those opposed to God or who fall short of his perfection. Idolatry is one of the most severe forms of uncleanness: it pollutes the idolater, the land, and the sanctuary. Such pollution, he observes, is the opposite of the life of God. God himself is full and perfect life, so that death is the very antithesis of holiness. For this reason, corpse impurity ranks among the most polluting types of defilement.

> If the quintessence of uncleanness is death, it becomes clear why corpses are regarded as so polluting. These apparently harsh regulations declare very loudly one aspect of God's character: he is life, perfect life, both morally and physically. He is opposed to death: those who willingly or even involuntarily embrace actions that lead to death separate themselves from God (138).

The *food laws* fit into the broader framework of cleanness and uncleanness. The distinctions made in the food laws between clean and unclean foods match the divisions among mankind, between Israel the elect nation and the non-elect Gentiles. They served to remind Israel of her special status as God's chosen people. Just as God had selected just one people to be near him, so Israel had to be selective in her diet. Through this system of symbolic laws the Israelites were reminded at every meal of their redemption to be God's people. Their diet was limited to certain meats in imitation of their God, who had restricted his choice among the nations to Israel. It served also to bring to mind Israel's responsibilities to be a holy nation. As they distinguished between clean and unclean foods, they were reminded that holiness was more than a matter of meat and drink but a way of life characterized by purity and integrity. But these laws not only reminded Israel of her distinctiveness, they served to enforce it. Jews faithful to these laws would tend to avoid Gentile company, lest they were offered unclean food to eat.

This overview of the OT thinking about purity and uncleanness allows us to assess the NT approach more clearly. The NT teaching fully underlines OT view of uncleanness, but in other respects transforms it. Transformation, rather than simple abrogation, is the NT's handling of uncleanness caused by disease, bodily discharges, and food laws. Instead of keeping his distance from those afflicted with uncleanness, Jesus touches them, thereby making himself unclean. Thus, he touches lepers, a woman suffering from a flow of blood, and even corpses, healing the former, and bringing the latter back to life (e.g., Mark 1:40-41; 5:21-43). In rather stark contrast with the OT, Jesus inaugurated the new creation and the eschatological reign of God, when God drew near to the sufferers and healed them personally. His miracles had the effect of including within the people of God those who had formerly been outside.

Drawing on the work of N. T. Wright,[3] Wenham maintains that the healing miracles are breaking in of the new order planned by the creator God, in which we glimpse something beyond the simple reconstitution of Israel, because when Israel was restored, the whole creation would be restored. This new creation, according to biblical and first-century Jewish thought, was to embrace not just Jews but all nations. Jesus' apparent disregard for the purity regulations signaled no disrespect for them, but rather was a declaration that their most fundamental values were being fulfilled. The purity laws bore witness to a picture of God who was the source of perfect life and wholeness: only those who enjoyed full and perfect health were judged fit to enter the temple and experience God's presence. But now, with the new creation inaugurated by Jesus, those healed were freed from uncleanness and were able to draw near to God.

These food laws reminded the Jews of their special status as the one people chosen by God. The clean (edible) creatures symbolized Israel, whereas the unclean (prohibited) foods symbolized the Gentile nations. But in the new creation, the people of God are comprised of all nations; hence, it is inappropriate for the food laws, which symbolized Israel's segregation, to be maintained. In Matt and Mark, Jesus' critique of the food laws (Matt 15:16-17; Mark 7:1819) is immediately followed by the story of the Syro-Phoenician woman (describing herself as a dog, i.e., unclean), whose daughter, possessed by an unclean spirit, was heated by Jesus (Matt 15:21-28; Mark 7:24-30). Thus, the reappraisal of the dietary laws, like that of unclean persons, is not seen by the NT writers as contradicting the OT so much as reaffirming the realization of its hopes with the coming of Christ and the inauguration of a new creation, in which there is neither

Jew nor Gentile, and everyone, including the unclean, may be restored to fulfill God's purposes.

New creation is also the key to understanding particulars such as the NT's modification of the OT regulations concerning marriage and divorce, especially in the revolutionary teaching of Jesus. In this particular respect, Jesus' transformation of marriage is like his treatment of the purity code. On the face of it, there is confrontation and abrogation of the old rules, but at a deeper level there is a reaffirmation of God's original creative purposes for the human race. The same goes for violence, which is anti-life.

In his Conclusions, Wenham underscores the pointedly eschatological character of Christian ethics. A Christian ethic is eschatological in two senses. On the one side, the reign of God has begun with the first advent of Christ. On the other side, the climactic phase of the kingdom is outstanding, and it is to this end that the OT narratives continue to find their relevance.

> The coming of the kingdom may be more apparent in the Christian era than it was before Christ, but it is still partial. The Church today, like Israel of old, still hopes and prays for the consummation. It still has to live in a world distorted by hardness of heart and not as it was in the beginning. It still lives in a world where sin and violence are endemic. Individual Christians and the Church are afflicted by both. They need the laws and narratives of the Old Testament to remind them of the creator's ideals and how to handle situations which fall short of these ideals. In this way the experience of the saints of the Old Testament has much to teach those of the New (154).

The book ends with the two outstanding points developed by *Story as Torah*. First, the OT witnesses to God's tolerance. The Lord urges Israel to love God and neighbor with all one's heart, soul, and might, and to be holy as he is holy (Deut 6:5; Lev 19:18; 11:45). But there is a great gap between these lofty ideals and the law. People were not punished for not loving God with their whole heart, only for brazen disloyalty expressed by active idolatry. Similarly, lack of love towards one's neighbors did not attract judicial sanction, only actions that seriously harmed them, such as theft, murder, or adultery. On such deeds the law came down very hard; but though God wanted his people to love him wholeheartedly and their neighbors as themselves, he put up with much less.

Closely related to the first point is the second: the narratives demonstrate God's faithfulness to his promises despite the unfaithfulness of his people. There are many episodes in Genesis where it is apparent that the patriarchs do not obey or show the faith they should; yet despite their slips, God remains faithful and indeed rescues them from the problems they create for themselves. This pattern is even more prominent in Judges.

> God's character as it emerges in the stories of the Old Testament is thus pre-eminently marked by tolerance and faithfulness. That is why St Paul could assure his readers that "whatever was written in former days was written...that by the encouragement of the scriptures we might have hope" (Rom 15:4). Read sensitively they may still do the same today (155).

2. Response

Wenham's book is a breath of fresh air in the study of OT (and NT) ethics. The central theses of the volume, as summarized in the Conclusions, are of particular importance and relevance in today's climate, particularly as regards the justification/sanctification debate. And it is just here that Wenham strikes the all-important balance between the demands of the law and the tolerance of the law-giver. Wenham, as quoted above, characterizes God as terribly demanding, looking for nothing less than godlike perfect behavior; yet despite human failing, he does not forget his covenant loyalty to his people. OT ethics are, therefore, as much about grace as about law: they declare that God, the all-holy, is also God, the all-merciful (4). This is a point well worth underscoring in view of the tendency of Reformed theologians to insist that the law functioned as a kind of "covenant of works" that had to be kept perfectly in order to remain in covenant standing.[4] Inevitably, "perfection," in this scenario, is defined in the modern, not biblical, sense of "sinlessness."

There is, to be sure, such a thing as perfection. But *biblically* speaking, perfection is a wholehearted commitment to honor the entirety of the Lord's revealed will.[5] Otherwise put, perfection is simply a David-like desire to seek God and follow his commandments with all one's heart (Ps 119:2, 10, 34, 69, 145). Perfection is exemplified by the godly Zechariah and Elizabeth, who "were both righteous before God, walking in all the commandments and ordinances of the Lord *blameless*" (Luke 1:6).

Luke hardly predicates sinless perfection of the elderly couple. What is in view the conformity of their lives to the will of God as the expression of their fidelity to him.

Since, then, perfection and covenant faithfulness are so closely linked, the comfort of a passage such as Rom 7:14-25 is that notwithstanding our many failures, there is no condemnation as long we as desire to remain within the covenant bond, true to Christ the Lord. In light of Wenham's findings, readers—and particularly teachers—of the OT will want to turn to its historical narratives to find examples not only of faith and perseverance but of godly living as well. As Wenham argues so persuasively, these narratives constitute a story *as* Torah. But to reiterate from above, we can be entirely grateful for the reminder that the OT world is one in which "there are few perfect saints and few unredeemable sinners: most of its heroes and heroines have both virtues and vices, they mix obedience and unbelief" (15).

The pastoral application of Wenham's reading of OT narrative ethics, therefore, is to the effect that a pietism that burdens the conscience unnecessarily by majoring on the observance of commandments and minoring on persevering faith is to be resisted at all costs.[6] The problem with the various ancient Jewish enclaves was not that they were "legalistic" but *pietistic*. The strenuous law-keeping of these groups, that often went beyond what is written, was grounded in a pietism that too often has been replicated in the history of the Christian church. If the essence of sin is idolatry, it follows that the essence of righteousness is fidelity. God forgives our weaknesses; it is only apostasy that makes it impossible to be restored to repentance (Heb 6:4).[7]

Some readers may be surprised at Wenham's claim of a gap between law and ethics. On a surface reading, it might seem implausible the historical narratives would present a "higher ethic" than the law itself. But it makes sense given his contention that law functioned as a civil code as well as an ethical code: civil law can be tolerant of behavior that an ideal ethic cannot. That an idea ethic is placed in the form of story rather than apodictic law is in keeping with the very character of Scripture as story. The story line of the Bible is the movement from creation to new creation, with the Christ-event as its central and pivotal occurrence. Or, as Witherington characterizes the theology of Paul, there is the story of a world gone wrong, the story of Israel in that world, the story of Christ, and the story of Christians.[8] From beginning to end, Scripture is structured in terms of a metanarrative (the big story), as subdivided by the various little stories. In other words, all the tributaries of salvation history flow into the mighty river of what God has done in history to effect a new creation out of the chaos of sin. To switch metaphors, this is the "big umbrella" of the divine speaking, first to the fathers by the prophets and now to us in his Son (Heb 1:1-2a).

With this study, Wenham has fully succeeded in whetting our appetites for more. The books of Genesis and Judges are but samples of OT narrative ethics. It is hoped, in time, that he will give us a volume encompassing the remainder of the historical portions of the Hebrew Bible and their relevance for Christian living.

---

[1] The image lies at the heart of OT and NT ethics. Wenham takes the nature of the image to be "elusive" (25). However, two recent studies, P. J. Gentry has shown that "image," in the setting of the ancient Orient, was a behavioral concept: *the king conducted himself like his god*. See Gentry, "Rethinking the 'Sure Mercies of David' In Isaiah 55:3," *Westminster Theological Journal* 69 (2007), 279-304; id., "Kingdom through Covenant: Humanity as the Divine Image," *Southern Baptist Journal of Theology* 12 (2008), 16-42); W. R. Garr, *In His Own Image and Likeness: Humanity, Divinity, and Monotheism*, Culture and History of the Ancient Near East 15 (Leiden: Brill, 2003), esp. 117-76; J. R. Middleton, *The Liberating Image: The Imago Dei in Genesis 1* (Grand Rapids: Brazos, 2005). This makes perfect sense of Adam as God's image—he and Eve were made to replicate God's activity in the world. Among other things, after the flood, man is allowed to avenge the murder of fellow humans just because he is God's image (Gen 9:6).

[2] Witherington, *Paul's Narrative World of Thought: The Tapestry of Tragedy and Triumph* (Westminster: John Knox, 1994).

[3] Wright, *Jesus and the Victory of God*, Christian Origins and the Question of God 2 (Minneapolis: Fortress, 1996).

[4] E.g., T. N. Schreiner, *The Law and Its Fulfillment: A Pauline Theology of Law* (Grand Rapids: Baker, 1993), passim; M. A. Seifrid, "Righteousness Language in the Hebrew Scriptures and Early Judaism," *Justification and Variegated Nomism. Volume 1: The Complexities of Second Temple Judaism*, eds. D. A. Carson, P. T. O'Brien and M. A. Seifrid (Grand Rapids: Baker, 2001), 435, 437; D. A. Carson, "The Vindication of Imputation: On Fields of Discourse and Semantic Discourse," *Justification: What's at Stake in the Current Debates?* eds. M. Husbands and D. J. Treier (Downers Grove/Leicester: InterVarsity/Apollos, 2004), 71.

[5] See my *'The Obedience of Faith': A Pauline Phrase in Historical Context*, Wissenschaftliche Untersuchungen zum Neuen Testament 2/38 (Tübingen: Mohr-Siebeck, 1991), 45; and *Exegetical Essays*. 3rd ed. (Eugene, OR: Wipf & Stock, 2003), 361.

[6] Still brilliant and relevant is J. D. G. Dunn's "Rom. 7,14-25 in the Theology of Paul," *Theologische Zeitschrift* 31 (1975), 264-73.

[7] See the excellent study of S. McKnight, "The Warning Passages of Hebrews: A Formal Analysis and Theological Conclusions," *Trinity Journal* ns 13 (1992), 21-59.

[8] See more recently, M. J. Gorman, *Cruciformity: Paul's Narrative Spirituality of the Cross* (Grand Rapids: Eerdmans, 2001); id., *Apostle of the Crucified Lord: A Theological Introduction to Paul and His Letters* (Grand Rapids: Eerdmans, 2004).

www.ingramcontent.com/pod-product-compliance
Lightning Source LLC
Chambersburg PA
CBHW071238300426
44116CB00008B/1082